THE GREAT ONE

*The Life and Legend of
Jackie Gleason*

THE GREAT ONE

The Life and Legend of
Jackie Gleason

William A. Henry III

G·K·Hall&Co.

Boston, Massachusetts
1993

GLE

**This Large Print Book carries the
Seal of Approval of N.A.V.H.**

Published in Large Print by arrangements with
Doubleday, a division of Bantam Doubleday Dell Publishing, Inc.

G.K. Hall Large Print Book Series.

Printed on acid free paper in the United States of America.

Set in 16 pt. Plantin.

Library of Congress Cataloging-in-Publication Data

Henry, William A., 1950–
    The great one : the life and legend of Jackie Gleason /
William A. Henry III.
        p. cm. — (G.K. Hall large print book series)
    ISBN 0-8161-5603-4 (lg. print : alk. paper). —
ISBN 0-8161-5604-2 (pbk. : lg. print : alk. paper)
    1. Gleason, Jackie, 1916–1987. 2. Television personalities—
United States—Biography. 3. Comedians—United States—
Biography. 4. Motion picture actors and actresses—United
States—Biography. 5. Large type books. I. Title.
[PN1992.4.G6H46 1993]
791.45′028′092—dc20
[B]   92-29549

For my equivalent of Jackie's gang at
Toots Shor's my pals, especially

Andrew Carron for his unfailing decency
Kevin Conroy for his universal compassion
Jon Nygaard for his unswerving loyalty
Tom Sabulis for his unflinching perception

and all of them for making me laugh

ACKNOWLEDGMENTS

One of the most gratifying things about being a journalist is how generous people are, for no reason other than their belief in the value of a truthful historical record. A very few of the hundred fifty or so people who granted interviews or otherwise assisted my research on this book had axes to grind, grudges to settle, pieces of terrain they wished to reclaim. But even they tended to be frank about their interests and fair about the facts. A few other people whom I would have liked to see declined me outright or turned me aside with brief unrevealing discussion. But the vast majority were giving in every sense. It is a tribute to Jackie Gleason that almost all of them, whatever the emotional residue of their experience, admired him intensely as an artist and viewed him compassionately as a man.

I am especially grateful to Jackie's fellow performers Art Carney, Audrey Meadows and Joyce Randolph of *The Honeymooners,* plus Milton Berle, Ted Bessell, Nandrea Lin Courts, Franklin Cover, Mercedes Ellington, Bob Fosse, talkmaster Larry King, Sheila MacRae, Jay Marshall, Robert Morse, Estelle Parsons, Trudy Carson Sales and Marian Seldes for their recollections of working with Gleason, and to the performers Jane Alexander, Dorothy Loudon, Malachy McCourt,

Burgess Meredith and Adam Redfield for stories of other exchanges with him.

From the world behind the scenes, producers Joe Gates, Robert Halmi Sr., Joseph Jacoby, Charles Joffe, Norman Lear and Jack Rollins, director Arthur Penn and the writers Larry Gelbart, Coleman Jacoby, Neil Simon, Leonard Stern, Peter Stone and Saul Turtletaub were especially valuable. So were stage managers Charles Blackwell, Gene Wolsk and Manny Kladitis, press agents Merle Debuskey, Frank Goodman and David Powers, and dresser Herb Zane. Harvey Sabinson, former press agent for David Merrick and now executive director of the League of American Theater Owners and Producers, was a treasure trove of history, as was Broadway historian Steven Suskin.

I learned much about Jackie's television career from the former CBS executives Mike Dann, Sal Iannucci, Oscar Katz, James Rosenfield, Irwin Segelstein and Frank Stanton. Also helpful were entertainment executives Robert Bennett, Dick Steenberg, Helen Brown of the CBS Foundation and Barbara Rudd of the late Sonny Werblin's office.

Within Gleason's inner circle, superagent Sam Cohn, attorney Richard Green, secretary Sydell Spear and especially press agent Pete McGovern gave me a vivid and affectionate understanding of a boss they adored. I appreciate the blessing of Jack Philbin, Jackie's producer and partner, and wish that circumstances had allowed us more than a brief conversation. The same applies to choreographer Peter Gladke, an assistant to June

Taylor in overseeing her dance troupe. Among Jackie's friends and acquaintances and their offspring, the pivotal figure was Flo Haley (widow of Jack Haley Sr.). I also thank her household assistant Norris Bennett, plus Mike Callahan, Michael Conniff, Freddie Hancock, Vincent McNamara, Linda Redfield and my brother-in-law, erstwhile Miamian David Manyan.

I benefited from the recollections of journalists Jonathan Abarbanel, Fred Bernstein, Les Brown, Dick Cavett, Charlotte Chandler, Richard Christenson, Robert Deutsch, Mel Gussow, Joe Franklin, Kay Gardella, Robert Lenzner, Gorden Manning, Dozier Mobley, Bob Sacha, Morley Safer, Arthur Unger and Linda Winer.

I learned much about Jackie's artistry from the musicians Phil Bodner, Max Ellen, Irwin Fisch and Frank Owens, among others, and something about his temperament from the painter Alfred "Chip" Chadbourne.

Any contemporary Gleason biographer owes a debt to Jackie's first booklength chronicler, Jim Bishop, especially for his research of Jackie's early years. I also thank another prior biographer, James Bacon. While I found significant factual shortcomings in both volumes, probably emanating from Gleason himself, the books enriched my sense of the man.

My own contacts with Gleason were fleeting. I saw him at the 1985 Tony Awards, at a press conference announcing the discovery of the lost *Honeymooners* episodes and at a press party for *Izzy and Moe*. At none did I have a real conversation. I have listened to dozens of hours of tapes of him being interviewed by others and have read everything I could locate ever published about him in any New York City newspaper or any Time-Life publication, amounting to a literal five-foot shelf of clips. Thus I owe a general debt to two or three generations of American entertainment journalists.

More specifically I owe thanks to president Robert Batscha and television curator Ron Simon of the Museum of Television and Radio, or the Museum of Broadcasting as it then was, which in 1986 commissioned me to write the main curatorial article for a catalogue of its Gleason exhibition, a testimonial that sadly turned into a memorial. It was the genesis for this book.

My mother, Catherine Henry, deserves thanks for matters ranging from providing the television set on which I first saw Jackie Gleason to copy editing my final manuscript. My wife Gail was as usual my invaluable first editor. At Doubleday, David Gernert commissioned and edited this volume and Renee Zuckerbrot helped guide me through the maze of the mechanics. Stephen Sherrill assisted me in research, especially document searches, and my esteemed colleague Rose Keyser of *Time* magazine was invaluable in photo research. I also had research help from Jim Burrus and Mark Mobley. My agent Michael Carlisle deserves the biggest thanks of all, for devising this deal and ladling it into my happy hands.

PROLOGUE: AND AWAY WE GO

He strode out of Sardi's restaurant and into the white Cadillac limousine that by contract was at his beck and call—and often was in use—all twenty-four hours of the day. He waited for the driver to open the door but, as always, ever since that day years before when a drunken pedestrian had called him a rich bum, he sat up front with the chauffeur rather than in the splendor behind. The trip to the studio was less than a dozen blocks, a short walk on this crisp and clear day. But the jaunty passenger was one of the laziest men alive. He might be a workaholic with an invariable multitude of projects under way, to cash in on his fame and to stave off his perpetual boredom. Yet he reveled in physical indolence. It was his credo never to walk when he could ride, never to stand when he could sit, and never to fetch anything for himself. There was always a flunky within earshot to light his cigarette, hand him a tissue or fetch a quart of whiskey, a gallon of chocolate ice cream and a brace of sausage pizzas to satisfy some sudden morning yen.

On this day, walking would have been out of the question anyway. The pasha-like passenger wore light makeup and a full costume suggestive of summer at the turn of the century in small-town Connecticut, not business in the heart of Manhattan in the wintry beginning of 1960. Besides, Jackie Gleason was, and had been for a decade, one of the most recognizable men in America, with a face as familiar as President Eisenhower's and a body, at two hundred fifty pounds and climbing rapidly, that was considerably more distinctive. For almost a decade every aspect of his life—from record-breaking deals with the CBS television network and its corporate sponsors to epic diets, a mid-broadcast broken ankle during a pratfall and a series of spiteful marital tussles—had been lived out on the front pages. In head-to-head competition for television ratings he had topped one after another of the industry's revered stars: Jimmy Durante, Steve Allen, Mickey Rooney, Perry Como. He had lured away the sponsors of the original Mr. Television himself, Milton Berle. For most of the decade only Lucille Ball had rivaled him for the honorific of television's biggest star. She played just one character week after week. Gleason often played four or five in a single night, always live, in performances marked by a spontaneous energy verging on hysteria. Yet unlike Ball he had also played, and written for himself, dramatic roles of great subtlety and poignance. Where other stars insisted on being lovable, he sought roles that exposed his flaws and tested the limits of the public's trust and devotion. And he poured much of his prodigious income back into his shows, regardless of profit, to enhance their visual appeal. His corporate credo, mounted on the walls of his penthouse suite, asserted, Barnum-like, "Three elephants are better than one."

Television could not contain him. As he emerged from Sardi's that day he could see his name across the street on the marquee of the Shubert Theatre, Broadway's signature house. He had been starring there for months in *Take Me Along*, a musical adaptation of Eugene O'Neill's only comedy, *Ah, Wilderness!* Gleason's character, the perennially drunk and occasionally repentant Uncle Sid, was secondary to the story, but in Gleason's hands it became, without undue indulgence, a star turn. He was conquering Broadway as he had conquered TV. Audiences came to see him and him alone, despite the Hollywood glitter of such co-stars as Walter Pidgeon and Una Merkel. On days when the ravages of Gleason's Falstaffian revelry (four bottles of wine at lunch on matinee day, for instance, capping a party still going from the night before) left him understandably unable to perform, theatergoers often rose from their seats during the overture, handed their tickets in at the box office and waited for another day when The Great One might be back in harness.

His fellow actors could not altogether resent his popularity, for it was keeping them in work. Although the show was only adequate and the reviews were just lukewarm, the Gleason name was more than enough to keep it running. *Take*

Me Along would last as long as he stuck with it—until the following October when, in an elaborate gesture of scorn for producer David Merrick, Gleason departed on a Thursday at the precise expiration of his contract, rather than routinely finish out the week. Then, despite his replacement by beloved TV and movie star William Bendix, the show would shut down just three weeks later. During the run Gleason would win a Tony Award, the only major acting honor ever to come to him, for a role that was both the beginning and the end of his Broadway stardom. He would never play the Great White Way again.

All that would remain of the epic performance in years to come was the bit he would record on emerging from the limousine this day. He was heading to CBS, the network that had made him a star, to film a spot for its self-celebratory special The Fabulous Fifties. A look back at the decade just past was unthinkable without the memorable presence of Gleason. But Gleason saw no value in nostalgia, no gain in merely reprising some bygone sketch. He wanted to promote his new show and his hitherto unknown musical-comedy talents. As always, he wanted to be paid handsomely for the privilege. CBS was already paying him one hundred thousand dollars a year for doing nothing, just to ensure that he would not appear on other networks. Although he insisted on performing a musical number from *Take Me Along* without rehearsal, to be recorded in a single take, he demanded and got what seemed to him an appropriate fee for a show celebrating the fifties—fifty thousand dollars. That might have been a plausible salary at the time for a leading actor's entire work on a movie. On this afternoon Gleason would secure it for a half-hour stint in the studio and less than seven minutes of screen time.

He breezed out of the limousine, into the studio building and up onto the stage. He quickly greeted the director, his fellow performers and the crew. He cocked his head, lifted an eyebrow and arranged his limbs into a look he later trademarked in stick-man cartoon form as the "Away We Go Shuffle"—one arm bent upward, the other bent down, his hips gyrating in a blend of soft-shoe cakewalk and duck waddle. The movements suggested the clownish grace of the jester, the pinpoint accuracy of the pool shark, the nimbleness of a stunt diver and acrobat—all of which he had been at some time. In technical training, Gleason was not a dancer at all, but Laurence Olivier would watch him perform this very number and say, admiringly, "He dances with such delicacy." The song was called "Sid, Old Kid" and it revealed that Gleason the singer was as robust and fearless, and hence as quicksilver-persuasive, as Gleason the actor and dancer. Through decades of penury and failure he had insisted, "I'm the world's greatest entertainer." Some part of him believed it, and that made him perfect this afternoon. Some part of him didn't, and that made him the lonely, inaccessible and deeply angry man who finished his number with a flourish, announced, "I left a beer on the bar at Sardi's and I want to get back before the head goes flat," and swept out. He was more in love with a bravado gesture than with the chance to savor—or repeat and polish—this sole enduring legacy of a triumphant time in his life.

The train engines were roaring but their noise was drowned by the hoot and holler of the Dixieland musicians. Performers and technicians, show business columnists and network executives thronged the aisles as the 1964 Great Gleason Express prepared to depart on one of the grandest follies ever undertaken by a celebrity ego. For a man whose lifelong ambition was to play, and for that matter be, Diamond Jim Brady, nothing better bespoke elegance than a private railway car—except perhaps, as with the elephants, two or three. To give a nonstop party, with bands playing around the clock and food and drink on tap at every moment, seemed to Gleason almost reward enough to make worthwhile the tedium of actually turning out a weekly show. In the fifties he had commandeered a train to Detroit as his perquisite for appearing at a charity event. For *Take Me Along* he had asked, and secured, such an extravaganza for the ride up to the opening tryout in Boston. In television seasons gone by, CBS had laid on a cross-country excursion or two.

But this was different. After more than a decade

of staging weekly television shows in New York, Gleason was moving to Miami, not merely voyaging there. He was uprooting more than two hundred employees and their families, and in effect relocating a significant part of television's most powerful network, simply to satisfy his whims about his lifestyle. He had fallen in love with golf and wanted to be able to play every day, an impossibility in the chilly Northeast. He wanted an adulatory press around him, not the snarling careerists of the New York City tabloids. He wanted to be Mr. Show Business in a town thrilled to get him, not an also-ran in, say, Hollywood. There he was made to feel like a fat freak and an interloper, and there—despite *The Hustler* and *Requiem for a Heavyweight* and *Gigot*, all made in the eighteen electric months between his glory on Broadway and his return to lucre on television—he could almost never control the circumstances of the deal.

To be sure, his financial advisers had found ways for him to extract services cheap or even free from the city of Miami and to charge CBS full price for them, turning the whole move into a multimillion-dollar bonanza. But the true cause for celebration aboard this train, for its roaring host at least, was that once again he had been able to show the bosses who was really boss. "All network executives must have one essential," he liked to snort, "and that is cologne." Henceforth, when the manicured villains wanted to harass him, they would have to do it on his turf and undergo a long plane ride each way into the bargain. Before his next birthday, in fact, one of the biggest of them would get very publicly sacked mere hours after misbehaving during one of these deferential trips down.

Television no longer fired Gleason's imagination. His "new" show was routinely repeating characters, even whole sketches, from his heyday in the fifties. He was relying, detail for detail, on the old opening format and on most of the same creative team. But audiences loved him more than ever. And on occasion he could even do some good. With him on the train, as it pulled into Georgia for a promotional stop, was the first black to join his precision tap troupe, the June Taylor Dancers. Her name was Mercedes Ellington, her grandfather was the composer Duke Ellington, and her hiring, in that era when civil rights advances were still regrettably novelties, had been the occasion for a feature article in *Look* magazine. She and Gleason were to become close friends. He loved jazz. He stood in awe of her grandfather. He admired her leggy beauty, her elegance, her poise and style—and the way she only laughed when he teasingly referred to her as "that colored girl," often to her face.

As the train reached the station in Georgia, newspaper photographers pressed forward and a crowd of fans and bystanders surged up to the train. One, spotting Ellington, who is the color of café au lait but recognizably black to a practiced segregationist's eye, shouted, "What are you doing here?" She felt, she recalls, that she was being told she ought to be in the kitchen, serving meals or washing dishes. "My first impulse was to hide. But Jackie pulled me toward him and made me stand next to him through the entire picture-taking session. I made my mind up about him then and we were friends for life."

"Ladies and gentlemen, The Great One."

No other introduction was necessary. The crowd at the 1985 Tony Awards ceremony stood and cheered. The body was somewhat smaller, the movements a little slower, the hair silver and the face altered by cosmetic surgery to smooth out bags and tucks. It was a quarter century since the man before them had been on Broadway, fifteen years since he had had a regular television series, and the movies he had made in the interim were numerous but largely forgettable. Yet they all remembered him, and many watched him every night in reruns of his immortal series The Honeymooners, the most successful single season of any television program in the history of the medium. The audience in the theater, and the audience at home, might question for a moment what connection Gleason had with the Broadway musical award he was about to present. They had probably forgotten Take Me Along and had surely forgotten his five Broadway musicals of the forties. But they had no doubt of his genius, no challenge to the grandiose title he had self-mockingly bestowed and accepted so many years before.

The prize granted, he proceeded to Sardi's, the scene of so many rowdy afternoons in younger days, to mingle with the press and then retreat upstairs. As always, he had an entourage in waiting. He recognized the name of one of the theater industry's executives, Harvey Sabinson, as that of the press agent for *Take Me Along*, and he had Sabinson brought upstairs to his table. "This," he said to friends, "is the guy who came to my dressing room and told me a couple of days in advance that I had won the Tony Award, just to make sure I would show up to get it. And I had to ask him, 'What the fuck is that?'" Gleason pumped Sabinson's hand, introduced him around and asked whether he still saw much of producer Merrick, an ego as big as Gleason's whose clashes with his star were titanic. "No, Jackie, I don't," Sabinson replied. "He's had a couple of strokes, you know."

"Ah." Gleason looked up with a grin of grim satisfaction. "Well, you know what they say. Three strokes and you're out."

Yesterday's anger was as fresh as yesterday's glory.

Jackie Gleason had a problem. He was in hock to the owners of El Rancho, a nightclub in the new desert resort of Las Vegas, for the gambling tab and bar bills he had run up the last time he had worked there. Now they wanted him to come back, for no pay, to clear his debt. That might be all right in itself. Nothing much was happening for Gleason in Hollywood in this year of 1948—or ever had, despite all of studio owner Jack Warner's promises and all of Gleason's own high hopes—and not much more was on offer in New York. Gleason could always get work at clubs in those towns, too, but never at the biggest places or with the best billing. And whatever he made would be squandered long before he dropped in for the occasional visit with his wife and daughters—scattered to the winds in buying drinks for strangers and making loans to deadbeats. No, the problem with going back to Vegas was not that it might be a bad career move but that it would be sheer torture to be surrounded by casinos and not have a buck to bet.

So Gleason hooked up with Leonard Stern, a buddy who had been a comedy writer for Abbott and Costello and for the Ma and Pa Kettle movies, a prematurely smart-ass veteran of show business at the age of not quite twenty-one. Stern was good company, courtly yet tough. More important, he had three hundred fifty dollars he was willing to risk, and he was prepared to share it with Gleason as equal partners. This was not as crazy as it might have sounded to people who did not know the loudmouth comic. He prided himself on being a man of honor, and he would scrupulously pay back any debt, even if it took him years. (He had once gone back three years after the fact to pay an Asbury Park, New Jersey, landlady on whom he had sneaked out because he had drunk up all the pay he earned entertaining at that seaside resort. The landlady had burst into tears, less shocked by the money than by the specter before her. She exclaimed, between blubbing, "We thought you drowned." Or so Gleason liked to say, although now and then he contradicted this story, as sooner or later he contradicted almost every colorful tale he ever told. Whatever the truth is in the case of the landlady, eyewitnesses known to Stern and others had definitely seen Gleason pay off years-old bills in restaurants and, most especially, bars.)

During working hours the frustrated thirty-two-year-old Gleason was unexpectedly enhancing his craft. "He performed," recalls the now gray-templed Stern, a prominent publisher and producer, "on a bill with Chas Chase, who had a genuinely unique act. Chase would come out elegantly dressed and smoking a cigarette, and the first thing he would do was eat the cigarette. Then he ate his cuffs, his shirt sleeves, and so on, all without saying a word. Now the audience would laugh anyway, but Jackie discovered that if he just came out and watched onstage, the laughter would quadruple. He learned then, I think, that he was a great reactor, that his eye-rolling and double takes and look of horror and exasperation needed a context to play against. I think he realized during that engagement that if he ever had a show, he would need a company around him."

In the off hours, Gleason was not so contemplative. He knocked back whiskey. He ogled women, and that wasn't all he did with them (although sex would always be more a part of his public mystique than his besetting private passion). And he gambled, especially with dice. Eating did not rate high among his yearnings of the moment. He was dieting down to a boyish one hundred seventy-five pounds, and for economy he and Stern did their serious dining at four A.M., when the casino served diehard patrons a free buffet.

On the night that would become forever after a symbol of their friendship, Gleason was hurling the dice while Stern kept track of the money. Jackie had a hot hand, and like every true gambler on a roll, he kept leaving all his winnings on the table to try for even more. He would back up twenty feet, sometimes thirty, set his elbows in a variation of that soon to be trademark shuffle and barrel up the makeshift alley between chairs and other playett like a bowler—or a charging rhino in full flight—bellowing in tones somewhere between exaltation and menace, "Load it on. Load it on." Time and again he staged this ritual, at last commanding the attention of the entire roomful of hardened, self-absorbed gamblers, as he wound himself up like a spring, surged forward and roared, once more, "Load it on."

The winnings mounted, dizzyingly for Stern. "We were up five thousand dollars and I had just enough of my wits about me to know that we had nowhere to go but down," he recalls. "A couple of times I tried to stop Jackie but each time he yelled at me, 'What are you trying to do, jinx us?' and he was so intense that I backed off, a little afraid of him. By the time I got him out of there we had lost back most of what we had won, but we were each still a few hundred to the good.

"The next morning—to be realistic, it was probably well after noon—I went around to see Jackie and give him his share and he said, 'Gee, thanks, that's great, pal.' As I talked to him I realized he had virtually no memory of what had happened the night before. It wasn't so much the booze, though he'd been drinking, or the gambling, though he'd had the fever, as it was the crowd and the performance. He had been living totally in that moment, totally for the show of it. When I told him we'd been up over five grand at one point, he said, 'Why didn't you stop me?' I don't think I could have, but I learned a valuable lesson for the future—that he always lacked a certain focus on reality when he was performing but that he might be persuaded to stop doing something if you said it was wrong and it made sense to him."

Gleason, too, seemed to have learned a lesson about himself from that moment of delirious, and costly, excess. Ever after, he would greet Stern with the phrase "Load it on, pal," an affirmation of intimacy and a winking reminder of a shared secret. Yet when Stern was invited in 1953 to come to work for Gleason, by then as big a star as there was on television, the darker side of this infectiously celebratory man began to emerge. "I was offered one thousand dollars a week for four weeks," says Stern, "to write episodes of *The Honeymooners* to appear within Jackie's variety show on CBS. That was a very high salary then, but the pay was so high partly because I would have to maintain two households, one in New York where the show was done and the other back in California, where I normally lived and worked. After I arrived, I guess some of the other writers found out what I was getting and complained, and Jackie himself called me in to try to bargain me down. I stood my ground. I said a deal was a deal and I pointed out my circumstances. Finally Jackie said, 'All right, Leonard, I'm going to give you your thousand dollars a week. But don't expect us to go on being friends.' Of course, he didn't really mean it, and I stayed on and off for three years. But he didn't really not mean it, either. I never reminded him of lending him that money in Vegas, never reminded him that I had helped bail him out of a jam. But I knew I had, and he knew I knew. And deep down that may have been something he couldn't forgive, that debt, that dependency."

Who was Jackie Gleason? To Art Carney, he was "the greatest talent I ever worked with," but far more a boss than a friend, so distant that he would be out of touch for years, until the next deal came along, and never once, as Carney's son Brian bitterly pointed out to friends, so much as a visitor to the family home for dinner. To Joyce Randolph, the original Trixie on *The Honeymooners*, Gleason was an unknowable man, hidden behind psychic walls, touchy and temperamental, whom she didn't even dream of inviting to her wedding. But to Audrey Meadows, Gleason was a man of boundless warmth and great restraint, a genius onstage and almost a saint off it.

To Gene Wolsk, the manager of Gleason's last cross-country tour, in Larry Gelbart's play *Sly Fox*, The Great One was "the worst person I ever worked with in forty years in show business." But to Manny Kladitis, second in command on the same management team, sitting in on almost all the same meetings and experiences, Gleason was just intoxicating entertainment, his tantrums and terrors the very stuff of which a star should be made. For Oscar-winning actress Estelle Parsons, who smoked pot with Gleason in the fifties and made a movie with him in the sixties, he was a sad holdover from the Damon Runyon era, an overdressed carouser who would rather be in a barroom full of men than alone with one beautiful woman. Yet to Kay Gardella, entertainment columnist for half a century at the *New York Daily News*, he was the courtliest of companions, a man who put women on a pedestal and treated even the hardest of them with deferential respect.

To Mike Dann, the longtime chief of programming during Gleason's heyday at CBS, he was "a true depressive," "the most self-destructive performer I ever knew" and a man so gluttonous for privilege that he would sometimes have three limousines waiting for him at three different entrances of the same building, all running up the bill for hours on end, so that he would not have to care which door he came out. Yet to superagent Sam Cohn, Gleason was the most generous of clients; he never once let his agent pick up the check for a meal in a quarter century of doing business together. "You never even saw the check to fight over it," Cohn recalls. "It was all taken care of before you ever arrived."

To talk show host Larry King, Gleason was an encouraging father figure, a loyal buddy and a fascinating conversationalist on almost any topic—but the meanest drunk in Miami, to be avoided at all costs once he had a bun on. To Flo Haley, widow of *Wizard of Oz* co-star Jack Haley and a savvy showgirl herself, Gleason was a born victim, turned tough over the years by the ceaseless disappointment of being exploited by so-called friends. To Coleman Jacoby, creator of most of the characters Gleason played for two decades of network television, The Great One was an ingrate, a credit hogger, a rewriter of history—and also an absolute genius who in the deepest sense was right that he owed nothing to anybody because he had done it all himself.

The more one digs into the life of Jackie Gleason, the hazier the truth becomes. He was many different things to different people and, moreover, many different things to himself. He was given to sweeping pronouncements about his life and views, and the grander the generalization, the shorter the time before he would somehow contradict it. Some years before his death he told a journalist that he had given an estimated five thousand interviews and that he felt honor-bound to say the same thing in answer to every basic question every time he was asked it. The estimate of total interviews was plausible enough. The ostensible philosophy of consistent answers was pure nonsense. Gleason did not just vary his stories and assertions from time to time; he did so almost compulsively, perhaps for amusement, perhaps for dramatic effect, but sometimes plainly for advantage. He was equally prone to false revelations and to concealment, sometimes in the same gesture. For a man who lived his last four decades almost entirely in the public eye and whose work was almost always autobiographical, he kept himself amazingly secret, often by the very device of making everything obvious, so that onlookers treated as just a joke the very deepest and most blatant truths about him. All of his art was a kind of confession, and applause was his absolution.

To journey through his life is to feel a bit like the reporter in *Citizen Kane*, discovering that many of the most carefully cherished myths and oft-repeated anecdotes are the most suspect. One keeps coming back, as the reporter in *Kane* did, to the image of a small boy, confused and just beginning to be frightened, standing and waiting in the middle of a snowfall. But in Gleason's life there is no Rosebud. There was no lost innocence, no lost hope, only a lifetime confirmation of a child's anger and intermittent despair. And besides, this boy's family was probably too poor even to provide him with a sled.

THE GREAT ONE

*The Life and Legend of
Jackie Gleason*

CHAPTER ONE

On the day Herbert John Gleason was born, February 26, 1916, there were three other members already in his family. Before he reached his twentieth birthday, all of them were gone—his sickly brother, Clemence, and his stoic mother, Mae, dead, his ne'er-do-well father, Herb, long since departed without even a goodbye. To the extent that factual circumstances ever explain anything as complicated as the human heart, this fact of abandonment explained Jackie Gleason.

He suffered a lifelong rage that energized his art and frequently poisoned his personal relations. He had an obsessive loyalty and a compulsive need to keep familiar faces around him, coupled with an almost total inaccessibility to affection and trust. He had a survivor's guilt that led him into both lacerating self-appraisal and deceitful self-mythologizing. He was obsessed with death and defied it in prodigious bouts of consumption and carousing, then bargained and atoned in ritual bursts of abstinence and self-improvement. He married three times officially and twice more without benefit of clergy, but with every mate save the last he fought as his parents had fought and ultimately split as his parents had split. In his mind, at least, they all abandoned him. He became a well-meaning but often neglectful father, as he had been an apparently loved but often neglected son. And, like both his father and his mother, he drank—excessively, often compulsively, claiming to be convivial but unleashing instead the sheer anarchic fury that was the deepest of all his passions toward the world. Yet during all of this pain and neurosis, he picked delicately through the attic of memories to create characters, almost all of them in some way deeply autobiographical, that struck John O'Hara as Dickensian, John McPhee as Chaplinesque and—more important to his success—struck ordinary viewers as reminiscent of their relatives, their neighbors, themselves.

Critics were apt to suggest, especially in later years, as America grew more cynical, that Gleason was a sentimentalist. In truth, the glimpses of misery in his art only hint at the prevailing misery of his early life. But no matter how far he moved in space and time and worldly goods from the cold-water-flat privation of his Brooklyn childhood, to the very end the roles that Gleason created or chose were roles that illuminated life's losers. The heroism of Gleason's characters lay not in triumph but in the quiet acceptance of failure and grief and pain. Sometimes the stories had happy endings. But the endings were never quite happy enough to transmute the losers into winners. Jackie Gleason knew better than that.

Anyone who has ever seen an episode of *The Honeymooners*, with its cramped walk-up flat, all but unfurnished rooms, noisy sink, battered icebox and miasma of poverty and despair, has some hint of the way Jackie Gleason grew up. He even gave the series' characters, the Kramdens, one of his childhood addresses, 358 Chauncey Street. But although critics have described *The Honeymooners* as the bleakest look at working-class frustration ever to reach a mass American audience, it turns out to have been almost giddily romantic in comparison with the real home life of the Gleasons.

To begin with, Gleason's idealization portrays a man perpetually determined to better himself, living with a wife who is for the most part proud and supportive and, at the least, relatively content with her lot. It shows marital quarrels ending in an embrace and shared expressions of faith. The central character, Ralph Kramden, knows he is going nowhere, yet his hope remains somehow unquenchable. And he and his wife find emotional fulfillment through close friends. None of this happened in the Gleason household. There weren't all that many laughs, either.

Mae Kelly was a girl of fifteen, Irish-born, educated only through primary school and with an unsophisticated adolescent's notion of love and romance, when she married Herb Gleason, a decade her senior, right at the turn of the twentieth century. She had no career, no trade, no ambitions beyond being a hostess to her friends and family and now and then going out on the town in distant Manhattan—a psychic pole vault from Brooklyn although newly part of the same unified metropolis. Her father was a sign painter, prosperous in a modest way, and she was the last of his five children. Her older sister Victoria was thrifty to a fault; she would sit in the dark to save money on the light bill. But Mae liked to spend. She longed for stylish clothes, elegant furniture. Yet all her married life she would eat the bitter crust of being a poor relation.

Herb Gleason had two things going for him in life. First, he was willing to work hard, within reason, so that even when he had wangled an office job he would try to hustle extra nickels by selling candy bars from his desk at lunch hour. Second, and a lot more useful, he had an older brother who was an executive at the Mutual Life Insurance Company of New York, and the brother dutifully supplied Herb with a minor clerical post and, eventually, raises and promotion. Once claims had been investigated by others at the company, all Herb had to do was get a check made out and bring it to the higher-ups, who would sign it for distribution. The work paid twenty-five dollars a week, and later thirty-five a week, at a time when that was enough to buy a good men's suit.

This income might have been enough to get by on—although certainly never enough to emulate Herb's brother, who commuted to leafy

4

Westchester County—if only there had been just the two of them to provide for. But by the time Mae was twenty, she had become a mother. Seemingly that event was a beginning to the joys of family life. It was really a precursor to destruction.

Mae, who was deeply religious, albeit in ways more often superstitious than theological—she had at least as much time for ghosts and ghoulies as for angels and saints—named her firstborn Clement, in honor of a succession of popes. For some reason she always called the boy Clemence, perhaps as a nickname, perhaps as a by-product of her distinct Irish brogue. From the start, the child was long, thin, pale and frail. His parents fretted over him constantly, as parents of a firstborn are apt to do, but their worry was not misplaced. They spent freely for a tonic called Beef, Wine and Iron, touted as good for a robust look and ruddy color. In keeping with the hygienic principles of the time, Mae also kept Clemence indoors most of the time, away from wind and weather—and from school yard sports and street corner revelry. She sent him often to church, supervised him closely the rest of the time and expected utter compliance. In all of this, she and Herb reflected the child-rearing values of their era, their class and their ethnic ancestry. If there was anything smothering or excessive in Mae's approach—as there was to be in years to come—no evidence of it survives. But none of her remedies accomplished much. Clemence remained weak and sickly. For Mae and Herb, the worry, the poverty and the frustration at Clemence's never getting much better all took their psychic toll. People of their era aged more quickly than in today's youth-extending culture. Mae Kelly Gleason was spending her twenties, the last few years of girlishness and laughter, in a losing battle to save a lost-cause child.

The arrival of a second son seems to have injected some joy and spirit into the household. Still, the birth, on February 26, 1916, was the occasion for yet another of the by now commonplace battles between Mae and Herb, this time over what to name the newborn. Mae once again wanted a religious name, John, in honor of the saint and baptist. Herb, not unnaturally, thought that with two sons to his credit at least one should be named for him. Mae told him she considered the name Herbert ugly and silly, hardly an assertion calculated to strengthen the marriage. When Herb at last wore her down, she proved a singularly stubborn loser. Although the child was registered as Herbert John Gleason, his mother never called him anything but Jack or Jackie and therefore, predictably, neither did anyone else. The new Gleason soon proved to have his father's glistening black hair but without the offsetting jug ears. He was quick-witted and funny in a bright-sayings kind of way. His eyes were a soft blue, like water in a swimming pool, and would keep their crystalline beauty all his life. He was plucky and adventurous, and his heart was full of mischief. While Clemence was admirably long-suffering, Jackie was fun.

They were not brothers for long. When Jackie was three, Clemence died at age fourteen of an illness—precisely what illness is undiscoverable now and probably was not known to the Gleasons at the time. Mae deeply distrusted doctors. She placed occasional faith in a homeopathic practitioner and none at all in any other kind. Neither she nor Herb had gone beyond the few years of grade school and, like many ignorant people, they tended to regard the art of medicine as akin to magic. Some peasants thought of doctors' care as benevolent wizardry; others, consciously or subliminally, feared that seeking medical help somehow amounted to defiance of God's will. Folk wisdom, moreover, equated physicians and death, because in most households a doctor was not consulted until so late in an illness that the only thing left for the medico to do was confirm the family's gloomy suspicions with formal diagnosis. Mae Gleason may have brought a doctor in, despite her misgivings, and hardened against medicine when it failed to save her son. Or she may not even have given the doctors a chance. If Jackie knew which was the case, he apparently never said. What is certain is that in later years, during Mae's own agonizing final illness, she would not allow doctors into her house. When well-meaning friends persuaded a young resident to pay a house call, Mae chased him away—and thereby ensured or at least hastened her demise.

The death of Clemence in 1919 transformed the Gleason household. Herb began to drink more heavily and more often, to disappear on benders for days at a time, to squander his meager earnings. Mae took to waiting for him outside the office on paydays, often with little Jackie in tow. Yet she also began to drink to oblivion herself. What in their youth had been a love of revelry together, of an innocent night on the town, had hardened in both Gleasons into a bitter yearning for escape.

They had plenty to get away from. The marriage was sour. Herb's career, lackluster to begin with, was further imperiled by his colleagues' growing awareness of how heavily he drank. His pay did not keep pace with inflation, an ever larger share of it was spent on booze, and to its other instabilities the family added frequent moves in search of more space and less rent—always in cold-water flats within a couple of blocks of Halsey Street, where the shopfronts were and the streetcars ran. On the day of Clemence's burial, as family lore had it, the Gleasons narrowly escaped the final tragedy of being altogether childless. While his brother was being prepared for burial, little Jackie was found to be missing and was located outside, playing a short kick away from the funeral wagon horse's hooves. He had come down, he explained, because he had heard that the horse had white socks—and with an impish grin he thrust out a fistful of the rubber bands with which he meant to hold those socks up.

Despite the gathering clouds at home, Jackie professed in later years to have been largely unaware of, or at least unaffected by, the misery around him. Soon after his brother's death he developed a habit of leaving the house at night, unannounced, to visit his cousin Renee a couple of streets away. His excursions may have been nothing more than the customary ritual journeys of childhood, undertaken by many a tot too small to have a proper sense of danger. And Renee was, to be sure, a lifelong favorite of Jackie's. But these trips may also have been psychically connected to his brother's death and to a fearful need to check on everyone else who mattered to him, so that they too did not die and leave. The nighttime treks may have been as well an assertion of independence, for what had been protective and possessive in Mae's handling of Clemence was quickly to become, with Jackie, well nigh pathological. She held her healthy son, as she had held her fragile one, suffocatingly close and kept him apart from the neighborhood children with their sports and games, their rough and tumble—all the social normalcy that lonely Jackie ached to join.

The adult Jackie Gleason, for all his public protestations of candor, was regarded by his closest associates as fiercely private and unconfiding. He loathed being described as a Pagliacci, a sad clown, and detested the way newspaper and magazine editors seemed to prefer portraits of him looking anywhere from brooding to outright desperate. He had a deep distaste for any psychoanalytic speculation, especially when it involved other members of his family. In the world in which he was raised, to criticize one's relatives, no matter what sins they had committed against you, was an unpardonable breach of taste. So he largely eluded meaningful discussion— throughout two authorized biographies, thousands of print and broadcast interviews and half a century of adult friendship—of any aspect of his relationships with his parents. His public posture was that his mother had deserved something close to canonization. "She had to work after my father was gone," he recalled, "and couldn't take care of the flat very well at the same time. The surroundings were dismal, just a round table and an icebox and a bureau that everything went into. The light bulbs were never very bright and the rooms were always bare. But she was a good mother and things were very pleasant, with a lot of affection."

In private, however, during rare confessional moments, Gleason had another story. He admitted to his longtime agent Sam Cohn, a friend and frequent drinking buddy during the last quarter century of his life, that Mae Gleason had been a deeply troubled woman with a propensity to booze and neurosis. "He said he had this bizarre childhood," Cohn recalls, "in which his mother sequestered him for his own protection from the whole life of the neighborhood. He saw her as the epitome of lace-curtain Irish, afraid he would fall in with the wrong elements, and as this obsessively sheltering figure."

She was to be only the first of a succession of women to set moral standards he couldn't meet. And her efforts were, predictably, counterproductive. As soon as he was old enough, Jackie ingratiated himself with neighborhood gangs and then became a regular at the pool halls, the nearest equivalent to opium dens to be found in the Bushwick section of Brooklyn. He and his friends were later to recall that he smoked by age ten, hustled pool games for money at eleven and sampled bathtub gin at twelve. If this was not precisely perdition by the standards of the neighborhood, it was not the hothouse innocence Mae longed for.

But those pursuits were relatively harmless, by objective norms if not by Mae Gleason's. The deepest harm that his mother's possessiveness visited on him was that Jackie did not enroll in school until he was eight years old. Although he read as well as his age-mates and would ultimately demonstrate a vast and various intelligence, this late start doomed him to spend much of his childhood as an academic misfit. Predictably, he became a class clown and a discipline problem. He hated school, did poorly and longed to leave. He rebelled against authority and lived only for the moments when he could, by dint of having crammed on a subject with an encyclopedia the night before, show up the teacher. That kind of triumph was only fleeting, however, and its inevitable result was to deepen the teachers' dislike of him and further mire his status at the bottom of the class. It could be argued that by temperament he would have been an irritant no matter what his mother did. But when he went to catechism class to prepare for Confirmation in the Roman Catholic Church, at about age fourteen, Jackie was at long last competing on an equal footing, with no stigma of a late start. He behaved well and ranked first in the class.

His brother's death was the first landmark event of Jackie's childhood. His father's departure was the third. Sometime between them came what for fellow Americans was the most momentous thing ever to happen to little Jackie Gleason, his introduction to the glories of show business. The problem in sketching this episode with the color and drama it deserves is that its central subject seemed unable to make up his mind about the basic facts. Gleason told the story in so many sharply different ways that one cannot be sure when it happened, or in whose company, or indeed for certain if it happened at all.

Gleason cited this epic little moment of self-discovery in countless interviews and numberless private conversations. He said it was the life event that persuaded him to be a performer or, rather, verified the existence of the thing he already intuitively wanted to do. In all his many versions, the locale of the story never varied. It was the Halsey Theater, where the child Gleason saw vaudeville shows and where the adolescent Gleason would later work as emcee on amateur night, his first paying job in show business. The essence of what happened never varied, either. The young Gleason was seated in the audience for his first show ever, jiggling with delight. He rose at intermission and joined in the general applause. Then he turned to look out at the audience spread behind him and abruptly thought, "No, this is the way to see it. I want to be up there and look out at them applauding for me. That is what will feel the most natural." The rest, of course, is history.

Like almost all of Gleason's other favorite stories about himself, especially those from his early years, this tale had a few holes in its logic and several shortcomings in its consistency. First, while the story may in essence be true, it doesn't actually reveal very much. Probably half the children who have ever been taken to a live show have had similar impulses, which reflect more a youngster's need for power and attention than any considered choice of career. The hunger for applause, moreover, goes a very short way toward explaining why Gleason became and remained a comic rather than an acrobat or juggler or high diver or song-and-dance man (all of which trades he also tried), let alone what made him any good.

13

The basic problem with the story, though, is that over the many times he told it, Gleason placed himself at any age from three and a half to nine. The significance of an experience varies enormously between those ages, one when a child is just emerging into communication, the other when he or she is nearing adolescence. It is hard to believe that Gleason could be so persistently hazy about so basic a fact concerning this transcendent day of his youth. Odder still, his recollections differed as to who brought him to the theater. Most of the time, he said he was accompanied by his father. But at least once, in private conversation with the radio and TV talk show host Larry King, a close friend for two decades, Gleason said his companion at that fateful show was his mother. The average person might possibly be in doubt about which parent did what in early childhood. But it hardly seems possible that Gleason would confuse the two, given that one parent would soon afterward abandon him forever, while the other would sustain him and die virtually in his arms. When attributing the adventure to his father, moreover, Gleason sometimes depicted it as a rare companionship and on other occasions as launching a regular Saturday ritual, one that routinely began with his father's stopping at an illegal but openly run Prohibition-era speakeasy to get snockered before attending the show. According to Gleason's first biographer, Jim Bishop, little Jackie was once left standing outside for so long that he was ques-

14

tioned by the police. He followed parental instruction and stayed mute. This episode, a memorable trauma for a child, seems not to have figured in Gleason's other versions of the story. But his other authorized biographer, James Bacon, asserts that Mae Gleason occasionally visited the same or a similar nearby speakeasy, although apparently not with Jackie beside her.

Whether Gleason actually had a flash of toddlerhood revelation—he told Bishop that learning he wanted to be a vaudevillian was his first conscious memory—beyond doubt he attended shows frequently at the Halsey. They gave him happy times in a less than joyous childhood. They also taught him show business lessons that he retained for a lifetime. One of the first was to be an impeccable dresser at all times, a standard he followed so compulsively that during his live network shows in the fifties and sixties he kept half a dozen replacement carnations for his lapel in a bowl of water just offstage, in case his gyrations knocked petals off the one he was wearing. He explained his fastidiousness to Pete McGovern, who spent two decades as his press agent, by recalling one of the first performers he ever saw at the Halsey, a juggler. "He was lousy," Gleason said. "I could do as much or more fooling around with the kids on the corner. But he came out in a full formal outfit, top hat, tailcoat, everything perfect, and when he kept three balls in the air at once the audience applauded as though he were W. C. Fields. The clothes meant you respected them, and they ought to respect you and your work."

Most of the comedians at the Halsey, and at every other vaudeville stop, were ethnic. They aped the accents and the stereotypic character traits of immigrant groups, which in Bushwick meant nearly everybody, either in the current generation or in the one just before. Around Halsey Street, most people were of Irish descent. A few were Italian. The Jews, derived primarily from Russia and Poland, clustered around Gates Avenue, a similar streetcar boulevard some blocks away. Ethnic humor was an accepted part of life, even in political campaigns, school shows and other sanctioned public events. By modern standards the mores of that era were shot through with overt prejudice, but to Gleason and his contemporaries, relations among the city's tribes were relatively benign. An example of what was tolerated—indeed, found funny—was the boyhood nickname of Thomas Robinson, a street corner pal who grew up to become a college professor of literature. In later life Gleason nicknamed Robinson "Bookshelf." But in childhood he was known as "Boogie" because neighborhood boys had decided that Robinson was "a nigger name." Robinson himself wasn't black, and it would be decades before Jackie Robinson would become a household name among Brooklyn Dodger fans. Yet Gleason would say, with apparent sincerity, "There was no bigotry where I grew up, none at all."

16

Ten days before Christmas, and about two months before Jackie's tenth birthday, Herb Gleason decided he had finally had enough. He was nursing a grudge from yet another fight with his wife. He was worn down by demands that he produce, out of his inadequate salary, the bounty of holiday presents that his complaining wife and any normal child would expect at that season. He could not stand the humiliation of being hauled home from work or dragged out of barrooms by his wife, often in front of his co-workers, and he was enraged at her hypocrisy, given how fond she was of drinking herself. The only real difference between them was that she liked to be drunk at home, alone, while he liked to be out at a bar with others, which at least seemed more normal and sociable. Divorce was out of the question. The laws of the state made disunion very difficult in those days. And for two practicing Roman Catholics, the laws of the church made it impossible. Whatever release Herb sought, Mae would doubtless fight him, for a divorced woman in that era was a figure of some disgrace, even scandal—and Herb was sick of fighting. Jackie, the namesake son who had never once used Herb's name, was sure to be lost to him. Anyway, Herb had had enough of responsibility. He needed a fresh start. Abandoning his family by stealth, he concluded, was the only course open to him.

He laid his plans as carefully as he could. Like

many a meek clerk in tales dramatized by Alfred Hitchcock, he proved—despite his modest education and intelligence, his drunkenness and general weakness of character—to be more than sufficiently cunning. First, he realized, he would need money. He resolved to wait until his twice-monthly payday, when he would get about seventy-five dollars. In advance he borrowed a hundred and fifty more, forging Mae's signature on the necessary forms. He also needed time to get away. So he plotted to depart the office just after noon and thus ensure himself a head start of three to four hours before Mae came looking for him. His co-workers would assume he was taking a long lunch or tying one on somewhere and would hesitate to point out his absence because he was the boss's brother.

Herb's final need was to avoid being traced. In that simpler day before computer cross-indexing and copious paperwork, the main way to find an ordinary man like Herb Gleason was through visual recognition. To elude detection, Herb would simply have to stay out of the path of people who knew what he looked like. He could have fled to another part of the country, but that would have used up most of his money and cut him off from almost everything he knew. So he chose a simpler expedient. Sometime during his last few evenings at home, he took away or destroyed every family photograph in which he appeared; he also spirited out the family photos he kept at the office. These maneuvers ensured that Mae would not have a likeness of her husband to give the police. That in turn meant that no photos could be distributed to hospitals, hiring halls or other agencies where Herb might turn up. Nor could they be reproduced in newspapers, where some stranger might see his image and connect him with the new employee or neighbor.

It is just possible, of course, that Herbert Gleason's disappearance was not altogether calculated and cunning. In one of the several versions of the story about the photos that his son told over the years, Herb started tearing up the family album during a fight with his wife. That might well have been a spontaneous outburst, however convenient it proved once he started to consider its ramifications. Similarly, it is remotely possible that he borrowed the extra hundred and fifty dollars intending to provide a lavish Christmas and forged Mae's signature so he could surprise her, only to succumb to the feelings of power and wanderlust that the wad of cash gave him as he stuffed it into his wallet. Herb may even have meant, as he left the house on the morning of December 15, 1925, to keep his promise to meet Mae at the workday's end and go into Times Square for a few drinks or perhaps a show.

But offering her that prospect of pleasure, and then standing her up, seems like a last act of spite from a man fully determined to go. In any case, however casually it began, Herb Gleason's flight ended as a perfect crime. He defrauded his cred-itors. He cheated his company of the loan money, an afternoon's work and a proper notice of his going. He left his wife and son penniless and be-reft on the eve of Christmas, standing in the cold for hours in the middle of a snowfall. And he never, in aftertimes, sent along so much as a com-forting or calming word. They never heard from him again.

Once she accepted that her husband was really gone, not just off on an extended binge some-where, Mae consented on a few occasions to view unidentified bodies at the morgue to see if one of them might be Herb. But within months she concluded that the effort was horrifying and pointless and refused to go again. One afternoon a former co-worker thought she spotted Herb, very much alive, among a crew of day laborers clearing up after a snowfall. But by the time the office worker had rounded up male colleagues to look with her, the Herb-like figure was gone. Some at the company thought it had been a trick of this woman's imagination. Others believed that the real Herb had been there but realized he had been recognized and had fled. Mae's handling of the whole situation was ambivalent. She never sought to have herself legally declared a widow, eligible for remarriage. But after Herb had been gone several years, she apparently started to date again, if chastely. According to some recollec-tions, one of her beaux was named Ralph—seem-ingly yet another autobiographical detail that

Gleason would eventually work into *The Honey-mooners*.

In optimistic moments, both as a child and as a man, Gleason would speculate that his father had been robbed or otherwise injured and was suffering from amnesia. He wanted to believe that what looked like cold desertion was in fact a shared tragedy of separation, suitable for some sentimental romance. But two incidents, both of which he did his best to deny through the years, argued compellingly against his sweet fiction. First, when Herb's older brother, the insurance executive and benefactor, died a few years after the desertion, some mourner not in attendance sent a wreath signed "From your loving brother." The only surviving brother in the family was Herb. This curious episode reinforced a dark suspicion among Mae's relatives that Herb's clan knew perfectly well where he was and might even have assisted in engineering his escape.

The clincher in dispelling any illusions about his father's desertion came many years later, during Jackie's first burst of superstardom in the early fifties. The all-powerful J. Edgar Hoover, director of the Federal Bureau of Investigation and a methodical currier of favor among the prominent, read of Gleason's sad childhood and ordered a trace put on Herbert Gleason. The search led to Connecticut, but there the trail ended: the quarry had died, at about age seventy, a few years before. He had lived long enough to know, if he paid any attention to such things,

21

that his son had become a star in nightclubs and had made a small splash on Broadway and in Hollywood. He had died too soon to see his threadbare home and its marital discord transmuted into video entertainment for millions.

The final whereabouts of Herb Gleason were promptly conveyed to his son—accompanied, Jackie recalled later, by a not too subtle bid for recompense in the form of a benefit appearance on behalf of the FBI. Gleason claimed to have scorned both the information and the request and to have thrown Hoover's agents out of his office. The whole package, he said, was so neat and slick that it ignited his mistrust. Viewed objectively, however, the information was fairly persuasive, and it became public through Freedom of Information inquiries after Hoover's death. But Gleason may not have wanted to view it objectively; throughout his life, he carefully avoided any direct criticism of the man who had abandoned him. At length he settled on a favorite locution, cunningly ambiguous: "He was the best father I'll ever know." The immediate overtone was affirmative. On a closer look, the phrase expressed no more than the poignant truth—that Herb Gleason, poor excuse though he might be, was all that Jackie Gleason would ever have to admire in that vital role. His alternatives were to protect the memory of that unhappy man or denounce him, and the latter would have been an unthinkable violation of the code of the Irish, the code of the neighborhood, the code of Mae

Kelly Gleason and the code of Jackie Gleason, the fiercely proud loner whom these influences shaped.

After the confusion and dismay wore off, the immediate effect of Herb Gleason's sneaking off was acute impoverishment. While he was still around, things were often tight enough that the Gleasons would take in a boarder, subletting space in a flat they only rented themselves and accommodating the paying intruder at the table at most family meals. This sort of arrangement was not altogether uncommon. While by present-day standards it would be a terrible invasion and indignity, in that era it usefully enabled the mother of a family to become a second breadwinner without committing the social solecism of taking a job outside the house, which few husbands, in their pride, would permit and which many employers forbade as an affront to conventional mores. Once Herb was gone, however, such niceties were secondary. Mae and Jackie had to find cheaper quarters, fast, and Mae had to have a real job. At ten, Jackie was still too young to make a real contribution (characteristically, he sometimes further sentimentalized the abandonment as happening when he was only seven or eight). Mae's options were limited by the hard economic times and by her own lack of education and skills. So she became a change maker for the BMT branch of the New York City subway system. This kept a roof over their heads and food on the table, but not much else. The hours were bad; some-times Mae worked an all-night shift. Working conditions were arduous; the change booth was broiling in summer and freezing in winter, and she stood on her feet the entire time. Clothing was at such a premium in the household that Jackie remembered seeing his mother borrow his leggings to wrap around her shins when she worked a night shift in winter, and he also recalled having only one set of underwear, which Mae would wash out at night in cold water (there was no hot water) and leave on the radiator to dry by morning.

The financial pressures on Mae were com-pounded by the emergence, in the months after Herb's departure, of what later became legendary in Jackie—his ravenous appetite. Bishop's biog-raphy reported, to Gleason's fury, that he became a compulsive, neurotic overeater in response to his father's desertion. Gleason repudiated this analysis in interviews and in conversation with associates. But he told some people that Bishop was wrong because he did not start eating heavily until much later, while he told others that Bishop was wrong because he had already become a fierce eater well before his father disappeared. Both disproofs could not simultaneously be true, of course. And what they were meant to disprove was in no way shameful. Indeed, people who might have dismissed Gleason as a sickening glut-ton were bound to view him with greater sym-pathy if they saw his behavior as the outcome

24

of childhood trauma. But precisely what enraged Gleason was this suggested connection, with its underlying premise that his actions might be in any way foreordained. He was determined to transcend Freudian predictability. To be understood could only make The Great One ordinary. In mystery and enigma, he felt, lay the wellspring of his persona and his art. Fittingly for a Roman Catholic steeped in the philosophical dilemmas beloved of his church, he centered every one of his enduring comic characters—from Kramden to the highborn Reggie Van Gleason to the pathetic Poor Soul—around the struggle to transcend circumstance through the exercise of free will. To become the adult artist he wished, Gleason had to reinvent his childhood, to break the bounds of cause and effect.

Yet whatever the psychoanalytic reason, a glutton he unmistakably became. He was not just a secret binger, like many obese people. Even in company he ate like a marauding animal. His first puppy love and lifelong friend Julie Dennehy, whose father managed the block of flats where the Gleasons finally lived, was occasionally a dinner guest in the Gleason apartment. She recalled that she and Mae always made a point of serving themselves all the food they might possibly want at the very beginning of the meal, rather than testing their appetite and going back for seconds. They knew that once they had filled their plates, Jackie would take hold of the platter and empty its contents onto his plate—or eat right from the main dish—not stopping for longer than a breath until everything was gone. No matter how high the serving bowl was heaped, it could not exceed his capacity. Unlike other families in New York City, the Gleasons could not count on Monday leftovers or Tuesday hash from a Sunday roast.

The other evident impact of Herb's desertion was to give young Jackie a lifelong hunger for male camaraderie. Having lost a father and a brother, lacking any male cousin with whom he was on terms of real intimacy and overseen by an increasingly possessive, dependent and alcoholic mother, he could have responded by becoming a mama's boy, fated to the long and lonely bachelorhood so common among the Irish. Instead, his stubborn and aggressive masculinity asserted itself more and more. He allied himself with playmates. He sought older boys as role models. He hung around neighborhood men, even those who, like Julie's father, regarded young Jackie as a wiseacre and future bum. As a sentimental gesture, Gleason would immortalize "Mr. Dennehy" as the unseen interlocutor of his Joe the Bartender sketches throughout the fifties and sixties. In real life the man may have been more curmudgeon than mentor to the fatherless boy, but his mere presence was apparently enough to endear him to a youth in emotional need.

Mae's possessive, smothering ways kept Jackie home much of the time, especially in the first few years after Herb left. In later life Gleason would attribute to these lonely hours the awakening of his imagination and the attuning of his senses. "My mother would go to work," he recalled, "and in the early morning I'd be sitting at the table and hear noises and be fascinated. I could tell who was coming into the tenement by the sound of their feet. I could tell what people were doing by the sounds they made. It was as though I could see them. If I even heard a mouse scratch, I'd be fascinated by that. And it got so that when I heard music, I could listen to the sounds in back of the melody, hear it all, how it was made."

But this sort of quiet contemplation, although it would remain a central and largely unrecognized part of Gleason's personality all his life, was not so strong in the budding teenage Jackie as was the yearning for company.

Like most big-city adolescents of his generation or later ones, Gleason joined gangs. Their principles were neighborhood loyalty and mutual cooperation. Their purpose was to have fun and raise hell. These were not gangs in the harsh contemporary sense or even the romanticized menace of, say, *West Side Story*. A Bushwick gang's idea of a crime spree was to hustle bets at a pool hall or hop the turnstile at the subway—the latter a sin Gleason always insisted he would not commit because it would somehow show disrespect for his mother's hard work making change for paying customers. Instead, the Four Original Eagles, the Nomads and Gleason's other cohorts were more like the alliances in *Tom Sawyer* or *Penrod and Sam,* youthful blood brotherhoods that began the maturation process of building emotional ties outside the family. That was especially urgent for the fatherless, brotherless Jackie.

He credited these bonds with developing his wit—"In Brooklyn, everyone was funny"—and with teaching him valuable street corner bargaining skills that later helped him hustle his megadollar network contracts. "With the network executives," he said, "it was threats to your security and kudos to your ego, that's how they operated. But I learned that game on the corner of Chauncey Street in Brooklyn when I was a kid. When a guy would ask me, 'Hey, you have a cigarette?,' I would say, 'Just one, and I have it in my shirt pocket,' and I'd pat it or take it out to show. Well, nobody takes your last cigarette, that's not done. But I'd have the pack with the other nineteen in my pants pocket. That would stand off the con from the other guy, and I carried that right with me into when I had to do business in television."

If the gangs were in themselves normal, relatively harmless and even in some rough-and-tumble way instructive, Gleason's membership in them helped establish in his mind two dilemmas that were to haunt his adult life. First and foremost was the conflict between the dull virtue of domesticity and the seductive conviviality of bad companions. The sense that being at home was suffocating, that the only real fun was to be had out on the town with the boys, would ultimately destroy his first marriage, estrange him from his children, lead him to squander his income on an epic scale and dissipate his talents. The second, closely related conflict was between the workaday routine of a job, the trap from which his father had so melodramatically broken free, and the unsteady exhilaration of earning one's keep by beguiling spectators. His Halsey Street cronies were Gleason's first testing ground for his hopes of breaking free by wit and charm, and the more they laughed at him, the more he loved and needed them. Throughout his life, Gleason would insist that the fundamental requirement for success in comedy was not wit but courage. "Look around this room," he said time and again. "Probably ten people here are as funny as I am. The difference is that I have the nerve to get up and do it in public."

The encouragement Gleason drew from his street corner buddies was not echoed at home. A CBS network press release from the fifties, presumably written with Gleason's cooperation and certainly reviewed and approved by him, credits Mae Kelly Gleason with sharing his show business dreams and spurring him on in his career. But by every other account, including Gleason's own on other occasions, this is simply not true. Although not educated herself, Mae believed in the redemptive and liberating power of education. Show business she regarded as a short path to the poorhouse. Despite Jackie's turbulent record in school, she dreamed fondly of his completing high school, even going on to college or—holy of holies for an Irish immigrant clan—studying law under Jesuit instruction. The priesthood might have pleased her even more, but some daydreams about young Jackie were simply *too* fanciful.

It was, ironically, in school that Jackie got the first solid confirmation of his talent to amuse and, at least as important to him, the first opportunity to prove it to his mother. His school, P.S. 30, planned a graduation entertainment called, prophetically for at least one class member, "Audio, Video and Radio." Part of its technological theme was a look ahead to television. But most of its content, naturally, was skits influenced by vaudeville and other popular entertainment of the time. Nothing in all his years of schooling had mattered as much to Jackie Gleason as being a part of that show. But he had been such a discipline problem that the staff had no intention of including him. Teachers turned him down, despite his entreaties. So did the principal. Finally Gleason got one last hearing and auditioned what he would perform: a Jewish dialect version of "Little Red Riding Hood," which would seem hopelessly incorrect on political grounds today but which wowed the faculty enough to make up for Jackie's many transgressions.

The experience of actually facing an audience wowed Jackie even more. "I got a laugh," he recalled, "and it was like, I guess, ten spoonfuls of cocaine. It was the greatest thing that could possibly happen to you, that instant critique of laughter, better than anything, even sex."

On the actual night of performance, the biggest and most memorable laugh came not from his rehearsed routine but from a throwaway insult, of the kind that would become his trademark for more than a decade in nightclubs. During Gleason's act, the microphone twice fell or was knocked over by his flailing, and the principal twice picked it up. The second time, Gleason shouted out, "That's the first time you ever did anything for us kids." Even the principal laughed. In later years, with this as with so many anecdotes, Gleason polished a little. He ceased to be the cause of the microphone's falling. It happened once, not twice, so his quip popped out the first time. And he reworded himself to "That is the first thing you have ever done for this school," which is rhythmically better and funnier because it is more grandiose. It has, however, the ring of the brashly mature Gleason rather than of an edgy fourteen-year-old. If he could, Gleason would probably have reinvented his personal history to have been a full-blown version of The Great One practically from the womb.

It is not merely a suspicious nature or the accretion of small contradictions that makes one skeptical about Gleason's autobiographical tales. Pete McGovern, his personal public relations man for two decades, admits he ghostwrote many of Gleason's articles, including nostalgic reminiscences, and he did so with only the sketchiest of instruction from his employer and no independent checking. On one occasion, Gleason accepted six hundred dollars to provide *Parade*, the Sunday supplement, with a Christmas remembrance from his childhood. He handed the assignment over to McGovern, who asked, "Do you want me to tell about anything in particular?" Gleason replied, "Just wing it," and McGovern did. "I just took an incident from my own childhood and moved it to Brooklyn," he recalls. "It had nothing to do with Jackie at all, except that I tried to have it sound like his voice. It won some kind of award and then, I think, Jackie finally bothered to read it."

With this in mind, one must at least mildly distrust such inspirational articles as Gleason's poignant description of how the family came to move into proximity with his first love, Julie Dennehy. This "memoir" from the early fifties describes how he concluded that a basement apartment that had become vacant in the building where Julie's father was superintendent, locally known as Dennehy's Flats, would be better, despite its lack of light, than the current Gleason quarters up six literally breathtaking flights of stairs. When his mother objected to the move on financial grounds, he said, he got a job as a delivery boy at a neighborhood grocery and started saving money to surprise her. (How Gleason could have concealed his job and wages from his mother or could have controlled his characteristically compulsive spending the instant he was paid, the article deftly does not address.) On the appointed day, when he planned to move between the time he got home from school and the time his mother returned from work, he and his friends began piling the household goods onto a rented cart. Too soon, his mother showed up.

"There stood my Mom, her face white, her eyes bugging out of her head. Something had gone wrong with the timing. Either she had gotten out of work early or we were working slower than we'd figured on.

" 'I wanted to surprise you, Mom,' I cried. 'I wanted to have us all moved before you got home.'

"She clapped her hand to her head and finally two hoarse words came from her. 'My things!' she cried.

"I turned around and seemed to see the wagon for the first time, see it with her eyes. Piled high behind a spavined horse was a wild jumble of Mom's prize possessions. There was the mahogany bedstead that had come with her from Ireland. The thick, corduroy-bound volume of family photographs. A set of hand-painted dishes tossed in a box. Her Sunday hat. Her lace curtains rolled in a ball.

"And beneath it all on the side of the wagon was painted the single word, JUNK.

"That Mom had pride was something that had never occurred to me before, but now I understood it with a sudden adult intuition. Her family had been fairly well off in Ireland and even here in America she had lived in ease until my Dad disappeared. Now she was a change-maker in an elevated station, but those possessions I had so thoughtlessly piled in the junk wagon were symbols of her dignity and pride.

"Dennehy Flats, where I was taking her, were noisy, brawling tenements compared to the house we lived in. All this I suddenly understood. I read it in her eyes as she looked at the junk wagon.

" 'I—I'm sorry, Mom,' I mumbled.

"Her arm went around me and she hugged me to her and smiled. 'Why do you want to move over there so bad, Jackie?' she asked. 'Is it because of Julie Dennehy?'

"She had guessed my secret. I blushed and looked at the ground."

" 'If it means so much to you, son, we'll move,' she said softly.

"Then with a wave of her hand she put the crew of movers back to work. Fifteen minutes later we rolled through the streets of Brooklyn, Mom sitting on the wagon seat beside me for all to see.

"Mom moved into Dennehy Flats for me. But she also knew that you can have pride and dignity no matter where you live."

Perhaps that is the way it went between Mae and Jackie Gleason, on some good days at least. Perhaps the careworn, drunken and angry woman was also gentle, intuitive and kind. But if so, it must have been a special moment. Nothing about the adult Jackie Gleason suggested a man who felt loved and secure.

If his graduation show triumph redeemed Gleason for his teachers, it did not redeem school for him. Despite Mae's dreams, his formal education ended a few months later. By law he had to continue somewhere—he was only fourteen—so he enrolled in Bushwick High in Brooklyn, where he professed profound boredom toward history and literature, and then after a couple of weeks switched to John Adams High, a trade school. "But the only trade I wanted to learn," he recalled, "was acting." Soon after the transfer, some adult male persuaded school authorities to allow Jackie to drop out altogether on the basis that he was a hardship case, the sole support of his mother. That was an especially compelling argument in the autumn of 1930, a year after the stock market collapse and in the midst of a deepening recession. Before his fifteenth birthday, before he came close to completing the ninth grade, and with little more than six years of actual time in a classroom, Jackie Gleason completed his first formal declaration of independence from authority.

The episode of his departure from school remains one of his more mysterious. By all accounts including his own, his mother wanted him to get an education. Why, then, did she permit him to shift to trade school and then leave altogether?

35

Who was the male adult who interceded with authorities, and how did that come about? The most circumstantial of several varying accounts, all emanating from Gleason himself in some way, has it that the man was his cousin Renee's husband. Renee was Mae's relative, and Jackie was living at home, so presumably Mae consented to all this. But by then Mae was drinking more often and perhaps Jackie's stubbornness simply wore everyone down.

The most inexplicable question of all, one that Gleason bitterly resented and ducked all his life, was this: If he was supposed to be his mother's sole support, then why, over the four and a half years between his leaving school and her death, did he never take a steady job to support her?

One answer is that he was Herb Gleason's son as much as hers and had no intention of starting what his father found himself unable to finish. Another is that he did earn his keep, at least a little, by doing occasional errands at a grocery store and other pickup jobs, by hustling pool bets and, above all, by working at vaudeville house amateur nights, first as a talent contestant and then as emcee. Pool opened his eyes to the pleasures of moneymaking. While still a kid he was good enough that his friends felt complete confidence in betting on him, one boy even going so far as to pawn his father's dress suit to raise a gambling stake. Gleason was skillful with the cue stick, and even more skillful with the psychology. He could size up and rattle an opponent while keeping his own demons hidden (a talent that provided his single most memorable moment on film, the all-night pool session with Paul Newman in *The Hustler*). Even when playing for money he had a prankish sense of humor. In the Brooklyn of that era, pool halls promoted appearances by a character called the Masked Marvel, a trick-shot artist who could take on all comers. Once, when he knew the masked man was coming, young Gleason got to the hall early, wearing his own mask, and was adroit enough to bring off the impersonation until the real Marvel showed up in the middle of Jackie's routine.

By his later adolescence, however, Gleason's focus shifted from pool, which offered minimal opportunities for real fame and money, to performing, which offered far more. He and a pal named Charlie Cretter worked up an act based on one of the hoariest vaudeville devices. Cretter appeared alone and professed to be confused as to where his partner was. Then Gleason appeared as if he were a member of the audience, shouting insults—once again in Jewish dialect—and in general bullying Cretter before joining him for a straight song as a finale. Then as ever, Gleason insisted on dressing up. It had to be tuxedos or nothing. Gleason was from the start the funnier of the pair (even though, in their first appearance, Cretter tried that comic standby of singing falsetto and wearing a dress), and he began getting calls to emcee one or more nights a week. He sang a little. He danced a little. Like almost every young comic everywhere in the world (including his future partner Art Carney), he did impressions of movie stars and other celebrities. But what made Gleason stand out was his spontaneity, his ability to be funny off the cuff, in response to situations as they arose or the ragamuffin amateur acts as they appeared. This was partly because he was a natural performer. He once attributed his getting hired permanently at the Halsey to his impromptu decision during his first performance as emcee to skid deliberately into some seltzer that had been spilled on the stage and take an extravagant windmilling pratfall. But his improvisation was so striking at least partly because his prepared material was by comparison so stale and thirdhand. All his life, he would be less someone who said funny things than someone who said things funny.

All this was very promising, but it was not paying the rent. On good nights Jackie would earn five dollars, but he didn't always get paid that much, and he certainly didn't get it five days a week. He was still appearing on amateur bills and was basically an amateur himself. Nearly all his work was in the evenings, and in the daytime he struck many of his neighbors as a well-dressed bum. He hung out on the streets and wouldn't take a regular job. He was always dandified, always as elegantly turned out as his budget would allow. It appeared that he spent much of what he earned on himself rather than on helping out his mother, who still owned almost nothing. Even her furniture was being purchased on the installment plan.

Many a poor boy has dreamed that one of the pleasures of success will be rewarding his mother for all her sacrifices. The happy ones get the opportunity. The saddest are those whose mothers die before the success comes, when the favors are all still flowing one way. Jackie Gleason was to be one of the sad ones. While he was still a teenager, his mother fell ill and slowly, over months, died in front of him. She was still young by the calendar—she was buried on what would have been her fiftieth birthday—but was prematurely worn down by depression, alcohol and poverty. The answer to why she let Jackie leave school, against her wishes, and also let him claim he would support her without ever actually making him do so is probably that she just didn't care anymore. She had been defeated by life.

The clinical cause of her death seems to have been anemia, brought on by an untreated infection called erysipelas. Bishop, relying on sources including Julie Dennehy, who was there, graphically recounts Jackie's failed attempts to extract a boil from his mother's neck and her subsequent deterioration. Mae kept working as long as she could and died quietly, as her son and his friends played cards nearby. In a ghostwritten autobiographical series published at about the same time as Bishop's biography, Gleason quoted neighbors as believing that his mother died of cancer, while he sometimes attributed the death to a broken heart—thereby effectively denying, without actually confronting, the truth that she died of a preventable infection accelerated by grubbiness and ignorance.

The same series, however, contains a staggering piece of self-indictment. Describing his mother's gradual worsening, Gleason says, "Some days she came home so tired she just made dinner and went to bed." Why, one might ask, admittedly with half a century of hindsight, did a healthy teenage boy, neither in school nor working, expect his mother to prepare dinner after a day's work, even if she was healthy? And why, if she were visibly ill, did he not postpone his budding show business career to find some kind of job and allow her to give up the exhaustion of standing on her feet for eight hours?

There weren't any good answers to these questions, and Gleason remained furious for the rest of his life with anyone who posed them—as, doubtless, he remained furious with himself for having failed to live in a way that could enable him to answer them comfortably. In the absence of a bearable truth, he invented a lie, the biggest and most self-excusing of his life, and the one he told most consistently and often. He reduced, by as much as six years in some conversations, how old he was when his mother died and he became an orphan. Instead of a young man of nineteen, old enough to work in a factory, old enough to be a soldier, old enough by the standards of his class and era to marry and start a family of his own, Jackie Gleason made himself a schoolboy of sixteen or even a Dickensian urchin of thirteen. Instead of a fully grown adult, nearly six feet tall and strong enough to find work as a stunt diver, he made himself sound like a soft, half-formed youth, a sort of Oliver Twist of Brooklyn. This lie was persistent. It was circumstantial. On one occasion he described himself as having been exactly "fifteen years, eleven months," which had the spurious ring of truth and implicitly added the heartbreaking detail of Mae's death and burial in cold January rather than the emergent spring of April. The misstatements showed up in some official CBS biographies, prepared under Gleason's direction. The falsification was part of countless interviews and ghostwritten autobiographical pieces. Gleason even apparently attempted to slip it past his second biographer, James Bacon, whose book includes the suggestive passage "Today, Jackie finds it hard to believe that he had turned nineteen when his mother died on April 12, 1935. He recalls feeling much younger at the time, probably because of his closeness to his mother. But the cemetery records, which Renee still has, authenticate the exact date of death." To nearly any journalist, that paragraph sounds like code language for "Gleason said he was much younger but I looked up the facts, confronted him and got this lame excuse in return."

The lie about his mother's death was accompanied by several others, varying slightly in the details from version to version but all meant to reinforce the image of Gleason as a self-made man who surmounted insuperable odds.

In the most unadorned version, Gleason departed from his mother's funeral (paid for through the charity of her co-workers) and headed straight into Manhattan to make his fortune with just thirty-six (or, sometimes, thirty-nine) cents in his pocket. For dramatic effect, Gleason would describe the slow wasting of his assets as he paid for a subway ride and a hot dog and then the elation when quite by chance he ran into the one person he knew in Manhattan—Sammy Birch, his predecessor as emcee at amateur nights at the Halsey, who was breaking into the lowest rungs of show business across the river. Through this miraculous meeting, Gleason found a place to spend the night, an agent and the first steps of his own career as a showman.

The thirty-six cents may have been true at his low ebb. And technically, once Mae Gleason died, her son was indeed all alone in the world. But he didn't have to starve. He had a married cousin, Renee, who would look out for him. He had neighborhood friends, who had sent flowers to the funeral and would help him find a job of some sort. He had the Dennehys, who had been virtually his second family for years and who would not willingly see him homeless—in fact, he apparently did move in with them for a short while.

None of these people, however, could be

counted on to support him indefinitely while he tried to make a go of show business instead of settling into a grocery or, with luck, an insurance office like his father. The price of their protection was bound to be conformity and the abandonment of Jackie Gleason's one and only dream. So he really did feel alone in the world, and desperate, and the lies he told years later carried with them a kind of primal emotional truth.

His meeting with Sammy Birch was not exactly happenstance, either. Gleason had stayed well informed of Birch's career moves and knew where to find him, even if they may have encountered each other by chance in the street while Gleason was on his way to attempt a scheduled rendezvous. But in this case, too, Gleason was conveying an emotional reality. Sammy's pickup jobs here and there weren't much—after Gleason moved in with Sammy and another aspiring performer, Walter Wayne, they slept three to a bed and often shared a single blue-plate special per meal, apportioning it among them course by course. Even so, steady work in show business in Manhattan was far beyond anything that people in the old neighborhood in Brooklyn considered attainable. No one else who knew Jackie could help him because no one else remotely shared his dream.

Of all the stories about the last days of his youth, the most melodramatic that Gleason told is apparently the closest to unadorned truth. After years at the Halsey Theater, he landed a new job as emcee of amateur night at the Folly, a slightly more upmarket house that would pay him six dollars per evening. He was scheduled to debut, and did, hours after Mae Gleason was buried. But if his mother was not there to see this step or the ones to follow, he would remember her. Most deeply, he would remember her doubt. She had never found him all that funny in the school show, or at the Halsey, or with Charlie Cretter, or at any of the other points along the way. Thus her memory would serve her son as every comic must be served—as an icon of a public that is ever skeptical, never satisfied, and that therefore hounds the laugh seeker to try harder, dig deeper, speak truer.

CHAPTER TWO

Whenever anybody asked the adult and successful Jackie Gleason to summarize the talents
needed to make it in show business, the one item
he always mentioned, usually at the top of his
list, was ego. Performing, he would explain, was
a sort of monstrous vanity, an insistence to a
roomful of complete strangers that you merited
their time, attention, laughter and applause. The
strangers wouldn't always agree that you were
worth it, of course. To a boy from the streets,
performing for other former kids from the streets,
the situation was like a challenge, them daring
you to prove yourself funny, you daring them
back not to be amused. "You're working in a
nightclub in some obscure part of a city," Gleason would say, "and they're throwing plates at
you. And if you give a guy a smart answer, you
may have to fight him. In that situation, only ego
would carry you through."

When contemporary performers use imagery
like Gleason's to describe a tough audience, they
are speaking in metaphor. They have grown up
in more sedate times and their testing experiences
have usually come in audition rooms or television
studios, quiet little boxes full of tension but no

tumult. When Jackie Gleason talked that way, he was speaking literally. During the decade and a half between his leaving Brooklyn to seek his fortune and his return there—and everywhere else—as a flickering black-and-white image on the instantly popular new medium of television, he made it to Broadway, opening three shows and quitting during previews or tryouts of two more. He made it to Hollywood, performing mostly secondary roles in six movies. But the majority of the time, he worked in nightclubs, nearly all of them of the variety known as "buckets of blood." The customers did not just heckle, they invited entertainers to step out into the alley to settle matters. Comics, who typically doubled as masters of ceremonies, did not limit themselves to a carefully crafted half-hour sitcom once a week but instead had to gin up (sometimes literally) the energy for two or three shows a night and be spontaneously witty enough to handle anything that happened. The tyranny of Nielsen ratings has never remotely compared with the stark terror imposed by audiences who booed or, worse, sat silent and by merciless managements who judged an act solely by its impact on cover charges and bar sales. To have a long run in these circumstances was to be held over for a second week. A player who couldn't make it in this rough-and-tumble could be fired between shows—and sometimes Gleason was.

The clubs were in a sense vestiges of vaudeville, the touring entertainment circuit of skits, music, dance and animal acts that flourished around the time Gleason was born and that collapsed at almost the exact moment when he started seriously looking for work. But vaudeville, of the kind that inspired little Jackie Gleason at the Halsey Theater back in Brooklyn, was conceived as family entertainment. Audiences in the clubs included no children and few virgins. The spectators were primarily male, generally half-drunk. They came to look at the legs of the women dancers if there were any and to hear bawdy stories if there weren't. For Jackie Gleason, who when he debuted may have *been* one of those rare virgins himself and whose audiences to date had always included neighbor matrons he wouldn't dream of offending, the nightclub business started out as a shock.

Just where he underwent this jolt into adulthood is, as ever with Gleason, a matter of some contradiction. In his *60 Minutes* autobiographical interview with Morley Safer in 1984, Gleason said with some anecdotal detail that his first-ever job was at a Newark, New Jersey, joint ambitiously named the Club Miami. But in the biography by James Bacon, for which Gleason was being interviewed at about the same time, he placed his start at the Tiny Chateau in Reading, Pennsylvania, followed by a summer in Budd Lake, New Jersey, with the Club Miami coming nearly a year later. The latter version seems to be correct, although the exact sequence isn't significant in itself. As a further indication of

47

Gleason's casual relationship with the literal truth, however, it calls into question the reliability of any of his vivid tales of those days. Doubtless they are accurate in broad outline. Equally doubtless, some details have been smoothed and sweetened for dramatic effect.

To get to the job at the Tiny, which was to pay nineteen dollars or so (on this point, too, Gleason had varying versions) for the scheduled engagement of a week, Gleason boarded a bus for what seems to have been his very first trip outside the confines of New York State. He got the gig in part because his roommates, Sammy Birch and Walter Wayne, didn't want it for themselves. No one could have called it a career move. There would be no agents in the house, no scouts for Broadway columnists, not even any secretaries to assistants to associates to producers. In a business where advancement depends on word of mouth, a gig at the Tiny Chateau offered absolutely no chance to generate any. On a per show basis the pay was worse than at amateur nights at the Folly or even the Halsey. But it was genuine professional work, so Gleason packed his blue suit and blue striped tie and a clean handkerchief for his breast pocket—he was still well dressed, and for this week no longer a bum—and took his first step toward what he was already assuring Walter and Sammy would be his certain, eternal stardom.

Cocky as he was among friends, who took his bravado and nervous energy as part of his charm,

Gleason alone or in a crowd of strangers could be as hysterically insecure as anyone in his trade—and comics are a notoriously angst-ridden lot. Theirs is the most naked style of performing. A singer on an off night still has the words and the notes. A dancer has the steps. An actor has the lines. A comic has only his jokes—*his* jokes, no one else's to share the blame—as defense against that deafening quiet of disapproval. Being funny is in large part a con game practiced on oneself, a sort of *self*-confidence game. It is much like sexual potency. Everything works fine as long as one avoids even considering that there might be a problem. Once one starts to worry, everything stops functioning and the fear becomes a self-fulfilling prophecy.

Gleason knew, as he sat through his seemingly endless bus ride to destiny, that by any objective standard he had plenty of reason for worry. He had never entertained anyone outside Brooklyn, so he had no proof that anyone would find him funny without that shared context of geography and folkways. The conflict between city and country has been one of the abiding battles in American history, and the cultural differences between urban and rural residents were far more pronounced half a century ago than they are in the television age. Moreover, Gleason had very little in the way of a formal act. Most of his experience as an amateur had been in skits with others or in spontaneous one-liners. What jokes he had were stolen chiefly from Milton Berle—

and mostly at second and third remove, for Gleason probably had not even seen Berle perform yet, although helpful friends had. Like most young comics, Gleason did some impressions of movie stars and other prominent figures. But while the young Art Carney's impressions, for example, were to be remembered as brilliant, Gleason's were by most accounts inept. His true gift was as a sketch comic, an acting comic, who could make you believe in the emotional reality of even the silliest or most formulaic situation. He remained to the end a subpar monologist because he could not get past the basic structural insincerity of jokes, and he remained a clumsy impressionist because his acting did not involve submersion into another character. It was instead based, Hollywood-style, on finding elements of the character within himself. He could not give the flavor of Cary Grant. But he could, and would, give the wrenched-out essence of Jackie Gleason.

In years to come, that performing style would make him a legend. In Reading, Pennsylvania, in 1935 it made him an opening night fiasco.

"I went in there," Gleason said decades later, "and I had this stale act of impersonations and a couple of real bad jokes and I completely dropped my Brooklyn style of kidding the audience. They were all miners in boots and I did the first show and they were a real rough crowd. They almost booed me off the stage. Then Tiny, who was, naturally, about seven feet tall, yelled

'Come here' as I came off. He took me over to the phone and dropped quarters in, one at a time, to call New York. A long-distance call to New York from Reading, Pennsylvania was a big event in those days, and this one had some added drama. Everybody turned around at the bar and watched and listened. He got my booking agent Solly Shaw on the phone and he says, 'How can you send me a bum like this?' Right in front of the audience. Solly must have said, 'Well, I'll send someone else down.' When Tiny hung up he looked at me and I guess I had that Poor Soul look on my face and he felt a little sorry. 'Come on,' he said, 'I'll buy you a drink.' So we had one, two, three—maybe fifteen—drinks and it's time for the second show. I went out and this time I killed the people. I did somersaults. I told jokes I never heard before. I played the piano, which I can't play. And when I came off this time, Tiny said, 'Why the hell didn't you do that in the first show?' I said, 'Well, you know, I'm just breaking in.' The next night when I came downstairs I tried to remember what I had done and I knew the only way to remember was to go to the bar and have about fifteen drinks and it would come to me. And I stayed there for about three months, always with ten or fifteen drinks to remember the act."

An alert reader may note a few things in this narrative that don't ring true. It's hard to believe that even a vigorous nineteen-year-old could perform so kinetic an act after so many belts of booze or that any club owner paying so little in salary would augment it with so much free hooch. The liberating and inspirational properties that Gleason attributes to alcohol, moreover, sound like the wishful thinking of a chronic and defensive drunk. Probably he did face his first professional appearance all but paralyzed with stage fright, and probably the shift to thinking that all was lost liberated him into a raffish, go-for-broke freedom of play. But whether spiritual or just spirituous, the transformation was not quite as magical as he remembered. True, Tiny undid the firing and let him finish the week. But Gleason was held over for just one additional week, not three months. After all, there just weren't that many new customers in a place the size of Reading, Pennsylvania, to be lured in to see him repeat essentially the same act night after night.

The Oasis in Budd Lake, New Jersey, Gleason's next professional port of call, employed him as a comic by night and a "penny boy" by day: in addition to performing, he had to make change for customers at the amusement arcade. This situation is memorable for only one reason. Gleason said he had his first big-time sexual affair there, with one Kiki Roberts, whom he recalled as formerly the great and good friend of the assassinated gangster Legs Diamond. Gleason said he met her by rescuing her from a boating accident—although he insisted to biographer Bacon, "She couldn't have drowned with those boobs." The incident brought them both tabloid publicity, something Gleason was savoring for the first time. But his gain was more enduring than a day or two of headlines. Roberts apparently went on expressing her gratitude, day and especially night, for the rest of the summer.

This wasn't first love for Gleason, and it may not even have been first sex. A boy who smoked at ten, hustled pool at eleven and sampled bathtub gin at twelve just might have been tempted to try a prostitute sometime during his teens. Brooklyn certainly had them, and it was something of a cultural norm in Gleason's class and neighborhood for a youth to have his first experience that way. But this was surely Gleason's first affair. He could not possibly have carried on a relationship of any duration in the old neighborhood without its becoming generally known. And in the intervening weeks since his mother's death he had been sleeping three to a bed, assuredly chastely, with Sammy Birch and Walter Wayne.

All his life, Gleason seemed to divide women between the good girls and the good-time girls. He was attracted to leggy blondes and married or made long-term mistresses of at least three of them, all former showgirls. But friends who knew the women in his life described them as more motherly than sexy. They were quiet, domestic and deferential, although they all laid down the law, or tried to, in matters of Gleason's health and indulgences. On the side, Gleason dallied with fallen women. In his youth there were plenty of showgirls of easy virtue, and he confessed to repeated infidelities. Later, according to professional associates, there were call girls, at times in multiple numbers, occasionally for small orgies, often just for obscene displays. One *Honeymooners* colleague remembers hearing about an episode in which Gleason induced a woman to copulate with a snake. But no matter how enticing Gleason found his companions for these quickies, he would never give them any kind of enduring place in his life. He believed unquestioningly in a double standard for men versus women when it came to sexual freedom and could not respect women who made men's licentiousness possible. He often described himself with apparent sincerity as a lifelong believer in Roman Catholicism although an erratic practitioner of it. A bombshell might be all very well for a summer of fun, but for a lifetime he wanted a woman more like a votive candle.

In fact, he had already picked one out. His early passion for Julie Dennehy had faded into loyal friendship, perhaps because she was too much a part of his sad past rather than his glorious hoped-for future, perhaps because her father still regarded Jackie, who liked to call himself the second Dennehy son, as a good-for-nothing. (Gleason cannot have endeared himself to the senior Dennehys by impersonating an older brother of Julie when she got into trouble at school and was ordered to bring in a parent or guardian—an episode that became common knowledge throughout the neighborhood.)

When Jackie was seventeen and emceeing at the Halsey, he met a pair of blonde ballerinas who billed themselves as the Halford Twins. They weren't twins, actually, just sisters who looked a lot alike. The one Jackie preferred was Genevieve, although some people rated her sister Geraldine as the greater beauty. Jackie's interest was immediate. He introduced Gen to his mother and kept her in mind as an ideal mate, although he was too young and certainly too poor to be rushing into marriage.

That changed when he landed his first more or less permanent job in show business, where nothing is ever really permanent, at the Club Miami. Elegant it wasn't. "The reason I got the job," Gleason recalled later, "was that I went into an agent's office, where a friend of mine brought me, and the two owners were sitting there. They didn't ask me if I had a good act, but whether I could fight well. Our instructions were, if we heard a glass crash out at the bar, the band would go into "Happy Days Are Here Again" and we would go to some location in the joint where we had stashed the leg of a chair and then go to the bar to see that the disturbance was quieted right away. Once, we were doing a three A.M. show, and I had had a couple of quarts of booze and I was telling some jokes and this guy kept yelling out all kinds of things. The guy was a bouncer at the Mirror Club or something but I didn't know him. He was going to fight for the heavyweight championship of the world, that was lined up already, and his name was Two Ton Tony Galento. But I didn't know who he was. And he kept going on, so I said, 'ladies and gentlemen, I'll be back in a moment.' Then to him I said, 'You, come on,' and we went outside. I was taking my coat off and the next thing I remember I was down in the cellar next to the furnace and I was saying to the owner, 'Why didn't you tell me who that was?' But the owner said, 'No, you're a wise guy, you can lick everybody.' That was a very bad experience and I was more careful after that."

For staying up half the night, scrapping with tough customers, devising (or swiping) all his own material and proving popular enough that he turned a dying night spot into a winner, Gleason was paid eight dollars a night to start, for weekends only, then thirty-five dollars for a full week. He was still sharing beds in rooming houses and cadging free food, and when he asked for more money the owners responded instead with more work. They gave him a forty-dollar-a-week gig at a burlesque house and Gleason still emceed at an amateur night in Brooklyn. In all, he had about eighty dollars a week coming in, and that was enough to prompt him to propose to Genevieve Halford in 1936, soon after his twentieth birthday. She helped the timetable along by arriving at the Club Miami one night on a date with another man. Had she known the misery and humiliation that were to follow, she would probably have let the brash, handsome kid comic from Brooklyn remain just a pleasant memory. Had Gleason sensed in the slightest how unprepared he was to be married, how unable he would be to discipline himself or live up to his commitments, he would likely have contented himself with boozing the nights away and seducing the occasional dancer. Legally, the marriage would endure almost four decades. By the most generous calculation, it involved only eight years together and about twenty-five apart. In practical terms, the union was over almost before it began.

Gleason performed at the Club Miami on his wedding night. The reception, such as it was, took place there too. No honeymoon followed. The couple's first home was the same rooming house where Jackie had been living as a single man. In short, nothing changed in Gleason's life. Nothing served to symbolize his new status and responsibilities. And nothing, and no one, could control his wastrel ways.

Of all the reasons the Gleason marriage could have failed—Jackie's drinking; his blatant philandering; his odd hours, frequent absences and general parental neglect; his and Gen's almost total intellectual incompatibility—the pivotal issue seems, in retrospect, to have been money. Gleason was not a bad breadwinner. But he was a terrible provider. What infuriated Genevieve, to judge from what she said in separation proceedings and in private remarks to friends, was never how much or little her husband earned but how he chose to spend it. Saving was not a concept in his vocabulary. Nor was the word *budget*. As soon as he got paid, he spent, compulsively, until it was gone. The only necessity for which he would set cash aside was not rent or even food, but clothing. "A new suit was always very important to me," he would say. He was his father's son, and Genevieve soon found herself wanting to act like his mother, camping out on payday to relieve him of his wad before he blew it getting into trouble.

Gleason loved to speak of "class" and "style," and he had a peculiarly blue-collar notion of what those meant. To him, class was picking up the check, no matter how many companions you had and how much more money they made than you. To him, style was buying a round of drinks for a barroom full of strangers, impressing them during a fleeting hour or two of acquaintance with the idea that you were a fine fellow and a hell of a sport. The more casual his connection with someone, the deeper his need to impress. He explained time and again to gossip columnists in his later, more flush years how he had learned in his youth what a big impression one could make by buying a round for everyone in the joint, at a cost of no more than, say, eighty dollars for this grand gesture. He never really explained why this hollow display should offer him enough satisfaction to justify blowing what was, in those days, a week's pay for him, or indeed why it gave him any pleasure at all. But throughout his life he loved empty, costly pomp, from custom-made pool cues to a special-order limousine that he boasted was the longest in America. The pleasure these things gave him seems not to have been inherent in their quality or splendor, but in their very cost and in the fact that he did not flinch at risking that cost. He seems to have reacted to the deprivations of childhood by waging a life-long battle against the tyranny of economic common sense. "I think everybody should make two fortunes," he liked to say, "one to blow, to really live it up with, and then the other for security." But the one for blowing always came first and mattered most. He loved buying things on credit. He was thrilled to be allowed to run a monthly tab at a bar or restaurant. "They were expressing confidence in me," he explained, "that I didn't have in myself." When he had money in hand, he would delight in paying off debts—the older and more long-forgotten, the better. "I even paid off people that had never lent me anything," he once said. "They'd come up and say, 'Remember when . . .' and I'd say, 'Oh. Oh, yeah. . . .' "

Until his talent proved so lucrative and his financial advisers so canny that not even he could piss it all away, Jackie Gleason was, understandably, often broke. He loved to tell of the time, early in his marriage, when he was so hard up that he resorted to taking an armload of promotional items from a store, big tin "coins" with a real penny in the center. On the pretext of passing them out at the Club Miami, he carted them home, where he and Gen methodically punched out all the pennies and accumulated enough cash to buy a modest meal. Two decades later, when his company had a CBS contract worth millions of dollars per year, of which his personal share topped three hundred thousand dollars, Gleason often had less than a two-hundred-dollar balance in his checking account. Some of this money went to taxes and management expenses, some to lavish business and personal suites, some to lush living. But the biggest uncontrolled item in his outgo was the endless party, either chez Gleason or at his home-away-from-home, Toots Shor's, with the fat comic as the ever bountiful host. Every time Gen read about one of these parties in the papers—she was hardly ever invited to attend—it burned her up more. Jackie eventually made so much money that there was plenty for everyone, and he was never stingy with Gen or their daughters. Yet Genevieve sued for more— not because she was profligate herself or even particularly needy but because it incensed her that her husband remained so in love with "entertaining" others. That vice, not any mistress, was the real home wrecker in their marriage.

The Club Miami may not have been the bottom rung of show business, but it came close. As a youth of twenty, Gleason was thrilled to be its house comic and emcee. Just a year after he left Brooklyn to pursue his crazy dream, he had proved all the neighborhood naysayers wrong. Already he was earning more than many, if not most, of them, and in his mind his work involved no drudgery, just fun. But after one further year, as a seasoned veteran of twenty-one, Gleason decided it was time to move on. To have a chance at real stardom, he had to be seen by lots of different managers and agents, and that meant working in lots of different places. Hollywood was his real ambition, as it was for almost any performer in that era, the heyday of the movies. But the vital first step to getting hired in California was to find a showcase in Manhattan. Gleason could go on forever circling the center of New York City, performing in its outer boroughs and suburbs, and do himself little good. Producers and studio executives did not entertain themselves in Newark or even Queens.

Gleason was not alone, however, in having figured this out. As a result, Manhattan was tough to break into, even at the nightclub level, and he spent the years from 1937 into early 1940 bouncing from gig to gig, out of work almost as often as he was in it. His asking price went up to seventy-five dollars a week, then a hundred. But on occasion he was reduced to working for much less, and with minimal dignity, as a comic diver at the Jersey shore or as a carnival barker at an auto stunt show. He even claimed to have been a boxer in fixed fights where the combatants would take it easy on each other and, win or lose, evenly split the purses. That stopped, he explained, when an opponent took the contest seriously and "beat the hell out of me." In later years he would sometimes boast of having been an Olympic-quality swimmer in his youth, although there is no evidence that he ever raced competitively. The tall tales he spun about his diving grew Bunyanesque. A thirty-foot drop into a six-foot-high vat of water, its sides greased so his body would slip in without laceration, evolved into a ninety-foot plummet into a foot-deep basin, a leap he survived but declined to repeat "because the salary wouldn't even pay for the mercurochrome." Similarly, he would sometimes claim to have been a stunt driver when in fact his job apparently consisted mainly of working up the crowd to see every sideswipe or fender bender as death-defying—and of trying to terrify freeloaders, who watched from beyond the end of the track, with warnings that they were being exposed to "stray pebbles traveling as fast as bullets."

His pursuit of more conventional club work took him, in tough times, as far as Pittsburgh and even Minneapolis, places where he was lonely and bored and seemingly more distant than ever from his goals. "When you begin," he recalled in later life, "you're sure you're going to be a success, a star. Then there are big valleys. You run into a bad audience and you say, 'What am I doing this for? I'll get another job, I'll do something else.' Then you hit a good audience and you're sucked in again. And it goes along like that." At times like these, Gen, especially after she was pregnant with their first child, Geraldine, might gently suggest that Jackie consider, just for a while, some steadier way of earning a living. This only enraged him. Despite his moodiness and frequent, lifelong fits of bleak depression, he was convinced that one essential for success was to have absolute faith in yourself and all your works. He required unwavering assurance from the people around him. But then, Gen wasn't often around. Even before she was a mother (Geraldine was born on July 31, 1939), Gen was discouraged by her husband from coming to the clubs where he worked. They were not fit places for a lady, he said. The roving, irregular nature of his work meant that the couple often lived apart for weeks at a time. Of course, for a very young man who was just beginning to discover the variety of sexual opportunities available to a headline performer, this separation was not altogether a burden.

Although at times it looked to Gen and even to Jackie as if he were going nowhere fast, in fact he was building up contacts that would prove significant for many years to come. At his first job after the Club Miami, at the Colonial Inn in Singac, New Jersey, he made the acquaintance first of Willie Webber, who became his agent-manager, and soon after of Bullets Durgom, who took over Gleason's management a decade later and guided him to triumph after triumph throughout the fifties. Gleason also met a skinny Italian kid from Hoboken, a singer named Frank

Sinatra, who became a lifelong friend and cheerful competitor in devising elaborate practical jokes. Less happily, while working at the Paramount in Newark, Gleason made the acquaintance of his longtime if uncredited writer Milton Berle.

Gleason had been stealing Berle's jokes, passed along to him by others, at least since his days at the Halsey. In later years he liked to recall that during his Halsey apprenticeship, neighborhood friends who made their way into Manhattan night spots were so loyal and naive that they reported back to Gleason about some Jewish fellow named Berle who was swiping Jackie's material. Gags were not copyrighted, of course, and the best of them were not shielded but were widely disseminated through gossip columnists, or Broadway columnists as they were then known. The performers spent time and money planting their one-liners, caring less about safeguarding a joke's fleeting exclusivity than about building up their reputations. In this climate, established comics were apt to overlook occasional borrowing by their juniors. If anyone could be expected to view such larceny indulgently, Berle could. He was already so notorious a purloiner himself that the king of columnists, Walter Winchell, had punningly dubbed him "The Thief of Bad Gags." But Berle blew up when he heard from a stagehand that some fat, brash kid in Newark was performing virtually his entire act.

Just where and how Berle conveyed his displeasure is murky. Born in July 1908, Berle is renowned among entertainers for the vivid detail of his recollections. But that color and clarity are not, alas, always accompanied by consistency. Over the years he has given several varying accounts of his first encounter with Gleason—two of them, sharply different, in the space of one month to this author. In our first interview, Berle said he turned up at the Paramount unannounced to confront Gleason: "I scared him so much he shit his pants, although he went out and did my material anyway. There were some fisticuffs afterward." In our second conversation, Berle said he telephoned Gleason from the International Casino on Broadway at Forty-fourth Street in Manhattan, where he was headlining, and reached the younger man backstage at the Paramount. "As soon as I said, 'This is Milton Berle,' he said, 'Uh-oh, I know what you're calling about.' I invited him to meet me at Dave's Blue Room in town, at Fifty-fourth and Seventh Avenue, where there were a lot of actors and a lot of mobsters. In came this good-looking kid, a little fat, very bouncy, and I instantly liked him very, very much. He said, 'I can't afford writers,' which was true at his stage in the business, and I sort of cooled off.

"The next time I saw him was out at the Colonial in New Jersey, where he was emcee, and he was *still* doing my material. After three or four jokes that were mine got big laughs for him, I stood up in the audience and bowed. But he

65

topped me. 'My pal is bowing,' he said. 'Little does my pal know that I am not the only one doing his material.' "

Not all of Gleason's act was stolen from Berle. The young comic had plenty of other pockets to pick. He did an impression of a man playing a pinball machine that gradually metamorphosed into an impersonation of the machine itself. This, Berle says, was swiped from a comic called Gene Baylos, although Gleason ultimately performed it better. Jackie still did movie star impersonations, but they had become more and more eccentric and satiric, including a Peter Lorre impression that seemed particularly inappropriate from one so young, tall, handsome and merry. Inspired by the silent-film comics, whom Gleason admired all his life—Chaplin, he said, "could make you laugh while throwing babies into the furnace"—he performed abundant pantomimes.

But the best part of his act was still his spontaneity. He could get laughs improvisationally, in nearly any circumstance, and his almost total independence from a script or monologue enabled him to be exceptionally responsive to a crowd. He also had two qualities that would prove invaluable in television: a physical grace at once preposterous and poignant in one so large and a manic nervous energy that lent emotional urgency to anything he said.

Berle claims credit for introducing Gleason to the owners of the Club 18, an oddball night spot located in the basement of a midtown Manhattan brownstone. Other accounts have it that Webber, Gleason's manager, booked him into a date in Queens for the sole purpose of luring the Club 18 management out to see him. Whichever is right—and maybe both are—Gleason made his yearned-for Manhattan debut in January 1940, a month before his twenty-fourth birthday. It was the beginning of a fireball eighteen months of glory. Although he would always think of himself as a knocked-about street kid from Brooklyn, Jackie Gleason actually was, for his time, as close as show business came to a true overnight success.

The Club 18 was a weird institution, a place where celebrities and socialites went to get insulted. Neither large nor especially lucrative, it was a prestigious place to appear because of its tony clientele. Onstage, however, the proceedings were anything but posh or even polite. Any man who arrived garbed in formal evening dress was apt to be asked where he worked as a headwaiter. If a stylish woman disappeared to the powder room during the show, one of the comics might demand, as she returned, whether she had been able to hear the show in there. As she replied, "No," with a certain bewilderment, the comic would happily snort, "Well, we heard *you* out here." When a particularly prominent customer arrived, the spotlight would swing right away from the stage—something no performer could welcome, even in fun—and remain on the glittering newcomer until he or she took a seat.

Gleason fit right in with the pandemonium, and the spotlight gag inspired him to an impromptu witticism that Broadway columnists were still quoting two decades later. Sonja Henie, the three-time Olympic gold medalist who first fused dance and figure skating, arrived in the middle of Gleason's act and made her way to her table. The fat comic feigned outrage at the loss of the spotlight and stormed over to Henie, demanding just what she did to rate such acclaim. When she meekly replied, "I dance on ice," Gleason mutely hoisted a champagne bucket, thrust it in front of her and said, "Do something." (In later years, recalling this episode, Gleason the inveterate rewriter turned the full ice bucket into a single ice cube, which he thrust toward Henie in the palm of his hand. As a concept, to be read about in an interview or as a column item, the ice cube was a literary improvement, much funnier than the bucket because of the absurd contrast in size between a tiny chip of frozen water and a full human frame. But in a dim and noisy club, with inevitably bad sight lines, the cube in the palm wouldn't have been funny at all, because most of the audience wouldn't have seen it, whereas the ice bucket would have been unmistakable and hilarious.)

The permanent comics at the Club 18 were Pat Harrington, Sr., Jack White and Frankie Hyers. Combative with each other, they closed ranks at first against the upstart outsider. Gleason fought back, with boasts and pranks and bravado, and was invited back on and off for most of the next year. In between, he could still be found at some of the old standby clubs in Queens and New Jersey. But he could also be found at occasional gigs paying three hundred dollars a week, a small fortune then.

And for a precious few weeks in the spring of 1940, young Jackie Gleason, just twenty-four, could be found on Broadway, co-starring with Jimmy Durante, Ray Bolger, Jane Froman, Ilka Chase, José Limon, the circus clown Emmett Kelly and an act called Dodson's Monkeys. Part vaudeville, part revue, *Keep Off the Grass* was more akin to early TV variety shows than to the storytelling Broadway musicals of today. The show ran briefly and Gleason's place in it was small, but nonetheless, just a decade after Mae Gleason's boy bulled his way into the eighth-grade pageant, he was a genuine Broadway actor. Reviewing the show in the New York Times, critic Brooks Atkinson (so esteemed a figure that he eventually had a Broadway theater named after him) found very little nice to say: "It gives Durante and Bolger room enough to fool around in. . . . run-of-the-mine stuff, with a few blatant obscenities that this column could easily get on without." Atkinson went on about most of the performers at length but did not mention Gleason, who had comic sketches, at all. Others recall Gleason as talented but raw and almost clueless about the basic rules of acting. He would break out of character, improvise asides, overtly acknowledge friends in the audience and generally depart from the text. In broad outline, the same bad habits would mar his live performances for the remaining four and a half decades of his professional life. But he would never—well, almost never—indulge them quite so crudely again.

Exultant as Gleason was to reach Broadway, an even bigger excitement soon followed. For years he had plotted to get to Manhattan as a stepping-stone to Hollywood. Within a year of his arrival at the Club 18, his master plan succeeded. Jack Warner, of the Warner Brothers studio, stopped in one night. Gleason, allegedly not knowing who this visitor was, insulted him mercilessly about his baldness and other physical shortcomings. Warner was so impressed that he took the management aside to ask whether Gleason was just having a fluky flash of brilliance or was always that good. The managers response must have been reassuring. Without even meeting Jackie offstage, Warner signed the comic for two hundred fifty dollars a week—not top money, and with no guarantees about parts. But for a guy just a couple of summers away from shilling for a bumper car show, it was pretty impressive.

Nobody was more impressed than Gleason himself. "I'll take Hollywood by storm," he boasted to his friends. "They won't know what hit 'em. I'm going to be the biggest thing that town has ever seen." Just as he had said goodbye to Brooklyn those few and infinite years ago, vowing never to return, so he started saying goodbye to friends and places around Manhattan. He would arrive in Hollywood and even have a big-budget movie in release, all before his twenty-fifth birthday. Once he took his rightful place on the silver screen, he intended to remain, from there to eternity.

CHAPTER THREE

Bullets Durgom, the manager whom Gleason met back at the Colonial in New Jersey and who would eventually make the fat man a multimillionaire, often said that his client's only intellectual interest was in show business. Everything to do with the craft, from lighting to makeup to costumes to choreography, Jackie would study intently, grasp at once and keep sharp in memory. Everything else, every other branch of learning from calculus to common sense, he had no use for and would forget at his earliest opportunity.

Durgom was mostly right. But there was a significant exception. Raised by a mother deeply interested in matters of the spirit, himself fearful of and almost obsessed with death, Jackie Gleason had a lifelong fascination with the supernatural. Everything that Shirley Maclaine was to explore in her exotic life and best-selling books had already been explored by Gleason, a touch more skeptically but with just as persistent curiosity, a generation before. Eventually he would read hundreds of books about extrasensory perception, telekinesis, teleportation, poltergeists, extraterrestrials, flying saucers and every other odd corner of cosmology. He would spend small fortunes on everything from financing psychic research to buying a sealed box said to contain actual ectoplasm, the spirit matter of life itself. He would contact everyone from back-alley charlatans to serious researchers like J. B. Rhine of Duke University and, disdaining the elitism of the scholarly apparatus, would treat them all much the same.

Yet Gleason must not have had a truly psychic or even superstitious bone in his body. If he had believed in omens and forebodings, he would surely have halted his trek to Hollywood almost before it began. Every decision he made in connection with the journey proved ill starred, and by the end of his time in those environs he was so soured on Southern California that once he achieved success, he spent most of the rest of his life looking for ways to avoid working there again.

The first basic decision he made was to leave Genevieve back on the East Coast. She apparently did not raise much objection. For one thing, she had her hands full with little Geraldine, who was about one and a half, and was already pregnant with Linda, their second and last child, who would be born September 16, 1941. Genevieve liked a stable home life and, in the repeated absence of a dependable husband, she had learned to rely heavily on her family and friends to provide it. She certainly didn't want to move three thousand miles to a place where she knew almost no one and then live there in conditions that would keep her from meeting anyone new. She might have worried that Jackie would stray if separated from his wife and confronted with temptation in the form of countless starlets. But she knew that Jackie was straying already, right in metropolitan New York, with a wife and child at home and another baby on the way. How much worse could he get? In effect, he had walked out already. Years later, she would say with some bitterness, "Jackie left me dozens of times. Every time he got successful, he left me." She had tried everything she could think of to persuade him to reform, above all religious guilt. According to biographer Bacon, Gen introduced Jackie to the Reverend Fulton J. Sheen, later a bishop and a television personality himself, for marriage counseling as early as 1937 or 1938, within a year or two of the wedding. (Others place this intervention by Sheen, which definitely happened, a few years later.)

But there was another aspect to the separation that both Gleasons failed to consider. However bad the relations between them had become, having Gen nearby exerted a moderating influence on Jackie's excesses. Apparently neither he nor she realized that with a whole continent between them, his drinking, carousing and financial recklessness might get much worse. Moreover, Gen served an even deeper need in Jackie. Despite his bravado and his constant assertions of fearlessness, his ego was fragile. He needed her encouragement, her support, her pride in his achievements and her unflappability during his setbacks. Before, he had never been able to get enough of it. Now he was going to get none whatsoever.

The second big decision Gleason made was to go out to California by train rather than airplane. In those pre-jet days, flying was a prolonged, noisy and cramping ordeal. For Jackie, it was also stark terror. "When one of those things is up above me, I start to shake," he would say. "Can you imagine me strapped into one?" Lacking even a rudimentary education in mathematics and science, he could not make sense of how a big, heavy metal object could ascend and stay aloft. So he genuinely believed, deep down, that at any moment, any plane might come crashing to earth.

The train was not in itself a terrible idea, although it made for an even longer journey. But Gleason chose to break his travel in Chicago, where he did up the town all night long with a young Lebanese comedian later to be known as Danny Thomas. As Jackie recalled it, the stopover was a whirlwind of pleasure—with one significant drawback. Characteristically, Gleason spent himself down to pocket change. He faced three days of riding with a colossal hangover, no hope of buying a "hair of the dog that bit me" and, to top things off, nothing more nutritious to eat than a pocketful of Baby Ruth candy bars. "I arrived in Burbank," he said, "full of pimples and despair."

Things did not improve much upon arrival.

Not only had Jack Warner not bothered to meet Gleason, he had not bothered to tell anybody that this new fat comic was coming. The gatekeepers had no record of Jackie's name and were reluctant to let him in. Worse, no one in higher authority knew about him either, so there was no waiting limousine, no apartment, no welcoming lunch and, above all, no part for him to play.

This was to be only a temporary foul-up. But it reminded Gleason, amid his happy daydreams, of practical reality. This California venture was at best speculative and could prove highly impermanent. Getting a contract was an enormous first step. But the studios signed many, many performers each year on terms similar to Jackie's and then decided after a tryout or two that most of them would never be crowd pleasers. Or, worse, production executives somehow never got around to casting these hopefuls, at least not in roles that gave them any opportunity to show what they could do. And so the onetime up-and-comers would be sent back home, to teach acting in Milwaukee or run a dance studio in Tampa or emcee at nightclubs in Singac, New Jersey, deflated from might-have-beens to the still baser status of tried-and-faileds.

Even after Gleason's contract was being honored, money became an almost instant, and then an immense, problem. In years gone by, when he was just a nightclub emcee in the boondocks of New Jersey, Gleason had already dedicated himself to living beyond his means. Now he was a genuine movie star, with a studio contract to prove it, and never mind that he hadn't actually made any movies yet. He was going to live it up, exhibit his class and style, prove himself a sport, tip the barman the equivalent of a week's pay for a single serving and in general impress every stranger in the joint. He was going to do it all on a bigger scale than ever.

The difficulty was that measly two hundred fifty dollars a week. It was a solid living for a young doctor or lawyer. It was five or six times what a young teacher might earn. But for Jackie it wasn't a gigantic raise, it was actually a substantial cut. He had made more at some New Jersey supper clubs. He had even made more during his tryout weeks at the Club 18, because the stingy hundred and fifiy dollars a week he earned then had been supplemented by an identical salary at a club in Queens to which he would shuttle nightly for a gig sandwiched between his early and late shows in Manhattan. Besides, in California he had a second rent to cover and a lot of other new expenses. In New York he had maintained only one household, even if he didn't actually go home all that much.

After the humiliation of his unheralded arrival at Warner Brothers, Gleason was jolted into elation by the glamour of his first screen job. *Navy Blues,* a full-blown musical comedy, was produced by Hal B. Wallis, the legendary mogul who would go on to discover and develop Shirley

MacLaine. The director, Lloyd Bacon, had made *Knute Rockne, All American* the year before (with Ronald Reagan as the Gipper) and had directed the non–Busby Berkeley sequences of that ravishing show business musical melodrama *42nd Street*. Much of the cinematography was by the celebrated James Wong Howe; the score was by Tin Pan Alley legends Arthur Schwartz and Johnny Mercer. The cast was equally impressive. The "four Jacks," as they called themselves during shooting—Gleason, Jack Oakie, Jack Haley and Jack Carson—were joined by Martha Raye, Ann Sheridan and, in smaller roles, Howard da Silva, Gig Young and William Hopper, the latter being the son of all-powerful columnist Hedda Hopper and later a TV star himself, as private investigator Paul Drake on the *Perry Mason* courtroom series.

Sadly, all this talent went into making a genuinely lousy movie. Of the one hundred eight minutes of running time, about fifteen are fun. The plot, a compendium of clichés, was credited to four writers including Sam Perrin, who later wrote extensively for Jack Benny. The story has Oakie and Haley as veteran seamen who have risked a lot of money on an upcoming gunnery contest and who therefore connive to ensure the reenlistment of a sweet, naive farm boy with a deadly aim, played by Herbert Anderson. Sheridan is the vamp whom the sailors employ to persuade their prey; predictably, she falls in love for real and then lives in fear that the farm boy will discover her role in the scheme. In the subplot that grates most on today's sensibilities, Raye plays Haley's wife, a figure of fun for no other reason than that she desires her husband's attention and affections rather more than he desires hers.

As for Gleason's role as a sidekick sailor, the most pointed and painful critique came from the eager young comic himself. Flo Haley, Jack Haley's real-life widow, recalls, "My husband didn't particularly care about *Navy Blues* and wouldn't go to the big Hollywood preview. Gleason said, 'Well, I never made one of these before and I *am* going,' so my husband said, 'Call me and tell me how it was.' When Jackie rang up, he said, 'Never mind how it was, I can guess. How were you?' And Gleason said to my Jack, 'I look like a guy standing on the street corner watching it being made.'"

This unflinching judgment was shared by studio executives and most reviewers. Bosley Crowther's tepid notice for *Navy Blues* in the September 20, 1941, edition of the *New York Times* does not even mention Gleason's name, except in the accompanying cast list. In typically mangled and overwrought prose, Crowther said of the film as a whole, "So you who are not averse to a lot of broad and unrestrained mugging—to a generous display of the Messrs. Oakie and Haley working harder for laughs than a bum vaudeville team in Omaha—and who like your musical shows noisy, this one should be all right."

But if *Navy Blues* was not a career maker, it served Gleason in four important ways. First, he did well enough that he went on to make five more films, at Warners or on loan to other studios, generally in support to major stars. Moreover, the debut movie introduced him to Martha Raye, who became for a while his West Coast version of Julie Dennehy, a surrogate sister with whom he could "go bouncing" from bar to bar. Raye shared his belief that life afforded no greater pleasure than accumulating a retinue of a dozen or more new "friends" for the evening and grandiosely treating them all to a spree—usually on credit from establishments that might wait a long while to be paid.

Third, this film introduced him to Jack Haley, who for the next four decades would be Gleason's closest friend in Hollywood, and maybe his closest anywhere. Of all of Gleason's intimates for the rest of his life, Haley was probably the only one who was a friend pure and simple and never also an employee on The Great One's payroll. Haley was seventeen years older and acted as a father, uncle or big brother to Gleason, giving him nononsense advice on money, marriage and general behavior. For some reason, no matter how headstrong he got, Gleason would tolerate from Haley the critical counsel that he would furiously reject from any other quarter.

Last, but not least useful according to Gleason, *Navy Blues* got him out of yet another of his chronic financial jams en route to New York for a conjugal visit. Having secured a leave between pictures, the story went, he set aside his phobias and agreed to fly from Los Angeles. But the aircraft had mechanical trouble and was forced to land in a desert airport near Phoenix. Told that a connecting flight had been arranged, the fearful Gleason refused to get back on board and opted instead for the train. He couldn't get a cash refund for his plane ticket; that sum would be mailed to him in New York. In an era before credit cards, he needed cash for a train ticket, and he didn't have enough. The railroad wouldn't accept his out-of-town check, and he went from storefront to storefront seeking someone who would cash it. He finally succeeded only because *Navy Blues* was playing in town. A hardware store owner agreed to go to the film, with Gleason buying both tickets, so Jackie could prove that he was who he said he was and that therefore his check was good. (The latter two points were not logically connected, of course. Indeed, if the hardware store manager had known a little bit more about who Jackie Gleason really was, especially about his reputation in matters of money management, the man would never have taken that check.)

The chronology of Gleason's life is somewhat hazy during this period. Stories that he told in interviews and to his biographers, including the airplane tale just related, appear to contradict studio records and other data about exactly when

Jackie was in Hollywood and when, if at all, he went back to New York during his year under contract to Warners. The disparities may be innocent or even nonexistent. But if Gleason was consciously or unconsciously twisting the truth, he probably had good reason. As with his misstatements about his age at his mother's death and his behavior toward her in her painful final months, he may well have had a significant domestic failing to cover up.

In the version he told Bacon, he waited to go to California until after his second daughter Linda was born. In the much more detailed version he conveyed to Bishop, he was back from California in time for the birth and indeed took a long enough leave to resume working at the Colonial Inn in Singac, New Jersey. He said he was onstage there one night when he got word that Gen had gone into labor. He headed over to the hospital in Jackson Heights, Queens, driven by friends and accompanied (across state lines!) by a skeptical policeman who had flagged down the Gleason entourage for speeding. The capper was that the labor pains turned out to be a false alarm—so Gleason left Gen in her hospital bed and headed back to work.

It would have been entirely in character for Gleason to plunge back into the nightclub scene if he were home ostensibly on a family leave. The money he earned was invariably needed. So were the companionship, the applause, the party atmosphere and the place to practice his craft. If anything, the Hollywood experience, with its humbling hierarchies and demands for kowtowing, would have made the club scene back East all the more attractive. In metropolitan New York, Gleason was a star, a hero to his barroom pals, and they were frankly awed by his movie career, making no distinction about the size of his billing or paycheck.

But self-critical as the little anecdote about his return home sounds, it doesn't seem to make chronological sense. Nor does what he told Bacon. *Navy Blues* was reviewed in the *New York Times* four days after Linda's birth. So Gleason certainly didn't wait until after her arrival to launch his movie career. Moreover, he is definitely known to have attended the film's West Coast premiere, which cannot have taken place much before the *Times* review, so it is hard to see how he could have come back in time to resume a club career, visit Gen during a false alarm and then be on hand for the actual birth. There simply wasn't enough elapsed time.

It seems more likely that Gleason was absent altogether for the birth of his second child, because he cared far more about his own career than about being a family man. He was to be an absentee father for decades to come, sending big checks and making lavish purchases but rarely investing much of his time, the commodity any child desires most. He told colleagues from Art Carney to agent Sam Cohn that he considered himself a failure at fatherhood. His daughters lamented to friends—from veteran film actor Burgess Meredith, whose manager is Geraldine's husband, to TV star Franklin Cover of *The Jeffersons*, who worked in theater with Linda—about how little they heard from The Great One. Even in their adulthood, his interest in spending time with them seemed to be sporadically intense but infrequent. But just as it would have looked lousy for a healthy nineteen-year-old to have exploited or neglected a dying mother, so it would have looked lousy for a professed Catholic family man to have bypassed the birth of a baby. Hence, one suspects, arose the welter of tales that confounded each other and that all defied the calendar.

What is certain is that Gleason was present in Hollywood enough during the latter part of 1941 to make the first one or two of the five films in which he appeared during 1942. The best of them, *All Through the Night*, a spoof of Nazi spy dramas starring Humphrey Bogart, was reviewed by Crowther of the *New York Times* on January 24. Once again Gleason worked with the biggest and most esteemed names—Bogart, Conrad Veidt, Jane Darwell, Judith Anderson, Peter Lorre and comics including Frank McHugh, William Demarest and Phil Silvers (who would later rival Gleason for TV popularity and lure away some of his best writers for a comedy series about the con artist Sergeant Ernie Bilko). The convoluted plot of the movie, making light of German infiltrators, concentration camps and a sabotage plot to blow up New York City's harbor, came to neighborhood cinemas at a highly inopportune moment, a month and a half after U.S. isolationism ended with the Japanese bombing of the Pacific fleet. Crowther acknowledged this bad timing in his favorable notice: "let it be said for the record that this is a pre-Pearl Harbor job, lest anyone raise the objection that it plays too fast and loose with a subject much too serious for melodramatic kidding in these times." With the passage of half a century, a modern spectator can appreciate the plot, credited to Leonard Spigelgass (later an Oscar nominee for *Mystery Street*) and Leonard Ross (a pen name of humorist Leo Rosten), as an engagingly elegant foofaraw. Once again, however, Gleason's contributions passed largely unnoticed.

Three months later he was up on the screen again in a comic caper, *Larceny, Inc.*, his second film for *Navy Blues* director Lloyd Bacon and his second in a row adapted by Edwin Gilbert, the scenarist who had reworked the Spigelgass-Rosten story for *All Through the Night*. Once again the comedy was top drawer; its source was S. J. Perelman's play *The Night Before Christmas*. And once again Gleason was working with true pros: Edward G. Robinson, Broderick Crawford, Jane Wyman, Anthony Quinn (who became a drinking buddy then and was so again two decades later when they co-starred in *Re-*

quiem for a Heavyweight) and Gleason's erstwhile *Navy Blues* co-star Jack Carson.

By the autumn, Gleason had made the jump from black and white into color in a high-profile but really dull musical. *Springtime in the Rockies,* for which Gleason was lent to Twentieth Century-Fox, was the first film to give Betty Grable number-one billing, and that is just about its only distinction. Grable and John Payne played Broadway performers who share bed-and-boards but can't stop quarreling. Drifting through the background were Carmen Miranda, Cesar Romero, Charlotte Greenwood, Edward Everett Horton (from whom Gleason said he took a postdoctoral course in scene stealing) and Harry James and his orchestra. Gleason played Payne's agent, once again without much notice from reviewers. Crowther summed up the general critical scorn with the closing sentence of his review: "For all its lavish trimmings, *Springtime in the Rockies* is just a second-rate song and dance."

Crowther was even more contemptuous of *Orchestra Wives,* another Fox release, which has its fans as a backstage story and as the final film appearance of swing-era bandleader Glenn Miller, who played, surprisingly enough, a bandleader. (A couple of years after the film's release, Miller was killed in a war-related plane crash over the English Channel.) Gleason was cast as the bass player in the band. He's not particularly funny on camera, but Ann Rutherford, who played the newest of the wives in the title, told interviewers in after years that he was a riot off camera, keeping the cast aroar between takes. Hollywood columnists, then and now a highly approximate equivalent to truth tellers, said Gleason was found howlingly funny even by Miller, who supposedly had a chronic pain in his side that kept him determined not to laugh. Whatever else Gleason may have done off camera, he made one acquaintance that in years to come would bring him millions of dollars in easy income. He developed both a professional admiration for and a personal friendship with trumpet player Bobby Hackett, who would be featured on albums of mood music financed—and ostensibly "composed," "conducted" or "produced"—by Gleason during the later fifties and into the sixties.

Amid all these supporting roles, Gleason got one chance at real stardom. Columbia teamed him with Jack Durant in an attempt to launch a new Abbott and Costello or Laurel and Hardy in *Tramp, Tramp, Tramp.* The film, just sixty-eight minutes in black and white and obviously meant to be the lesser half of double-feature bills at neighborhood cinemas, had the illadvised premise of being a World War I–era comedy released in the midst of real-life World War II anxiety and heartbreak. The leading men play barbers who see their business dwindling as their customers head off to war. Attempting to enlist, they are rejected. So they form a home guard unit and run afoul of some murderous thieves on the lam.

As dreary and hapless as it is implausible, this bomb was treated by critics as beneath contempt and pretty much sealed Gleason's fate. When *Time* magazine did a cover story about him in December 1961, it noted that although he had once been under contract for a year, "Warner Brothers today does not even remember that he was there."

It would be eight years before Gleason made another movie and a decade after that before he made any more. He would never stop bad-mouthing Hollywood, and he would never entirely forgive the studio executives who jerked him around. He would often tell interviewers that during his time at Warners he was told to lose a lot of weight and in return he would be given a shot at conventional leading-man roles. So he dieted—fasted, really—and dropped fifty pounds. Or, in some versions of his story, a hundred or even more. And when he had slimmed down, the very people who had told him to lose the weight said they were sorry, but they were no longer interested. Thin, he just wasn't funny.

The young Gleason was a strikingly handsome man, better looking than his daughter Linda, who became a movie star, or his grandson Jason Patric, who not only became a movie star but won the heart (and broke up the wedding plans, just days before the event) of reigning nineties sex symbol Julia Roberts. Gleason had a winning smile, deep and delicate blue eyes and finely cut features without the least shortfall in masculinity. Art Carney remembers him as "a good-looking Irishman who was always attractive to women." Flo Haley, who knew Gleason since he was twenty-five, recalls more than a trace of physical vanity in him. "He would take off a few pounds and come here to show my husband. He'd say, 'See,' and pull in his waist, and then he'd start to shimmy and strut and give it that stripper thing." He hated being stereotyped as a fat comic and would periodically diet just to give himself a new image and shake up public expectations. Toward the end of his life, in his *60 Minutes* interview with Morley Safer, Gleason claimed to have been all but unaware of his weight as an issue:

"I never thought I was fat. I never worried about it. The only thing about being overweight that bothered me is that I always liked to look nice in clothes. I always liked to buy expensive clothes, have them made in London and all of that stuff, and when you're heavy you don't look as good in clothes as you do when you have less weight. But that is the only thing. I never walked like I was a fat guy. I was a pretty good dancer. I never thought about being fat."

This disclaimer was nonsense from a man who went on a diet virtually annually, sometimes more often, and who cumulatively lost at least a thousand pounds during his lifetime. To the end, Gleason believed that only his weight had kept him from becoming his vision of a *real* movie star, that is, a sex symbol, the guy who got the girl. But after a while, Flo Haley says, he more or less made his peace with his proportions. "Eventually his only reason to go on a diet was healthwise," she says, "if he had a pain or was having trouble breathing. He knew that half the comic appeal he had was to be plump and pleasing."

Apart from the Haleys and assorted drinking pals, Gleason built alliances while in Hollywood with his old acquaintance Bullets Durgom, by now primarily a music promoter, and with Durgom's ally Leo Talent, the head of Glenn Miller's music publishing company. Just as Durgom was fated to become the Svengali of Gleason's television career, so Talent was to become the guiding spirit of Gleason's mood music business in decades to come. But for immediate purposes the most important contacts Gleason made were at Slapsie Maxie's, a sort of rough equivalent of the Club 18, named for a former middleweight boxing champion who was the restaurant's front man and the signature comic of its stage shows. Slapsie Maxie Rosenbloom was battered-looking and ostensibly punch-drunk, but he handled his duties profitably. The real behind-the-scenes manager was a man called Sam Lewis, who hired Gleason as a comic at a hundred fifty dollars a week and eventually raised him to three hundred twenty-five a week. Gleason's West Coast life was starting to look more and more like his New York existence—he was working two jobs and spending the equivalent of six or seven paychecks.

Warner executives were less than delighted that Gleason, a very busy actor by day, should find so much energy to perform at night. They were convinced he was shortchanging them somehow, especially because he had a third full-time occupation as party boy and lush. But he came to work on time and conscientiously did his job. In later life he would often say that film acting is absurdly easy: "You wait until they yell 'Action,' stand where they tell you to, and just say your line."

For Gleason, indeed, it may have been that simple. Some of his film performances are oversized, but not one is stilted or boring. Flo Haley recalls that her husband, Jack, whose own memorable work in *The Wizard of Oz* seems entirely fresh half a century later, told her that Gleason was "maybe the most natural performer he ever saw, always believable, even when he was onstage with a pure genius like, say, Frank Fay. My Jack would say, 'He just has it in him, a sincerity that you don't see in other actors, even the biggest stars.' "

Whether film acting seemed easy or natural to Gleason, it wasn't, at least in 1942, very creative or satisfying. That was probably the main reason he could be found onstage most nights at Slapsie Maxie's. There, as at the Club 18, he didn't do a set act. He just got up and winged it. The thrill of live, improvised performance, with nothing to fall back on, no script to protect him, gave him an adrenal excitement of danger. Some of what he did fell flat. Some was outright weird. If he had seen a movie within the past couple of days, he might go through the whole plot, enacting all the characters himself and also supplying all the sound effects. This sort of imitation is a staple of stand-up comics today, and movie star impersonations were standard stuff then, too. But other comics would take off on big, popular movies that most of the audience had already seen or at least heard about. Gleason was often doing something small and unfamiliar, or maybe a film so new that it was still in studio previews. There was no way his audience could appreciate the wit and satire of his rendition.

What appealed to him about stand-up was that he shaped the material to fit himself. He was always doing something appropriate to his talents, style and demeanor. The maddening thing about the movies was that Gleason had been hired as a comic but was then expected to perform as an actor, often in roles that did not suit him. He had never been to acting school; he had hardly been to school at all. His professional life before Hollywood had been centered on the development of a recognizable, consistent persona; acting was premised on the idea of submerging oneself into someone else. On Broadway he at least had a chance to be spontaneous. In films, he was required to do take after take until he achieved the director's version of the scene, not his own, and that was the only one the audience would ever see.

By the time Gleason would return to movie-making in earnest, two decades later, he would be cast with great precision and care. Roles would even be written, or at minimum rewritten, specifically to suit his talents and needs. That self-impersonation was the kind of acting Gleason enjoyed, and even the kind he admired.

In off-camera conversation with Safer for *60 Minutes* he said, "Take a guy like Clark Gable. Now, they said he wasn't a good actor. He did the same part a hundred times and was good every time he did it. That takes acting ability. They said Gary Cooper wasn't a good actor. He did the same picture eight hundred times, walking up the middle of the road with the gun coming out and all, and he did it good enough to entertain audiences all over the world. Now that's acting. I'd like to see anybody else do as many pictures as Gable did that have the same plot, the same quality, and still exist."

That was Gleason's *sotto voce* answer to critics who said he always played some version of himself and offered no surprises. To do just that and still be entertaining, he thought, was the hardest thing in show business.

If he had learned one lesson from the disappointing year at Warner Brothers, it was that there was no satisfaction to be had—no glory and no fun—in standing where you were told, saying what someone wrote for you and trying to submerge yourself into a character that was, inevitably, a lot less interesting than you were. Inevitably, that is, if you were Jackie Gleason. Another performer might have been crushed by the setback. Perhaps some part of Gleason was. He said, in old age, "I think you make your hell right here on earth and I think real hell is having everything you want as soon as you first want it." But the most interesting part of Jackie Gleason was not crushed. It was inspired. He was too fat, too thin, too good-looking, not good-looking enough, too much this and too little that and too thoroughly the other to become an ordinary, garden-variety star. So he went back to Manhattan and methodically turned himself into The Great One.

CHAPTER FOUR

For fans of the image of Jackie Gleason as the total party animal, the forties must surely rank as his heyday. He had celebrity and popularity without crushing responsibility. He had the youth and vigor to party all night, to shake off hangovers and broken bones with equal aplomb. Marriage and fatherhood did not encumber him because he barely acknowledged his status as a family man and most of the time he did not even live at home—he just dropped by for short, awkward visits. He earned plenty of money and was able to spend far more than he earned because he found a succession of friends willing to bankroll his glorious excess.

These benefactors figured he would pay them back someday, especially if he struck it rich. And if he didn't, they found his company so amusing that they happily paid for the privilege. They were sure he would be equally generous if the situation were reversed. In fact, Gleason made a habit of demonstrating his generosity to them with their own money. He was notorious for cadging a loan of a couple of hundred dollars, slapping the cash down on the bar the instant he received it and roaring in gleeful abandon, "Drinks for the house!"

Gleason considered a night deadly dull if its revelry ended before dawn, and his favorite fellow carousers were Dixieland jazz musicians, because he loved their sound—its brassy insistence, its gay exuberance, its ability to penetrate the most sullen and moody of silences. When he was living apart from Genevieve, he generally resided in hotels because he had neither the ability nor the inclination to tend to his creature comforts. But he was often reprimanded, even evicted, for throwing all-night jam sessions in his rooms, to the disquiet of other guests. He received such chastisements entirely without shame. In fact, he bragged about them. Like many adolescent boys of all ages, he seems to have done almost everything he did not so much for the pleasure of the experience itself as for the sheer joy of recounting it to the boys afterward.

He liked to tell, for example, of the time his wife called him at a hotel room just as he was about to leave for his standard night on the tiles. Fully clothed, he jumped into bed, pulled the sheet and spread up to his chin and solemnly assured Genevieve that he was already in bed under the covers. It was a tale with a peculiarly Roman Catholic sensibility, about a lie that could parade unabashedly before the Almighty as the truth.

Often, Gleason descended from the witty to the raunchy. He considered it hilarious to get so drunk that he would actually throw up on his friends. He did that to the celebrated sports columnist Jimmy Cannon in a restaurant and to Frank Sinatra at a baseball game—and in later years was to appear at times to be on the verge of doing so to his agent, Sam Cohn, and assorted senior programming executives at CBS. This, too, Gleason bragged about, in what must surely have been yet another manifestation of his underlying anger toward the same mankind that in his cups or on the air he so sentimentally professed to cherish.

It is little wonder that Genevieve, who grew ever more settled in her rectitude, wanted as little as possible to do with him. In her mind, Gleason had abandoned home and hearth for the sins of the flesh. In his mind, she had more or less thrown him out by imposing rules that had nothing to do with the young man he had been when they met or the public man he longed to be now. Sometimes Jackie would accuse Genevieve of willfully refusing to understand the nature of show business. It was not enough for him to perform and go home, he would explain. There was no dividing line between social life and professional life. The men he was out carousing with were business contacts of the kind that had led him to most of his past jobs and they might well lead him on to still greater glory. Besides, he couldn't be funny if he was relaxed and sober. And once he was keyed up and drunk in order to perform, surely it was better for him to go out and have the party he yearned for after the performance rather than come home and disturb her and the children. in all of this was a small kernel of truth—wrapped, as Genevieve quickly spotted, in much self-justification and deceit. Other men in show business had wives and families and paid sincere attention to them. Jackie was abandoning the family because he didn't want to be there—and perhaps because he had learned in his childhood that what fathers do is quarrel and depart.

He made periodic attempts at reconciliation, the last in about 1948. But none lasted very long. Flo Haley, who was present for some of these attempts and who also intervened periodically to bring together Gleason and his daughters when he was in California and under her sway, says the marriage was misconceived from the beginning: "They were just not a good match. Some other girl would have been great for him and some other guy would have been great for her. Gen was devout and truly good but she had no tolerance and no sense of humor. She had no special feeling for show business. I'm surprised she was ever in it, even as a kid. It wasn't important to her the way it was to him. When you're a comic, you have to have an audience at home to try stuff out on. She wouldn't do that for him.

"I thought he tried to see things her way, but she didn't make it easy. When I first heard they had trouble, I could see her point, what with all of Jackie's drinking and his careless ways with money. But I remember we were out with them in New York one time when he was trying to be sober and really holding it in. He got up and started to go from table to table, saying hello to this one and that one, the way you do in a club, especially if you're in show business. And Gen said, 'Are you going to start *that* again?' She was a real hounder. And my husband turned to me and said, 'You see what I mean? It's not all his fault.' "

The estrangement from Gen meant that Jackie became a virtual stranger to his daughters as well. Even on Christmas Day, he might be around for no more than half an hour. But he found himself another family in the saloons of New York, and by about 1944 he had found the replacement for Genevieve, the next great love of his life.

The new object of devotion was not a blonde showgirl but a tall, fat, big-nosed, craggy-faced, homely Jewish man called Toots Shor. Gleason's bond with him was assuredly not sexual or romantic—indeed, despite all the bygone theorizing about the effects of absent fathers and possessive mothers, there was never any suggestion of even the faintest, most subliminal trace of homosexuality in Gleason. But his need for male bonding was intense, and for at least a decade and a half, from the early forties through the late fifties, he was to center his life on a ceaseless effort to tease, amuse, trick, top and otherwise entertain Toots Shor. He spent more cumulative time with Toots than with any of his wives or mistresses until the last one, and he probably valued Toots's opinion more than he did any woman's, partly because Gleason was a male chauvinist, partly because The Great One had decided that Toots spoke candidly for The Great Unwashed. "I prize him for his absolute honesty," Gleason would say. "Other people will tell me how terrific the show was. I'll walk in on Toots and he'll say, 'You weren't so good tonight in such-and-such number.' And his opinion will invariably be my own."

No social history of Manhattan at midcentury would be complete without mention of Shor, the barkeep-turned-celebrity who was described by *The New Yorker* in a November 1950 profile (adulatory at such length that it ran in three installments) as "the burly, impudent, hard-working, high-spirited, sentimental proprietor of the restaurant at 51 West 51st Street that bears his name." Just as in the cinematic vision of Casablanca everybody went to Rick's, so in the real-life New York City of World War II and the decadeplus that saw itself as "postwar," everyone went to Shor's, to eat, to drink, above all to see and be seen. Everybody was not, of course, really and truly everybody; it never is. Shor's was not for the literati, the left-leaning or, naturally, the ill-to-do. It was not for the café society of tuxedoed gentlemen and gilded debutantes. Rather, Shor's was for saloon society, the self-confident men of attainment in sports and journalism and entertainment, plus their hangers-on, admirers and gawkers. The in crowd at Shor's were men's men, prowling stallions who would have had trouble absorbing the very concept of "macho" because to use that label might imply that their tussling, raucous masculinity represented an ideological choice, just one of a range of legitimate options, instead of the eldest state of nature, wild. Most of these men were married, and many of them, including Shor himself, were said to hold quite domesticated views about the importance of their duties as husbands and fathers. But in their world, a world where Jackie Gleason quickly became a central figure, a kind of upper-level court jester, men derived most of their sense of self-worth from winning the esteem of other men.

Toots's was a world of celebrities, commingling all sorts of people whose common bond was being famous. Long before television turned life's assorted achievers into interchangeable "talking heads," the newspapers and especially the columnists implanted in the minds of the public— and of the noted themselves—some sense of the equivalence of different kinds of fame. And just as being "mentioned in Winchell" was a vital hallmark of this status, so was being moved to the front of the inevitable waiting line at Shor's. Sports heroes had the place of highest honor with the proprietor. Joe DiMaggio and, later, Mickey Mantle were esteemed regulars. So were Mel Ott, the New York Giants slugger for whom Toots once snubbed Sir Alexander Fleming, the discoverer of penicillin, and the golfer Ben Hogan, who gave the Jewish Shor a pair of gold cuff links made from Roman Catholic medals of St. Christopher. But gangster boss Frank Costello also frequented the place; Harry Truman dropped by as both senator and vice president. Entertainers mobbed the bar, among them Frank Sinatra, Charlie Chaplin, George Jessel, Pat O'Brien, Bob Hope and film studio owner Louis B. Mayer, who complained about being kept waiting for a table, only to be told by Toots that at least the meal would be better than some of the Metro-Goldwyn-Mayer films the restaurateur had waited in line to see.

Just as important to Shor's reputation were the newspaper columnists, most of them locally based but many of them nationally syndicated at a time when New York was far more central to every aspect of national life than it is today. Shor's attracted all the big names—Louis Sobol, Leonard Lyons, Bill Slocum, Bill Corum, Ed Sullivan, Frank Conniff, Earl Wilson and a host of others, including the grandest and snidest of them all, Walter Winchell. These journalistic power brokers worked the tables at Shor's to get glittering celebrity items for their columns, often accumulating a whole day's worth of material in the course of lunch. The celebrities, in turn, worked the tables at Shor's to promote their careers. Shor smiled benignly over the whole process, knowing that the publicity generated long waiting lines of would-be stargazers who happily paid steep bills.

Beyond this practical advantage, Shor welcomed the famous out of sincere snobbery. He genuinely believed that the acclaimed deserved to be fawned over, unless and until they showed themselves to be "shitheels"—a favorite derisive term that his buddy Gleason quickly took to using too. Toots was regarded as a crude but accurate barometer of how one's career was going. He had the kind of sixth sense that movie casting executives pray for. The warmer his greeting, the faster one was rising; the more perfunctory his handshake, the quicker one's impending fall. Given this alert attention to status, it is all the more impressive that Gleason so quickly became a fixed favorite, at a time when he was a recently failed movie actor and still a second-tier nightclub performer.

It would be unfair to leave the impression that the scene at Shor's was strictly about social climbing, the way it is at a few favored film industry hangouts in Los Angeles today. The famous had a genuinely good time at Shor's (and so, if they did not expect too much democracy in treatment, did the not so famous). Although he made enemies aplenty, Shor made many more friends, and they regarded him as a genuinely lovable man. His personal byword was *loyalty*. He operated his business, especially in the early years, more on the basis of boozy camaraderie than on sound principles of cost accounting. He let friends have credit; he even advanced them cash; he barely kept track of what went into their glasses at the bar, and portion control of food was a notion that would never have lodged in his gutter-savant vocabulary. In effect, what Shor provided was a private men's club for the headline makers of New York, with two enormous advantages over more formal versions of such institutions. First, even if a DiMaggio or Mantle, a Jimmy Cannon or Jackie Gleason could persuade the usual Upper East Side club to overlook a lack of background, education, polish and savoir faire on the basis of raw achievement, the unfortunate inductee would soon find himself adrift, surrounded by a phalanx of moneyed, mumble-mouthed Chaunceys and Reginalds, with not a kindred streetwise spirit in sight. Second, in a conventional club, the members collectively share the burden of maintaining the overhead. At Shor's, the wide-eyed visitors from Omaha took care of that responsibility.

For Gleason, whose financial recklessness was matched only by his envy and resentment toward those born to privilege, the setup at Shor's was ideal. He basked in the affection of the proprietor, who in turn largely brushed off the sort of educated, steadily employed and financially sound types who made Gleason uncomfortable. More important, Jackie could dip into the till practically at will. For the first decade of his relationship with Shor there was scarcely a moment when he was not running an interest-free tab in the hundreds, if not thousands, of dollars. Shor merely sighed, or even laughed, when the already indebted Gleason would ask for a couple of hundred dollars and then immediately hand half his borrowings to the headwaiter with the explanation, "Toots, I hadn't tipped him in a long while." On one occasion Gleason's conscience apparently began to nag him—or he may just have been trying to psych Shor out—and he announced he wouldn't be dropping around for a spell because his tab had gotten too high and money was still too tight. Shor implored Gleason to keep coming and assured him he could sign for everything, tips included. At the evening's end, as he wrote his name with a flourish, Gleason added a five-dollar tip, a small fraction of his accustomed grandiosity. "I'd leave a lot more," he explained to the help, "but I'm signing for Toots, and you know how cheap he is." Like many of Shor's regulars, Gleason looked for ways to reduce the notional obligation of a signed bill to no debt at all. One favorite method was to challenge Shor to a drinking contest. In this display of misguided macho, winning or losing didn't much matter. The main point of the contest was that the drinks of the combatants were on the house.

From time to time, even Shor got disgusted with Gleason's excesses. Once, when Jackie passed out near the bar, Toots ordered the help, "Leave that bum there. It'll teach him a lesson." For hours the waiters and customers meticulously stepped over the sprawled form of the comic, who snored heavily in plain view. In its career impact, this may have been more than just a prank. Although attitudes toward alcoholic overindulgence were certainly more tolerant then than now, Gleason had already begun to develop a perilous reputation as a boozer. He was often impaired while working; sometimes he was simply too drunk to go on at all. Producers were often reluctant to hire him. To have word get around of his being passed out for hours in a place as public as the barroom floor of Toots Shor's was bound to have some adverse effect on his job prospects—as both he and Toots would have been well aware.

Gleason, too, sometimes let playfulness slip over into malice. When a practical joke involving a concealed live piglet went awry—the delivery team dropped the unhappy animal down the cellar stairs and fatally broke its neck—Shor was forced to leave the decaying corpse in place over a weekend until appropriate city regulators could verify that no law had been broken and condone the removal of the remains. Gleason delightedly went from table to table deflating Shor's food sales by touting the diners, already queasily aware of a faintly off aroma, to try "fresh pork—we dressed it ourselves." Far worse, by the standards of their shared macho code, was an affront that was to come much later in the relationship. Returning from a sojourn out of town in the late fifties, Gleason heard that Shor had been bemoaning not having heard from his pal. Jackie sneered that Toots was "like a woman—you have to tell her where you are every minute." The bond between them survived even that slur, although in after years Shor was far less visibly a part of Gleason's life.

Insult and humiliation were central to the style of the friendship, so it is not surprising that each sometimes crossed the line into incivility. An illustrative anecdote appeared in the *New Yorker* profile of Toots (it is noteworthy as well for the way the story identifies Gleason, who is clearly presumed to be unknown to the readership despite his five movies, half dozen Broadway shows and national tours, and television appearances on *The Life of Riley*, which was then airing): "Shor once told his good friend Jackie Gleason, a stage comedian, that he had the face of a pig. 'And you got the body,' Gleason replied." In a wisecrack of somewhat later vintage, after both men took up golf Gleason boasted that he was superior to Shor through a simple conjunction of optics, physics and excess poundage: "If he puts the ball where he can see it, he can't hit it. And if he has the ball where he can hit it, he can't see it."

The one-upsmanship extended to elaborate practical jokes. After tiring of hearing Gleason brag endlessly about his prowess at pool, Shor, who had been a juvenile hotshot at the billiards table himself, brought in a friend "from the garment business" to challenge Jackie in a game for money. In classic hustler fashion, the "garment executive" let Gleason win a couple of games for relatively low stakes and then pleaded for a chance to win his money back by upping the ante. He proceeded to clear the table before Gleason got in a single shot, whereupon the fat comedian figured out he had been had. "I don't know who I've been playing," Gleason said, "but he sure ain't who he says he is." Jackie was right—his opponent was the sport's foremost champion, Willie Mosconi. According to Milton Berle, Gleason's old pal Frank Sinatra was in attendance for this comeuppance. In Berle's recollection, Sinatra turned to Gleason and said, "That'll teach you not to bet strangers on trains and not to brag so fucking much." Gleason told a slightly different version of events—indeed, in characteristic fashion, several slightly different versions, depending on what narrative point he was trying to make at the time.

The same haze of contradiction enshrouds the finer points of what was certainly the most publicized exchange between Gleason and Shor, their celebrated footrace around the block. After trading a series of barbs about how fat and out of shape they were, the men challenged each other to circle the rectangle of land bounded by Fifth and Sixth avenues and Fifty-first and Fifty-second streets. The reported stakes were anything from twenty dollars to free drinks all night to an all-night party for a flotilla of friends. For reasons never explained in any version of the story but essential to its punch line, Gleason slyly suggested that the combatants run in opposite directions, one clockwise, the other counterclockwise. Shor agreed, and therein lay his undoing. As soon as Toots had lumbered off Jackie lifted a hand, calmly hailed a taxi, circled the block and strolled back into the restaurant. He was sitting there, serenely sipping, when Toots burst in, puffing and sweaty. Only after the astonished loser had paid off—anywhere from a few minutes later to the next day, depending on which of the innumerable variations Gleason was telling—did Shor suddenly wheel on his rival and shout, "Hey! You never passed me!"

The best part of this story, the most illustrative of the relationship, is that Toots was amused and delighted, not enraged, by Gleason's chicanery. He made no attempt to get his money back and he described Jackie as a wit, not a welsher. Indeed, just as Gleason loved to tell the tale of how Toots had hoodwinked him with Willie Moscone, so Toots enjoyed recalling how Jackie's treachery had left him literally gasping for breath.

Toots was not Jackie's only partner in ribaldry, nor Shor's his only hangout. In the later forties, Gleason could often be found at Kellogg's, a gathering place for second-rank comics (the really famous ones went to Lindy's). A group of cronies there egged Gleason on to one of his more outrageous escapades, a saga that would surely seem suspect except that other participants assured the gag writer Coleman Jacoby that it was true. Learning that a friend would spend a much-anticipated night of romance—in some versions of the story, his wedding night—at the Hotel Wentworth, Gleason contrived to get into the room in advance and hide under the bed in the company of a goat. He and the animal waited quietly until lovemaking commenced. Then Gleason began squeezing intimate parts of the goat to cause it to bleat, while up above, the love-sick swain took these noises for cries of passion elicited from his beloved by the vigor of his attentions. In the most detailed and ornate version of the story, Gleason and his vocal assistant managed to stay hidden, and to maintain the deceit, until the intercourse was complete. The incident was said to have ended his friendship with the rightful occupants of the room at the Wentworth—but to have brought in a big wad of cash from bets with the crowd at Kellogg's. Like so many of Gleason's tales about his exploits, this one loses plausibility on close scrutiny, beginning with the image of fat Jackie wedged under a bed. It all sounds more like vaudeville than like life—unless, at minimum, those involved were very, very drunk, which in Gleason's crowd was altogether possible (but surprising in a goat). In any case, it surely says something about Gleason that he wanted friends to believe that this smirky, school boyish episode was true. For a married man, Gleason in the forties (and in his own late twenties and early thirties) was singularly lacking in discretion. Milton Berle recalls of that time, "Gleason screwed a lot and he wanted you to know. Some guys fuck a lot but they don't talk about it. Gleason talked."

Just as Shor's was not Gleason's only hangout, so Toots was not his only personal banker. Jackie was almost invariably in hock to his manager, Willie Webber, and he borrowed from the Club 18 and any other employer that would lend him money. For a while in 1943 he conned the management of the Hotel Astor into giving him a corner suite rent-free and periodically advancing him wads of cash. He was no more respectful of the clubs' or hotel's largesse than of Shor's. His idea of a grand joke was to hire a limousine to take him half a city block—better still if he had the chauffeur pull up to a street corner hot dog stand, where Gleason never ordered fewer than half a dozen franks—or to toss hundred-dollar bills at a nightclub band to persuade them to play the same song half a dozen times in a row. Anything perverse, anything nihilistic, appealed to Gleason. Well before Eugène Ionesco was writing theater of the absurd, Gleason was living it.

As reckless as he was with money and booze and sex and reputation, Gleason was most daredevil with his own body. He was determined to display no fear and acknowledge no limits. In November 1943, while exiting a club in Philadelphia, he fell down a flight of stairs and broke his arm. A doctor set the break temporarily, in the wee small hours, but instructed Gleason to rest and then return the next day for a more proper setting. Jackie did not. Instead he rounded up friends, drank and partied till dawn. On recovering from the predictable hangover, Gleason telephoned to secure himself a booking (and a five-hundred-dollar advance) back at his old standby the Club 18 in New York. To the consternation of management there, which had not known of his injury, he insisted on going onstage with a broken arm, defying audiences to laugh at a man who was, at least temporarily, a cripple. Gleason's inadequate attention to the break left him with permanent nerve damage in his hand and, ironically, may have helped save his life by contributing to his exempt 4-F draft status during World War II. Yet Gleason was unchastened, every bit as headlong and nervy as before. In 1944, Berle recalls, his *Ziegfeld Follies* team played softball opposite a team featuring Gleason and showmates from *Follow the Girls,* a Broadway musical with a mild military theme. Says Berle, "I have many fond remembrances of Gleason. That one is unusually frightening. It was just a casual game but he played his heart out. He broke a bone in his foot sliding into me at first base. Sliding. At first base. And in softball!"

The determination to test limits, or better yet prove there really were none, was one of the most persistent of Gleason's character traits and one of the most adolescent. All his life, his sense of humor revolved around finding someone's sore spots and then pressing them, harder and harder.

As for conventional constraints on behavior, in deference either to health or to common sense, Gleason acknowledged them readily enough, but invariably with an insistence in the next breath that they did not apply to him. He would brag that his physical and emotional fiber was so much greater than other people's that he could comfortably withstand strains they could not. He would also convey his impatience with moderation, his sense that a well-controlled existence was hardly better than being dead. About his eating or his drinking or his epic smoking (five to seven packs of cigarettes a day, not to mention the more than occasional cigar), he would snap, "I want to live, pal." That yearning to survive, which was the very reason his contemporaries were scaling back their youthful excesses, was Gleason's battle cry to persevere. For him, life had to be a larger-than life. Eventually that sensibility would inform many of his enduring characters on television and in movies. This autobiographical resonance would doubtless be part of the reason that Gleason would ultimately proclaim, in defiance of the facts, that he had in effect written all his characters himself. For a full decade before he brought the personas of Ralph Kramden and Reggie Van Gleason and Charlie the Loudmouth and so many others to the small screen, he was living much of their essence on the barroom floor of Toots Shor's or underneath a bridal bed in the Hotel Wentworth.

The gut unhappiness for the self-proclaimed "world's greatest entertainer" during the forties was that the rest of the world still didn't know he rated that honorific. In fact, within show business Gleason was acquiring the hazardous reputation of being a first-rate "table comic." The term meant that Gleason was funny when he came to your table and beguiled you over drinks, absolutely free—but that up on a stage, where he had to have an act and captivate a paying audience, he just couldn't deliver. For at least the first half of the decade, Gleason was content, if not elated, to earn five hundred dollars a week, at a time when the top club comics, like Milton Berle, commanded five thousand or more. Only on rare occasions did Gleason come anywhere close to that kind of money. He picked up a few weeks as emcee of the stage show at the Roxy, a theater that combined live entertainment with movies, at three thousand dollars a week. Gleason often said he got his agent's price despite having blurted out to the Roxy management, in the presence of the horrified agent, "But I'm not worth three thousand dollars a week." If he indeed had such a flash of modesty, it was gone by 1946. That year he was appearing at Billy Rose's Diamond Horseshoe for thirty-five hundred dollars a week when he came down with laryngitis. Billy Rose himself, the almost legendary showman, prevailed on Gleason's model and nemesis Milton Berle to pinch-hit. Says Berle, "I filled in between my own shows at the Carnival and I was already getting a paycheck so I didn't ask for any money. Rose thanked me when it was over but Gleason didn't. In October of that same year *I* got laryngitis and Toots and Frank Sinatra asked Gleason to fill in with an act of fifteen or twenty minutes. Billy Rose agreed but Jackie said he wanted to get *my* salary, which by then was ten thousand dollars a week, the biggest money in clubs. He appeared for five days out of the seven in the week, so they gave him five sevenths of my ten thousand dollars." Berle adds, "But I forgave him for that," in a tone that makes abundantly plain he still hasn't.

Gleason being Gleason, not enough of these bursts of cash went to Genevieve and the girls, and almost none was set aside for a bleaker day. Yet he should have known from experience that his brief flirtations with high finance were almost invariably followed by demotion back to the small change department. The gig at the Roxy, for example, was succeeded by a stint on radio in a "sustaining" program—meaning one without commercial sponsorship—that paid a hundred and fifty dollars per week. The Club 18, his steadiest employer, apparently never paid him more than six hundred dollars per week at any time during the decade. Slapsie Maxie's in Los Angeles, to which he still repaired occasionally, seems to have treated him no more extravagantly. In any case, whatever salary nightclubs might grant, they did not offer him much of a future.

In the longer run, the clubs were a poor bet

because they were a dying institution. Just as talking movies and, even more, radio had supplanted vaudeville, so the experimental medium of television was going to knock off the night spots by providing equivalent entertainment at home, free of charge. The mechanics of TV were demonstrated by RCA at the 1939 World's Fair. By the mid-forties, a few visionaries realized television's commercial potential. By 1948, Ed Sullivan and Milton Berle were already established as the medium's debut stars. Gleason, by his own later admission, was not among those who first grasped TV's implication. But he and his managers must surely have realized, when TV was still mostly a scientist's speculation, that the clubs were the wrong place for Gleason. The clubs emphasized what he did least well, the stand-up monologue, and afforded little or no opportunity for Gleason to display his real gifts in comic character sketches. Despite the disappointments of *Keep Off the Grass* and the movies, Gleason had to resume acting.

He returned to the stage in 1943 in *Artists and Models*, a revue assembled by Lou Walters, a sometime nightclub impresario, now better remembered as the father of TV newswoman Barbara Walters. The most important thing about the show was that it earned Gleason a favorable plug, apparently his first, from *New York Daily News* columnist Ed Sullivan, whose paper had the biggest circulation by far of any in the United States. About a decade later, in his other career as television presenter, Sullivan would introduce the firstever glimpse of Gleason on their joint network, CBS. Gleason followed *Artists and Models* with a national tour of *Hellzapoppin,* the Olsen and Johnson revue, in which he and a fellow carouser named Lew Parker had the temerity and bad judgment to replace Olsen and Johnson. But his first substantial success onstage came in April 1944, with the debut of *Follow the Girls,* produced by the soon to be august David L. (then billed as "Dave") Wolper. Nothing much about the text won raves, although the book was credited in part to Guy Bolton, P. G. Wodehouse's erstwhile collaborator on many charming musicals, and the sets and lights were by the esteemed Howard Bay. Like many musicals of that era, *Follow the Girls* was a pastiche as much akin to vaudeville as to a play. Although *Oklahoma!* had opened the year before and introduced the then novel concept of a completely integrated show, in which even the ballet dancers were characters rather than animated wallpaper, Broadway audiences were still prepared to tolerate the flimsiest of narrative.

The locale of the action was a naval training station on Great Neck, Long Island. As in *Navy Blues,* Gleason—whom the real military had rejected as, among other things, one hundred pounds overweight—appeared in uniform and joshed the serviceman. (To his credit, Gleason never confused his show business time in uniform with actual combat, unlike such actors as Ronald Reagan and John Wayne. Nor did he ever claim

117

to have volunteered. He was drafted and rejected.)

The show's top-billed star was Gertrude Niesen, a torch singer whom veteran press agent Frank Goodman recalls as "a minor Sophie Tucker." Goodman made Gleason's acquaintance during the run of the show and remembers him as "always on"—show business parlance for performing at all times, in an intense and hyperkinetic way that more or less precludes everyday conversation. Niesen's big numbers included a ballad, "I Wanna Get Married," with what were considered very racy lyrics in those tame times (for example, "I wanna order twin beds, then only use one"). She was cast as a stripper who entertained the troops, and Gleason played her love interest, such as it was. Audiences apparently readily accepted him as a well-rounded form of leading man.

Critics at last responded to Gleason too. Burton Rascoe of the *World Telegram* said, "Jackie Gleason, Miss Niesen's fat and comical vis-a-vis . . . is a good-natured and likable pantaloon with some of that engagingly honest naiveté which made Sonny Tufts such a pleasant addition to the ranks of movie players. Gleason does his stuff in an off-hand, apparently effortless manner, with none of that frantic, scenery-biting horseplay which some comedians indulge in. He has one stock gag which, surprisingly enough, is always surprising and funny." The gimmick, as the doyen of critics George Jean Nathan recorded, went this way: "The fat comic curves his right hand over his head and ejaculates, 'What the hell!' " Wilella Waldorf of the *Post* enthused, especially about a drag sequence: "Two-ton Jackie Gleason injects some roistering comedy into the proceedings. Jackie is funnier than we have ever seen him. Perhaps his high point of the evening was a terrific struggle getting into various garments officially worn by the WAVES. He made a very large WAVE indeed, almost a tidal WAVE." Lewis Nichols of the *New York Times* was less enthusiastic about the comic opportunities—he described Jackie as "working practically without material"—but added, "Mr. Gleason is rotund, with a fat man's beaming face: some day when he gets the words he will be wonderful instead of just very good." Jackie even rated a mention in *Time* magazine, then the most powerful media institution in America, which said, *"Follow the Girls* has a number of virtues and two faults—its music and its book. It boasts a lot of good people [including] likably loony comic Jackie Gleason."

Although he started out with fourth billing, on a line with fellow comics Buster West and Tim Herbert, Jackie soon moved up to second, ahead of them, singer Frank Parker and ballet dancer Irina Baronova. He was described in the program as "a 4-F redwood that grew in Brooklyn who has never walked away from a third helping of roast beef or lost a chance to convulse a customer." The paying public apparently agreed. The show ran 882 performances, something over two years; Jackie moved on some months before the end of the run.

Gleason's stage career brought him much-craved attention from the columnists and began to open new opportunities for him in the biggest entertainment medium based in New York—radio. While still at the Club Miami, Jackie had had a local radio show in Newark for a little while. But he was thrown off the air for inviting his friends into the studio and turning the broadcast into a loud, drunken party—not an impossible concept for a show and one he would later attempt, more elaborately and at great expense, for CBS television. He had appeared occasionally for Edelbreu Beer, mixing music and comedy on a local New York station. By August of 1944, he had become big enough to appear on NBC network radio and to have a joke banned as too political. Given that Gleason was, then and later, determinedly among the least topical and controversial of humorists, this was a little ironic. The gag had Gleason describing an appearance at a nightclub called El Cellardooro. "Dark?" he asked rhetorically. "It was so dark that John L. Lewis walked in and tried to organize two of the bartenders." This kidding reference to the wild-eyebrowed head of the United Mine Workers seems almost childishly mild today, but in that era the radio networks were determined to avoid offending union members on the one hand or union opponents on the other. In noting the incident, columnist Earl Wilson referred to Gleason, then twenty-eight, as "a top U.S. comic." Wilson's praise was not only extravagant but in some regards plain wrong. He went on to portray Gleason as "under contract to get $50,000 in one year for two pictures for Twentieth Century-Fox." Not so. It would be more than five years before Gleason made another movie and nearly seven before he would have a contract paying him fifty thousand dollars a year. That would not be in the movies at all, but in the still-to-emerge medium of television.

By late 1945, Gleason knew it was time to seek another venue to succeed *Follow the Girls*. Whenever a performer leaves an established hit for the speculative risk of a new show, onlookers question the performer's judgment especially when the new venture turns out to be a fiasco, which is the incontestable description of Jackie's next big vehicle, *The Duchess Misbehaves*. But he had sound reasons. To begin with, he was bored almost beyond endurance by playing the same scenes night after night. Although he capered and cavorted and in general maddened co-star Niesen with his improvisatory departures from the text, he still chafed at the inevitable abundance of repetition. This is far from uncommon among actors, but the sentiment was especially intense in Gleason. Thus he generally avoided working in live theater in his later years.

On a more commercial level, it did not require genius or even special insight to recognize that the end of World War II made the text of *Follow the Girls,* especially its setting at a naval training facility, hopelessly dated. It is always humiliating to have a show close, and in his television years Gleason made a fetish of refusing to commit to another season until the network had publicly professed its yearning to renew him. He could be fatalistic about the whimsical nature of show business success, but he preferred not to have to. Far better to walk out on a show than have it close around him—and according to Broadway reference books, that seems to be what he did. (Both Bishop and Bacon, however, imply that he stayed with *Follow the Girls* until it closed. But then, either through Gleason's lapses of memory or for other reasons, Bishop significantly garbles the chronology of Gleason's stage career, and some of his errors recur more or less verbatim in Bacon's version. Both, for example, place *Along Fifth Avenue,* Gleason's last Broadway show of the decade and indeed his second to last ever, during World War II instead of in 1949.)

Perhaps the biggest factor in Gleason's thinking, however, was ambition. The second to top billing in *Follow the Girls* was nice, and so was the thousand-dollar weekly paycheck. But he wanted much more. The ideal next step would have been to have a show built around him, the way *Girls* had been built around Niesen. In concept, *The Duchess Misbehaves* sounds like a sublime moment for the Gleason of the television years. He was to play a timid sign painter (think of the Poor Soul) working in a department store who is knocked on the head by thieves stealing Goya's famous nude of the Duchess of Alba. (Set aside for a moment the logical questions about what a masterpiece is doing amid the cosmetics counters and lingerie displays.) The painter has a dream in which he is Goya (summon up Reggie Van Gleason in a rare sober moment) and in which the woman he fantasizes about in his sign painter life becomes both his fantasy partner and the duchess herself. It is easy to understand how Gleason, still a few months shy of thirty but already a seasoned knockabout, could have envisioned this cheery nonsense (a conceptual rip-off of Cole Porter's *DuBarry Was a Lady*) as the career-confirming showcase of his own dreams.

The problem, as with every previous stage show and film he had done, was the script. It didn't make much sense and it wasn't very funny. At Gleason's urging, a writer named Joe Bigelow came in to craft new jokes and develop some situations in which Gleason could exploit his gift for interpolating oddball movement. Nothing helped. During its out-of-town tryout in Philadelphia, the show bombed. Gleason began to panic and tried to get out of his contract. The management refused. He was the star; the show depended on him or someone like him; it was far too late to find a replacement who could be ready and whose name would sell tickets. Jackie had a run-of-the-play contract, which meant that in the unlikely event the show caught on, he was legally obliged to stay with it until it closed.

On January 31, 1946, it was reported that Gleason had sprained his ankle onstage and would have to miss performances. The next day, he returned. But ten days later and just two days before opening, Gleason pleaded continued pain in the leg and a possible stress fracture (attested to by a cooperative physician) and finally and irrevocably quit the show. After an inconclusive medical exam, the producers reluctantly agreed to accept his going and abandoned their threats to have him called up on charges before his union, Actors' Equity. That was on February 11. In an unsung moment of theater heroism, comic Joey Faye stepped in and opened the show, letter-perfect in every line, just two days later.

While Faye's memory was perfect, nothing else in the show came close. Gleason's judgment had been right. Critics took pleasure in flaunting their wit at the expense of a stinker. Vernon Rice of the *New York Post* said, "Misfortune has befallen *The Duchess Misbehaves* almost since its inception. Last night, however, it had its greatest misfortune. It opened." Louis Kronenberger of *PM* cracked, "Kicking its eighteenth-century heels on West 54th Street is one of the most maddening musicals of the decade. I can't conceive what *The Duchess Misbehaves* was even trying to do. It is all a noisy and witless mess. . . . The leaden jokes pile up on the Adelphi stage until it would take ten husky stevedores to lug them away." With eight resounding pans and not one even tempering review to quote to customers or to bolster confidence backstage, *The Duchess Misbehaves* closed after just five performances (not counting previews, in keeping with Broadway custom). It left behind only one witticism, and that from offstage—the slightly hyperbolic claim that this had been a show so bad the star had deliberately broken his leg to get out of it.

It's not clear to what extent *The Duchess Misbehaves* soured Gleason on Broadway and to what extent his own considerable misbehavior soured producers on him. His abrupt and seemingly deceitful departure compounded his image as difficult, temperamental and unreliable. Yet the agony of floundering onstage had reminded him of how dependent actors are on writers. For a decade, he had enjoyed mounting success in nightclubs while still not having an act. His wit and charm and ability to read an audience could save him. But in a formally scripted scene, no performer could ever be much better than his material. That grated on The Great One's pride.

Whatever the mix of reasons, for the next three years Gleason did not open on Broadway in any show. He made no movies. He had no major and lasting radio showcase. He just worked at clubs and the few holdover vaudeville houses, the latter mostly featuring a mix of movies and live entertainment. He had no fixed asking price. He took what he could get. He traveled from city to city, rarely in the company of his wife and children. For a time he went back to Slapsie Maxie's in hopes of renewing interest at the film studios. But he was still a man whom executives applauded at night and ignored in the cold light of day. In later years he would boast of having walked away from lucrative dates because he was not given the proper billing. In one instance, he explained, his name on the poster was only one third as big as his friend Jimmy Dorsey's, instead of the promised equality. The story rings true. Gleason had volcanic pride and temper. But this was surely a futile, almost nihilistic gesture from a performer who was chronically in debt, erratic as a provider to his estranged family and stalled on the ladder of advancement at a point well beneath his dreamed-of destiny.

Flo Haley remembers attempting a reconciliation between Jackie and Genevieve. She and her husband, she says, paid for a bungalow in Beverly Hills and provided train fare for Gen, Geraldine and Linda to travel West because Gleason seemed so guilt-stricken at his parental absence and so hopeful that he could somehow reform. She is vague on when this happened and on whether Jackie lived steadily under the same roof as his family, but the timing would appear to have been 1947 or early 1948, when Gleason was back trying his luck at Maxie's.

In self-critical moments, Gleason would say that Gen was on her way to sainthood, while he was born to be a hoodlum. At other times he would bristle at being forever depicted as the bad guy, insisting that his escapades were merely boyish and fun-loving. From the perspective of conventional values, one has to wonder why Genevieve persisted so long in attempting to restore the marital bond with a man so unrepentant. She knew of Jackie's infidelities. He had confessed them to her. She knew of his drinking, his lunatic spending, his rackety up-all-night partying. They clashed repeatedly over religion. She was a devout Catholic. Gleason was, from day to day, a believer, an agnostic, an atheist and every other kind of spiritual searcher. He read voraciously about his own religion but also about all the others, which to Genevieve seemed little short of heresy. Gen devoted much of her life to charitable work. Gleason was to become widely known in show business for his resistance to benefits and giveaways. (He did write occasional impulsive checks to the needy in later years, often in circumstances that afforded no tax deduction, and he would sometimes astonish an acquaintance by agreeing to show up at a communion breakfast or other two-bit event. He seems to have done these acts as a genuine penance, insisting there be no publicity for his good deed. But even his agent Sam Cohn recalls, "It was hard enough getting him to agree to show up for pay. Doing it for free was out of the question.")

Three things kept Gen involved with Jackie: her religion, which said marriage was for life; her faith that any sinner can mend his ways and be forgiven; and her daughters' need for a father. Presumably she also longed for some companionship herself. She was still very attractive, barely into her thirties, determinedly unprovocative yet the kind of woman whom men would notice and admire. She may not have ignited much sexual spark in her husband. His insistence on assorting women into whores and madonnas —and finding only the whores titillating—probably kept him from feeling full satisfaction within the bonds of matrimony. Gleason apparently needed to have his sex be a little dirty, or at least somewhat forbidden. He also wanted from a wife the same kind of smothering attention he had had from his mother, although offset by enough adult authority of his own that he not be kept at home against his will. Gen offered the maternal demand that he be housebound without any of the adulation. On the rare occasions when she came out to see him perform, Gen was apt to be the only person in the audience not laughing. By way of explanation she would reportedly sigh and say, "I've heard these jokes before." It is striking that two children were conceived within the first five or so years of the Gleason marriage, despite Jackie's frequent absences, but none thereafter. As a devout Catholic, Gen was not likely to have practiced birth control. It may be the sad truth that in sexual terms, the marriage had broken down irretrievably by the time Gen turned twenty-five.

Whatever their sexual relations, other communication was certainly bad. Bishop reports that in 1947, shortly before Gleason went out to Los Angeles and attempted his last serious reconciliation with Gen, the fat comic suffered appendicitis, underwent emergency surgery and nearly died. Bishop adds, "Nobody thought to tell Gen the news that day. Nobody." This underscores how little standing she had among Gleason's managers, Club 18 colleagues, Broadway drinking buddies and other friends.

Just after this sojourn in Los Angeles, Gleason made his comeback to Broadway. But *Heaven on Earth* was pure hell, even more ignominious than *The Duchess Misbehaves*. The show was just as big a bomb, although it limped along into a second week before it, too, succumbed to a barrage of uniformly hostile reviews. Brooks Atkinson in the *New York Times* said the show "sets a very high standard for mediocrity." John Lardner in *The Star* called it "the biggest sleeping pill in town." Even worse than the failure was that once again Gleason didn't make it to opening night. He left during the tryout and, according to theater historian Steven Suskin, was replaced not by a man but by a woman, Wynn Murray. That casting stroke suggests just how flimsy both his part and the whole enterprise must have been. The crowning indignity was that Gleason had slipped back from top billing and the central role, which he had occupied during his brief association with *The Duchess Misbehaves,* to third billing. He still didn't have an act, and he still hadn't established himself as a star. When *Heaven on Earth* folded in September 1948, it was seven years and more since Gleason had debuted on Broadway and headed off to Hollywood. Like his marriage, his career consisted of dashed hopes, unfulfilled promise and roles that, however freely chosen, never seemed quite to fit.

Nothing but his own fierce faith would have suggested to Gleason or to his small if solid band of loyalists that a truly triumphal return to Broadway was just four months away. Only wild optimism would have persuaded him that within a year or so after that, he would be back in Hollywood, costarring in a splashy Technicolor movie. And although his hero and demon Berle had already debuted on television, on what was to become *The Milton Berle Show*—just days before *Heaven on Earth* closed on Broadway—it certainly did not cross Gleason's mind that within a year he too would be seen nationwide in the title role of his own series on the new medium—in fact, on the same night as Berle, Tuesday, and the same network, NBC. When it all happened Gleason would, of course, be labeled an overnight success. And like almost every entertainer who has had that experience, he would remember with something of both rage and bafflement all the brushed-aside years of worry and struggle and humiliation that preceded his "instant" success.

The Broadway show that triggered everything

else was called *Along Fifth Avenue,* and it was not intended by its producers to star the temperamental Gleason. A revue, it featured sketches by an assortment of writers, prominently including Nat Hiken, who a few years later would create one of the most enduring of all television series, the Sergeant Bilko connivances and misadventures starring Phil Silvers. Nancy Walker was hired to be the principal comedienne, and longtime vaudevillian Willie Howard was booked as the principal male comic. But Howard fell ill and died during tryouts. Gleason, known as a quick study and a skillful improviser, was hurriedly summoned as a replacement.

Ironically but not surprisingly, Gleason let his ego and temper flare to the point of potentially derailing this vital career move. He threatened producer Arthur Lesser with a walkout, which would have been his third pre-opening exit in a row and would have all but guaranteed that he would never be cast in another Broadway show. What caused Gleason to blow up was a certain slowness in adjusting the house boards—giant posters at the entrance to the theater—and the accompanying photographs so that they would feature him to his satisfaction. The delay was partly his own fault. He had demanded bigger billing than Willie Howard had been getting, which could have forced the producer to renegotiate the contracts of all the other stars. (Gleason was far from alone in his morbid fascination with the size and play of his name on the posters and programs. Billing is a vital part of almost every star contract, and the conflicts can be legendary. In one of the best remembered, Jimmy Durante and Ethel Merman agreed to appear in *Red, Hot and Blue* only if their names were played as intersecting diagonal lines, one from bottom left to top right, the other the inverse—and even then, they insisted that they swap placements every few weeks, just so their equality was absolute.) Press agent Frank Goodman volunteered to meet Gleason at the theater and prevail on their past amity, established during *Follow the Girls,* to placate the comic. Howard had been billed fourth. Goodman was empowered, in an emergency, to sound out Gleason about second billing, on the same line as Nancy Walker or in large type at the bottom, with his name preceded by "and," a meaningless inclusion which performers for some reason feel makes them seem more important. Gleason just raved. At one point he was so angry that he kept shouting "Bullshit" and proposed that his name appear in giant type among the names of the choreographer, lighting designer and so on. He didn't mind the illogic of the location. He thought his big type, compared with their smaller type, would make him look more impressive. Recalls Goodman, "He got his way. It didn't last long, and everybody laughed at it within the cast and crew, but in his mind he had better billing that way."

Gleason, whose weight bounced back and forth throughout his early adulthood (even in maturity it pingponged between about two hundred twenty and three hundred thirty-five pounds) was an almost gaunt-faced one hundred seventy-five pounds for the opening of *Along Fifth Avenue*. His physical humor depended on his cocked head, lopsided grin and wide, rolling eyes rather than frisky plumpness. In one scene he appeared with a blonde lovely named Joyce Matthews, just his type, in what for him must have been distressingly un-natty attire: a crumpled boater hat, a too-tight coat with one sleeve torn away, his shirt collar curled in on itself, his tie loose and askew. In another sketch, however, he claimed to have worn a uniform run up specially for him by Brooks Brothers (an inherently unlikely source for a Broadway costume shop) and to have developed many of the mannerisms and postures that he later used for the playboy Reggie Van Gleason. The scene appears to have had only one joke. A group of thirsty and bedraggled French Foreign Legionnaires lies in distress in the desert. Gleason arrives, perfectly groomed, accompanied by a shapely blonde (presumably Matthews) who carries his golf bag. As he dismissively sweeps past the weary soldiers, he asks in an upper-crust trill, "Do you mind if we play through?" Gleason remembered it as surefire, bringing down the house every night.

Brooks Atkinson of the *New York Times* didn't see it that way. Of the show's nine major newspaper reviews, five were positive and four not, with Atkinson among the naysayers. He described Gleason and Nancy Walker as wasted assets but added praise of a kind actors pine for: "Jackie Gleason, serving as second buffoon, will starve to death if his diet ever gets much leaner. [Atkinson presumably meant a dual reference here, both to Gleason's slimmer frame and to the show's consommé-thin script.] Mr. Gleason is a cheerful wag with laughing eyes and a droll map. He knows how to inhabit burlesque costumes. He can also move—which is a priceless accomplishment in a man who wants to be funny on stage. But there seems to be no place in *Along Fifth Avenue* where he can let go with the slapstick properly and entertain the customers royally." John Lardner in *The Star* was less friendly, lamenting the passing of Willie Howard and speculating that he would have been much better than Gleason. Still, the show ran 180 performances, or nearly half a year, at a time when the show business newspaper *Variety* considered 100 performances sufficient to qualify a show as a hit. For the first time since *Follow the Girls*, which he had left almost three and a half years before, Gleason was reestablished as a Broadway star.

His response to that status at the end of the forties was exactly what it had been at the beginning of the decade: to go to Hollywood and attempt to use his new celebrity as a springboard into mass stardom and big money. The vehicle for which he was first hired was, he later acknowledged, a mistake in three ways. He took over a role already made famous on radio by another actor. He played a persona entirely different from the street-smart, hard-edged wisecracker he had been for years. And he worked on film, without the stimulus of a live audience. The combined effect of these factors was failure.

The Life of Riley was not a fiasco. It survived twenty-six weeks. It won, ironically, an Emmy Award as best series (competing with other programs on film), something no subsequent Gleason show would ever do. But despite the enormous popular appeal of Gleason, the *Riley* episodes have gone largely unseen for the four decades since they first aired. The role of Chester A. Riley, well-meaning but dim-witted aircraft riveter and family man, remains forever tied in the public mind to William Bendix, who first shaped it on radio and then resumed it, in a longer-lived revival of the TV version, in 1953. (It was a sweet irony for Gleason, surely, that Bendix would eventually replace *him* in *Take Me Along,* on Broadway, only to have the show close within three weeks.)

Riley was a supremely amiable dope, so dense that the plot of an entire episode could be built around the not so mysterious temporary disappearance of his coat from the front hall closet. In social class terms, Gleason was a good choice to play Riley, an embodiment of the ordinary blue-collar working man who prospered in the years of economic expansion just after World War II. But in every other way Gleason was wrong. The show was set, and filmed, in the tract houses of suburban Southern California, while in accent and outlook Gleason was unmistakably tenement-row New York. Riley was a prototype of the dumb daddies much remarked on in critical analysis of fifties TV. Where Riley fumbled, Gleason both offstage and on prided himself on being cunning and quick. Riley was as sweet and protective as a sheepdog, a character who could not conceivably be imagined enjoying adultery, flimflammery or any kind of meanness. The Gleason stage persona, like the man himself, had an edge of self-absorption, indulgence and anger. Riley had some elements of the persona that Gleason would develop into Ralph Kramden a couple of seasons later: a thin-skinned quickness to hurt, a slight hint of paranoia (although Kramden's was far more acute), an overdeveloped jealousy and a hair-trigger insecurity. But the essence of Kramden was anger; the essence of Riley was doting affection. The psychic makeup of Riley was ultimately too passive for Gleason to be at his most effective. Even his gentlest characters in later years, such as the Poor Soul and the title role in the film *Gigot,* were initiators of action. They might be mute, they might be long-suffering, but they always had an objective.

Gleason may also have found Riley uncongenial for a simpler reason: unlike Jackie, Riley was a family man whose first interest in life was the protection of his wife and children. The life of Riley was the life Gleason professed to believe in. But Gleason did not practice what he preached. He seems to have made yet another stab at reconciliation during this California sojourn, however, moving Genevieve and the girls out to Los Angeles once again for what turned out to be the better part of a year of work. At least part of the time, they all lived with the Haleys.

From *Riley*, Gleason went into *The Desert Hawk*, a movie in which he played, in color, a blue-eyed Arab camel driver called Aladdin. The romantic leads were Yvonne DeCarlo and Richard Greene, the latter soon to become a TV star himself as Robin Hood. Bosley Crowther's amiably dismissive review in the *New York Times* was typical: "Vaguely, within the memory of this reviewer (who saw the film an hour ago), there flickers a fading jumble of inchoate images." Most of those images, it seems, concerned scantily clad, bare-midriffed maidens. When the film was released in August 1950, Jackie missed the premiere. He was on his way back to New York for a quick job.

His agents had had a call from DuMont, a struggling fourth television network with outlets in a limited number of cities. The company's talent was regularly raided by the big three networks, NBC, CBS and ABC, which could pay more. DuMont had successively lost Jack Carter and Jerry Lester, each employed as host of its principal variety show, *Cavalcade of Stars*, both to NBC. It wanted to try Jackie in that emcee slot for two weeks—his agents ultimately bargained the deal up to four weeks, on the basis that he was making an arduous, coast-to-coast train trip—at a salary that would have been barely acceptable from a nightclub and wholly unacceptable on Broadway, just seven hundred fifty dollars a week. Still, work was work. And in contrast to *Riley*, this television would be live. It would resemble nightclub or vaudeville work in format. It would surround him with musicians. And, of course, it would give him a perfect excuse to party for a few weeks, out from under the watchful eyes of Genevieve.

Seeing him off at the station was manager Sammy Lewis of Slapsie Maxie's, who still wanted Gleason on his payroll whenever he was available. "I'll see you in a few weeks," Gleason jauntily called to Lewis as he boarded the train.

The next time Gleason was to work in California would in fact be almost fifteen years later. In the meantime, he would make himself an icon of American popular culture. Like a schmaltzy diminuendo ending to one of the Dixieland pieces he loved so well, this cheerful wave for this seemingly ordinary trip was little sound and no fury, yet signifying everything.

Herbert John Gleason, urchin, orphan, high school dropout and selfthwarting drunk, was thirty-four years old. His whole country was about to discover him as a genius.

CHAPTER FIVE

Television was a tiny, almost folksy business in 1950, and Gleason found himself installed in one of its smaller and odder corners. The owner of his new network, Allen Balcom DuMont, was the infant industry's first millionaire. Indeed, six months after Gleason arrived, the DuMont operations were reported to be grossing more than seventy-five million dollars per year (a figure that should be at least sextupled to provide a sense of its equivalent today) and they had an estimated net worth of more than twenty million dollars. Half of that value belonged directly to DuMont. The other half belonged to his co-investor, Paramount Pictures, the film studio, which had extracted generous terms in exchange for an infusion of a mere fifty-six thousand dollars at a strategically vulnerable moment of DuMont's early entrepreneurial expansion.

These robust financial returns had little to do, however, with the scrappy upstart TV network, which instead was an almost incidental part of the DuMont empire. The bulk of DuMont's revenues came from manufacturing television equipment, ranging from giant transmitters used by TV stations to the receivers, or sets, used in individual households. Chief executive Allen Du-Mont was an engineer, not a showman, and was far more concerned with how clearly a picture came in than with who or what was actually on the screen. Like many radio pioneers, he apparently believed that the potential profit in new technology would come mainly from the sale of machinery to consumers; programming, and the advertising opportunities it offered, struck him as simply a necessary nuisance, the means by which the less scientifically minded could be induced to buy his ingenious assemblages of cathode ray tubes.

Other technological pioneers of television had been visionaries. Philo T. Farnsworth, commonly credited as the father of American TV for experiments he conducted in the twenties, maintained an almost naive faith in the educational, cultural and diplomatic implications of his brainchild. Farnsworth's widow, whom this writer met in the seventies, said her husband would have deplored latter-day American commercial TV as worse than a Roman circus. If DuMont cherished similar dreams or agendas about the content of the medium, he failed to communicate them to any of the journalists who wrote about him.

As a result of their boss's detachment from programming, DuMont subordinates spent sparingly on shows, even by the parsimonious standards of the era. Worse, during the early, formative years of the industry, they passively let slip whatever opportunities may have existed for lining up enough affiliate stations to carry these programs. Hence the DuMont network never became enough of a force and it was subsumed into other entities by the mid-fifties. In fairness, it must be admitted that greater aggression would not necessarily have enabled DuMont to survive, even if its owner had also had much deeper pockets and the show business instincts of P. T. Barnum. For nearly two decades after DuMont folded, conventional wisdom held that television was "a two and a half network business," with perennial also-ran ABC being the half network. There simply wasn't enough advertising demand to prop up number three, let alone a putative fourth. And unlike its three larger competitors, the DuMont TV network lacked the vital advantage of being rooted in an established, popular radio network.

Predictably, Allen DuMont had little if any personal contact with Gleason or the network's other stars. In contrast to his counterpart owners, such as William Paley at CBS, DuMont saw no great need to coddle performers or inflate their egos. If the owner and the clown had ever become acquainted, Gleason would surely have regarded DuMont as a mystery. Despite great wealth, the inventor-executive lived with only a modicum of opulence at home, while at the office he maintained the same battered furniture he had always had (in part, he explained, to discourage his underlings from ordering lavish accommodation for themselves). To Jackie, all this would

have denoted a shameful lack of "class" and
"style."

The absence of a personal bond between tycoon and star might not seem important. But
it contributed to Gleason's ultimate itchiness to
leave *Cavalcade of Stars,* which took hold before
he was halfway through his eventual two-year
contract. Gleason always set great store by loyalty, in others and sometimes in himself. He always craved deference or at least attention from
the man at the top. He wanted the money men
to be glad to have him around. He wanted the
illusion that they regarded him as a peer. Du-
Mont and his network made Gleason the star
he had always dreamed of being. But in his mind
they did not treat him like one.

Jackie Gleason's first live television appearance,
a date of transforming importance in his life and
of considerable significance in the life of American popular culture, came on *Cavalcade of Stars*
on Saturday night, July 8, 1950. No video record
of that program exists. Nobody, in fact, remembers quite what Gleason did that evening, not
even the people who produced it—they just remember that it wasn't very good. Jackie Gleason
would become an overnight sensation, all right,
but not over that particular night. His pratfall
of destiny was still a short while away.

To call *Cavalcade* understaffed is a triumph of
modesty. Its entire conceptual team consisted of
the producer, Milton Douglas, who was also re-

sponsible for a companion show, *Cavalcade of Bands;* two bookers, one for bands, the other for vaudeville acts; Joseph Cates, a general factotum who booked actors for the sketches, pitched in on writing and directing, drafted the emcee's remarks on *Cavalcade of Bands* and even acted small roles now and then; and a secretary. Technically, the shows did not belong to DuMont. Instead, the network provided a distribution system and production facilities to the owner and sponsor, Drugstore TV Productions, an affiliate of a twelve-store pharmacy chain. The pill pushers had a touching innocence: the ad copy at the end of one *Cavalcade of Stars* installment referred to pharmacy as "the world's oldest profession," a term traditionally reserved for the likes of the scantily clad working women patrolling the street a few blocks away on Ninth Avenue. The lewdness of the allusion was surely unintentional; else, it would have been wholly unallowable by the standards of the times. Another measure of the operation's pervasive mom-and-pop quality is that advertisers were enticed onto *Cavalcade* with the pledge of window space and counter display in the chain's dozen drugstores; after all, no one yet knew whether TV was an effective selling tool, but exposure next to the cash register certainly was.

Gleason was not the first choice of host for *Cavalcade* or even the tenth. When Jack Carter and then Jerry Lester decamped, the latter in some haste after a fight with the drugstore chain over the suitability of a comedy routine that involved spitting on camera, producer Douglas and dogsbody Cates and the vaudeville booker Benny Piermont spent long, frenzied hours debating the merits of practically every comic and storyteller they had ever seen. Some names they pondered were not available; some wouldn't work for seven hundred fifty dollars a week; some feared the new medium of television, because in a week or two it might use up and render shopworn an act that had stayed fresh for decades in the live theater, where audiences were numbered in hundreds instead of millions. At last the producing team settled on Peter Donald, a genial Scot who had a charming way with a narrative. Flattered, Donald weighed the offer for a bit, then declined. He judged himself too mellow, too slow-spoken, too low-key. But those are exactly the qualities we want, the *Cavalcade* creators replied in urging him to reconsider.

Well, perhaps. Yet when Donald continued to say no, they turned instead to a performer of high-voltage intensity. Gleason could have his mellow and low-key moments. But they were grace notes. The rest of him was a brass band marching. And his new employers knew it. Cates and Piermont had seen Gleason in full cry at the Club 18. Douglas had seen him just a year before on Broadway in *Along Fifth Avenue*. While none of them, Cates recalls, had actually seen Gleason in *The Life of Riley*, they all knew he had done it with urgency and some success. They wanted Gleason because he could act as well as do stand-up. Although the host would "front" the show and do an opening monologue, the bulk of the hour would be given over to sketches. The host needed to be funny and plausible when portraying a character. "Without any question," Cates recalls, "of the available options, we felt Gleason had the best potential. But of course none of us had any idea how exceptional he would prove to be."

Before actually offering the job, Cates asserts, Douglas tipped off a friend named Herb Rosenthal, who thereupon called Gleason and touted himself to become the comic's new agent, saying he thought he could get Jackie some work on television. This tip-off call cost Gleason the agent's fee, ten percent, which amounted to three hundred dollars over the initial four-week deal and ultimately much more: Rosenthal and his associates, at an evolving succession of agencies, represented Gleason for decades. Perhaps Jackie never learned of the initial subterfuge. Perhaps he just didn't mind, on the theory that at the top levels of show business, every deal is done through agents anyway. Perhaps he blew up when he found out, as he was wont to do, and then cooled off just as quickly, as he was also wont to do. Or it may be that the whole incident didn't happen. Although Cates's memory is vivid and circumstantial, it conflicts on a few fine points with the recollections of others who were around for Gleason's first flight to glory. They are all, moreover, recalling events from four decades previous.

Just as some key moments in the first part of Gleason's life remain hazy because he was the sole source of information and was for various reasons unreliable, so some nuances from this Golden Age of early TV must also remain hazy because there is an abundance of sources but they are often contradictory. For most things, however, multiple concurring witnesses survive. Knowing this did not deter Gleason, then or later, from his habitual rewriting of history, which was to recommence within months.

Once Gleason signed, the first order of business was to find writers for him. At long last, Jackie would have an act. A fresh one every week, in fact. He wouldn't have to steal jokes for his monologue or rely on the chemical reaction between his improvised drollery and an audience's insobriety. In the character sketches, he would have the best of both worlds, as he had never had on Broadway or in movies: real emotions and human needs to act, but complete freedom to depart from the script in search of a laugh, with no director or headlining star to bully him. The show was his; he was the top banana; whatever made him look good was by definition good for the show.

Finding able writers who want to defer to a performer in this way has never been easy. The best writers of dialogue and characters typically turn to fiction or perhaps the theater, where they can control the situation, or to movies, where they are no better treated but make far more money. Those who stay in television usually become producers and in that capacity can protect the narrative and tell the actors what to do. In the case of *Cavalcade of Stars,* not only was the situation odious, but the task was Herculean and the pay almost negligible. Nowadays a single half-hour sitcom episode may pass through the hands of five to ten writers (some operating under the subterfuge of executive labels such as story editor). The budget for *Cavalcade* allowed just four hundred dollars per episode for writers, barely enough for one two-person team who would be expected to crank out enough original sketch material for a whole hour of air time—as many as five or six brandnew, finished items each week. They would also have to contribute gags to Gleason's monologues and, as a practical matter, participate in the hurried staging and rehearsing of the skits as they were readied for the air. The show had a director, Frank Bunetta, but he was primarily a director of camera shots and control room supervision, not a seasoned director of live theater.

The writers who got the job, Coleman Jacoby and Arnie Rosen, had been working together for three years, mainly as joke writers for stand-up comics. Jacoby, at thirty-three the older by five years, had spent almost a decade of his youth in an orphanage and had a tough, noisy exterior concealing a basic sweetness. In those respects, at least, he and Gleason were much alike. Rosen came from a more middle-class background and was college educated. Neither writer had any significant background in the theater or any major credits in the shaping of characters and narrative. When they showed up for a meeting with Gleason at his hotel apartment, their most obvious qualification for the job was that they had not automatically ruled out working for the subpar pay.

Jacoby recalls that before Gleason gave them the least hint of what kind of show he wanted or began to extract their ideas, he launched into an accurate polemic of how show business seemed to be changing for the worse. "Pals," he said, "before we start this interview, I gotta tell you how bad things are. Nightclubs are closing all over the place. Comics who never got laid off now find they can't get arrested. Television has made bums of them all. Me, with a wife and two kids, I'm worse off than any of them, because there's no money in television either. I mean, I've never seen things worse. I've been broke before, but not like this. I mean . . ."

Before he could finish the next sentence of the jeremiad, Jacoby leaped from his chair and shouted in mock alarm, "Let's get the hell out of here, Arnie. This is no audition. It's a touch."

Rosen laughed. Jacoby laughed. Gleason roared. Fighting for air, he gasped, "You've got the job."

If the decision to hire Jacoby and Rosen was

indeed as impulsive as Jacoby recalls, that was altogether typical of Gleason. He always jumped to conclusions. He liked to believe that his instincts were impeccable, in part because it was less work to respond to intuition than to reason and research his way through a problem. The method worked well for him nearly all his adult life. Few choices he made were shrewder, or at least luckier, than bringing in Jacoby and Rosen. They stayed with him only about a year full-time, although they returned sporadically to the fold through 1955, and Jacoby did some unproduced writing on commission for Gleason in the sixties. In that brief tenure, they created the format and most of the characters that made Gleason a television star for twenty years. As if that were not enough contribution, they also suggested hiring, for the very first sketch they prepared, a promising young comic actor, then unknown to Gleason, called Art Carney.

For this invaluable help, Gleason expressed his undying gratitude by shortchanging them on money, reneging on promises and cheating them of any writer's most cherished possession, credit for creative work. As the years passed, Gleason would become ever more vehement in claiming their inventions as his own.

Cates thinks Jacoby and Rosen were hired before Gleason went on air but had to bypass the opening week's show because they needed time to get started. Jacoby thinks they were engaged after Gleason was already on air and that he appeared at least twice without their help. The difference doesn't matter much, except as an illustration of the vagaries of memory. The main point is that Gleason was floundering before he got sketches from Jacoby and Rosen, and for the old, familiar reason: he was performing material not originally intended for him. In those days, writers maintained portfolios of vaudeville-type sketches, tried and true audience pleasers, that they rented out. For a fee, a TV host could obtain the sketch and use it for an evening, just like any nightclub comic. The networks didn't yet have big enough budgets to buy the material outright, and television didn't yet have a wide enough reach—at least on the DuMont network—for a single broadcast to render the material dated and dead. So Cates and company picked up a couple of sketches—he has no idea who wrote them, but one, he recalls, involved a hat check room—and brought in Hank Ladd, one of Gleason's co-stars from *Along Fifth Avenue* the year before, to perform with him. At this point there was no thought of assembling a permanent company around Gleason. The plan was to hire actors week by week, as the sketches dictated, and certainly not to develop any ongoing themes or sidekicks.

Jacoby and Rosen changed all that. They were shrewd enough to realize that it would be far easier for them to fill an hour of live television each week if they did not perpetually start from scratch. They also calculated that Gleason, however imaginative, was bound to begin resorting to trademark gestures and catch phrases. Every comedian does that; Jackie had done it already in *Follow the Girls* and *Along Fifth Avenue*. Surely it would serve everybody's purposes, they argued, if they developed recurring characters. This was not absolutely unprecedented. Both Milton Berle and the rapidly rising Sid Caesar were in the process of developing the same idea. But no other early TV comic took the idea as far as Gleason did. Within the first few months of their tenure, Jacoby and Rosen thought up the Poor Soul, the well-meaning loser who goes through life forever thwarted yet poignantly hopeful (they dubbed him the Bachelor, but despite the change in name neither the character nor the music-without-dialogue style, a nod to silent films, would ever really alter; the Poor Soul style would also reappear in 1962 in *Gigot,* Gleason's personal favorite among his films). The writers introduced Charlie Bratton the Loudmouth, a lout whose nickname says it all. They came up with Rudy the Repairman, another hyperaggressive type whose assertive manner is exceeded in aggravation only by the extra damage he causes in the futile pursuit of his job. On a gentler note they shaped Fenwick Babbitt, a nebbish like the Poor Soul, but a worm who eventually turns; his long suffering invariably triggers a violent retribution. And in "The Man of Compunction" (originally titled "The Man of Extinction," a play on the Man of Distinction advertising campaign then

151

popular), they brought to life "that devil-may-care playboy" Reginald Van Gleason III.

In Jacoby's personal archives at his East Side townhouse is an artifact that any collector of Gleason memorabilia would be thrilled to own—the author's personal typescript of the introductory Reggie sketch, doubly significant because it is the very first live TV sketch of any kind written specifically for Jackie Gleason. Jacoby, who seems oblivious to the commercial value of the script, kindly lent it to this writer. Even the most cursory reading makes plain that Reggie's basic nature had been fully formed in the minds of Jacoby and his partner, and that, despite Gleason's later claims of authorship, whatever creative input Jackie provided was within the normal range of contribution by any actor.

The Reggie sketch appeared, according to Cates's calculations, on a July 15, 1950, episode of *Cavalcade* that also offered guest appearances by Gloria De Haven, Eddie Fisher, and others, including a comedy juggling act. The week after, which is when Jacoby thinks the sketch aired, the biggest name guest was Ella Fitzgerald. Right from the beginning, television was able to attract marquee talent. When Jacoby and Rosen showed up with the first sketch, they were warmly congratulated by Douglas and Cates but were greeted with what would eventually become invariable skepticism and worry by the star. "Some of this is funny, pal," Gleason said of the Reggie pages. "But who are we going to get to do it with me? That photographer is going to have to be a hell of an actor."

Jacoby and Rosen suggested Art Carney, a thirty-two-year-old former stand-up comic and impressionist who was playing a waiter at Morey Amsterdam's Club Amsterdam, the fictional setting of a half-hour variety series, recently moved from CBS to DuMont. Carney was hired, proved himself indeed to be one hell of an actor, and was promptly told by Gleason to return the next week. When Jacoby, Rosen, Cates and Douglas pointed out that the next week's material did not even exist yet, Gleason said, "Find something for him. He's great." Thus was born a partnership that brought great joy to millions, if not always to the two main participants. Thus, too, Gleason's showcase became, at his instigation, something of an ensemble vehicle.

The premise of the sketch is that Reggie, as a society figure, has consented to appear in a high-prestige endorsement campaign for a whiskey company. Carney, the chief photographer for the advertising agency conducting the campaign, fussily awaits Van Gleason's arrival. He bustles up to greet Reggie, all charm and deference—and in the first gesture that Jacoby and Rosen imagined for Reggie, the haughty aristocrat "flicks his cigar in Carney's outstretched hand." As he does so, he speaks just one word, the dismissive comment-to-no-one "Swine." The essence of Reggie—his rage and his crass exploitation of his privilege—merges whole within those few seconds.

The action in the rest of the skit has Carney taking shot after shot of Reggie while Reggie takes shot after shot of the product—that is, for the sake of realism, Van Gleason is urged to sample the product he is endorsing, until he ends literally falling down drunk. This inebriation is supposed to be a welcome novelty for him. As the character explains to Carney the photographer, "I should tell you, I don't drink. Mother won't let me, because of father. You know, father drank six barrels of whiskey." Carney asks, by way of clarification, "During his lifetime?" Reggie replies, "On the day he died. That's why I abhor the stuff. Mother is only permitting me to do this [advertising] because it's fashionable."

However unconsciously, Rosen and Jacoby had given Gleason, in his most autobiographically named character, a personally resonant truth about the horrors that boozing could visit on family life—a topic Jackie understood as both sorrowing child and sodden parent. Had Gleason been a more serious artist in those days, he might have invested even this silly sketch with a sting of awareness. But Gleason did not aspire, then or ever, to dark and unsettling art. Throughout his career he remained a happy-endings man. Instead, what he brought to the sketch was pure style and visual imagery. He decided that Reggie should wear a top hat tall enough for a stovepipe, a cape as sweeping as draperies and a thick rectangular mustache. (Gleason had a fixation about mustaches. He associated them, at various times and in conversations with various people, with vanity, villainy, elegance and excess. In his relations with Jacoby and Rosen, as he tried to determine who really controlled the team, he eventually concluded, "Ah, I see, it's Arnie who pulls the strings. Coleman fooled me by wearing that mustache.") Moreover, Gleason enjoyed playing that drunk scene so much that it became a trademark gag for the Van Gleason character, as inherent as his wealth or his cavalier cruelty. This shift was at least partly Jackie's idea, and it was a smart show business maneuver. Jackie's double takes and lurching walk proved popular with audiences, and in this eponymous role they helped reinforce what proved a very marketable persona for Gleason the performer—as carefree carouser and lord of misrule. Whatever Reggie did on camera was presumed to be indicative of what Jackie did off camera. And it was taken as cute and funny, not self-defeating or pathetic.

Reggie was to become, by Gleason's repeated assertion, his favorite character—ahead of the Poor Soul/Gigot, which was his most delicate and winsome work, even ahead of Ralph Kramden, the character that was to give him something akin to immortality. This wasn't because the Reggie sketches were deeper, truer or even necessarily funnier; Jacoby is the first to say they were not. But they apparently resonated deeply with Gleason's inner personality. Reggie, one suspects, is the man Gleason would like to have been from earliest childhood. The most salient fact about the character is that he is rich. He has no apparent money worries (save in one early sketch where he seems to have been engaging in fraud and imprisons a bank auditor in a vault). As a result, he can be as rude as he likes to whomever he wishes to abuse, including his parents—he commonly greets actress Zama Cunningham, in the character of his mother, with the sneering appraisal "Boy, are you fat!" He never shows deference; his anger is always near the surface. He is also able to womanize with impunity and he dresses with preposterous formality, forever in cape and top hat as though headed to the opera. Above all, he drinks relentlessly, and every sip of liquid consolation is accompanied, in the sketches, by a twanging noise resembling the striking of a distant gong. Not much is likable about Reggie Van Gleason, but one fact, at least, is poignant. He is always deeply alone. Even in a sketch that has him departing in the company of some cuddlesome lass, there is no suggestion of a merging of hearts, a meeting of minds. This will plainly be a brief encounter. The Poor Soul is lonely, too, but he is forever trying to break through to others. Kramden, whatever his frustrations, is married and has friends. Reggie wants to be alone with his bottle, his hostility, his deep depression and anger toward the world. If this was Gleason's favorite character, that sad fact illumines the morose recesses of his soul.

Perhaps this close psychic association accounts for why Gleason went out of his way, in such elaborate and various fashion, to claim the creation of Reggie as his own. Sometimes he said he had an uncle like Reggie—although it is hard to discern anyone in the families of Mae and Herb Gleason who could fit that unlikely assertion. Biographer Bacon, in another version plainly derived from Gleason, says that Jackie "invented" Reggie by appearing as the playboy in the sketch in *Along Fifth Avenue,* although that character and Reggie had nothing in common except a society wardrobe. Gleason told his longtime public relations aide Pete McGovern that he had based much of Reggie on President Franklin Roosevelt's son Elliot, with whom Jackie had had a run-in at the Club 18. Almost never, once the two writers had left the payroll, did Gleason credit Jacoby and Rosen for what they had put on the page. As Joe Cates recalls, "Gleason believed he created these characters by playing them. And he did contribute some of their mannerisms and certain aspects of their appearance. Any great characterization is in part the work of the personality who performs it. But with Reggie, Gleason was basically playing the role as written by Coleman and Arnie." Jacoby notes with some asperity, "For him to say that his performances made the characters come to life and thus somehow entitled him to claim authorship is asserting a principle that would have let Lee J. Cobb say that his performance of Willy Loman gave him the right to claim Arthur Miller's writing credit and royalties."

Jacoby and Rosen suffered countless torments and humiliations in their one full year with Gleason. Every week he would glance through the script and say with a contemptuous wave of his hand, "There's nothing there." After the show, when at least some of the sketches had worked as written, and often worked rather well, Gleason would give them the benediction of faint praise, followed immediately by a fearful, accusatory question about what they could come up with for the next week. Gleason enjoyed playing mind games. "We were sitting one day," Jacoby recalls, "trying to figure out a technical problem—a plot moment, a bit of business, something about how to end a sketch. Suddenly Jackie yelled out, 'I got it.' Then he got this strange look and said, 'But writing is your job, so I'm not going to tell you.' And he didn't. To this day I don't know if he had a good idea or a bad idea or if the whole thing was a put-on just to get to us."

Because his own marriage was failing and his carousing schedule often kept him up until dawn, Gleason thought nothing of calling his writers at three A.M. to discuss something. "And those calls were usually demanding or hostile, not warm and friendly," Jacoby says. Yet this original team of writers enjoyed something almost none of Gleason's later writers did—access, in both

158

business and social settings. Jacoby would generally direct the sketches, coaching Gleason on movement and acting during rehearsal or prompting him with lines during performance. After the show, the two of them might sit and talk with Jackie at Toots Shor's—or even upstage him there. Once Gleason walked toward the two of them and Rosen genially said, "Sit down, Jackie," then added drily, as Gleason reached for a chair, "Not here. At some other table." They were witness to his late-morning breakfast binges of takeout Chinese food. They visited him in the hospital during one of the first of his periodic stays to lose weight. In fact, on one occasion they dressed as Dr. Kildare and his cranky, wheelchair-bound adviser and proclaimed the diagnosis that there was "nothing wrong with this man Gleason that a famine wouldn't cure." The putdown that Jacoby remembers most fondly had a harder edge to it. On one morose occasion Gleason began to explain away some of his hostile, bullying behavior by telling how his father abandoned the family when Jackie was only eight (in reality, of course, he was nearly ten). Rosen feigned a look of sympathy and gently asked, "Gee, how did he stand you for *that* long?"

Subsequent writers not only were denied the chance to sass Gleason that way but were frequently denied the chance to see him at all. Neil Simon, who worked for Gleason for several weeks a few years later, recalls asking on the day he came to work, "When do I meet Jackie?" The answer was, "You don't." And indeed he didn't. Many of Gleason's writers told of having to slip their scripts under the door for him to read, rather than getting the opportunity to deliver them in person. Even Leonard Stern, who had been Gleason's friend for years and was his gambling partner in Las Vegas for the memorable "load it on" episode, said he never felt comfortable with Jackie once he worked for him as a writer. "I think he resented us because we did something he knew he needed and couldn't do for himself," Stern says. "He could act, he learned to direct after a fashion, he certainly became a producer, he called himself a composer and conductor. But he couldn't write. He could imagine a situation, even outline a story. He could not turn out dialogue. He wasn't even a great editor of writers, the way Jack Benny was, choosing and shaping material for himself. I remember the first year I worked for him, he would thank everybody in his curtain speeches. Once he even thanked 'that wonderful group without whom none of this would be possible—the ushers.' But he never once mentioned the writers."

With Jacoby and Rosen, the biggest issue would eventually be financial. They agreed to keep working for Gleason and DuMont, at the same pinchpenny four hundred dollars a week, even after becoming the talk of the industry (*Cue* magazine profiled them in March 1951 as "among the most inventive humorists in the business"), on the basis that they would retain ownership of their creations. Jacoby still has the contract, which later became the linchpin of a suit that he and Rosen filed against Gleason and CBS. There are a few things wrong with the contract as an enforceable document. First, it is with Drugstore Productions, of which Gleason was just another employee, not an owner. Second, it provides for Drugstore to have the sole right to use the writers' creations for it, thus effectively negating any alternative market. Third, it guarantees them compensation for reuse but creates no mechanism for determining the amount. Fourth and most crucial, it never establishes whether the protected creations are the characters and situations, however used, or just the specific sketches, for which Gleason was always willing to pay on revival. The underlying question in the suit, which ultimately went nowhere, was whether Jacoby and Rosen were the authors of their work or whether Gleason was. Morally, the writers were right, and Gleason knew it. In the practical world, he could and did prevail. Surely this challenge—to the very core of his ego, his claim to be a universal creator, the World's Greatest Entertainer—helped make him determined to keep all future writers firmly embedded in their place.

In Gleason's first months on the job, Cates recalls, there was little of the epic self-indulgence and self-importance for which The Great One later became renowned. "It was a job. He was detached, not attempting to boss everyone and control everything. He showed up on time. He rehearsed a normal amount—something that he would eventually become famous for refusing to do at all—and he performed. No bullshit, no prima donna stuff. He made no big fusses about the script. Maybe he would change a line or two." But as Gleason started to get popular, he began to exert control. He wasn't legalistic because he had no contractual right to control. But he was a master of tantrums. "He was given to odd angers and eccentric, unyielding demands," Cates continues. "He knew how to punish you when he wasn't getting his way by imposing extra time and trouble. Once we did a skit that involved a baby carriage and he must have made me bring in sixty of them. Each one wasn't quite right, it wasn't what he had in mind. In the end, we used the very first one I had brought. And in retrospect I realized that whatever that was about, it was not about the appearance of the baby carriage."

As he made himself more of an impresario, Gleason also began to contribute more to the show creatively. Some of his whims were merely egotistical. Some served a real purpose. He conceived and sold to Drugstore Productions the role of the June Taylor Dancers, who remained a part of his variety show for as long as he had one. He had seen a Taylor troupe while touring in Baltimore years before and was impressed by their precision and professionalism. He had a vision of opening the show with a big, fast, gaudy routine à la Busby Berkeley, with lots of tap and patterns, and of his walking out at the end of their number into the welcoming midst of the applause earned by the dancers. That assured him a high-energy entrance. It diminished the pressure on his opening monologue, which remained the weakest part of his repertoire as a comedian. It lent an aura of nightclub conviviality and sex appeal to his homey hour of sketches. And it provided an opportunity for him to flirt, on camera at least, with lots of leggy young women, enhancing the devil-may-care playboy image of both Gleasons, Reggie and Jackie.

On a more thoughtful note, Gleason insisted that a sketch be written featuring him as a small-town boy made good in the wide world of entertainment, returning to his tank town for a one-night stand and spending a poignant few minutes in his dressing room with his former girlfriend, whose horizons had never stretched beyond the boundaries of that small place. The skit had no laughs and not much lasting value, save that it provided a young actress called Joyce Randolph with her first exposure to Gleason. She was hired, both she and Cates recall, because Cates originally had been sweet on her roommate, who was also an actress but was unavailable for an earlier commercial that Randolph got instead. Randolph handled that well, and then in the hometown skit made enough of an impression on Gleason as an actress that when he was casting Trixie Norton in *The Honeymooners*—having tried and not liked Elaine Stritch—he ordered Cates to "get me that serious actress." Randolph got the part and, in a career that otherwise never achieved lasting stardom, the role of Trixie gave her a legion of fans and a place in history.

Gleason was both impatient and impulsive. If he had an idea, he wanted it carried out immediately. What he liked about the combination of live television and stardom was that it permitted almost boundless spontaneity. "late one night, the day before a show," Cates recalls, "Jackie called and woke me up to say he had had an inspiration and wanted to throw out the main sketch. Instead, there would be a tag team wrestling match featuring Reggie Van Gleason and a midget who appeared in the Rudy the Repairman sequences versus a couple of wrestlers from the pro ranks, real big names. He told me, 'You can get the ring from Ridgewood Grove over in Brooklyn, it's portable and it's available for rent.' So at midnight I called an agent from William Morris and said, 'I need eight wrestlers for tomorrow afternoon, two to play the parts and the other six to carry Reggie's sedan chair.' And they came. Well, the ring was enormous, it swallowed up the stage and everything else in front of the curtains. We couldn't have a June Taylor dance number, just Joe the Bartender, Jackie's opening monologue and a couple of singers— only the solo acts that could stand out by the microphone. It also turned out that I had to pay one of the wrestlers an extra two hundred dollars because Jackie wanted Reggie's team to win. The wrestler said, 'No, I never lose. I'm the champ, that's the idea.' The money shut him up. Well, at the end of the afternoon we finally had a dress rehearsal for this routine and Jackie did a tumble and dislocated his shoulder. So I had to disassemble the ring, pay off the wrestlers and send them home, and in a panic I called up Morey Amsterdam and asked him to fill in that night—television was a much smaller and folksier business then, you could never do something like that now. I put back in the June Taylor Dancers and told everybody to do an extra number. Morey said okay and asked, 'What do I bring?' meaning his clothes. I said, 'Bring about forty minutes of material, because that's what we have to fill without Jackie.' Well, it went off all right. But the next day, and this is absolutely typical of what made Jackie both impossible and a genius, he called me and said, 'Get the ring back for next week and we'll do it again.' He was tough, really tough physically. He knew the routine was funny. And so, even though the doctor told him he should stay in the sling for weeks, he rehearsed that wrestling for two days, with the tumbles and all. We were careful but we did everything we originally planned. And it worked. Another time, he had me hire eight firemen and he jumped down forty feet into a net they were holding. He was incredibly demanding, but he was especially demanding of himself."

As Gleason became more assertive, he grew

particularly insistent in matters of casting. He preferred, whenever possible, to give jobs to old friends. But inasmuch as most of his buddies were nightclub stand-ups rather than sketch comics, or were in California, there weren't many for Cates to accommodate. One was Jay Marshall, then a magician and sometime sketch actor, now the owner of a Chicago magic shop and a leader in a local organization of onetime vaudevillians. Marshall had gotten to know Gleason at Kellogg's, the club for lesser comics, in the late forties. When both were on Broadway in 1949— Gleason in *Along Fifth Avenue,* Marshall in the ambitious Kurt Weill–Alan Jay Lerner musical *Love Life*—Marshall recalls, "We used to see each other on Forty-sixth Street going to work and exchange dirty jokes." In one early appearance on *Cavalcade,* Marshall worked into his dialogue a plug for a Lewyt vacuum cleaner and received a case of whiskey in gratitude from the manufacturer. "Another performer on the show had done something similar," Marshall recalls, "and Jackie called a meeting because he knew about it and didn't like it happening. He said that sort of thing had to stop." Gleason may have been protecting the priority of a sponsor or the artistic integrity of the show. But it seems more likely that he was simply asserting the star's right to claim all the graft: several accounts from that time, including published column items, indicate that Jackie was up to exactly the same shenanigans.

Certainly Gleason was looking for ways to make money. He had been to see his friend Fulton Sheen, soon to be named a Roman Catholic bishop, at least once during the opening months of the show in an attempt to secure an annulment of his marriage—an indulgence that the church was not going to grant. The hierarchy had no reason to help a scapegrace, the father of two children who would thus be rendered in effect illegitimate and the rightful husband of a loyal, Mass-attending wife. Gen, meanwhile, put renewed pressure on Jackie to return. Jacoby recalls seeing Gleason take a call from her and, on finishing, compulsively bolt down a half gallon of chocolate ice cream. Now that he had a steady and public paycheck, Gen moved to annex a fixed percentage of it for herself and the girls. By the time Gleason paid his agents, his managers and his family, he felt that nothing was left for him to have fun. At the end of the first season, Cates recalls, "Jackie asked for an advance of ten or fifteen thousand dollars. That amounted to nearly half a season's pay for him. In fact, it was virtually the entire budget for an episode of the show, which we were doing for twenty thousand dollars an hour, or about two percent or less of what it would cost today. The show just didn't have that kind of money, so Gleason's people went to the head of sales and offered to extend Jackie's contract from two years, which is what he had agreed to after the four-week tryout was a success, to five years. That would have been one of the great show business bargains of all time. Even if DuMont hadn't used him, the network could have gotten its money back several times over just to let him out of the deal. But the DuMont people came back and said, 'We have very limited money for programming and we would rather spend it on a pilot of a dramatic series starring Joseph Schildkraut.' So Jackie didn't get his loan, which made him very angry, and in his mind he was free to go."

If DuMont did not appreciate Gleason's value, the rest of the industry did. CBS corporate president Frank Stanton recalls a telephone call from four decades before as though it happened yesterday. He was on his way to an important business lunch when he got an urgent plea from Jack Van Valkenberg, a subordinate who headed the company's TV network division. "He was on my private line and said, 'I've got to see you right away. I've got the hottest piece of talent in my office. You won't believe it. But I've got to make an offer right away.' We would later get used to that about Jackie. Everything had to be done right then; once something was settled he couldn't bear to wait. To me, he was no more demanding than a Jack Benny or a Lucille Ball or an Arthur Godfrey—or a United States senator. They're all pretty demanding. You can't give them too much attention—such a thing doesn't exist for them. Anyway, my lunch date was already there and waiting, so I asked Van Valkenberg to come up and give me the details quickly. They were pretty impressive. Jackie wanted fifty thousand dollars a week to produce the show and a thirty-nine-week guarantee. We couldn't buy him out. We'd have to air them all, no matter how bad, no matter what the ratings were. Now, this was at a time when we were buying the entire *Ed Sullivan Show* for fifteen thousand dollars a week, talent included. Jackie was asking the top end. I thought Gleason was good, but I won't pretend I knew what he would mean for the network. I just considered Van Valkenberg a very competent manager and I knew he was red hot to make the deal, so I gulped and said, 'Go ahead.' I didn't even meet Gleason at that time. Bill Paley liked to pretend he had discovered Gleason but he had nothing to do with it. He was not involved, no question about it at all. When he heard about it, he said of Gleason, 'Who is he?' "

This was never Gleason's version of the story. He told many people, including Morley Safer in a *60 Minutes* interview for CBS near the end of his life, that Paley had been so dumbstruck with Jackie's talents that he had said, "Get me Gleason." The idea that Jackie might actually have made his deal with a subordinate two or three tiers down—and in a meeting he himself instigated, while simultaneously shopping himself to NBC—would have been too ego-deflating for him to believe and remember, even if it were true. Stanton could have his own reasons for downplaying Paley's role: he was forced to obey company retirement rules that owner Paley did not apply to himself, so that Stanton never got a crack at being CBS's unfettered boss. His departure was emphatically not friendly. But Paley biographer Sally Bedell, who is certainly alert to these nuances, accepts Stanton's version as fact.

Gleason also might not have wanted to remember—or not have been able to remember—the upshot of his meeting with Van Valkenberg. As the executive reported to Stanton later, Gleason was "drunk when Van Valkenberg came upstairs and absolutely in the soup by the time he got back down a few minutes later. It seemed that Gleason had found the hospitality bottle and helped himself to more of what he didn't need any more of. Later we would worry a lot more about that in a performer, especially because Gleason was so expensive. We were projecting profits for the entire network division of about five hundred thousand dollars that year, and a fiasco with Gleason could have entirely wiped that margin out."

The CBS deal with Gleason became public knowledge by November 1951, when it appeared as an "exclusive" simultaneously in several different newspaper columns. The items seem to have been planted by Jackie himself, making full use of his contacts from Toots Shor's. Characteristically, Gleason spread the word that this was a deal for nearly two million dollars. Technically, that was correct. But his fifty-thousand-dollar weekly producer's fee was to cover the entire payroll and production costs of the show. His personal take would be a more modest, though still impressive, three hundred thousand a year or thereabouts—less the substantial portion that his agents, managers and estranged wife were entitled to claim. It was always a point of pride with Gleason, throughout his two decades of television stardom, to command and get top dollar. He seemingly cared far less about the actual amount than about whether anyone else might be getting more. Money was mainly a way of keeping score. In an interview about his prospective role as impresario, Gleason was quoted as saying, "The additional responsibilities don't frighten me. It's the opposite—I've always wanted to travel first class."

Actually, Gleason was doing that already. He was living in a penthouse apartment decorated with, among other memorabilia, a framed photograph of himself as Reggie Van Gleason in World War I costume, with the insignia "Our Founder." A gift from Cates and the DuMont crew, the photo remained an essential part of Gleason's home or office furnishings at least through the fifties. He described his surroundings this way: "I've got a sable-lined dump on Fifth Avenue for myself and my friends, which needs only a pool table with dead cushions to make it home sweet home." The swaggering sardonicism of "sable-lined dump" expressed the Gleason style, honed during the lean years and about to be sustained through the bounteous ones. But perhaps the most revealing aspect of the wisecrack is the phrase "myself and my friends," with its evident omission of his wife and daughters. Seemingly Gleason had given up even the pretense of being a family man.

Although Gleason had already departed in spirit from *Cavalcade of Stars,* he still had a contract for the rest of the 1951–52 season to fulfill. Whether out of pride in his craft, duty to Du-Mont or pragmatic fear of dissipating his audience before he ever got to CBS and the big money, he kept working with the same manic intensity and creative zeal. He was still, and would remain ever after, a generally undistinguished monologist and joke teller. Within a skit he had the conviction of character, but in stand-up scenes he was literally the kind of comic who shakes off each joke with a head wag and shoulder roll before starting the next, sometimes actually saying, "That was a gag" or, worse, "But, seriously, folks . . ." As a stand-up on television he did not dare try the insult comedy, directed toward the audience, that had served him so well at Slapsie Maxie's or the Club 18. He understood the era's, and the medium's, prevailing rules of niceness and wholesome restraint, and he exhibited an almost naked need to be liked: self-conscious smiles, nervous laughter, a too-hurried delivery and an almost pleading form of address to his listeners.

The only traces of that erstwhile brashness can be heard in his catch phrases ("I feel gooooood," "You are a dan-dan-dandy crowd to-night") and in his baiting the orchestra leader about the contrast between his vibrant wardrobe and his bland personality, in a fashion later adopted by Johnny Carson on *The Tonight Show.* Fearful of censors and never much of a crusader by temperament, Gleason militantly avoided controversy, both in the skits and, especially, in his stand-up appearances. One can search in vain through show after show—or decade after decade—for a reference topical enough to establish even what year it is. On one *Cavalcade* show from the second season, for example, Gleason admonished his audience, "It's National Brotherhood Week, so be kind to your brother and any one of your friends." He was not merely laughing off but standing on its head, the message of tolerance and acceptance toward the very people who were *not* one's brethren or friends, and he seemed unrepentant throughout his life about having bypassed this and many another opportunity to promote good causes. Some of this reluctance may have reflected a lack of conviction. Flo Haley, who says that Gleason started out as a New Deal Democrat and evolved into a Nixon Republican, adds, "I don't think he ever liked any of them who were too certain about things, like McCarthy, because he wasn't ever so certain himself." That may be why he disliked doing monologues in his own identity and preferred playing characters—including the rowdy public roisterer whom this shy, dispirited man had invented and called Jackie Gleason.

In any case, the monologue shrank to an almost pro forma element at the beginning of each show. More weeks than not, audiences were treated to Reggie, his teetering walk and brush mustache bringing to mind a portly, dipsomaniac Charlie Chaplin. Despite the declaration in the opening sketch that Van Gleason pere had passed on to that great squash and tennis club in the sky, the role of Reggie's father was written into subsequent sketches and played by Carney. In one installment, Carney asks reprovingly of his idle boy, "Son, do you know what time it is?" Gleason retorts with unshakable certainty, "Yes, it's time for another" and belts back what looks like a lethal dose of spirits.

Gleason also appeared frequently as Fenwick Babbitt, the sweet and earnest long-sufferer with the delayed-action fuse. In an October 1951 sketch, aired at just about the time he was opening negotiations with CBS and later repeated on his new network's *Ed Sullivan Show* as a way of touting him to the nation, Gleason spoofs game shows with a baroque challenge called "Can You Do This?" The successful contestant has to skip through a maze of tires, step on bells, shoot at a target, catch and heave a basketball and take a flying leap through a hoop, all without smashing an egg stuck down his drawers. Fenwick wins, only to be disqualified because he is a nephew of a sponsor. Gleason rolls his eyes murderously (a look later taken up as a trademark by John Belushi, among Jackie's countless admirers and imitators) and shoots the smarmy host, played by Carney, stone dead. The lack of adequate rehearsal for *Cavalcade* is evident in this sketch, which is preserved at the Museum of Television and Radio in New York City from the personal collection of Snag Werris, one of the writers in the second season and on and off for years thereafter. As Carney spiels off the rules, midway through the sketch, he forgets about inserting the eggs. Gleason has to remind him by "noticing" the eggs and asking where they come in, while staying in character as a dim and meek contestant.

Many of the one-off sketches relied on Gleason's manic energy and capacity for menace. A sequence in an Old West saloon has him playing a chickenhearted new sheriff, a garden-variety braggart and coward, whose most creative moments come when he comprehensively trashes the local bordello in his fake death throes. Among the genuinely timeless sequences, however, are almost everything featuring the Poor Soul. Written without dialogue but with elaborate gestures, like silent movies, these sketches usually end with the saintly, wide-eyed innocent being victimized for someone else's crime or for none at all. It is hard to understand how the police could be so persistently mistrustful: his coat buttoned tight across his vast girth, his chin lowered so that his neck disappears and his jowls flow straight into his chest, his button eyes as imploring as a beagle's, the Poor Soul looks mildly retarded, not in the least evil-minded. Yet he has an unerring instinct for trouble. A particularly deft episode from the *Cavalcade* era shows the pathetic creature attempting to elope at three A.M. To arouse his beloved, he throws a heavy object through a window—the wrong window. An angry man throws it back and brains him. As he reaches the right window and readies himself, an alarm clock inside his suitcase goes off, rousing the neighbors and even the police. He wins everyone over by unpacking and showing off the His and Hers nightshirts he has secreted for his and his bride's getaway. The crowd disperses, he pushes a ladder up against the housefront and the alarm goes off again. Finally reaching the window, he takes his girlfriend's suitcase, her second and even bigger case—a trunk, really—and helps her down. At that moment a robber on the lam races by and drops his swag bag. Of course the police arrive and arrest the Poor Soul, who sadly hands his fiancée her ticket so that she can elope alone while he heads, as usual, off to jail.

Ed Sullivan displayed another superb Poor Soul sequence, set in a movie theater. Without seeing it, no reader is likely to believe how much humor Gleason could wring out of the business of a couple trying to find two seats together in a crowded local cinema. After endless commotion, including having to pass a spaghetti meal back and forth between an elderly immigrant woman and her husband, the Poor Soul settles in to watch the film and fails to notice that his date has sneaked off with the better-looking man to her left. Another woman has taken her seat and when the Poor Soul reaches over affectionately, she beats him with an umbrella until, of course, the police arrive to take him away.

Of comparable quality was another silent sequence from *Cavalcade,* although in the character of the Bachelor, a gentle and often frustrated but less inept and pathetic figure than the Poor Soul. The Bachelor's appeal was his sad loneliness, tempered by his perky determination to cope, in a post-World War II era of widespread marriage, suburbanization and the baby boom. In this installment, while doing his own laundry, Gleason grins in self-satisfaction. Attempting the trick of pulling out a tablecloth without disturbing the dishes arranged on it, he succeeds only halfway. Preparing to wash his laundry, he sits by accident in scalding water and then by intention in the refrigerator to cool off. He loads a tub with lots of soap powder, immerses the clothes and takes them out. Might his jacket shrink? Inevitably. One item he hangs up is a dress. In an inspired moment, he talks to it in pantomime as though it were a woman and then in a flush of mortification realizes that he is in his underwear and runs off to put his pants on. He dances with the dress. At the end, a very ugly guy in drag shows up for a date and Gleason thumps down from dream to reality with a poignant "What can you do?" face.

Perhaps the best of the Poor Soul sketches came a little later, in a 1953 installment of CBS's *The Jackie Gleason Show.* The antihero goes to a skating rink and waits for his girl, a fat, homely, pointy-chinned, but seemingly good-natured sort who just might bring him happiness. Once inside, he chivalrously helps her with her skates, only to wind up knocking her over and unintentionally exposing her underwear. A moment later, each with one skate on and one off, they dipsy-doodle perilously across the floor. When at last he is out-fitted to skate, he falls down three times. Dispatched to get his girl a cup of coffee, he returns, sneezes, and spills the coffee all over her. Lifted and whirled around by a show-off skater, he falls anew and, while dazed, is evicted from the rink for supposed drunkenness, once again involuntarily leaving behind his girl.

Success has many fathers. But most of them can't pass the blood test for paternity. There are almost as many claimants to a role in the creation of *The Honeymooners,* the single most enduring sketch idea in the history of American television, as there were employees and hangers-on in the vicinity of *Cavalcade of Stars.* Only three things can be said with anything approaching certainty about the origins of the storied Kramden household. First, no one involved had any idea that this would become Gleason's most popular, signature work, so no one kept much in the way of records. Second, the first *Honeymooners* skit, which aired on *Cavalcade* on October 5, 1951, and was later repeated on the *Sullivan* show, was a primitive cousin of what Americans later came to love. It was lacking in laughs and almost entirely devoid of sentiment and was played on a single rising note of rage. Only time and experiment would soften the sketch material into its eventual form, equal parts cartoon farce and subtle psychological study. Third, whatever else Gleason may have unjustly claimed authorial credit for over the years, he was unquestionably in at the creation of *The Honeymooners*—although it, too, ironically arose from Gleason's effort to take up someone else's idea without credit.

The gist of the original sketch—a husband and wife locked in all but mortal verbal combat—was hardly new. It had been a staple of classic comedic theater from the Romans to the Restoration. More recently, it had been a mainstay of network radio, in the persons of a couple aptly named the Bickersons. That series was off the air but some of its sketches had been adapted to the stage. On the September morning in 1951 when Gleason arrived for a meeting with his production team, *The Bickersons* had newly provided a theatrical triumph, in what little remained of the vaudeville circuit, for Gleason's erstwhile co-star in *Hellzapoppin,* Lew Parker. "Gee, that husband and wife bickering, that's a great idea for a running sketch," Gleason said. "Do you want us to rent *The Bickersons?*" Cates asked him. "Fuck it," Jackie replied, "we'll make up our own."

Gleason, of course, would be the husband. For his wife, the *Cavalcade* team settled on Pert Kelton, a meaty, battered-looking matron whose appearance suggested that she really had been through the marital wars and had given as good as she got. While Kramden would eventually be sentimentalized into a doting if splenetic husband, full of threats but, in Gleason's phrase, "more likely to put his hand through a wall than to lay one finger on the woman he loved," the first sketch seethes with the real likelihood of domestic violence. It pits a wife who feels overworked and underappreciated against a husband who speaks those most familiar and least welcome words of accusation, demanding to know what she has been doing all day. He wants bread for dinner. She tells him to go to the store for it. He says he has been working all day and expects dinner ready when he arrives. She tells him she doesn't eat bread, and if he wants it, he had better fetch it. And so it escalates. Whatever its roots in *The Bickersons*, this acrid sketch has the feeling of close observation of domestic life, of true pitched battle between Herb and Mae Gleason all those decades before. Jackie seems every inch a laboring man who cannot believe that his wife's unpaid duties remotely compare with his contribution. Kelton is unmistakably a drudge so sullen that she has no intention of accounting for a day too miserable to remember. Although

the sketch ends, as they all would, with a reconciliation, there is scant evidence of affection
between these two. The union feels cold and economically based. The battle over who should buy
the bread seems to be in truth about who will
be able to dominate and crush the other's spirit.
Although the squabble is silly and its resolution
mawkishly sentimental, the atmosphere is un-
comfortably real, an aching evocation of the tin-
derbox nature of borderline poverty and of
humans' universal capacity to maul those who
are closest.

The most striking omission, for those who
know what *The Honeymooners* would become, was
the leavening of friends and friendship. In this
opening episode there were only Kramdens, no
Nortons. The miserable pair were made even
more unhappy because they had to depend on
each other for all their emotional needs. Carney
appeared in the sketch, to be sure, but in a virtual
walk-on as a policeman. He was nothing more
than a sight gag—an irate authority figure, coated
in flour from the climactic gesture of the fight,
the flinging of a much needed (and for this poor
couple, costly) foodstuff out the window to hit
the street below. His appearance, as an image of
the calling to account that confronts all thought-
less transgressors—and that provides the capstone to countless classic comedic routines—got
laughs yet reinforced the sense of ill fate hovering
over this household. Placating the policeman, or
being punished by him, would be simply the next

in a skein of travails. It is, in retrospect, surprising that Gleason let so doomstruck a script pass, although he probably believed that its acerbity was relieved by the hokey reconciliation. What is far less surprising is that, once *The Honeymooners* caught on, he quickly altered the sketches from a fairly accurate glimpse of what his home life must have been like to a sanitized, cheered-up version with the danger and menace removed.

When Gleason announced that he was deserting DuMont and Drugstore Productions for CBS, nobody seemed particularly surprised. More strikingly, no one seems to have made much of a legal effort to stop him. The deal with CBS presupposed that Gleason would be able to transport with him substantially the same show he was offering on DuMont (by now on Friday rather than Saturday nights) but on a bigger budget and as head man rather than employee. But the show wasn't really Gleason's to transport. The format had been developed by Drugstore Productions. The characters had been created primarily by Jacoby and Rosen, secondarily by their second-season replacements, including Snag Werris, Joe Bigelow and Harry Crane. June Taylor's style belonged both to her and to Drugstore. The cast included a lot of semiregulars, of whom only Carney was considered vital by the people around Gleason. It might have been just as easy, and certainly legally cleaner, for Gleason more or less to start over. A bigger payroll was sure to make a broader range of outside talent available to him. Yet then and throughout his life, Gleason remained fond of the tried and true, preferring something essentially familiar, even if ordinary, to something that might be excitingly new. He was acutely aware of the fickleness of popular taste. If something had pleased the crowd before, he would cling to it until it had plainly lost its power to enchant. This held true for characters, formats, catch phrases and personnel. So he set about offering deals to lure practically everyone involved with *Cavalcade* to CBS.

Most of these promises he honored and kept. One, conspicuously, he did not. Partway through the second season, Cates decided to leave *Cavalcade*, where he was earning three hundred dollars a week, to become the chief producer for bandleader Sammy Kaye's variety series. Gleason tried to dissuade him. "Well, pal," he said, "you're stupid. I don't know why you'd want to do that, after putting up with this small-time short money for so long, when I'm going to take you with me to CBS as my producer at five hundred dollars a week." Cates asked whether that was a real and firm offer. Gleason assured him it was. "So," Cates says, "I turned the other job down. But for the last six months with Gleason, as he got more and more full of himself, I had a migraine headache every Friday night before the show and it didn't go away until I threw up. When I left *Cavalcade*, the headache went away, too."

Toward the end of the summer of 1952, Cates was summoned to meet with Gleason to discuss his future at CBS. "I came into a room and here was Jackie playing yet another role, the chairman of the board and chief stockholder. He was sitting at a long table with all his crowd around him, the guys he went drinking at Toots Shor's with. When they explained that I was there to discuss my terms, I said very firmly that I didn't know what there was to discuss. Jackie had promised me that I would be producer and get five hundred dollars a week, and as far as I was concerned those were the terms of the deal. 'Well, pal, I guess I did, in a moment of generosity,' Gleason said. 'But things have changed.' He said he had 'sort of promised' the title of producer to Jack Philbin, who had been a manager in the music business and had gradually become part of Gleason's entourage, along with his chief manager, Bullets Durgom. So I said, 'Fine, you can call one of us producer and the other executive producer. I know the line operation of the show better than anybody and Jack can run the business side.' And Jackie said, 'Well, pal, I sort of promised the other job to Jack Hurdle,' who had been a producer in radio but for the past year had basically been Jackie's companion, cooking for him, driving him around, overseeing his personal affairs. The upshot was that he offered me the same job title I had before, associate producer, and a very slight raise, to three hundred fifty a week. 'But you've got to give me an answer quick, pal,' he said, 'because we've got to move on.' I was furious, but all of Jackie's agents and managers—Bullets, Herb Rosenthal and Herb's assistant Jerry Katz—all told me to take it. 'You know how Jackie is,' they said. 'In a couple of weeks he'll bump you up the extra hundred and fifty a week.' But the next day I went back and told him I had a mental picture of being forty or forty-five, and having Gleason be finished with TV or having TV be finished with him, and still being an assistant with nowhere left to go. Sure enough, the guy who took the assistant job instead, Stanley Poss, got a raise within a month or so to five hundred dollars a week."

Cates never regretted his refusal. He went on to produce hundreds of hours of TV specials, from circus shows to Emmy-winning variety hours and the prestigious Tony Awards telecast. But he always kept wanting to believe in Gleason. In 1955, when Jackie planned a summer tryout of what eventually became *Stage Show*, the first series Gleason produced without starring in it, Jackie offered Cates the job of mounting the pilot. "I said I'd produce it for no salary whatsoever, on one condition—that I got to do the whole summer, and the season, if it continued. I did it and, sure enough, Philbin and Hurdle and the rest took over again and Gleason sent me a check for five hundred dollars for my efforts on the pilot. He had one of his agents call me to explain that Jackie's regular people didn't want to be out of work for the summer and he felt he had to take care of them. So I wrote him a letter saying, 'There will be no third time. You've gone back on your word twice.' A couple of years after that, he tried to make it up to me in his fashion. I was doing a pilot for a sort of stunt and game show and I wanted him to shoot pool. I knew the footage could never air because the show was for NBC and he was under exclusive long-term contract to CBS. But I thought the NBC executives might get a kick out of it and that would help sell the show. Jackie said yes and he did it, as I remember, for free."

Cates and other backstage talents, whatever their moral claim on Gleason, struck him as replaceable. The vital person for him to sign, it seemed then and it is certainly clear in retrospect, was Art Carney, who had become Gleason's principal foil. Most of the people who worked with the two men liked Carney considerably more. He was gentle and kind and polite. He had a dry and modest wit, unlike Gleason's braying one. His humor was supremely benign. Like Gleason, he was Irish. Like Gleason, he drank, sometimes to excess—although Gleason was a frequent but functional boozer, whereas Carney went on the occasional helpless bender. The major difference was that Gleason was driven to succeed, to dominate, to be the boss. Carney had a quiet pride but no macho urge to overpower. Gleason was an unforgettable presence, always and unmistakably himself. He was a star the way John Wayne or Clark Gable or Cary Grant was a star, instantly recognizable as himself within a hundred different roles and contexts. Carney was more of an actor, far better at submerging himself into a character and a situation. Gleason was percussion. Carney was strings.

As early as spring of 1952, before their supreme comic creations of Ralph Kramden and Ed Norton were fully evolved, before they had done any specific work that would endure much beyond the moment of its live telecast, Gleason and Carney already struck many people as a natural comic team—the next Laurel and Hardy, to cite the types they most resembled in movement and temperament, or perhaps the next Abbott and Costello. Instead, they were, and remained, star and second banana. Carney admits now, "I always hated that second banana business and wanted to get away from it." But Gleason was far too fierce an ego to share center stage, top billing, star money and creative control without a fight. And there was no fight in Carney. "He was the boss," Carney says, "and I never said or did anything to challenge him as the boss, and we got along fine." Gleason was, in Carney's judgment, generous in front of an audience. "He was the only star I ever worked with who said, 'Go for more.' If you got a laugh, that was fine. If you got two laughs, that was better. He didn't worry about me upstaging him or showing him up—although when it came to being spontaneously funny, he was pretty damn fast on his feet, let me tell you."

Three factors, Carney says, persuaded him to take Gleason's offer to come to CBS. First, the two men worked extremely well together: "There was always a special chemistry between us. We brought out the best in each other." Second was the range of opportunities: "Of all the roles I played with him, and maybe of all the roles I ever played, Ed Norton was my favorite. I developed the costume and movements. I developed a lot of the character's attitudes. Norton was very extroverted, where I'm shy, so it was great to get out of myself that way. If I didn't get quite as many other sketch opportunities as I might have liked, that was Gleason's business. He was the star and it was his show. But it was also a very good deal in terms of outside work. It allowed me to do two other roles on other shows every thirteen weeks, provided there were no conflicts with air time or sponsors, so I got to do a lot of dramatic parts right away and show my range." Third, and not least, was money: "I was getting a couple hundred bucks a week at *Cavalcade*. When Gleason got the CBS deal, he came right up to me and said, 'I just want you to know that I want you to come with me for . . .'"—well, I don't like to talk about money but he named a very nice sum, it was a big, fat raise" (to seven hundred fifty a week, according to other members of the ensemble, and soon thereafter one thousand a week).

Another factor, which Carney does not discuss in detail but colleagues from that era do, was his drinking. As a boozing man himself, Gleason was extremely tolerant of Carney's binges, which now and then would reduce him to incapacity. They often ended with Carney seeking refuge at Gleason's penthouse apartment. Although Gleason was less than three years older, he acted in this regard like a big brother. Whatever the blows to his ego at remaining second banana, Carney apparently felt it would be risky and ungrateful for him to strike off on his own. Gleason, consciously or not, manipulated those feelings to keep Carney close at hand, in the position where he did Jackie's career the most good.

The image of Gleason and Carney as bosom buddies proved tremendously marketable and was carefully cultivated over the years. The reality was that the men saw little of each other outside of business and, when not working together, were frequently out of communication for years, even decades. Carney's wife, who reportedly did not like Gleason very much, says tartly, "They were not very close, except for work and parties, which is not much of a basis for insights into a person's real inner life." Carney's son Brian has told friends that it was a source of some family bitterness that Gleason never once visited Carney in any of his various suburban residences, in Westchester County outside New York City or in Connecticut. The senior Carney says, "In fairness, I never asked him, because I knew that he'd

189

turn me down." By the last time he and Gleason worked together, more than three decades after *Cavalcade*, there was essentially no off-camera relationship left.

But in the summer of 1952, when both men were young and their hopes were high and fame and fortune at CBS beckoned, they set out on what Carney still remembers as their happiest time together. Indeed, he says it was almost the only time when they were around each other long enough outside of work to think of themselves as friends. To capitalize on the renown of the DuMont show, to build an audience for the CBS version, above all to earn some welcome income during the dry summer months when the variety series was out of production and the paychecks stopped flowing, Gleason and Carney and a handful of others embarked on a five-week, vaudeville-style tour across the United States. The work was tedious: multiple shows per day, day after day and week after week, of the same Reggie sketch and the same *Honeymooners* sketch. "We were performing four or five times a day," Carney says, "and when you do that, you basically live together. You are never offstage and awake long enough to be much out of each other's company. I look back at those five weeks very fondly. We had an awful lot of fun. I didn't really know Gleason. After the show in New York, he would go his way and I would go mine. He turned out to be a delightful companion. We didn't discuss anything serious—no politics, no religion, no philosophy, nothing about our families. When Gleason was partying, it was all frivolous and fun talk, trying to top each other. He was very good at that.

"The other thing I remember was how many people showed up and how enthusiastic they were for the Reggie sketch and the *Honeymooners* sketch. I had really had no idea before how many people loved those Friday night *Cavalcade* shows. It made me think that this CBS job might amount to something and last a little while."

CHAPTER SIX

Despite CBS's big gamble and subsequent ten-month hype of anticipation about his arrival, Jackie Gleason remained considerably less than a household name when he debuted on his new network from eight to nine P.M. Eastern time on September 20, 1952. Television had begun making its own superstars already, but Gleason was not yet among them. His old rival Milton Berle was already far ahead, having become the first craze inspired by the medium in 1948 and having earned (or bestowed on himself) the honorific of Mr. Television by the dawn of the fifties. Berle was merely foremost among a host of comics in an era when comedy was king. During Gleason's second and final season on *Cavalcade of Stars*, Berle, Sid Caesar, Red Skelton, Lucille Ball, Jack Benny, Groucho Marx and Arthur Godfrey all had series rated among the top ten by the A. C. Nielsen research company. Godfrey, in fact, had two.

Neither Gleason nor any other DuMont performer rated even among the top twenty, primarily because the network reached too few metropolitan areas. (Before Gleason came to Cavalcade in the fall of 1949, the show had ranked tenth on a Nielsen list. But in those days, very few people owned television sets, and the affluent minority who did tended to be concentrated in the handful of major cities that DuMont served.) In cities where DuMont had outlets, Gleason still had faced tough competition in his time slot, spending his second season opposite CBS's situation comedy *Mama*—one of the first and best examples of that form, in which warmth of heart and depth of sentiment are just as important as the evocation of laughter. That show, a reminiscence about Norwegian-American family life, was based on John Van Druten's Broadway play *I Remember Mama,* which had been derived from Kathryn Forbes's memoir *Mama's Bank Account.* Thus its roots were in the high culture of theater and books, while the Gleason show emanated from vaudeville, nightclubs, pool halls and street corner slanging matches. Moreover, the characters on *Mama* were rounded and realistic, at a time when the sketch figures on *Cavalcade* and all the other variety shows atop the ratings tended to be buffoonish and broad. But the gap between a show like *Mama* and a show like Gleason's would soon narrow. Alone among early variety shows, his was about to metamorphose into a true situation comedy, *The Honeymooners.*

Gleason's profile had been boosted a bit by his guest appearances on Ed Sullivan's show (then known as *Toast of the Town*), but that Sunday night fixture did not yet enjoy either the prestige or the popularity that it would attain later in the decade. To the extent that CBS viewers remembered Gleason at all, it was, ironically, most likely for his appearance on NBC, in *The Life of Riley* a couple of seasons before and on the *Colgate Comedy Hour,* which had no permanent cast and which featured Gleason repeatedly as a guest star during his second season on *Cavalcade.* Jackie, in fact, had been the "guest host" of the season-opening show for *Colgate* in September 1951; he appeared with Rose Marie in a sketch about commuters that NBC officials had ballyhooed as the first of a nine-show commitment by him. (That plan was somewhat curtailed once he made his series deal with CBS, after having first approached NBC and having been turned down as too costly.)

Influential critics and columnists had been routing Gleason ardently throughout his time on DuMont. Jack O'Brian of the Journal-American, hardly the most literate but surely one of the most powerful early reviewers, hailed Jackie as early as March 1951 as "this year's comedian." O'Brian added, "He's a gifted maniac with a future, we hope, that could nicely place him in the company we've reserved a paragraph or two upstairs for Miss Beatrice Lillie." During the second *Cavalcade* season, several critics professed to see a maturing of the Gleason persona; one unsigned snippet spoke of his "graduating from out and out slapstick and throwing his weight around to more polished and sympathetic humor." For a decade, Broadway gossip columnists had delighted in retailing Jackie's eccentricities and wisecracks (or, at least, what publicists asserted were Jackie's wisecracks, although some of these sallies, like most other celebrity bon mots of the time, probably originated with hired gagsmiths). Now that television was beginning to confer on Gleason a broad public recognizability, the columnists' interest intensified. They were particularly receptive to Jackie's tales of his Brooklyn childhood, many of which carried a characteristic whiff of enhancement. For example, Jackie recalled his pal Crazy Googenham's implausible reaction on seeing Mother Googenham be carried off to the hospital in an ambulance: "We can throw a big party! There won't be anyone in the house." One favorite Gleason story, an attempt to evoke the flavor of the macho bravado of his neighborhood, described two men who decided to pawn a big old cabinet radio—and delivered it to the pawnshop by taxi. Although Gleason meant this tale to show how Halsey Street men always insisted on class and style, he apparently reconsidered it and decided a lot of people would regard a big radio as much too cumbersome to carry long blocks by hand. Thus the later version of this vignette had a single man arriving at the pawnshop by taxi and being glimpsed from across the street as he went in to pawn his wife's engagement ring. That retelling is certainly better for making Gleason's point about conspicuous consumption in the face of adversity—like his own borrowing to hire limousines and overtip headwaiters. But as the columnists would have recognized if they thought for just a minute, there was no way for Gleason, no matter how eagle-eyed, to have spotted an object the size of an engagement ring from across the street. In spirit, Jackie was back in catechism class from his Catholic childhood, teaching morality through parables, striving not for literal truth but for a higher one.

On a less elevated plane, the columnists had carried plenty of items during the *Cavalcade* days about Jackie's struggles with his weight, which continued to whipsaw between trimness and morbid obesity. During one reported sojourn at Doctors Hospital, which Jackie would leave only to rehearse or perform the show, he lost eighty-six pounds, for a time shedding the excess at the asserted rate of two pounds a day. Around this time columnists also began to report that Jackie maintained three separate wardrobes, identical but for size—the personal equivalent of the "small," "medium" and "large" displays in a clothing store—to accommodate any phase of his gorge-and-repent cycle. Over the years, Gleason would on some occasions vehemently deny this three-sizes-fit-all-Jackies tale and then cheerily affirm it in some subsequent interview. He was certainly a Beau Brummel, having not only suits and shirts but overcoats made to order, in rich but flashy fabrics—plaids, houndstooth checks, pink cashmere. He never crossed the line into bad taste, but he was always sporty. Like many fat people, he found that wearing well-made, custom-fitted clothes enabled him to lie successfully about his weight. Published accounts rarely if ever pegged him above two hundred eighty, a figure he frequently topped by fifty pounds or more.

If his colorful way of life and his Runyonesque tales of youth made Gleason distinctive enough to have a hope of attracting attention amid the clamor of competing comics, most of his other traits made him, as CBS executives belatedly began to realize, a bit of a risk. He was aggressively hot in a medium that Marshall McLuhan would soon characterize as cool. He was volatile and difficult to deal with off camera and spontaneous to the point of chaotic on camera. He was willful and stubborn and he had been granted a degree of creative control enjoyed by almost no star before or ever since. He was typically at least a hundred pounds overweight, appearing on a medium that made trim people look fatter, and he insisted on grabbing the leading-man roles in sketches even—perhaps especially—when they required a measure of sexual attraction. He was an alternately angry and morose man—over and over, colleagues now characterize him as a "true depressive"—whose darker impulses often pervaded, despite his best efforts at sublimation, his ostensibly lighthearted comedy. And above all he was a problem drinker. At *Cavalcade,* colleagues say, he had occasionally been tipsy for a rehearsal, but never for a performance. He had, however, shown up smashed for the *Colgate Comedy Hour* on NBC. Arthur Penn, the floor manager for that show and later the director of such films as *Bonnie and Clyde,* recalls, "It was definitely a bit of a problem. His drinking was really heavy then, and you could see him getting increasingly drunk as we got closer and closer to air. He was always professional. He never actually missed a performance or really loused one up. But he made us nervous." If word of such behavior reached CBS, as it had to have done in those hothouse days of the industry's beginnings, it must have made executives there rather nervous too.

Outwardly, of course, the network's posture about *The Jackie Gleason Show* was one of unalloyed confidence. A *Life* magazine feature, published to coincide with Gleason's debut, focused on spectacle and splendor. At the center of its narrative was the audition for the June Taylor dance corps, with hundreds of young women being seen, thirty-six selected as finalists and, ultimately, twenty getting the coveted jobs. Jackie was portrayed as the final arbiter in the process, and he explained his man-in-the-street standards: "I want pretty girls who can hoof. No ballet stuff. The folks in Utah don't know from *entrechats.*" The cast of the debut show was reported to include one hundred twenty-four performers in front of the camera, assisted by a behind-the- scenes crew of forty-seven, although these numbers may have been a bit inflated by CBS or by Jackie, as the alleged sixty-three-thousand-dollar-per-episode budget certainly was (CBS had contracted for fifty thousand, according to Stanton). *Life* also said that Gleason owned seventy suits (in those days, a researcher might well have gone into his closet to count) and an unspecified number of sports shirts with his trademark phrase "Mmmmmm Boy" embroidered on the sleeve. In one sketch, *Life* reported, Gleason sang, "I don't care for ham on rye/Or apple, peach or pumpkin pie/But I love girls." Although that particular lyric might have sounded absurd in the mouth of a fat man, *Life* claimed that Gleason had dieted his way down from two hundred fifty pounds to two hundred for the opening show (all Gleason weight figures being, of course, compounded of reality, public relations and daydream).

The most important preparation that Gleason made for his new show, however, got almost no press attention. Its significance had not yet become clear. Pert Kelton, the original Alice Kramden, had suffered heart trouble—aggravated, no doubt, by attempts to blacklist her as an erstwhile leftist, which the apolitical Gleason had nobly resisted. Kelton had to be replaced for the *Honeymooners* sketches; based on their popularity during Gleason's tour with Carney, they were likely to appear almost weekly, and she simply wasn't up to that much work. Audrey Meadows, a lively daughter of a missionary who had been appearing with radio comedians Bob Elliott and Ray Goulding in one of their short forays into television, landed the job. Just how she did so remains a matter of substantial dispute. Meadows tells a detailed and circumstantial story (it seems to have become more detailed and circumstantial with the passing of the years) in which she went to see Gleason once about the part, was rejected as too young and too pretty and then presented herself (in person according to one of her quoted versions, in a photograph according to another) as frumpily dressed, without makeup, her hair unkempt and askew. Gleason, supposedly fooled into not recognizing her, pronounced her the Alice Kramden of his dreams and then asked who she was. Other people who were involved with the show do not remember anything so elaborate taking place, and some have suggested that Meadows started at an ordinary cattle call audition, a suggestion that she told this writer she finds deeply offensive. One thing is certain: Gleason did not take the casting of Alice as seriously as Meadows did. Several colleagues, from agent Sam Cohn to publicist Pete McGovern, quote Gleason as having said in later years, "I could do *The Honeymooners* with any Alice Kramden and any Trixie Norton that I picked up off the street. But I couldn't do it without Art Carney."

While Gleason was readying the creative side of the show, CBS was trying to sell it to advertisers. At first, things went very badly. Owner William Paley, who had not been part of the original deal making with Gleason and who had viewed the commitment as excessive from the start—especially the proviso that Gleason could not be bought off but must be provided with his full thirty-nine episodes of air time—became almost hysterical as the opening date neared without a sponsor. The main problem was the show's enormous budget, which the sponsor was expected to defray. When added to the purchase of air time for commercials, that meant a splurge on television advertising far beyond the means, or needs, of most corporations. Stanton recalls, "It was grim. I couldn't get Paley to focus on anything else in the company except the financial risk that Gleason represented and why no one was buying it. Then Billy Hylan, a sales executive, came in and asked if I would accept partial sponsorship. I said yes, and ultimately we agreed to sell the show in twenty-minute segments and alternate weeks, so that a sponsor need take on only one sixth of the show. This was a big break in the way we sold time and opened the doors to a lot of smaller advertisers. Once we did it, Gleason sold out in a week. In a way, it was a move toward how the business eventually went, in which advertisers buy spots and hardly ever sponsor or cosponsor a particular show."

The advance unease at CBS was not much relieved by the reviews for Gleason's opening show. Harriet Van Horne of the *World-Telegram* began by mourning the absence of Ken Murray, the comic whose show Gleason's had replaced. It went down from there: "Now Mr. Gleason is a highly amusing fellow, likable and distinctly gifted. Last season on a DuMont show called *Cavalcade of Stars* he showed the wide range of his talents. He built a good rating, too. His easy flair for pantomime, mimicry, pathos, as well as the broadest, baggy-pants comedy indicated that his way henceforth would be onward and upward. A CBS contract seemed only a logical step in the inevitable direction. But in the stepping, he seems to have lost something. He appeared tense and ill at ease on this premiere show. His material was far below expectation. For want of a better word, I guess you'd have to say that the entire show lacked class."

Van Horne then proceeded to dissect the material, sketch by sketch. She described a particularly lovely Poor Soul routine in which the hapless man attempts to paint a picture of a dog but is constantly interrupted—by a brass band, a Boy Scout troop, a street cleaner and a postman, all of whom knock down his easel, upset his paints or otherwise discombobulate his finicky arrangements. Then a policeman arrives to arrest him for bringing the dog into a public park. Because the piece was moody and wistful rather than boffo-funny, Van Horne termed its placement at the show's opening as flatly "a mistake." Of Audrey Meadows, debuting as Alice Kramden, Van Horne dismissively said, "I shall never forget how funny Miss Meadows was on the Bob and Ray show. But I liked Pert Kelton's gravel-voiced Alice much better. It was earthier." Van

Horne termed Reggie "a cross between King Farouk and Groucho Marx" but brushed off a skit in which the caped one became a shoe salesman, with a bottle of whiskey cached in seemingly every shoe box, with the judgment "Too much slapstick and too little genuine wit made this interlude a heavy one." Van Horne's only praise was for the second banana: "A special word should be said for one of Mr. Gleason's colleagues. That would be Art Carney. He makes the smallest bits memorable and I wish he had a show all his own."

Jack O'Brian of the *Journal-American* was not much more encouraging. Although referring to Gleason as "a clown we're particularly high on," he added, "Jackie hardly is the king of the monologists, and his approach to that opening habit of joking with the bandleader has not much changed, nor has it much improved."

This negative coverage was a new experience for Gleason. In the past, when he was a secondary player, he had often been overlooked by reviewers, but he was rarely condemned. The press had been generous and supportive when he was on DuMont, giving him the benefit of the doubt because he was a newcomer and was appearing on a struggling, low-budget network. Besides, many journalists who frequented Shor's considered Gleason a friend. A few, such as columnists Bob Considine and Jimmy Cannon, were steady drinking buddies. Others, such as Kay Gardella, a *Daily News* entertainment reporter then in the first flush of her celebrated beauty, came in only occasionally but were accustomed to having Gleason greet them warmly and invite them to sit at his table. "We met during *Cavalcade of Stars*," Gardella recalls, "and it was a typical meeting when you're starting in the business, where you go and interview the big star and are expected to pretty much just write down what he says. But there was a wonderful chemistry between us right away. I'm part Irish Catholic myself, the rest is Italian Catholic, and like him I was always interested in metaphysics. I knew he was this brash, insulting nightclub comedian and a heavy boozer, but I struck another side. I always appreciated his more perceptive view of a complete situation and of human beings than you would expect. I also saw his kindness. It was like he was lending his celebrity to you. He knew it would mean a lot to a young girl on a beat to sit at Toots Shor's with him and Bob Considine and Mickey Mantle. He just took a liking to me and was inclusive and protective. By being available to me, whenever I asked, and allowing me to interview him he was helping to give me a better position in the business, and he knew it. He had a nickname for everybody, and he always called me Clara Bow, I don't know why—I must have looked pretty different when I was young. Although it was business, it wasn't just business. I remember once I was scheduled to interview him, and the interview turned out to be going on a date with him and his little girls, at his treat, to see Edith Piaf sing." Gleason's platonic flirtation with Gardella seems to have been a sincere bond, and it lasted a lifetime. But other relationships appear to have been based on mutual use. According to publicist Pete McGovern, Gleason had been appreciative enough of Jack O'Brian's favorable reviews and columns to send him an expensive watch as a Christmas present, either during *Cavalcade* or at the outset of the CBS show. O'Brian, operating by the far more permissive ethical standards of the time, accepted the watch. But when O'Brian started writing more negative pieces, Gleason, who apparently thought he was purchasing coverage rather than honoring friendship, demanded that O'Brian send the watch back.

Apart from that outburst, Gleason's response to the newly critical press mirrored the response of aggrieved stars since the dawn of reviewing. He sneered at the journalists as low-paid no-talents, asserting that if they had any real gifts they should go into show business. Their criticism, he said, was just a bid to attract attention or an attempt to avenge themselves on their economic and artistic betters. This sort of diatribe rarely intimidates critics—quite the opposite, in fact—but it may make a star feel better. Gleason also invoked another theme beloved of stars who have been badly reviewed: he described himself as seeking to please not some snobbish elite but the common people. About this, he seemed to be right. He was certainly greeted warmly by a crowd estimated (perhaps optimistically) at an eye-popping two and a quarter million people for the Macy's Thanksgiving Day parade in 1952. As official parade marshal, he sat on a throne of an American eagle float and repeatedly bellowed what was fast becoming his most popular catchphrase, "And away we go." The response from homes surveyed by the Nielsen Company was less dramatic. Gleason's show did not crack the top twenty. But it did knock out of the top twenty his NBC opposition that opening season, a four-year-old, firmly established variety series called *All-Star Revue* (frequently hosted by Jackie's old Hollywood drinking buddy Martha Raye). By the end of the season, NBC moved Raye's show out of the time period, an admission of competitive defeat; once away from Gleason, *All-Star Revue* promptly regained its top-twenty ranking.

In 1953, *The Jackie Gleason Show* won the first of what would become a passel of Emmy Awards. The prize was not given to the show itself, which never won in any of its incarnations over the next couple of decades, nor to the writing, nor to the star—Gleason received several special honors from the Television Academy over the years but never a regular, competitive Emmy. The victor in 1953 was Art Carney as best supporting actor in a series. That was the first of five Emmy Awards that Carney would win. He repeated as best supporting actor in 1954 and 1955 and was awarded Emmys for individual achievement on his triumphal reunion with Gleason in the 1966–67 and 1967–68 seasons. All five awards came basically for Carney's pixilated portrayal of Ed Norton in *The Honeymooners.* Gleason always claimed to be delighted that Carney was so honored and insisted he felt no jealousy toward Carney or toward Audrey Meadows, who in 1954 won as best supporting actress in a series. Yet repeatedly over the years, including in his interview with Morley Safer for *60 Minutes* some three decades later, Gleason went out of his way to point out the anomaly that the star who showcased the others went forever unhonored. "I was nominated for an Emmy once," he told Safer, "but that's as far as it went. It's strange that in the business that I devoted most of my endeavor to, there shouldn't be some award. Now Audrey, I believe, got an Emmy. Art did. June Taylor did when we were doing the variety show. Everybody got an Emmy but me. I don't know why that is. They started a television Hall of Fame, and I made it, but not in the first group. They like safe performers, and I'm a dangerous one. But the award really isn't that important because if you ask someone who won the awards last year, not very many people would know. As a matter of fact, you may say, 'Remember when I got an award this past year?' and they say, 'Oh. Oh yes,' even if you didn't. It doesn't make any difference." This rambling explanation had the quality of protesting too much, of covering avid yearning with indifference. Gleason spent much of the fifties overtly expecting to win an Emmy, as he spent most of the early sixties expecting to win an Oscar. He speculated aloud about his chances, especially for the Oscar, to friends, colleagues and journalists. He craved that certification—perhaps not as much as he craved the more vulgar distinction of being the highest paid star on television, but passionately nonetheless.

The first few years of his association with CBS brought Gleason countless joys and opportunities. He began to etch a reputation as a serious dramatic actor. He claimed standing as a composer and conductor, both for television and in the recording industry. He became so big a star that CBS offered him a guaranteed one hundred thousand dollars a year for fifteen years, back when that was real money—whether he appeared on the network or not, as long as he would forego appearing on any other network. He at last upstaged his old rival Berle, surpassing him in the ratings, stealing away Berle's sponsor, Buick, and extracting a vastly bigger contract than Berle had ever seen. Everything Gleason did was news, from attending other people's weddings to getting fined five dollars for running a red light in a small town. He even became the subject of a biography by a best-selling author whose other book-length subjects included Abraham Lincoln and Jesus Christ. But of all the things that came to Jackie Gleason in those years, none mattered more to him, or endured longer, than love.

Of sex, Gleason already had plenty. He had been enjoying for years the easy availability of showgirls and, even more, of would-be showgirls. What was not available free he had never balked at paying for. His surging stardom meant he could afford more easily whatever pleasures he wanted yet would be more apt to receive them free and with the donor's gratitude. Had Gleason been merely the braying playboy that he liked to project, his satisfaction would have been complete. What he lacked, however, was a companion in life. He yearned for affection and support, for the unstinting applause of someone special at home whose devotion was more dependable than that of a cheering but fickle public. He wanted, and needed, a measure of mothering. He liked to be catered to, clucked over, fetched for and even, on certain limited issues having to do with moderation and his health, nagged just a little. He wanted, aptly enough for a man nearing forty, a little domesticity.

Returning to Genevieve was out of the question. He still put up periodic, halfhearted attempts. But by now the accumulated anger between them made any attempt at communication almost hopeless. Her anger was compounded by the fact that her daughters were growing up virtually fatherless. Jackie stayed in touch by letter—and especially by check—but he was a barely glimpsed presence in the everyday existence of Geraldine and Linda. For that, Genevieve blamed show business as well as Jackie.

She could never heap on him the praise he so yearned for, when the most obvious result of his success was to make him even more distant from the girls.

Like many a career-obsessed man in midlife, Gleason found the replacement for an unwanted wife right to hand at his workplace. She was, again fitting the cliché, the same physical type as Genevieve—a sweet, soft blonde with a dancer's legs—but a decade younger and somewhat in awe of the boss. Her name was Marilyn Taylor. She was the younger sister and chosen choreographic instrument of June Taylor, and she had been one of the highkicking, quick-tapping, collectively selfless corps of dancers since virtually the beginning of *Cavalcade of Stars*.

Just when and how the relationship shifted from employer and employee to something more intimate is hard to say. Neither Jackie nor Marilyn ever publicly discussed the beginnings of their romance in much detail. In the face of scandal, brought on by an eventual public outburst from Genevieve, June Taylor dated the start of the romance to the later months of 1952, at about the time Gleason debuted on CBS. But even this claim may have been unreliable, for reasons having to do with the Roman Catholicism of all the principals, including Marilyn, and Marilyn's consequent fervent wish not to be seen as a home wrecker, still a potent accusation today and a morally disfiguring one back then.

In deference to this concern of Marilyn's, Gleason always made a point of emphasizing that their affair did not begin until after he was formally separated from Genevieve in the eyes of the law and with the knowledge of the church. Maybe so. But there is substantial reason to think that the affair predated, and indeed triggered, Gleason's formal moves toward separation.

Having worked out a separation with Genevieve in the late forties that was legally, if not realistically, nullified by his temporarily rejoining the family under one roof, Gleason formally sought another split in December 1952. He worked through lawyers and the courts but also, indeed primarily, through the church. Diocesan officials met separately with him and Genevieve in January of 1953, apparently accepting as a given that the marriage had broken down irretrievably but feeling that the church could at least sanction proper protective arrangements for the financial needs of the children. Completion of the legal arrangements, including settlement of a financial pact with Richard Green (Gleason's lawyer until the end of Jackie's life and now for the estate), dragged on for more than a year. But as Gleason told the story, initiating the separation was enough to allow him to feel free to pursue other romantic entanglements; only then did he turn to Marilyn.

Colleagues from *Cavalcade* and CBS remember matters a little differently. Joe Cares, Coleman Jacoby, Joyce Randolph and others believe they recall Marilyn's being involved with Gleason a year or more before he sued for separation. Cates's memory is particularly compelling on this point because he and Gleason had acrimoniously parted company over the broken contract terms by late spring or early summer of 1952, half a year before the time when Gleason said his romance with Marilyn started. Even June Taylor, in speaking for her sister to the press after the blowup with Genevieve in early 1954, dated the romance as having been going on for "a year and a half," or several months longer than Gleason's official version. In fairness, it should be noted that different sources had widely varying understandings of the nature of Marilyn's relationship with Jackie. Both Cates and Jacoby thought, or at least hoped, that it was not overtly sexual, partly because they didn't like Gleason very much anymore but regarded Marilyn as intelligent, pleasant and every inch a lady. Randolph and Art Carney understood the passion to be more physical, although they claimed no firsthand knowledge. Randolph recalled having heard on the set a story about Marilyn spending a night or weekend with Jackie, asking, "When do I get the ring?" and discovering only at that moment that he was already married. As the literal truth, this tale seems next to impossible to believe, if only because June was well aware of Jackie's situation and was emphatically close to her younger sister. But as a metaphor, the story may well express what happened. Marilyn and Jackie probably embarked on a romance with each well aware that his marriage was for all practical purposes long dead, but with Marilyn insufficiently aware of Gen's resistance to divorce and with Jackie insufficiently attuned to Marilyn's urge for marriage. Having belatedly discovered the need to regularize his situation, they kept their romance discreetly hidden from Genevieve while Jackie initiated his paperwork.

Gleason may have sensed that Genevieve would be more bitter about being supplanted by a genuine, abiding romance than she was about his innumerable flings. Biographer Bishop reports at least one awkward encounter when Gen and Linda showed up, uninvited and unexpected, at one of Gleason's penthouse parties and announced that he had a dinner date with them. In attendance at the same party, and expecting to be his center of attention through the evening, was Marilyn. Whether Jackie really had made conflicting dates or whether Gen was responding to rumors and surveying the landscape for potential rivals, the incident led to at least a temporary cooling in Gleason's new courtship. Marilyn was embarrassed, and began to sense the immovable obstacle that Gen presented. So she pulled away. After a time, however, Marilyn relented and the courtship resumed. She was still seeing Gleason professionally at least a day or two a week. And there was between them a bond of sympathy and commitment that, with noteworthy detours, would last to the end of Jackie's life.

The big blowup came almost incidentally, as a result of a headline-grabbing accident during a live telecast. Jackie was appearing in a sketch of his own devising, one he had forced on his writers against their will. Dressed as a cross between Little Lord Fauntleroy and Buster Brown but playing his own notion of Peck's Bad Boy, Jackie pantomimed opening radiators to spoil a party from which, as a child, he had been excluded. A careless stagehand left the nozzle of a radiator pointed downward and the steam (actually carbon dioxide foam) formed a slick puddle on the floor. While carrying an electric fan and a bag of flour for the next of the character's pranks, Gleason took a skipping step and went flying, crashing off camera with his leg and ankle contorted in agony. Horrified cast and crew members crowded around as Gleason was hoisted onto a stretcher and taken to the hospital. Writer Leonard Stern, one of those who had been overruled about the desirability of the sketch, remembers Gleason's looking up at him—numb with pain and acutely aware that he had only himself to blame—halfpleading and half-ordering, "Don't say anything."

Jackie was taken to Doctors Hospital, his favorite weight loss clinic, and was ultimately diagnosed as having dislocated the right foot, torn all the ligaments in the ankle, separated the ankle joint and broken both a bone in the ankle and the lip of the tibia in his shin. He was told by doctors that he would be off the air for at least a couple of months. As usual, Gleason was determined to prove them wrong. He vowed to reporters that he'd be back performing the next week. This defiance of ordinary physical limitations contributed richly to the mystique, if not the reality, of what happened next.

Marilyn, as Gleason's steady girlfriend and companion of choice, installed herself in the hospital at his bedside. Genevieve, as his legal wife and the mother of his children, not unnaturally thought it her proper place to visit Jackie in the hospital and saw no need to telephone first. She arrived to find Marilyn and Jackie engaged in what subsequent gossip ambiguously, and suggestively, termed a "tête-à-tête." Gen exploded. Righteous indignation just reinforced her strongest emotion, a shocked pain at this latest public humiliation. She had been shown, in front of the world, that Jackie no longer regarded her as the real Mrs. Gleason—and, worse, that he had chosen a replacement. Her fury was directed at Marilyn at least as much as at Jackie. Do you know he is a married man, she demanded of Marilyn, and if so, what are you doing here? The harangue went on until Gleason summoned a doctor, who managed to calm Genevieve and break up the supercharged triangle.

The only thing that could make matters worse happened next. The story of the hospital confrontation broke in the newspapers. Eventually every major publication in New York City, not to mention those elsewhere, ran its own version

215

of the cross fire between Genevieve and Jackie (Marilyn, nearly everyone agreed, had been quiet and passive, devoutly wishing she were some-where—anywhere—else.) The battle lasted for months, shattering the privacy of all the partic-ipants. No two stories were alike. Some hinted that Genevieve had walked in on Jackie and Mar-ilyn actually in the midst of sexual congress; in-deed, some Gleason insiders believe that version to this day (although this author, coincidentally, had a remarkably similar injury at a similar age and can attest that as a result of pain, shock and limited mobility, sex remained for some weeks the furthest thing from his mind). Some versions had Jackie threatening to divorce Genevieve and the piously Catholic Gen, hurt and fed up, initially willing to cooperate. Some stories amounted to Jackie's belated defense of himself once Pandora's box had been opened; some were Marilyn's self-defense via sister June; a few em-anated from Genevieve, who for several months broke her longtime vow of silence toward the press to advance her economic interests and de-fend her own good name.

Some public figures actually take a perverse delight in scandal. Gleason was not among them. When Pete McGovern had become Gleason's publicist upon Jackie's arrival at CBS (working first on the network payroll and later on the comedian's personal staff), Gleason issued firm instructions: "I don't care if the newspapers say I drank six quarts of whiskey, ate at seventeen different restaurants and laid sixty-eight different women in one night. But if they print one line about my family, my wife or my daughters, that's your ass." Gleason was not so unreasonable as to blame McGovern for this ruckus appearing in the headlines; he knew he had brought it on himself. Jackie was, however, painfully aware of the impact the scandal would have on the sensibilities of his two conservatively raised Catholic girls, both just entering adolescence—and both hearing Gen's side of it in full.

Marilyn, aghast, left town when the headlines broke and skipped at least a few weeks' performances. Jackie made a typically brave and foolhardy effort to appear on air in at least a token way the week after the accident. But the jolting involved in transporting him from the hospital to the studio so that he could come on camera for three minutes made him white and nauseous with pain and, the doctors said, surely set back his recovery.

The one who kept the spotlight trained on the episode was Genevieve, all her hurt and rage and punitive passion at last flooding out after years of restraint. Ostensibly her battle was only about money. But as always in a divorce—for that is what the court conflict amounted to, although Gleason would not obtain formal legal release for nearly two decades—the money carried enormous symbolic significance. Genevieve wanted the courts, and the watching world, to tell her that she was right and her husband was wrong.

She wanted to see Jackie's wild living and his wanton indulgence of people she regarded as virtual strangers forcibly curtailed. She wanted him to feel that his talents and achievements were family assets, nurtured through mutual sacrifice, rather than his alone. And of course she wanted to be able to spend as she chose without having to ask permission. Jackie had never been ungenerous, but she disliked being a supplicant. Perhaps most important, she wanted direct control of all money spent on the girls, so as to bind them closer to her. Like many an abandoned mother, she stormed at the idea that her affluent husband could use gifts and other powers of the purse to win his way into the affections of children he had walked out on. To all of this, Jackie responded with grim forbearance and at least a semblance of contrition, only occasionally lashing out in private about the frustrations of being cast as the bad guy in a situation where he felt no one was really at fault.

Court documents filed by both sides recorded a long history of conflict over money. As far back as 1943, Jackie had obtained a separation decree in Los Angeles Superior Court, providing that Genevieve receive four hundred dollars per month plus a two-hundred-fifty-dollar payment of legal fees. The separation was based on "mental cruelty and failure to provide," and on both counts Jackie manfully shouldered the blame. Just seven weeks after that agreement, however, Genevieve had been back in court demanding more money because Jackie had been hired for a new engagement at a higher sum. She knew how fleeting and unpredictable show business salaries were. But she was determined that she and the girls should get a fair share—and, seemingly, a large enough one to prohibit Jackie's carousing. That plea of hers had resulted in an out-of-court settlement. Thereafter, Jackie had rejoined the family periodically, and financial transactions had reverted to a more informal, less adversary basis. But by 1946 Gen was suing again, charging that Jackie was two thousand dollars in arrears. He was ordered to increase his payments by one hundred dollars a week. Later that year, there was another out-of-court settlement.

Gen dated the final departure as having occurred in 1951, while Jackie was on *Cavalcade*. "When he left me," she said, "he began paying $1,000 a month plus my rent and all department store bills. In 1953 he began paying me $1,500 a month, without handling the rent [he continued to pay the other bills]. Since February, 1954, his sole contribution to our support has been $ 1,750 a month." She sought a raise to five thousand a month, almost double the previous New York State record award to an estranged wife—the twenty-eight hundred dollars a month temporarily granted to Eleanor Holm on her breakup with impresario Billy Rose. Genevieve's attorney argued that such a sum was entirely reasonable from a man whose income the year before had been more than $336,000 (impressive, although considerably less than the two-million-dollar producer's fee for the whole show that Gleason liked to tout as though it were his personal take). Moreover, her attorney argued, because Gleason's federal and state income tax brackets were so high, the increase to Gen would cost him, net, only about four thousand dollars a year. In addition to the sum she sought monthly, Genevieve asked for five thousand (later twenty thousand) dollars in attorney's fees, a sum that compelled Jackie to go his beloved first class, this time in matters entirely to his detriment. Her court papers, to Marilyn's discomfort and Jackie's fury, specifically referred to Marilyn as "a shapely assistant choreographer."

In making her case, Genevieve argued, "He has not only publicly admitted that I have been a good mother to our children but has made statements that are a matter of public record that he is no longer in love with me, but is in love with a female performer on his television program. His dissatisfaction with our relationship, and his decision to separate from me is, in my opinion, solely attributable to his inability to adjust gracefully to the tremendous success he achieved as an entertainer in the past few years." She went on to note, with particular acidity, that he "is known to entertain lavishly" and added, "He has a fabulous wardrobe and very expensive jewelry. He lives a life of complete splendor and spends money with reckless abandon." The fixed stare of her disapproval can be glimpsed behind every phrase of the petition.

Jackie, having been caught figuratively if not literally with his pants down, made the strategic error of arguing that his neglected wife and budding daughters were asking too much money. It is a measure of his remarkable popularity with audiences that his career survived the court contretemps, with its battle of headlines in which Jackie was clearly the loser. After Gen made her proposal, Jackie countered that meeting her demands would leave him "destitute," with about three thousand dollars a year to live on. He claimed that during their last period living together, in 1951, he gave Gen his entire paycheck and that he had provoked many a violent argument simply by asking her for ten dollars for pocket money—presumably, if his claim was true, because he was going to use the cash to drink, gamble or hang out all night with friends when she wanted him home like a normal husband.

Gleason further explained that his gross income of $336,679 was reduced by business expenses—including payments to his agents, managers and attorneys—to just $63,798 for 1953 and that he had given Genevieve $31,161 of this, or approximately half. The proposed alimony and the irritating legal fees he termed "confiscatory and excessive." He added, on a more personal note of justification, "It is true that I have publicly stated that my wife has always been a good wife and a good mother to our two daughters. I shall never get into any public row with her if I can conceivably avoid it because she is the mother of my children and I consider their welfare far more important than our quarrels. As a matter of fact, although I practically live in the public eye, the world never knew through me that Mrs. Gleason and I were living separate and apart [a debatable if just possibly defensible claim]. I never discussed this anywhere. It was only when Mrs. Gleason informed newspapermen of the fact, after I had broken my leg in an accident on my TV show, that the story ever got into the press." Gleason described the marriage as having endured just two separations, from 1943 to 1948, by formal legal arrangement, and again since 1951. Like his age when his mother died or the authorship of Reggie Van Gleason, this was, of course, a polite fiction. Jackie had been absent more than present from the very beginning.

Ultimately the lawyers for both sides, who could view the whole sad mess with some emotional detachment, arrived at a settlement. Rather than grant Genevieve a specific amount and face the prospect of being taken to court for a raise every time he had a new success—or of having to sue in court himself for a reduction if his popularity faded as quickly as it had flourished—Jackie agreed to hand over a fixed percentage of his income. Genevieve would receive 12.5 percent (exactly one eighth) of Jackie's pretax earnings, plus a separate maintenance fee of 1 percent per daughter until each reached the age of twenty-four. "That is so they could go to college, which I hope will be the case," Jackie said. (Both girls eventually enrolled.)

On the even more sensitive question of a divorce, things remained at an impasse. At first Genevieve was willing to let Jackie divorce her, if he could, although she would not seek a divorce herself. "He has my permission if he wants one," she said. "As for me, I'm a Catholic. I want to live and apply my Catholicism. She—that girl—says that she and Jackie can be married after a divorce. I don't know how. Jackie's a Catholic, too, and she says she is one. The Church forbids it. I know I'll never marry again." According to Genevieve, Jackie had said during the hospital confrontation, and immediately after, that he was ready to seek a divorce and risk the wrath of his church.

But he was not. This man who sought out Archbishop Fulton Sheen as a friend—and of whose theological thoroughness Sheen said with sincere respect, "The Jesuits tell us there are seven St. Judes, but Jackie genuinely knows seventeen"—simply could not risk eternal damnation. Throughout his life, however filled with doubt, he always came back to Catholicism, if not by practicing it himself, then by asking others to pray for him. He could not bring himself to believe wholeheartedly. He had what humanist intellectuals call healthy skepticism and what adherents term a tragic lack of faith. Yet he could not bring himself to disbelieve, either. He always described himself as a loyal member of the church even if he was a poor example of its teachings. So he told reporters, "We are Catholics, Marilyn and I, and the church does not recognize divorce. We cannot hope for an annulment because we have no valid grounds for one. In the eyes of the church I will always be married to Gen and that means I will never remarry." Two other factors may have colored Gleason's revelation. First, as a practical matter he might well have found it hard to secure a divorce under the restrictive laws of the time as the offending rather than the aggrieved party. While Gen might be willing to let him get a divorce, as a practicing Catholic she would never have initiated one. Second, Marilyn again accommodated herself for a while to the idea of being merely Jackie's girlfriend or common-law wife. She returned to the show. She traveled with him to Europe at the end of the season. She remained his consort for a year and more after the scandal erupted, enduring damage to her reputation of a sort that had driven Ingrid Bergman out of Hollywood just a few years before. At that point Marilyn left, in large part because she wanted to marry, become a mother and have a decent, respectable life by the norms of the era, something Jackie by circumstance was unable to provide. But to her disadvantage and perhaps regret, she did not issue an ultimatum at the crucial moment when both Jackie and Genevieve might have been psychologically poised to yield to it.

In addition to deepening the public rift in his marriage, Gleason's broken leg indirectly led to backstage ill will in his career. After his misguided, momentary appearance the first week following the accident, Jackie accepted that he had to remain off camera for nearly two months. The first question that arose in the minds of critics and programmers concerned his replacement. The logical fill-in, it seemed, would be Art Carney. To make him guest host for all the intervening installments would gratify audiences and reward the loyal co-star with a showcase for the full range of his talents. Colleagues had been expecting for years that Gleason and Carney might evolve into a full-fledged partnership of peers or that Carney would get a show of his own, and this was surely the chance to test how center stage would suit him. But Gleason instead opted for a rotating succession of guest hosts, so that Carney got a little more exposure, but not *much* more.

Carney, a lifelong peacemaker, accepted this situation philosophically then and still does now. He emphasizes that he never wanted a comedy or variety series of his own—his ambitions lay in dramatic acting, he says—and indeed he did not attempt a weekly lead role even in a drama until the short-lived detective series *Lanigan's Rabbi* in 1977. His explanation: "No guts, I guess." Given his problems with drinking, nerves and what he once described in a *New York Daily*

News interview as "a manic-depressive thing," he wanted to avoid the added pressure. Yet he also detested being typecast as a second banana—specifically Gleason's, but he says he would have found it just as objectionable to be anyone else's.

In the minds of other people on the show, Gleason was being meanspirited and selfish in not showcasing Carney during the weeks when the boss was away. Jackie, however, had his reasons. Knowing that Carney was an invaluable foil, a career-lengthening buttress to his own work, Jackie not unnaturally wanted to keep Carney on the series rather than promote him into stardom in some other venue. A couple of onlookers, who decline to be identified but who were very much in a position to know, are convinced that Gleason went beyond the bounds of decency in preserving this self-interest. They believe that Jackie consciously set out to sabotage Carney, setting him up for media coverage that would peg him a second banana forever.

For the hour that aired five weeks after the accident, Gleason at last agreed to let Carney be the substitute host, just this once. But by all accounts, even then he did not strive to display Carney's talents. He showed up day after day—at the very same rehearsals he scorned to attend when he was actually appearing on the show—and took over the roles of writer and director as well as impresario. Hurtling down the aisles in a vast wheelchair, he literally tore up sketches that might have benefited Carney and substituted ideas of his own that the cast—and, a few days later, the critics—labeled utterly unplayable. He flatly forbade the appearance of Carney in the character of Ed Norton because he would not be accompanied by Jackie as Ralph Kramden. No *Honeymooners* without me, Gleason commanded. That dictum deep-sixed a fully written and very funny quasi-documentary spoof of "The Private Life of a Sewer Worker" that was the longest sustained material then, or ever, developed to highlight the character of Norton. In its place came a sketch of Gleason's own design that had Carney, as proprietor of a pet shop, talking in monologue to a lot of empty cages. In another solo, also devised by Jackie, Carney was supposed to play the harried teacher of a classroom full of hoodlums. As Gleason presented these sketches, which had little in the way of wit or even dialogue and no real opportunity for acting, others on the production team watched the blood drain from Carney's face. One says, "It was the worst thing I've ever seen in half a century in show business. It was the next thing to a willful attempt to murder a man's career." As the week wore on, morale backstage dropped steadily. Everyone loved Carney, and everyone sensed he was about to be humiliated. What Jackie gave, he would take away.

Carney's guest stint was widely reviewed and, sure enough, the critics all termed it a failure. If Gleason really had set out to hamstring Carney, he had succeeded. Jack Gould of the *New York*

Times said that the problem was that Carney was being compelled to do Gleason material—literally including the opening monologue, the "Away We Go Shuffle" and Jackie's boisterous brand of sketch. Said Gould: "He was cast in perhaps the one part he could never play: the part of Mr. Gleason. . . . [He] had nobody to play to or with. He was caught in a couple of running vaudeville gags and had no real opportunity to illuminate a situation with his comic warmth." Gould added, with almost prophetic insight into what had been going on backstage, "It was almost as if the producers of the program were a little frightened by talent." *Variety* was characteristically terser and less insightful but had much the same opinion: "Carney came insufficiently armed and with weapons not particularly suited to him. . . . He was left out on a limb by the writers." The headlines continued to be hurtful to Carney in weeks to come. On April 18 the *New York Times Magazine* ran a profile with the banner "TV's No. 1 Second Comedian: Art Carney Is to Jackie Gleason What Tonic Is to Gin and Tonic." On May 23 the *Pictorial Review* carried a syndicated piece from King Features labeled "TV's Most Contented Comedian: It's Not That Art Carney Lacks Ambition—He Just Isn't the 'Top Banana' Type." Gleason had his subordinate just where he wanted, and needed, him.

Carney, it must be said, does not confirm that this incident ever happened. But his recollection may be as polite as the rest of his behavior. He

228

professes not even to remember the issue of his guest hosting, let alone the reviewers' references to him as a born second banana. And as ever he is diplomatically careful in his choice of language. In three conversations with this writer on the subject of Gleason's alleged perfidy, he invariably stopped short of flat denial. "I certainly wasn't aware of it," Carney said—a phrase that conspicuously allows for the possibility of the betrayal by Jackie having happened, without compelling this characteristic conflict-avoider to confront it.

Gleason loyalists generally insist that this reported episode is a fiction, absolutely unthinkable, at least as a deliberate act. They quote their man's innumerable private repetitions of what he said publicly—that Carney was the ablest, most imaginative and most stimulating performer he ever worked with. But some of them concede that at a level below the conscious, the street-smart survivor in Gleason might well have done what he thought was necessary to protect his own career. If he did, Carney of course shared the blame for remaining entrapped. Something in him shied away from the burden of carrying a weekly series and from the added burden of even greater fame than he already knew. Carney was, of the two men, more delicate and subtle in his thinking, more gifted as an actor, better able to submerge himself into a character. But Gleason was the larger and more robust personality, better able to engage the crowd, more eager to wear the public mantle of genius. It is noteworthy that when Carney divorced his first wife he had, by his own description, a sort of nervous breakdown. He retreated into private pain. Every time Gleason had major marital trouble, throughout his life, he gave interviews.

Gleason's cries of poor mouth at the time of the 1954 settlement with Genevieve, however unconvincing they may have sounded to tabloid readers or to a judge, were not entirely unjustified. By any reasonable standard he was, of course, awash in money. But Gleason never, ever lived by any reasonable standard. He dwelt, as a de facto bachelor, in a penthouse apartment variously described as occupying ten, eleven or twelve rooms in a midtown Manhattan hotel. Eventually this space became a lavish office and he acquired still grander personal quarters. Having just finished redecorating the first residence at great expense during his opening season on CBS, he immediately began tearing it all out to embark on a new scheme of decor. He explained to columnist Earl Wilson (a supposed friend who would later break the story of the battle between Genevieve and Marilyn in the hospital) that he had realized he was hopelessly unfashionable. "Oh, it's new all right," Jackie said, "but what kind of furniture do I have? Just stuff to sit on. It has no motif, and these days, they tell me, you can't live without a motif." The chosen style of renovation featured vivid earth colors—heavy on the orange tones, some verging on Technicolor—and ultramodern, angular wooden items, many of them built-ins. Having sneered for years at the prep school and fraternity circuit, the WASP elite with its hereditary grasp of privilege, Gleason explicitly felt no desire to ape their ways once he joined, or surpassed, their economic ranks. He would not dress like them, or furnish like them, or entertain like them. In common with the old-money crowd, Gleason spent a lot on personal services, but his manservants were more apt to resemble characters from *Guys and Dolls* than Jeeves from the pages of P. G. Wodehouse. And Gleason was just as apt to pal around with his factotums as he was to sit serenely back and give orders, for although he acquired all the imperiousness of the grandest star, he feared losing the common touch, which had been the wellspring of both his identity and his career. What meals he did not eat in restaurants were generally delivered from them to his apartment. Cooking there was a rarity, a task he almost never performed. His tastes were plebeian, if gargantuan. He would order two wagon-wheel-sized pepperoni pizzas and eat both at a sitting. He would have two steaks, each big enough to have been carved off a brontosaurus, for dinner and then tell a stunned waiter that for dessert he would have another steak. Sunday dinner for Gleason and a female companion on a diet was sometimes a five-pound boneless roast of beef—with no leftovers. His idea of an adventure into Continental cuisine was spaghetti with meatballs. The only exotic food he much favored was Chinese take-out, which he was apt to eat for breakfast; on other occasions, he arose to a morning meal of five or six stuffed lobsters. It should not have required immense sums to feed Gleason, despite the size of his appetite. His palate was far from discriminating. But he *liked* the idea of paying top dollar for simple meat-and-potatoes fare. That was class. That was style.

His personal payroll kept growing as he expanded into new enterprises. There was always need for one more aide to fetch and ferry and flatter. The maids, secretaries, drivers, accountants and general henchmen multiplied. As his multifaceted operations reached their peak, he had more than two hundred regular paychecks to provide. Some of his undertakings were profitable. Some were not. All were a bit eccentric. When Gleason decided in the mid-fifties that there would be a market for a record album featuring mood music played by forty strings and a single trumpet, Jackie's manager Bullets Durgom could not find a record label willing to finance the project, even with a guarantee of copious on-air promotion. So Jackie and Bullets underwrote the studio session themselves. The result was a mess, universally agreed to have no commercial potential and, far worse to Jackie's ears, bearing almost no resemblance to the sound he had in mind. Doggedly he started over again with a new arranger. This time even Bullets wouldn't go along. He saw no point in throwing good money after bad. So Jackie paid for it all himself in exchange for reaping what he alone believed would be the profits. He was right. He had extraordinary intuition about what the common man would want. The purpose of his music, he explained, was seduction. If Clark Gable on the wide screen needed background music to help him pitch woo at the critical moment, then surely the poor slob in Brooklyn did too. When trying to convey the sound he sought to musicians, Gleason often resorted to vulgar or overtly sexual imagery: "Like the sound of pissing off a high bridge into a teacup." "It's five A.M. and you see her body outlined through her dress by the streetlight and you get that 'Mmmmmm, I want to come' feeling." Somehow, it worked.

The debut album, *Music for Lovers Only,* was the first of more than forty that eventually sold a collective total of more than one hundred twenty million copies, reaping Gleason's j. g. enterprises a royalty pool that sometimes topped one million dollars per three-month reporting period. The television exposure certainly helped. As early as November 2, 1952, in the dawn of his first season on CBS, Gleason used the show to promote his music. Ethel Waters and Deems Taylor were guests and the highlight was Jackie's "Lover's Rhapsody," which was credited as having been composed and conducted by Gleason and performed by forty-six orchestra musicians and sixteen dancers. Gleason's return after the onstage accident in the spring of 1954 displayed him conducting his songs "Romantic Jazz" and "You Can't Pull the Wool over My Eyes." And so it went, several times per season. Gleason was credited with composing the theme music for the show and for most of the individual characters, as well as more formal orchestral offerings. On May 28, 1955, Gleason conducted four of his compositions with three different ensembles, one featuring a twenty-member mandolin section as part of the so-called Lonesome Echo Orchestra. One repeatedly performed composition, a ballet called "Tawny," featured Marilyn in a solo sequence choreographed by June.

In music, as in acting and directing and writing, Gleason presented himself to the public as a natural-born, fully formed genius. He admittedly could not read a word of music or play any instrument, although at a party he would like to pick up a horn and improvise or nudge aside the drummer and crash out a solo. Sometimes he called himself discreetly a "purveyor" of music, a term employed in one of his cautious press releases from the midfifties. More often he exulted in his status as conductor and composer. One memorable stunt, at the height of his fame, had him agreeing to appear in a nightclub, but not as a comic. At a bolte de nuit called La Vie en Rose, he came out in formal dress, bowed to the audience, then turned his back to them, lifted a baton and presumed to lead a twenty-piece string orchestra in numbers including those announced as his own. The public adored the gig, although the string orchestra cost so much to hire and took up so much floor space normally occupied by paying customers that the engagement lost the owner a bundle and nearly put his club out of business permanently.

Given the success of such odd ventures, it is not surprising that Bullets and the press took seriously what can be seen in retrospect as obvious pipe dreams. Having fallen in love with Dickens's *A Tale of Two Cities*, which may have been the first of that author's novels he read and which he certainly discovered only as he reached his forties (while his contemporaries had read it in high school), Jackie announced plans to hire dozens of actors and a full orchestra to record the complete, unabridged text, with a phonograph playing time of thirty to forty hours and a cost comparable to an entire set of encyclopedias. There is some basis for doubt as to whether this extravagant vanity production ever took place. Jackie gave countless interviews describing it as a fait accompli, but this writer was unable to locate a single review or feature reflecting anyone's ever actually having heard the recording. What is certain is that the line of business of which it was meant to be a forerunner—the complete classics of world literature on vinyl, issued under the Gleason label—never remotely materialized.

Another of Gleason's recurrent schemes (almost as outlandish, arrogant and get-rich-quick-oriented as those spun by Ralph Kramden on *The Honeymooners*) had him designing the ideal hotel supper club. In a plan that betrayed a certain ignorance of architecture, geography, regional differences in market and other practicalities—while reflecting sublime confidence in himself—Jackie proposed to specify the precise decor, ambience, menu and entertainment program for hotel restaurants and lounges around the United States or, better yet, the world. His notion was an extension of the standardized bedrooms offered by major hotel groups and the standardized menus soon to be featured by fast-food chains. In Gleason's vision, a visitor from Tuscaloosa could find in Toledo a supper club exactly like the one back home, without the faintest ripple of unsettling novelty. Everything would be exactly reproduced, down to the light fixtures and ashtrays, and it would all be to the taste of Jackie Gleason—who, after all, surely understood the common man's wants and needs better than anyone else alive. Years later, in Florida, Gleason would be hired as a consultant by local hotels and country clubs, although there is no evidence that he ever imposed a unique vision. Some of his thoughts—soft piano music during dinner, a menu emphasizing steak—were standard stuff, at least for their time. Others—such as an emphasis on orange and other earth colors in decor—were not so widely adopted and in any case came straight from the decorators who had done up his penthouse.

The biggest business Gleason got into, other

than music, was the production of television programs beyond the ones he would star in. A number of performers have made the transition from headliner, which is lucrative enough, to mogul, which pays far better. Lucille Ball and Desi Arnaz did so with Desilu Studios. Gleason's old pal Danny Thomas had several hit series as a producer. Eventually, development deals for series to star others became a standard part of salary for performers as diverse as Johnny Carson and Michael Landon. But Gleason had no luck with such ventures. Despite the enduring phenomenon of his record sales, in general it seemed that the public was less enchanted with Jackie Gleason's taste than with the presence of the man himself.

A further disadvantage to Gleason as a producer is that a poor manager can lose a lot of money quickly even on a successful show because the scale of operation is so large, the variables affecting cost are so numerous and complex and the product is in effect reinvented every week. Gleason, a temperamental perfectionist and procrastinator, was not meant to work under such constraints. And he was a terrible businessman.

In his producing, just as in his private life, he took a perverse delight in displays of needless, nihilistic extravagance. He loved splash, the more pointless the better. For a pilot idea called *Cafe Mardi Gras* he spent tens of thousands of 1950s dollars to re-create a nightclub within a network studio, complete with full sit-down dinners and an actual working bar. This lavish event did not, and from the start would not, go on the air. It amounted to nothing more than a very expensive party for network executives and advertising agencies plus assorted Gleason friends. Recollections differ as to who nominally paid for the evening. But the reality, which Gleason never really accepted, was that even if the network officially picked up the tab, its accountants were watchful and skillful enough to bargain the money back out of him in other ways. The funds he spent were, in the end, invariably his own. Often his demands verged on the irrational and were seemingly motivated more by the traditional star's desire to prove he can get whatever he wants than by any pragmatic or aesthetic necessity. For *Stage Show*, the half-hour variety series that briefly reunited him with Joe Cates in the summer of 1955 and that was then paired with *The Honeymooners*, seen in half-hour sitcom form, to replace Jackie's variety hour on CBS for the 1955–56 season, Gleason insisted on re-creating the capacities of the old Paramount Theater stage in Newark, where he and Frank Sinatra, among others, had appeared at the outset of their careers. Jackie remembered fondly the way the microphone could rise from the floor to reach a speaker's exact head height and also how the stage apron could be detached mechanically to come thrusting out toward the audience. The problem with achieving the microphone effect in the Manhattan theater that had been converted into a network studio for *Stage Show* was that the floor beneath was solid concrete. Eventually, to placate an enraged and insistent Jackie, CBS officials jackhammered out a hole in the concrete and, in the absence of an appropriate raising and lowering mechanism for the microphone or enough time to design and install one, Cates himself hunkered below, pushing the microphone up and pulling it back down at the appropriate moments. "I had to do it, even though I was the producer," he recalls, "because I was the only one who knew the sequence and timing of the show well enough. So I couldn't even watch the show I was producing. When I saw a kinescope later, it was hilarious, in an embarrassing sort of way. I'm no machine, and the microphone was bobbing up and down, wavering from side to side. It looked just awful, horribly distracting. But you just couldn't persuade Jackie of that."

Having appalled Bullets Durgom and Jack Philbin, his in-house voices of financial reason, by insisting on employing a corps of sixteen June Taylor dancers for the opening season (the advisers contented themselves with the calming thought that Jackie would come to his senses in a week or two and scale the number back to eight), they saw him not only stand firm but expand. The dancers alone cost two thousand dollars a week in salary, not to mention costumes, rehearsal time and other expenses. In the second season Gleason swelled the pulchritude budget by adding seven "portrettes"—long-legged lovelies whose sole function was to pose inside picture frames and look inviting. However much this spending reflected a sense of what the common man would enjoy, more of it seemed to be rooted in a compulsive yearning toward danger and extremity. Like another hard-drinking, up-from-dirt show business success who was emerging at about the same time, Richard Burton, Gleason seemed to feel an absolute need to empty his pockets, to spend every penny as soon as it came in, as though his integrity and identity lay in having to fend and forage, as though stockpiling for the future were the act of a dishonest man. Freedom from want, he seemed to say, lay in the scorn of wealth rather than the accumulation of it.

For all the opulence and grandeur of his life, all the aura of stardom, Jackie still loved best the nightly crawl from bar to bar, growing ever louder and more skunked, immersing himself in sentimental renditions of the Dixieland and saloon songs he loved. For a time in 1953 and 1954, he became addicted to a robust, sexy, sweet-faced and lumpy-grinned young blonde named Dorothy Loudon, later a Tony-winning Broadway musical star in *Annie* but then just an awestruck small-town New Hampshire girl on the loose in Manhattan in her early twenties. She was belting out old standards nightly at a place called Jimmy Ryan's on the East Side, not far from the hallowed if unsanctified Club 18 of yore, and after Gleason and his entourage happened upon her

240

act one night they came back again and again. "They wanted 'Cottage for Sale' and Toots Shor's favorite, 'Oh, You Beautiful Doll' and other numbers like that. Now, for someone twenty-one years old even to know all these barroom songs was really rather unusual," Loudon recalls, "and they liked me and got to calling me 'the Kid.' The place closed at four A.M. and you just knew, as sure as anything, when those doors slammed open at three-thirty A.M. and a fresh crowd came in, it would always be Jackie Gleason and his pals. I remember one particular night—he had come in before and he came in again, but this was the only night he ever came in either alone or reasonably sober—he called me over to his table and told me he would put me in touch with the Ray Bloch organization and get me a job. You remember Ray Bloch, one of Jackie's orchestra leaders. Jackie always called him 'the flower of the musical world.' Well, I didn't really believe any of this but when I got home I still called my mother up in Claremont, New Hampshire, and told her. That very day I got a call at the club from someone in Ray Bloch's office asking about signing me and the next thing I knew, within about a week as I remember it, I was singing on the radio on CBS. I sort of feel I owe my career to Jackie Gleason." (The sad irony, Loudon says, is that although she remained a lifelong fan, she never got to work with him, never even saw him again after Ryan's. In the midsixties, after seeing her on *The Ed Sullivan*

Show, Gleason telephoned to offer her the role of Alice in the musical revival of *The Honeymooners,* but she had just signed to take another role. In the eighties, when Loudon was appearing in a Tony-nominated role as an aging comedienne in the farce *Noises Off,* Jackie attended one night and sent along a congratulatory telegram in time for the next performance. But to Loudon's sorrow, he did not come backstage—perhaps because he had been spooked a short while before by being mobbed by an overeager crowd of fans as he left another Broadway show and failed to find his limousine waiting.)

Bursts of generosity, of the kind he showed Loudon, were common with Gleason. But so were episodes of dictatorial cruelty. Gleason had a mercurial temper, a ferocious will toward self-expression and an absolute need for control. At times he was the stereotypical sentimental Irishman come to life. He read newspaper articles about an unemployed man who had killed himself and offered to pay for the funeral and to give the widow six months' income, provided his charity remain secret—a stipulation in keeping both with Catholic tradition that true charity eschews pride or praise and also with the practical consideration that well-publicized kindness begets entreaties for more. On other occasions, his virtue was more public. For Christmas 1955, he showed up at the Lighthouse for the Blind as "the only Santa in America who didn't have to wear a pillow." He appeared for the March of Dimes, the City of Hope and Catholic Charities. On hearing that a young girl needed blood donated for an operation, Gleason ended a 1955 installment of the variety show with a plea on her behalf and prompted five hundred New Yorkers to go out to Columbia Presbyterian Hospital that very night, in winter rain, to volunteer. Throughout his life he remained a soft touch for sad stories in the newspaper, an inveterate impromptu sender of checks. Yet his friend and agent Sam Cohn acknowledges, "Jackie wasn't big on the charity circuit" and sometimes, when people thanked Gleason for having appeared on behalf of some worthy cause, he not only denied knowledge of having done any such thing but appeared to reject the idea that he ever might consider doing so, in tones of persuasive indignation. This may have reflected genuine confusion, his odd sense of humor, fear of being asked again or some strange form of penance.

He was equally erratic as a boss. He tended to remain loyal to those who worked for him so long as they showed even minimum competence, and he maintained such tight bonds with his cronies from the fifties that ultimately the majority of them joined him in living, and dying, in Florida. Indeed, Gleason had hardly any intimates other than his business friends—and like many entrepreneurs, he therefore had no close comrades who did not ultimately work for, and hence defer to, him. Save for Jack Haley, he had no one to tell him off.

When Gleason did have the occasional rupture with an ally, whether it was publicist Lee Myers or manager Bullets Durgom or writer Leonard Stern, the issue was almost invariably money. Gleason regarded the people who built his career as leeches and exploiters unless they showed sufficient respect for The Great One. The idea that they, too, might be competent professionals in their sphere did not count for enough with him. Stanley Poss, the man who succeeded Cates in the slot as associate producer (and later, briefly, as producer of one of Gleason's successive variety series), is described by friends as often having gone home in tears. Audrey Meadows and Art Carney were so frustrated by Gleason's refusal to rehearse that they used to get together in secret to shape their scenes. Lee Reynolds, Gleason's personal secretary in the fifties, told reporters, "It's nothing for him to call me up at any hour of the day or night because he suddenly remembers there is something he wants me to do for him. At first it was difficult to understand why he couldn't let this ride until business hours in the morning. But that's Jackie. He's got so much on his mind that he might forget if he waits until morning. It is nothing for Jackie to call me when I am miles away on a weekend to ask me to remind him to do something on Monday or to ask me to call him at a certain hour to keep an appointment he's made. And there are all the little

244

chores that I sometimes find myself doing, anything from shopping for wild materials for the apartments to buying red flannel pajamas in the heat of summer to play a gag on a friend."

At one stage, briefly, Gleason owned a pink convertible, and he wore a pink shirt to drive the car on its maiden voyage, exulting, "I'm on TV in black and white but I live in color." He offered a ride to a production staff member, then changed his mind because he decided that the fellow's yellow shirt would clash. On the morning that Pete McGovern first reported for work, he watched Gleason hold a series of meetings with writers, rejecting one after another of their ideas in tones of contempt. As the comic and his new publicist headed over to Toots Shor's for lunch—traversing the six sunny blocks by limousine rather than on foot—Gleason turned and said, "Mac, I can tell you didn't like what you saw today. You're a writer yourself and you side with those guys. Well, let me tell you, I pay every one of them a thousand or fifteen hundred or two thousand a week, and they'll hate me until they get the next paycheck. If I don't push them, if I don't keep demanding that they do better than what they think is their best, then the show will suffer and we'll all be out on the street." McGovern found this argument persuasive and still does.

But even with the writers, much of Gleason's abuse was mere ego and swagger. While the rest of the writing staff labored in Gleason's office suite, Leonard Stern and his partner Sid Zelinka stayed in a personal apartment two blocks away, overlooking Central Park. This anomaly cost the show no money but caused Gleason no end of annoyance. It wasn't that he met with the writers very often—sometimes he just had them leave the scripts under the door and then returned them so fast, with dismissive but not specific comments inscribed, that the writers and much of the cast doubted that Jackie had even read them. (Art Carney is sure he had not.) Still, Gleason wanted his writers on hand, where he could watch them if he chose. "You're taking walks in the park," Gleason would complain. "I know you are. I can feel it." Stern insisted that wasn't true. He pointed out that they were always available by phone, that Gleason and his minions had never once failed to reach them if they were wanted and that by actual time test they could make the journey, apartment door to apartment door, in something under five minutes. As it happened, if they actually were taking walks in the park, that might well have been a constructive way to work through a plot. But they weren't. Time and again Gleason fumed, raised the issue, was dissuaded by logic and subsided—only to build up to fury again. As the accusations about strolls through the park kept recurring, Stern got a little annoyed at the insult to his honesty and said so. Gleason heard him out manfully and said, "All right, Leonard, I accept that. You're not taking walks in the park. You say you re not, and

I believe you. But I *think* you're taking walks in the park." And as Gleason confessed this measure of lingering paranoia, half-laughing, half-domineering, Stern saw the wisdom of giving up the battle. "Against the irrational part of Jackie," he says, "there was nothing to do but give in. We moved over the next week."

Part of Gleason's cantankerousness may have been caused by uncertain health. By the end of 1955, he had undergone four abdominal operations in a decade, mostly for the removal of cysts or adhesions, but each imposing the strain of recovery, compounded by the complications of cutting through so much fat to get at his muscle wall. The arm that he broke in Philadelphia in the forties still gave him occasional trouble. So did the ankle he tore up on live television. The up and down swings of his weight burdened his mood, and more than once friends came to visit him while he was dieting at some hospital, only to be told by a nurse at the desk, "Mr. Gleason wasn't feeling well, so he checked out and went home." Health worries were augmented by the irritation of knowing that reporters hunted after every tidbit, no matter how minor, about Gleason's hospital stays. Indeed, for one of his abdominal operations, a few months after the broken leg and the flare-up between Genevieve and Marilyn, Gleason went off to Europe, explaining with a sly smile to the disconsolate Manhattan press that "strange things seemed to happen" when he was treated in New York.

For the most part, however, Gleason was difficult simply because he could be. As his show climbed to the top of the ratings and he became the biggest male star on television, he grew ever more assertive. He boasted more and more openly about not rehearsing (the record minimum, he said, was one hour and fifty minutes to prepare a one-hour show) and whenever he was crossed or irritated he threatened not to appear for the actual broadcast. Once, Leonard Stern recalls, he returned late to a Friday night rehearsal after having gone to a Broadway musical on a long-planned date with a visiting friend, only to find the rehearsal studio in darkness and the cast sitting around outside it in nearly catatonic gloom. Gleason abusively demanded to know how anyone expected him to perform an unplayable sketch and asked whether Stern had attempted the physical actions specified. It turned out that Gleason had misread the script, ignoring the standard left-right split between movement and dialogue, and after a bit he grudgingly admitted his error. In fairness to Gleason, Stern admits that on at least one other occasion he did script a bit of business that proved literally unplayable.

The closest Gleason came to not appearing, however, was the Saturday in October 1955 when director Frank Satenstein chided a colorfully cursing Gleason with the reminder "Mrs. Van Valkenberg and her friends are listening." This was news to Jackie. The ladies were not in the theater. His rehearsals were closed, meant only for the edification of the people involved in creating the show. He began to ask pointed questions and discovered, to his fury, that every top CBS executive, led by Jack Van Valkenberg, the man who had hired him, had a closed-circuit live telecast of the rehearsals piped into his office. In Van Valkenberg's case, because his wife had a neuromuscular disease that made it hard for her to get out, a second wire led to his home, both for her convenience in watching and for his own in staying on top of live telecasts and rehearsals while looking after her. Frank Stanton describes the closed-circuit arrangement in retrospect as "a mistake" and says that Van Valkenberg was particularly in error. No comparable arrangement exists now. But the real tactical error had been in not telling Gleason—presumably because of fears that he would have refused to abide by such an arrangement. If he did refuse, and got away with it, Van Valkenberg had to wonder, what performer would continue to comply?

Gleason's response was instantaneous and decisive. "There will be no show tonight," he said. He ordered the stage shut down, the cast and crew sent home. Agents and CBS executives began telephoning each other, with both the rank of the officials and the panic in their voices mounting as the afternoon progressed. The only hope was that Gleason's fury, which grew fiercer by the hour, was so volcanic that it would burn itself out. Because of a few cool heads among the cast and crew, including the iron professional Audrey Meadows, the team stood by and waited. CBS officials tried not to show their hysteria, but in those days before videotape, they lacked the technical facility to rerun an old Gleason show and had nothing of an appropriate length to put in place of the live hour. To throw in a movie, assuming one was available, would have made a hash of the entire evening, alienated viewers and ensured a major public humiliation. Worse, had Gleason actually walked out, the network would have been obliged to describe itself as publicly in the wrong, which Paley would have found close to intolerable, or to discipline Gleason, which would probably have destroyed CBS's relationship with one of its most lucrative properties. As Stanton recalls, "When Van Valkenberg came to me and said, 'We might not have a show tonight,' I told him, 'My first advice is to get over there and make your peace with Jackie in whatever way you can. Don't rule-book him, for Christ's sake.' I stopped short of telling him to admit to Jackie that the network had been wrong—although I thought Van Valkenberg had erred. The issue of the wife was secondary, in my opinion, although it turned out to be the basis on which Jackie forgave everything. What Gleason really resented, understandably, was having network executives spying on him. He didn't like them very much. He constantly wanted to show who was boss. This was bound to create trouble."

The broad outlines of Gleason's threatened

walkout inevitably became public. But because it was only an approach to catastrophe rather than an actual, visible one, the press and public didn't much care. If anything, the incident strengthened the reputation of Gleason and company as indomitable troupers. Jack Gould, *New York Times* television critic, said of the resulting performance, "The show, as it went on the air, was pretty ragged in spots but, as so often happens in such backstage flareups, not too bad."

About any such fireworks or falterings of virtue, Gleason remained spectacularly unapologetic. He believed that his assertive, egotistical style endeared him to the audience, and he had no yearning to be considered nice or proper. He was surely thinking of himself when he wrote to sports columnist Bill Conn in September 1955, "In the golden Twenties, the public wanted their heroes on a level with themselves. They wanted to think that their man contained the same faults and foibles their own skins encased. However, in recent years a change has taken place. Heroes were placed on a pedestal and stripped of their glamour. If it was whispered that they drank, gambled, winked at a filly or did any of the other human things to which humans are addicted, they were pulled off the pedestal and replaced by the next immaculate. Gusty glamour is the IT that fills sports arenas. I give you Babe Ruth, a great human being but surely not a plaster saint. P.S. I am available to pitch any game of the World Series for either club and with either hand."

(Ruth's opulent persona, a blend of natural talent and undisciplined excess, was of course the closest equivalent in the sports world to Gleason's own. It is notable that Ruth died in 1948, only a couple of years before Gleason vaulted into national consciousness. Perhaps something in the American character requires that a celebrity figure be available to embody these traits.)

As Gleason broke into the top ten of Nielsen ratings during his second season on CBS and reached second place, outranked only by Lucille Ball, during his third season, he appeared to have arrived at a formula that needed no tinkering. Although television and the audience it reached would both change immensely over the next couple of decades, many of Gleason's competitors during that 1954–55 season would linger long, unchanged. Ed Sullivan, whose series beat Gleason's to the 1955 Emmy for best variety show, would hang on until 1971. Lucille Ball, whose *I Love Lucy* gave way to her divorce from Desi Arnaz, would bring back her character on *The Lucy Show* and *Here's Lucy* for twelve more seasons, all but the last in the Nielsen top twenty. Jack Benny would persist a further decade with what was in essence his radio show, barely altered. Had Gleason been content to keep doing what he had been doing, and had the same principal cast members stayed with him, he too might have accumulated an uninterrupted two-decade run on network television.

But that wasn't what he wanted. After five seasons in variety, two on DuMont and three on CBS, Gleason was getting bored. He was profoundly tired. He felt almost unbearable pressure. He found it harder and harder to get enough good writing out of his staff each week, or at least he found it harder and harder to voice any faith in what his writers had done. He wanted more money and less work. He wanted more respect. He wanted the prestige that comes to dramatic actors but that is largely denied to comedians. And he wanted to go back to Hollywood, this time as a star. He could have made movies, despite the film community's persistent belief in that era that spectators would not pay to see someone they could watch free on the small screen; Lucy and Desi, for example, had achieved moderate success in *The Long, Long Trailer,* as extensions of their TV selves, in 1954. But Jackie wanted to make arty pictures of his own devising, dramas that might get him Oscar nominations, certainly not takeoffs on Ralph Kramden. He wanted to achieve in Hollywood what he enjoyed in television: control of the circumstances of production.

Toward this end, Gleason made two moves. At the end of the 1954–55 season, he dropped his variety show, to CBS's considerable annoyance, to make a season of episodes of The Honeymooners as a conventional situation comedy. They would be recorded before an audience, without pauses or corrections of errors, in a process Gleason wanted to call "live on film." The network did not allow that designation because viewers would not understand it. Gleason believed, however, that his method would preserve the virtues of live performance without enduring its major technical disadvantage, its impermanence. This season of *The Honeymooners* that he was planning would, he hoped, have some life in reruns and thus would give him something to sell to generate income while he shifted his career in other directions. That concept was largely untested, of course, and only time would tell whether it was worth abandoning a comfortable variety show for the risk of *The Honeymooners.*

The other thing Gleason did was to branch out, almost as soon as he arrived at CBS, into dramatic television. During his first three seasons he starred in four major television dramas. Each of them holds up, nearly four decades later, as splendidly natural and subtle acting from an unlettered and largely self-taught man. The projects were done at all chiefly because Gleason was Gleason, a major star. They were done so well because, as Jackie had insisted to an unheeding throng for so long, he really was a genius.

The first of these to air was *The Laughmaker,* on May 18, 1953. A chilling portrait of a star on the rise, it may have helped inspire Elia Kazan's great film *A Face in the Crowd,* but it deserves resurrection from the archives of the Museum of Television and Radio for more than this scholarly value. Gleason enacts a comic who uses everyone around him, male and female, without the slightest reciprocal loyalty. He is a compulsive performer, always "on," given to unpredictable vacillations between generosity and pique. The show has some conspicuous holes in logic: as the comic's adoring sister, Marian Seldes intones in accents as crisply upper class as Gleason's are brayingly lower class, and as a journalist assigned to write a magazine profile of the comic, Carney permits himself to get emotionally involved with Seldes and other members of The Great One's entourage in ways that must have seemed ethically dubious then and that are wholly implausible today. Gleason doubtless loved the danger of playing a role so unattractive and so suggestively close to himself and he may have valued the morose cynicism of the best speech in A. J. Russell's script (certainly Russell remained his favorite writer thereafter and was at one stage the writer of choice for *Gigot*). In the apt and fitting words, Gleason (called Jerry Giles, so that he even has the same initials) declaims, "You work, you hope, you do without things, you finally make it. And what have you got?" The answer, of course, is nothing, save perhaps, if one is forgiven one's sins, friendship.

Seldes vividly recalls the time with Gleason. "I don't think it was one of the happiest periods of his life. Art Carney was doing it primarily to make Gleason comfortable, to keep him calm about doing a dramatic part, and they broke each other up a lot the first few days. But mostly Gleason would look morose and Art would lean over to me and say, in this gently satiric way, 'Fat people are happy.' Gleason so obviously wasn't. I didn't know whether to laugh with Art or be sad. Jackie sat sipping all day from a coffee container that held nothing but booze. After knocking back a lot of whiskey he would send out one of his henchmen for a gallon of chocolate ice cream. He would see me looking in astonishment at how he could eat all that after drinking all that and say, 'It's to put out the fire.' Looking back, I can see he was self-destructive, but then I thought he was invincible and marvelously daring to do such a part. He didn't handle it like a comedian. He handled it like an actor. He was not drunk during rehearsals or the actual performance. He was not smashed. Rather, he was mulled— easygoing, red-eyed, tipsy. I never saw his famous temper apropos the show, although I heard it on the telephone plenty with his associates. I should register how lovely he was to me. He certainly thought of me as the remote intellectual and was courtly. But a cute bimbo was a cute bimbo and he of course approached them in a wholly different way."

Gleason's next major dramatic role, a year and a half later, came in *Peacock City*, based on an actual corruption inquiry in Phenix City, Alabama. Gleason was cast as a prosecutor whose achievements were considerable but whose motives were suspect. Once again he made himself somewhat unattractive, although hardly with the confessional clout of *The Laughmaker*. Two months later Gleason appeared for the first time on television in a classic American play, *The Show-Off*, by Pulitzer Prize winner George Kelly (uncle of Princess Grace of Monaco). The play was Gleason's favorite throughout his life and he seemed to have been born to play the title role, despite a few cavils by television critics of the era. Indeed, Gleason had apparently enacted *The Show-Off* at least once in summer stock. According to Joyce Randolph, he had gotten the role during one of his fallow periods in the forties, at a playhouse in Rhode Island that was linked with a nightclub where all the actors were also expected to perform. The job, Randolph says, was secured for Gleason by one of the Kean sisters, which explains, in Randolph's view, why Jane Kean won the part of Trixie in all the *Honeymooners* revivals of the sixties and seventies, even on the rare occasions when both Audrey Meadows and Art Carney resumed their original roles. As Aubrey Piper, the title part, Gleason epitomized the kind of disruptive intruder that every family fears its daughter may marry: a nobody at work, a spendthrift at home, fancying himself helpful when he only muddles whatever he touches. Aubrey is perfectly capable of borrowing a car, wrecking it, injuring a traffic officer, resisting arrest, sneering at court proceedings and coming home not only indignant but confident of ultimate vindication. The plot, predictably,

257

turns this good-for-nothing loudmouth into a hero by the final scene. For audiences to believe that ending, they must want it to happen, and that dynamic requires an actor to be likable even while doing wholly unlikable things. Gleason had that ability as Kramden and as Reggie; he certainly exhibited it in *The Show-Off* dominating an all-star cast including Thelma Ritter, Carleton Carpenter and Alice Ghostley. Martin Manulis produced and future Oscar nominee Sidney Lumet directed.

For sheer sentimental appeal, Gleason may never have been better in his entire career than in an unheralded little tale, like *Peacock City* and *The Laughmaker* an offering of the Golden Age original drama series *Studio One*. The first drama ever to be based on an original idea of Jackie's, *Uncle Ed and Circumstance* begins in classic Golden Age fashion with glimpses of two small boys on a front stoop intercut with arty shots of the feet of unseen people coming in. As these family members arrive, they are introduced by one boy to the other, each with a tale of his or her accomplishments and heroism as a Staten Island Ferry captain, policeman, fireman, or nurse. When the last person to arrive clumps in, the boy refuses to say anything about him at all. This, it turns out, is the universally scorned and barely tolerated Uncle Ed, a silly-looking fellow with an unbecoming mustache and a too tight coat buttoned all the way up, just like the Poor Soul. In this really nasty family, seen to particular disadvantage in overhead shots of the grasping and snarling at the dinner table, Uncle Ed serves as a sort of communal wife without portfolio, fetching and carrying and making menial repairs in lieu of holding down a job and kicking in a paycheck. Uncle Ed's sole interest in life is the movies, all of them, from the industry's beginning, and he knows so much that he decides to try for a spot on *The $64,000 Question*. The family, sure he will fail and humiliate them, forbid him to audition and then insist that he not appear. They almost prove right the first week when a dazed-looking Uncle Ed answers a question with the words "My mind's a blank. I know it's Marilyn Monroe, I just can't say it." Each time Ed wins, his family want him to stop and take the money. They all have plans for how to spend it for him. Each week Ed quietly, passively resists and goes on. He wins. And wins. And wins. And when he has made it all the way to the top, he is asked what motivated him to try and replies, in words that are spoken straight yet laden with irony, "My family."

In a more realistic story, Ed might have shot every single member of this loathesome clan long before getting to appear on television. In Gleason's parable, the newly rich Ed packs his bag to go off to a new life as a movie columnist and researcher, and only after he has left, with his family shouting into the street about his ingratitude, do they realize he has left behind the check and signed it over to them. He is grateful

259

for their taking care of him all those years when he was not productive. He is grateful, too, for their compelling him to grow up, stand on his own and go his own way.

From a distance he looks back through the misting rain, smiles ruefully, then laughs. Like the eighth-grade graduation play emcee who stood glorying in the applause and shouted, "I told you, Mom, I told you," this character devised and inhabited by Gleason smiles with the serene peace of one who knows he can make his living doing the one thing he has always loved.

Little more than five years earlier, Gleason had been a second-tier performer at second-rank nightclubs, still dreaming of that one big break and hoping that the blown opportunities on Broadway, in movies and on *The Life of Riley* did not mean that his full share of big breaks had already come and gone. In October 1955, Jackie Gleason was beyond breaks into stardom, even legend. He had already become the subject of a biography by columnist Jim Bishop, the stuff of a thousand headlines, a Saturday night habit for nearly half a nation. *Uncle Ed* aired on October 10. Just nine days earlier, Gleason had taken the step that could have pushed him back toward obscurity—but that instead vaulted him into something approaching eternity. On October 1 of that year appeared the first of what were to be thirty-nine installments of a half-hour situation comedy version featuring his most popular sketch character, and the only one Gleason could legitimately claim to have had even the "original idea" for, Ralph Kramden. Any artist is lucky if he produces one enduring work. Gleason was about to produce thirty-nine. They would all be called *The Honeymooners*.

CHAPTER SEVEN

When asked in his final years why *The Honey-mooners* shows had remained so popular for so long, Jackie Gleason avoided all the pop sociology and domestic psychology so beloved of scholarly critics and answered with four terse words: "Because they were funny." The judgment was entirely typical of Gleason, who turned his questing if undisciplined intelligence to everything from politics to UFOs, from Roman Catholic metaphysics to reincarnation and ESP, but preferred to remain intuitive rather than introspective about the craft in which he made his living. Jackie never let himself get drawn into discussions of the larger implications of Ralph Kramden's yearning for recognition, much as it may have prefigured the American celebrity culture soon to come. Nor would he ponder the larger meaning of Alice Kramden's unyielding insistence on her equality, much as it may have foretold the march of American women out of the kitchen and into the workplace. Gleason professed to see no political agenda in his depiction of the poverty and thwarted materialism of the working classes. His own striving life belied the analysis of those who saw the show's emotional theme as the unbearable curse of ambition. Time and again Gleason asserted some variant of what he eventually told Morley Safer for *60 Minutes:* that Ralph Kramden was no symbol, no metaphor, just "a poor moax" who loved his wife and wanted to please her but had no money to shower indulgences as he wished. The vanity Kramden displayed, his vainglorious claims and schemes were all meant toward one end—obtaining this woman's respect and justifying her continued devotion, Kramden wanted nothing for himself per se, Gleason would insist, but only as a means to impress the woman he loved. Like most of Jackie's sweeping statements, this one was only partly true. There are numerous moments in *The Honeymooners* where Kramden envisions leisure and luxury as desirable in themselves. But Gleason was right in emphasizing the personal rather than the universal. However much it may have served in later years as a kind of archeological artifact illustrating its times, *The Honeymooners* initially connected with audiences on a down-to-earth, emotional basis. Spectators saw themselves in the foibles of the Kramdens and Nortons.

While it seems inconceivable that there is any American adult who has not seen at least a few of the thirty-nine episodes first aired during the 1955–56 season, this writer will bow to convention and offer a brief description. Ralph Kramden is a bus driver. His upstairs neighbor Ed Norton is a sewer worker. Both are childless, yet both expect their wives to stay home and would be deeply insecure about their working (Alice does work, briefly, at one stage in the series, and the economic challenge to Ralph's manly status as provider is compounded by his fits of raw sexual jealousy). Both relationships are affectionate. Neither seems faintly erotic. Alice is more like a mother to Ralph, and Trixie is more like a keeper to the dotty, occasionally sleepwalking Ed. The Nortons live in relative comfort, if gauche taste, because they have bought household furnishings on credit (they would call it "buying on time"). The Kramdens live in Spartan deprivation, without so much as a refrigerator or even a permanent telephone. (Gleason vetoed that instrument on the basis that writers would be too tempted to provide exposition by telephone call rather than devising scenes that would compel the characters to interact.) In the middle of the postwar economic boom, neither couple seems to be experiencing much financial uplift; although the Ricardos of *I Love Lucy* were only about a year away from moving from a nicer but still cramped apartment to suburban ease, which they did in 1957, the Kramdens and Nortons seem mired in tenement squalor. In the midst of the baby boom, neither couple makes much noise about becoming parents, save in an episode where the Kramdens briefly take in an infant, only to be forced to return custody to a social service agency. In practical terms, these arrangements allowed Gleason to keep his show different from the proliferating family sitcoms and also to avoid the professional risks of being upstaged by pet animals or cute children. The basic division between the two men of the cast echoed what Gleason plainly thought was a basic division in the world—between the Ralph Kramdens, who yearn and struggle to get ahead, and the Ed Nortons, who believe that no reward is worth the angst of ambition. The basic shape of virtually every episode was the same: Ralph tries to change his world for the better and is humiliated for his pains. His ego, as enormous as his waistline, is punctured; his wife and friend, whom he bullies and sneers at, have the last laugh. But all is always forgiven.

In one installment, typical of the *Honeymooners'* capacity to echo universal experience, Ralph gets into an argument with a landlord and suffers through a shutoff of the heat, a barricade that prevents him from getting food and, finally, an eviction, all to protest paying a few dollars more of monthly rent. By the end he sits in the street surrounded by his sticks of furniture as snow starts to fall. At long last ready to give in, he insists he is not doing so because he was wrong or because he has hugely inconvenienced himself for the sake of a dubious principle, but because he must be solicitous of the health of his wife. Surely almost everyone in the audience has experienced some similar moment of minor madness when he or she attached absurd importance to a point of honor (or to a whimsical preference labeled honor) and then found himself or herself painted into a corner, longing for a graceful, face-saving exit.

The particular incidents of this and most other episodes were extreme, bordering on the unbelievable. But they were outgrowths of normal human behavior, exaggerated just enough that people who could not laugh at themselves were able to believe they were laughing at someone else. The essence of *The Honeymooners* was that kind of duality. It was, as Art Carney recalls, "caricatures and cartoons of behavior, certainly not realistic." But it was also, as Coleman Jacoby admiringly describes it, "living tissue."

All great dramatic art, tragic or comic, achieves this kind of heightened reality. It is plainly not the literal truth but it seems more true than the literal truth. It portrays incidents that are implausible, if not impossible, but it invests them with an emotional urgency and candor that make them seem expressive of fundamental human nature. Even the most realistic writing for the stage (or the screen, small or large) is never precisely true to life. It is, inevitably, compressed in time frame and intensified in emotional richness. It is more articulate than real life, and also more explicit, more self-revealing. In effect, the aspiration of dramatic literature is to make audiences see an absolute equivalence between the metaphor of art and the reality of life. This is, first and foremost, an attainment of writers. But it is also the highest calling of actors. *The Honey-*

mooners has survived, among other reasons, because its writers were very good and its three principal actors were extraordinary. Gleason, in his over-the-top way, was the most remarkable of all. He got laughs from the physical pain of slamming a window on his hand as readily as from the psychic pain of getting caught in a lie. He performed in an elaborate, almost Kabuki-like language of double takes and slow burns and eye-rolling and apoplectic roars, yet he learned to make this seem like ordinary, off-the-street behavior. Within the undiminished rage one saw his frustration, self-doubt and yearning to be loved.

Part of the reason this outlandish activity could seem so grounded in the everyday world was that Gleason, more or less unconsciously adopting the Method so widespread among performers of that era, had rooted the Kramden character emotionally in his own half-cynical, half-slushy view of life. Leonard Stern, Gleason's friend and writer, concluded that all of the sketch characters were at heart embodiments of maxims that Jackie had come to believe about the world: "Reggie showed that the exploitative and hostile people of this world would come out ahead. Fenwick Babbitt demonstrated that you would invariably be punished for working hard. The Poor Soul stood as proof that society doesn't appreciate anyone who tries to be helpful. In contrast to all of these characters, who could be reduced to an essence, Ralph was both the active and passive principles, the doer and the done upon. He would act very aggressive but it was always Norton who was invading *his* apartment. He would rage and bluff but he would never act. Jackie would do that, too, of course. There was a lot of Jackie in Ralph."

By the same token, there was a great deal of Jackie that *wasn't* in Ralph. The fundamental difference is that Kramden was a thwarted man who still believed that fame and money would solve all his problems, while Gleason was a rich and famous man who had no illusions about money buying happiness. About a third of the *Honeymooners* episodes focus on some effort by Ralph toward social climbing, advancing himself in a career, garnering celebrity status or getting rich quick. Gleason, who had made it to the penthouse, really had to be an actor—or have a very vivid memory of his hungry days—to bring alive Ralph's faith in future fulfillment. Although Marian Seldes, in making *The Laughmaker* with Gleason in 1953, spoke of its seeming not to be a happy period in his life, what she saw was reasonably representative Gleason. Stern, who stayed in touch through the years, says, "I don't think he had a lot of fun with his success. But then, most comedians can't enjoy what they are doing, although they may enjoy it in retrospect." Carney, whose working life with Gleason spanned thirty-five years, puts it with uncharacteristic bluntness, if absolutely characteristic compassion: "It used to make me miserable to see how little joy he got out of everything he had achieved."

Kramden was a happier man than Gleason in another, perhaps equally important way. He had a successful marriage that was the center and purpose of his life. Gleason had a failed marriage that he couldn't legally escape and that served as an insurmountable obstacle to his establishing a conventional home life with anyone else. Despite the disappointments of his own married life, Gleason fiercely defended the devotion and optimism in the Kramden household. "Comedy writers are almost always more comfortable writing lines of attack," Stern recalls, "but Gleason insisted that we never leave Ralph and Alice in a state of cynicism, mistrust or regret. There had to be resolution. I think he viewed that marriage as his message to the world that he was not a bad person, whatever may have gone on in his life. He was saying, 'I may brag and bluster, but I'm really decent.' It was a covert plea for understanding."

Even the relationship with Norton was at best an idealization of Gleason's bonds with his friends. His "pals" certainly "meant the world" to him, but in contrast to Ralph's unswerving loyalty (if occasionally marked by irritation and bullying) toward the man from upstairs, Gleason's real-life friendships with the gang at Toots Shor's featured enough bullying, verbal abuse and prankish practical jokes to suggest an underlying streak of sadism. Besides, Gleason's friends were mostly people whom he employed or people so rich and successful as to need nothing material from him. On *The Honeymooners*, Ralph Kramden and Ed Norton provided each other with a haven of moral and sometimes financial sustenance in an overpowering world.

As a sociological document, *The Honeymooners* was severely limited. Stern, who went in 1956 from *The Honeymooners* to the Phil Silvers show about the conniving Sergeant Bilko, recalls that his new employer "had a social conscience and tried to touch on race relations and the other issues of the day. *The Honeymooners* certainly didn't." Save in one or two episodes, the series barely acknowledged the ethnic stew that was Brooklyn, and it scrupulously avoided politics of any sort. That may be one reason why it survives so well for contemporary audiences: very little in its plots is specific to its era.

Beyond mere survival, of course, the series has penetrated the national consciousness to the point of qualifying as a cultural icon. References to Gleason and Kramden are obligatory in any history of television and usually form one of the two or three defining visual images, whether in print in such magazines as *Life, Lear's* and *TV Guide* or on television. CBS's memorial tribute to its founder, William Paley, included nine separate references to Gleason or *The Honeymooners*. When *60 Minutes* celebrated its twentieth anniversary, it revived much of its Gleason interview and highlighted his talking about *The Honeymooners* in its promotion. Numerous other television shows, from the caveman cartoon series

The Flintstones to the blue-collar comedy *All in the Family*, have acknowledged their indebtedness to *The Honeymooners*. More playful allusions also abound, from a pair of felines in a 1991 advertisement for cat litter who are named Alice and Trixie to a 1991 John Goodman movie about a sleazy Las Vegas nightclub entertainer who becomes hereditary monarch of England, titled *King Ralph*. A New York City nightclub calls itself The Raccoons, for the fraternal order to which Ed and Ralph belonged. A society of fans termed the Royal Association for the Longevity and Preservation of *The Honeymooners*, acronymically RALPH, drew thousands to conventions in the mid-eighties. When the Museum of Broadcasting (now the Museum of Television and Radio) in Manhattan unearthed some *Honeymooners* sketches from the CBS variety series in the early eighties—items not seen in decades because they were apart from the canonical, syndicated thirty-nine—the institution drew its largest crowds ever, stretching for blocks. Then came a cable bidding war for Gleason's secretly maintained vaultful of such old *Honeymooners* sketches, resulting in a sale in which his personal take exceeded six million dollars, with more to come.

The most remarkable thing about *The Honeymooners* is that almost nobody thought it was a good idea at the time the half-hour series was made. CBS disliked meddling with the success of the variety hour and believed that variety shows, not situation comedies, were the bulwark of television scheduling. Save for Ed Sullivan, who was a pure presenter rather than a performer himself, Gleason was by far the most successful variety entertainer the network had yet employed (or would in years to come, at least until Carol Burnett arrived to give the format its last hurrah from 1967 through 1978). The writers of the Gleason show regretted the loss of flexibility they faced in having to make all the stories about the Kramdens and their neighbors the Nortons the same half-hour length, instead of letting the running time vary from a few minutes to a full hour as the content warranted. Both the writers and the actors were additionally appalled that Gleason decreed that the shows would be rehearsed as minimally as before and then recorded without pause or correction—and at the needlessly demanding rate of two episodes per week instead of the normal one. Once the episodes started airing, critics opined that Gleason was confining his multifaceted talents and was contributing to the lamentable loss of live performance on television. His contention that the shows were "live on film" did not persuade them.

Most striking, in light of the later popularity of the series and of its numerous revivals and reunion episodes, is that the viewing public received the show with considerably less than wholehearted enthusiasm. After three seasons of steadily rising ratings, the reconfigured Gleason series dropped from second to twentieth in the

Nielsen list for the 1955–56 season. The sponsor, Buick, which had deserted Milton Berle and committed to Gleason for eleven million dollars over three years, bowed out of backing *The Honeymooners* at the end of its first and, as things turned out, only year. None of the principals involved in creating, producing or presenting the show seems to have had the least awareness at the time of creating a classic, or even a commercial, commodity. Only Audrey Meadows, for example, negotiated perpetual residual payments for repeats of her work, and that bit of shrewdness, she explains, resulted simply from her brothers' having been lawyers.

The deal to make *The Honeymooners* had been launched with exuberant hyperbole. In reporting the Buick contract, which amounted to eleven million dollars for Gleason and at least five million more for CBS, *Life* magazine hailed the frisky fat man as "by financial standards, at least, history's greatest comedian. . . . No other actor in the world ever had it so good." Gleason liked to sweeten the triumph by saying he had nodded off during negotiations over this whopping sum. The numbers were accurate but, as always, inflated by being taken out of context. For fees of three and a half million dollars for each of the first two seasons and four million dollars for a planned third season, Gleason's production company undertook to cover all expenses of supplying thirty-nine episodes per year of *The Honeymooners* plus an additional thirty-nine episodes of *Stage*

Show the musical half hour that Gleason planned to precede his situation comedy. That worked out to an equivalent of just under ninety thousand dollars per hour of the variety show, a solid raise for Jackie but no more, according to Stanton, than the network would have expected to pay for another season of a show so elaborate and so highly rated. Jackie was unquestionably the highest paid star on television. But in real purchasing power, he was not netting as much as the biggest stars in the heyday of the movies. And in accumulation of capital assets, he was not keeping pace with his CBS colleagues Lucille Ball and Desi Arnaz, who owned a whole studio and were compensated in a different way. Still, in the *Life* piece and similar articles about his breakthrough, Gleason detected an undertone of envy and a hint that maybe he wasn't worth so much. He complained to columnist Sheilah Graham, "Success is like a blue serge suit. You pick up the lint of your critics' behavior. People seem to think I should be ashamed of making $11 million. I'm not. I didn't rob a bank." To another columnist he said, "The people like it big and funny and that's what I try to give them. I'm not ashamed of this and I'm not modest about it. I came a long way in a very short time and I still remember the lean years and the hopeless years. There is no point in kidding anybody by hanging my head coyly and murmuring, 'I was lucky.' I was lucky only in getting the DuMont break. After that I've sweated for perfection and for any success I've

On-the-set portrait for 1969's
Don't Drink the Water, inscribed
to producer Charles Joffe "Dear Charles,
Believe me, Kleenex is included in
the budget— The Great One."

(Charles Joffe Collection)

When Carney rejoined Gleason to reprise
The Honeymooners in 1966, Art proclaimed
himself no longer a second banana.

(Everett Collection)

With Hope, Marilyn and former President Gerald Ford at a
sixty-first birthday party for Jackie at Inverrary in 1977.

(News Pix International)

On a rare visit home, a 1951
family portrait with Genevieve and
daughters Linda and Geraldine.

(Jerry Cooke Photography)

He sometimes reduced Audrey to tears,
but she adores him to this day.

(Joe Franklin Collection)

The lazy boy's version of the on-deck circle.

(Dozier Mobley Photography)

won. But I don't take all the credit. I still stop in at St. Patrick's Cathedral and get on my knees and say, '*You're* the greatest.'

What imperiled *The Honeymooners* from the start, however, was neither Gleason's arrogance nor the frets and doubts of his colleagues. The show's problems arose almost entirely from a network scheduling practice, now much diminished but hugely influential in the days before personal videotaping machines, called "counterprogramming." That is the term for placing shows with strong popular appeal directly against each other rather than against weak opposition. The practice reduces a network's chances for making a show a big hit but affords the opportunity to kill off, or at least dampen, a competing network's best offerings. In his first three seasons on CBS, Gleason had been confronted on NBC by Martha Raye and Jimmy Durante, among others, on *All-Star Revue;* then by *Ted Mack's Original Amateur Hour;* then by Mickey Rooney. None could compete with Jackie. (ABC's inconsequential entries posed no threat.) But for the 1955–56 season, NBC offered a variety hour of precisely the kind that Gleason was giving up, starring a personality as different as possible from the frenetic Gleason. Perry Como, an Italian-American singer with a genial kindness and an almost sleepy demeanor, was as relaxing to watch as Gleason was energizing. Como did a little light comedy, but his specialty was song, and he ranged from romantic ballads to comic novelty items. Robert Williams, contrasting the two in the *New York Post,* wrote, "Gleason is a big, upholstered monument of a man. Como is a stocky scale model. Gleason is quick-tempered, outspoken. Como seldom finishes a sentence. Gleason is a man talking in a bar. Como is the man listening." Como had also built up visibility on smaller-scale television shows, including five seasons of fifteen-minute appearances several times a week following the early evening news on Gleason's own CBS. Como was good—at season's end, he and Gleason would share the George Foster Peabody Award for best entertainment programming, the only major competitive award in television that Jackie ever won—and he was enduring, appearing weekly through 1963 and in popular seasonal specials for decades thereafter. Como wasn't quite as popular as Jackie. During the half hour that *The Honeymooners* was on, it beat Como's competing half hour every week of the season but one (or, according to some sources, two). But Como was much more popular than *Stage Show,* which generally lost its half hour to him by more than two to one. That allowed the Como show to finish just ahead of *The Honeymooners* in the ratings for the year, nineteenth versus twentieth—although the real point is that neither show's rating was remotely as high as its public esteem.

Gleason and Como were, ironically, social friends, although their manners and lifestyles could not have been more different. They had been long acquainted through entertainment circles. The singer lived on Sands Point, Long Island, one of the settings for *The Great Gatsby;* Gleason had taken a summer place there with Marilyn at least one year during the mid-fifties, and the two households had socialized. (Indeed, this Gleason house was the locale for an unlikely and certainly unverifiable story told to this writer by Audrey Meadows, a fervid Gleason partisan and a fierce critic of Genevieve. According to Meadows, while Jackie and Marilyn were away from the house, Genevieve arrived unannounced, looking for them. On being told they were not present, Meadows says, Genevieve demanded that Marilyn's pet dog be brought to her—the implication being that she meant the animal some harm. Apart from sounding as though it were a direct lift from the climax of the Broadway melodrama *The Barretts of Wimpole Street,* this tale in no way jibes with the vision of Genevieve evoked by anyone else who knew her. But the conflict got so bitter during the separation hearings and financial negotiations that Meadows could be right.)

Throughout the ratings tussle, the press tried to lure Gleason and Como into saying provocative things about each other. Both men refused. Como was in the habit of calling everyone a "nice guy." Gleason wasn't, but he recognized that the wiser course would be restraint. "The columnists," he said, "have been positively bloodthirsty. They've called me to try to get me to say something against Como. They've done the same with him. But both of us know the futility of it all. We've been friends for fifteen years. Ratings can't interfere with that. Besides, there may come a time when I might have to borrow a few bucks from Perry."

It was a measure of Gleason's disquiet that jokes about money trouble started to seep into his conversation more and more. He began telling again in interviews a story he had dusted off periodically since his first break, about how he had shipped a trunkful of clothes to a theater in Newark where he used to work, with money for a rainy day pinned inside each garment. The more he told it, the more money was involved and the less likely the story got. But it reflected his surging worry. He fretted to columnist Leonard Lyons, "When success comes, inhibitions set in. You're being watched. Inhibitions make you sad." In the same conversation, he added, with classic Brooklyn bravado, "The measure of your success depends on your indifference to it. If you seem indifferent, they pursue you." Gleason also pointed to his golf cigarette lighter and case and told Lyons, "I bought these for myself. But I never put my initial on anything I buy. I might have to hock 'em someday."

The reality of Gleason's situation was bad enough. The misinterpretation of the press, which in those days (and, truth to tell, in these) could be very unsophisticated about ratings, made it worse. *Time* magazine, for example, reported a few weeks into the season that Como had burst into the Nielsen top ten and that Gleason "was nowhere to be seen" on that roster. All this really meant, of course, was that the bandleaders Jimmy and Tommy Dorsey, co-hosts of *Stage Show,* were not as popular as Como. Nor should they have been; neither had ever had a series before, while Como was a veteran. But in the fifties as in the nineties, media perception had a way of becoming reality. People overlooked the scheduling issue and judged that, at minimum, *The Honeymooners* as a stand-alone show was a failed idea and that, in all likelihood, its star was rapidly fading back into the obscurity whence he had emerged.

What might have seemed, in later times, to have been Gleason's greatest year was thus surely one of the worst of his adult life. And at about the time that *The Honeymooners* started up, Marilyn Taylor left him to seek a more normal, married existence. For some time, Jackie was alone. Then he took up with another showgirl, Honey Merrill, once again a sweet-natured blonde with nurturing ways. Columnist Dorothy Kilgallen said of Honey, "She appears to regard Jackie as romantic even if he does make a dozen telephone calls to cronies while he's breakfasting (or lunching, or whatever meal it is he's having at 4:30 in the afternoon) with her by his side, 'digging' his half of the dialogue." Honey was to be his companion for thirteen years, and in the view of some Gleason intimates the great love of his life, until she, too, opted for marriage and stability. Before all that, however, and just when the pressure on him was greatest, for a longish while Gleason found himself abruptly alone.

Fat and out of shape and beginning to feel the onset of middle age, Gleason was exhausted by the physical and psychic demands of performance. Carney remembers, "The pitch was a lot higher than on anything else I ever worked on. Gleason's whole style was chaotic, high tension, with a special electricity. He thrived on it and I didn't realize it, but I guess I did, too." Part of the nervous energy was Gleason's unfamiliarity with the script. He claimed he had a photographic memory and could recall the text after one reading. In truth, his memory was very good but not perfect. He could cover forgetting a line fairly well, and so could the rest of the cast—he was ferocious about insisting that they remain in character, come what may—but improvising movement and physical business was harder. For that, Carney and Meadows developed a sort of body language, combining symbolic gestures (if Meadows rubbed her stomach, for instance, Gleason was supposed to head toward the refrigerator) and simple pointing or nodding. Gleason further alleviated the problem by designating a special Gleason camera, the operator of which was charged simply to follow his movement, wherever he went and at whatever pace.

At the show's end, Gleason would thank the live audience (filmmaker Joseph Jacoby, a frequent spectator in those days, recalls Gleason as being far more polite and solicitous to his public onlookers than, say, Milton Berle). Then he would collapse into a chair and suck oxygen from a tank. Says Stern, "After a show, Jackie sat like a dethroned king. He would be in the dressing room, his hair matted down, his shoulders and neck draped with a towel." Gleason's own description to a journalist was similar: "When the show is over, I'm like a tub of damp putty. I want to go off to Toots Shor's or some place equally friendly and sit and drink and swap guff with the boys. I want food, too, in family size portions. I want to laugh. I want to be with guys I don't have to be careful with. All of a sudden, I'm not thirty-nine any more. I'm nineteen. And life is serene and beautiful." The rhetorical flourish of "nineteen" versus "thirty-nine" may be its own justification for his precise figure of speech. But it is striking that Gleason should mention the very age at which his mother died and his responsibilities to anyone but himself ceased. His real life at nineteen had not been "serene and beautiful," of course, but full of fear and privation. Still, it is probably human nature, and it was certainly Gleason's, to sentimentalize.

These sprees at Shor's rarely involved other members of the cast. Carney joined Gleason occasionally, but mostly he went home to Westchester. Meadows once came to a Gleason party, prudently chaperoned by her sister, and Randolph attended one or two. But for all the appearance of devotion, these were business relationships. Both Meadows and Randolph got married during the season. Neither invited Gleason, or for that matter other cast members, which led to tabloid flurries of rumor about a feud. The truth was that Jackie was the boss, not an intimate for his colleagues. Carney says, with careful neutrality in his tone of voice, "It all revolved around him. He was the star figure." Meadows—who is so defensive of Gleason that former CBS programming chief Mike Dann drily describes her as "running for office" on the subject—insists that she never saw him angry, depressed or difficult. But even she pauses and adds, "Unless the person deserved it." According to friends, Audrey more than once told her sister Jayne Meadows that Jackie had reduced her to tears. But she denies recalling any such episodes now.

Stern, who was Gleason's only social friend among the creative team, asks a surprising question: "Did he like other people at all? I don't know. I always felt Jackie was retreating when he was not performing. You sensed he was exiting. You just didn't know when that door would be closing. On a personal basis, I think he liked me. But I don't think he would have missed me. I don't think any of us shared any intimate moments with him. I was alone with him fairly often, but those moments were static and superficial. A visit with Jackie was often a vow of silence. On Christmas, he would come to wish you well [a courtesy extended to very few colleagues] and he would sit there for twenty or thirty minutes, often with his hat and coat on, almost monosyllabic in his conversation. But he was there.

"The truth is, I don't know if I ever met Jackie Gleason. I know I met some portrayal of him."

It might be possible to dismiss Stern as a disappointed former friend who saw nothing more in Gleason because Gleason chose not to share it. But in fact Stern continued to enjoy Gleason's company and trust—enough to participate in what became a classic story of Jackie's ego and eccentricity. In 1954 Gleason resolved to take his first trip to Europe and invited the more worldly Stern to be his traveling companion. (On the sly, Marilyn traveled over separately in the wake of the hospital fiasco.) "I was to go to London," Stern recalls, "and then meet Jackie in Paris for some time in France and Italy. He told me over and over how much he wanted to get away from all the publicity, all the newspapers, all the fans, how he wanted to be just an ordinary person for a while. I guess it says something about my innocence that I believed him, although I think he believed himself. On my first night there, I got a call from Al Barnett, owner of the Stork Club in London, who said, 'Your guv'nor's here.' I thought he meant Thomas E. Dewey. I showed up and it was Jackie.

"He had arrived in Paris, started walking down the streets and, of course, being an American television star rather than a Hollywood star, in a time when there weren't nearly so many American tourists, he had gone totally unrecognized. He had flown on to Rome and the same thing had happened. So he wanted to give me my tickets and go home."

In fact Gleason stayed on to complete the trip, partly because he had surgery scheduled. But he continued to miss the attention and the creature comforts of home. He proclaimed Italian food in Italy inferior to that in New York—and it may have been, for postwar Europe still suffered from problems of rationing and scarcity. He thought Paris beautiful but was unimpressed with the food and the wine (he drank grand reds chilled, or even on ice, to the horror of waiters and, for that matter, proprietors who could never afford to savor such bottles themselves).

Stern did not end up among those writers who felt abused or hated by Gleason. He did believe that Gleason resented his writers for possessing a talent that the World's Greatest Entertainer did not. Comedians as a class suffer from this resentment more than dramatic actors. No audience member thinks that the man in the codpiece reciting blank verse actually invented those glorious lines of Shakespeare. But an audience tends to assume, intuitively, that a stand-up comic is telling his own jokes. Some writers who worked for Gleason felt, as Neil Simon did, that "nobody who respected our contribution could have treated us that way." Sid Zelinka, Stern's partner, bristled when, on a rare occasion, Gleason actually included the writers in his post-show talk to the studio audience. Jackie said, "I want to thank my writers Marvin Marx, Walter Stone, Leonard Stern and . . . and . . . don't help me, I can see him . . . the guy with the pipe." He could not recall Zelinka's name.

Other writers, however, seemingly thrived on Gleason's unmanageability. Marvin Marx, who was Gleason's leading writer for a couple of decades, used to swig antacids regularly as he met with Gleason, especially when offering jokes for a monologue (the writers called the process "our weekly humiliation festival") and attempting to deliver them in an approximation of Jackie's style. Says Gleason's agent Sam Cohn, "Maalox. That was the currency of that relationship."

What happened, in Stern's view, was this: "Marvin was the guiltiest of us, the most vulnerable to Jackie's moods, and Jackie knew it. When Jackie wanted to exploit us, to work out his anger at his dependency and wreak punitive damage, he would make Marvin guilty." Still, Stern points out, "Gleason's trust in his writers was ultimately unequaled in my experience. To rehearse that little means that you basically go out and do the material as written. And although Jackie could be mean and loud and uncommunicative, I never felt there was any deep animosity. Plus I know for a fact that he paid a little better than everyone else, because he wanted our loyalty. That was important to him, even if he had to buy it."

Although *The Honeymooners* filmed at night twice a week, on Tuesdays and Fridays, Gleason never once showed up drunk for a performance. On at least one occasion, he did have a hangover so severe—"four colors in key," he called it—that it impaired his normally impeccable timing. He tried to get himself in better shape, going off at one point to training camp with heavyweight prizefight champion Rocky Marciano. After purchasing about seventeen thousand dollars' worth of equipment, Gleason huffed and puffed his way through the first quarter of one day of Marciano's roadwork, told the champ he would meet him back at the camp, canceled his fitness program and donated the gear to a home for orphan boys. He also tried to keep his mind active. As though producing and starring in two shows a week and assembling the occasional record album were not enough, Gleason began to make plans to appear on Broadway in *Volpone,* Ben Jonson's classic English satire. Orson Welles, who was to direct, envisioned an elaborate opening pantomime of Gleason arising late, surrounded by musicians and manservants, ostentatiously looked after, handed a delicate porcelain cup of cocoa to bring him into the day. "I've been living like that for years already," Gleason replied, "only without the cocoa." Welles pledged to act as well as direct but said he would remain subordinate to Gleason. Revealingly, Jackie replied, "Sure, sure, I know what you mean. It's like on my show when they laugh at my subordinate Art Carney, that dirty so and so. I smile when Carney gets those laughs, but you should see my insides."

The *Volpone* plans fell through, for lack of financing and of Jackie's availability. So did Gleason's bid to play the fading Irish mayor Skeffington in a film version of Edwin O'Connor's wonderful novel about Boston politics, *The Last Hurrah*. The role went instead to Spencer Tracy, who would almost certainly have won an Oscar nomination for it had he not been nominated instead for the title role in an adaptation of Hemingway's *The Old Man and the Sea*. Gleason was more successful substituting for Edward R. Murrow on Person to Person, interviewing an actual New York City bus driver (and *Honeymooners* fan) and NBC programming chief Sylvester "Pat" Weaver, originator of the *Today* and *Tonight* shows. (Gleason had been pondering publicly the idea of inverting the order of his two series, assuming that *The Honeymooners* would provide a better lead-in than *Stage Show.* Weaver, acknowledging that this might be effective, asked Gleason on air whether NBC shouldn't counter by shifting Como's start time to seven-thirty. "I wouldn't do that if I were you, Pat," Jackie shot back, "because we'll just keep moving up until we're on at noon.")

A few weeks later, in March, *Studio One* presented a show for which Gleason was credited as providing the story, although he did not star. Red Buttons took the title role in *The Tale of St.*

Emergency, a story of an angelic intervention to clean up a corrupt town. It is hard to know how much of the honor was deservedly Gleason's, and how much the dialogue writer's, but Jack Gould of the *New York Times* said with enthusiasm, "The program's virtues were simplicity, humanity and a moral delicately made. It was eminently worth seeing."

Even *Stage Show,* although it continued to be disastrously unpopular, demonstrated Gleason's show business acumen. Ed Sullivan's better-rated show would later grab the glory for introducing Elvis Presley, but in fact the first network TV show to feature the fast-rising Southern singer was actually Gleason's benighted review. Odd as it may be to imagine an amalgam of the Dorsey Brothers' big band swing and Elvis's pelvic rock, the man whom Gleason characterized as "Brando with a guitar" was booked six times in eight weeks—and, unlike the Sullivan hour, *Stage Show* apparently let Elvis move his hips on camera. Although the record company was hoping Gleason would highlight the song "I Was the One," Jackie preferred a number called "Heartbreak Hotel." Presley sang it on the show three times and it hit the top of the charts. Said Jackie, "If I booked only the acts I personally liked I'd have nothing but trumpet players on the show. It was and is my opinion that Presley would appeal to the majority of people." Gleason was no mean spotter of talent. He also gave early or debut exposure to Barbra Streisand ("she looks like midnight but she sings like dawn," he said) and Wayne Newton.

But despite Presley, *Stage Show*'s ratings continued to lag, and CBS forced Gleason first to relegate it to the second half hour, after *The Honeymooners,* and then to cancel it altogether. After further discussion, Gleason and CBS decided for 1956–57 to go back to a full-hour variety show, with *The Honeymooners* once more just an anchoring sketch element. Even so, Buick wanted to get out of its contract, and CBS, loath to offend so major an advertiser as the parent General Motors, compelled Gleason to agree.

The last blow of the season was the publication of Jim Bishop's biography *The Golden Ham,* about which Gleason had been as excited as a child at Yuletide. The expected treat of a detailed study of his life by a celebrated, best-selling writer turned instead into a nightmare of exposure and disgrace. After reading the text prior to publication, he sent a letter of manly forbearance, refusing to take issue with passages he considered wrong or unfair. Bishop then printed the letter at the front of the book, which amounted to both an advertisement for the book's revelatory toughness and an endorsement of its general accuracy. Gleason had been poorly advised to commit anything to writing. When Bishop's publisher asked Gleason to help promote the book, the comedian snarlingly refused, explaining that it invaded the privacy of his marriage, gruesomely depicted his childhood and his mother's death, and above all accused him of cheating on his filial duties in her final illness. "You're asking me," he said, "to help sell a book that says I played cards with my friends as my mother died. You're crazy, pal." Even this rebuff found its way into print, in a leak to a *New York Herald Tribune* column, reinforcing the (correct) idea that Gleason had something to hide and that Bishop had revealed it.

Despite his determinedly plucky exterior, events began to weigh Jackie down. Columnist Louis Sobol reported on spending an evening at Toots Shor's, where the company included Massachusetts Senator John F. Kennedy and radio personality Ed Gardner, which Sobol called "Gleason's Nite O' Gloom." The comic was in his cups, muttering, "It don't amount to nothin'. Just nothin'. Whaddaya get out of it, let's face it, whaddaya get out of it?"

What Gleason got was defeat and, in the suspicion of many observers, the end of his career. He jauntily began the fall season in 1956 by saying, "I want to thank Perry Como for making me appear live again." He was acutely conscious of the generally bad press that the *Honeymooners* season had received and said of critics, "They present panaceas for problems the audience doesn't even realize exist. They're Freudian analysts. They'll say, 'He told his joke because his mother took a fall back in 1910.' We're not trying to win Pulitzer Prizes here. We're trying to entertain people." Some critics responded sympathetically to this more muted, seemingly chastened-sounding Gleason. Ben Gross of the *New York Daily News* wrote, 'There are sixteen statuesque Glea girls this season, every one of them a looker. Although not contributing much in the way of entertainment, they are a balm to the eye." But Jack Gould of the *New York Times* reviewed the season debut more harshly, "Viewers may feel that whatever the mode of reproduction [live or film], Mr. Gleason's talents are notably circumscribed. This season's premiere was by and large a very dull affair." He noted the ballyhooed presence of Charles Laughton, Peter Lorre, William Boyd ("Hopalong Cassidy"), E. G. Robinson and Zasu Pitts, saying that they were "introduced for about a minute each and then excused. Seldom has the celebrity-conscious set owner been so wantonly conned."

Before the season was very old, Randolph and Carney recall, they began to suspect that it might be the last one. Their feelings about that were at worst mixed. Randolph was happy in a new marriage and hopeful of better opportunities, preferably in productions where the star approved the script and allowed it to be delivered to the other actors sometime sooner than the day of performance. She was also eager for less draining negotiations about pay. She had started at two hundred dollars a week at CBS and finally made it up to two hundred fifty per show after two years of waiting. When at last Jack Philbin informed her of her raise and she said, "Gee, Mr.

Philbin, that's not very much," he retorted, "We'll get another girl." In retrospect, she realizes they probably would not have, but she believed Philbin then. Moreover, Randolph was never allowed to play any other part in sketches and for shows in which the Trixie character didn't appear she received only a one-hundred-dollar retaining wage (in the first years it was nothing at all). Meadows, whose pay had moved from five hundred to seven hundred fifty dollars per week, and Carney, who had gone from seven hundred fifty to a thousand dollars, were happier in financial terms. But they were also ready for other challenges.

Gleason's behavior, always arrogant, got more erratic. Jay Marshall, the comic and magician who had appeared on the show several times, was brought in once again. "I was used to Jackie's overbearing ways by now," he recalls. "Although Reggie Van Gleason had a magic act and I was a professional, Jackie never asked me how things were done. He would have us go on with no rehearsal and scream if we missed a cue. But this time it all went well and he apparently thought so, too. He sent a message through an intermediary: 'You were wonderful tonight and I'm never going to use you again.' And sure enough, he didn't. I never found out why, or if there *was* a why."

Throughout his career with CBS, Gleason wanted to be the one to jump rather than be pushed. By late winter he had started floating talk of "retirement," an oddly premature term for a man of forty-one. In response, as Marie Torre of the *New York Herald Tribune* reported, "The program insiders at CBS have been conspicuously mum." Gleason's manager, Bullets Durgom, insisted in interviews that Jackie was not worn out, an image that might suggest his comedy was also stale. "It's not that Jackie wants to cut down his work," Bullets said. "He's just concerned about having good vehicles. He'd even go on for fifty-two weeks next season if CBS found the right series for him."

Jackie's case for renewal, or for some other life at CBS, was not helped by such antics as his nationally publicized ejection from Manhattan's Stork Club in March 1957. Gleason maintained that the incident resulted from a vendetta between the club's owner, Sherman Billingsley, and Jackie's bosom pal Toots Shor, or perhaps from Jackie's support of the musicians' union, which was on strike at the Stork. Billingsley acknowledged disliking Toots, whom he was suing for libel, but said he ousted Gleason because he was drunk, boisterous and "obscene."

Gleason's real problem, though, was that he was up against Como again. This time there was no gainsaying it: the laid-back singer was much more popular. Como's variety show ranked ninth in the Nielsen ratings. Gleason didn't make the top twenty. By May, Gleason had already given up the battle. The *New York Times* reported that Jackie had taken two three-week vacations during the season and was about to take another that would cause him to miss the last three shows, on which such visitors as Polly Bergen would emcee. Gleason explained later, "It wasn't that I was fired. I was just irritated at the monotony of that continual pressure of holding meetings and rehearsals and having to be there on Saturday nights. You know, if you don't like what you're doing, you give a bad performance. You find yourself fighting two things, your material and your attitude. Then the odds against you just become too big. But at no time did I feel the public had gotten tired of comedy, or of my comedy. I always think I give a great performance or I wouldn't put on a show. What it is, is this. You make a lot of cabbage and after you've piled it all up, *you're* what's cooked. You didn't think what it was you wanted to do with it. Unless a person has some other target than a materialistic one, it's ridiculous to be successful."

At another confessional moment, he lamented to friends, "Chaplin wouldn't have lasted in television, and he was the best."

Try as he might to suggest that his departure was all his doing, CBS was happy to show him the door. CBS President Stanton recalls, "It was a mutual kind of thing. With even the best talent, there is a fatigue factor that sets in on the part of the audience. We thought it was time. There certainly wasn't any wringing of hands around here that Jackie was going off—which, looking back from the perspective of his successes in the sixties, there should have been. We probably should have tried going back to doing another season of just *The Honeymooners,* but no one seriously considered it. We knew we had Jackie under long-term contract. We didn't know if he would be a hit again for us. At least we knew he wasn't going to embarrass us by succeeding anywhere else."

Through it all, Gleason had just three comforts—four, once Honey arrived on the scene. The first was golf. The game came to obsess him, so much so that his move to Florida in the sixties would be prompted by a yearning to play year-round. What Jackie really liked about golf, he explained to friends, was that it was so frustrating, that one's best performance was always so far from perfection. The object of the game in its ideal state—to sink a ball into a hole in a single stroke by hitting it from a great distance and then do so seventeen more times in a row—is of course impossible, altogether unattainable. Success in golf consists of the roughest, most compromised approximation of the ideal, and it seemed to Gleason a satisfyingly accurate metaphor for the rest of his life. On a more practical level, he liked the game because he was comparatively good at it. He was big and strong enough to drive with real power when he got his weight into his swing. He was practiced enough with a pool cue to be a real danger man when chipping and putting. And he was schooled in psychological warfare. One of his favorite tricks was to praise, in apparent innocence, a particular element of an opponent's swing. Gleason's compliments would be so lavish that they would prompt the opponent to start thinking analytically about that element, in hopes of learning something he could use in other aspects of his game. And of course, once the opponent's swing became an object for study instead of something easy and natural, its effectiveness disappeared. Gleason's own style was, to put it politely, untutored. He gripped the club as if it were a baseball bat and eventually had special clubs made in which the handles resembled fungo bats. In three decades of avid playing, he never mastered a conventional style.

Gleason's second big comfort was his exploration into the paranormal. A frequent insomniac, he would stay up half the night reading (or rereading) some of the hundreds of volumes in his library, nearly all having to do with the metaphysical or the occult. He tried not to be gullible. He liked to read contradictory books on the same topic so he could make up his own mind. But in the absence of much formal education, he lacked many of the analytic and other intellectual tools to distinguish between serious and shoddy research, and thus he was easily taken in by lively, populist writers. Every branch of the arcane appealed to Gleason, from space aliens to telekinesis. Part of him believed. Part of him refused to. The once abandoned child had an understandable lifelong difficulty in committing to anything—a woman, a job, an idea.

Gleason's last great comfort was his own pervasive cynicism and pessimism. When things went badly, that was only what he expected. And in the end, it was easier to prepare himself for glum tidings than to go through the painful, perhaps unachievable mental surgery of turning himself into an optimist. In any case, he thought contentment and resignation were classier than the last-ditch battle. He told columnist Sheilah Graham, late during the *Honeymooners* season, "The secret of long life in show business is to know how to lay an egg gracefully."

CHAPTER EIGHT

The whirlwind stilled. The great noise fell silent. The force of nature that for twenty years had been Jackie Gleason in the full cry of ambition turned, in the months following his humbling departure from television, into an almost perfect vacuum, a black hole, entropy. For more than a year he did almost nothing to get his name into the newspapers or his face onto the television screen. He did not return to Broadway or Hollywood or even, so far as can be reconstructed, to what remained of the nightclub circuit. The polite version is that after two decades of almost invariably working two or more jobs, he took a long overdue fifteen-month vacation. The blunt version is that Gleason teetered on the brink of despair.

Honey Merrill, the new woman in Gleason's life and the first to accompany him almost all day long, almost anywhere he went, devoted herself to restoring his health. As always, Jackie's heft ricocheted across a hundred-pound range, and his mood was even more volatile than his waistline. Without irritating him in the way Genevieve had, Honey fretted constantly about his weight, his drinking, his lack of exercise. About his smoking, which averaged five packs a day or more, there was nothing to be done. Gleason had no desire to constrain his nicotine habit and, more important, if he were to return to television, he would diminish his sponsorship options if he started offending cigarette manufacturers, who were among the leading advertisers.

Honey was not alone in worrying that the fat comedian was on his way to shortening his life. During Gleason's sabbatical, columnist Hy Gardner poignantly called Jackie "the forgotten man of television," a label that must have hurt despite its benign intentions, and added, "Intimates are proud of the aggressive manner in which Jackie has gotten a grip on himself and feel that his walking a long, straight line on the golf course has added years to his life." Gardner, alas, was operating on false presumptions. He asserted that Gleason had stopped drinking, which was almost certainly not true and was in any case not true for long. And he assumed that Jackie's playing golf actually involved exercise. This simply wasn't so. Gleason sometimes managed to pack in seventy-two holes, four complete rounds, in a single day, because he rode in a motorized cart and relied on a caddy for everything save the actual contact between club and ball. As feature writer Atra Baer reported in a syndicated article, "The caddy fixes the tee, places the ball on same and, when Jackie sinks a putt, even if he's standing a foot and a half from the cup, the caddy retrieves the ball. Needless to say, this is the best-tipped caddy in the country."

Now and again Gleason would show up in his old saloon haunts and thereby appear in the gossip columns as well, Several writers savored a moment at Shor's when the much-married Mickey Rooney showed off a wristwatch that he explained had been given to him by his father-in-law. Jackie cracked, "Which one?" But generally he stayed out of sight. Most baffling of all to his old gang, this Brooklyn boy, tenement born and bred, began extolling the virtues of the countryside and eventually acquired a dozen or so acres in Peekskill, north of New York City, where he had an old stone farmhouse and envisioned building an ultramodern retreat for parties. As though his crowd would party in the middle of the woods!

Gleason had income and assets to devote to such newfound pleasures, despite his best efforts to squander his pelf. The record albums, by now numbering more than a dozen, brought in a steady income that was unspectacular only by Gleason's Lucullan standards of consumption. The library of thirty-nine *Honeymooners* episodes, which Gleason had made on film so that they would afford him some future value, was sold to CBS for a sum variously reported as from $1.2 million to $4 million. The smaller figure is almost certainly the more accurate; the larger total is apparently a gross price, from which a payback to Buick of more than $2.5 million and certain other participants' fees had to be deducted. But this was still a tidy sum, especially by the un-inflated dollar values of the fifties, and in tax terms it was surely eligible for preferential capital gains treatment, which meant that Gleason got to keep most of it. The day would come, and soon, when Gleason would have to start earning more or spending less. But he could certainly afford the retreat that his psyche needed—and that the CBS network and the public seemed to have urged upon him.

At about this time Gleason started to listen a little more closely to the advice his friend Jack Haley had been dinning into his ears for years about not shortchanging his children and himself through mismanagement of money or excessive trust in others. As Flo Haley recalls the homily, which was repeated time and again between the two Jacks, it went something like this: "Count your own money or it isn't yours. Put it in the bank yourself. You're not worth it if you can't keep your own watch on it and put your own hands on it. Forget all this stuff about 'I don't know money matters, ask my lawyer, ask my ac-countant, ask my agent, ask my business man-ager.' If you can earn it, you can control it. If you have to put it into someone else's hands, it belongs there."

Gleason did not take all of this advice to heart. He moderated his excesses somewhat, and he ad-mitted to feeling a little shaken that on an annual corporate income of three million dollars or more a year he had seemed to go ever deeper into debt, by a yearly twenty thousand or so, which was worse than in his hardscrabble days. But he continued to believe, in business at least, his dictum "The easiest way in the world to waste a lot of money is to try to save some." And given his fondness for the grand gesture, he was probably wise in ignoring Haley and continuing to rely substantially for the rest of his life on his lawyer Dick Green, his producer and business manager Jack Philbin, his tax lawyer and de facto accountant Dave Shulman and his various agents. Sam Cohn, the last and longest-enduring of the agents, who represented Gleason for the final quarter century of his career, says, "Jackie never did learn to be responsible about money. But he was responsible enough to surround himself with people who cared deeply about his not finding himself broke in his old age and who worked very hard to ensure his financial future despite his best efforts at living for the moment."

The first fruit of those advisers' efforts came when the variety show folded after the 1956–57 season. Jackie did not have the money—or, more important, the need—to maintain an office staff as large as the dozens who served him when all his projects were in production. So after carrying many employees for months of almost total inactivity, Gleason reluctantly faced up to the necessity to put them out of work and "reorganized" in early 1958. By all accounts Gleason found the business of firing people distasteful, painful and guilt-inducing; it brought back the miserable memories of his own childhood of poverty. A core staff, including Philbin and publicist Pete Mc-Govern, stayed on. Some others, including secretary Sydell Spear, kept themselves available to return to the fold as soon as Gleason geared up again; Spear, who had been part of Gleason's music operation, would return to become his personal secretary and stay for three decades, until the end. Others from the production side, including Stanley Poss, the writers Marvin Marx and Walter Stone, director Frank Satenstein, set designer Phil Cuoco, dresser Ed DeVierno, and general factotum Joan Canale, preferred working with Gleason to any other opportunity and held themselves in readiness through the comings and goings of the next few years. They did not much mind Gleason's moodiness, his emotional inaccessibility, his offhand and last-minute way of doing things. They considered him a genius and found him fundamentally kind. They were prepared to accept the bumpy, unpredictable life and the constant late-night telephone calls of demand in exchange for the stimulation, the variety and, of course, the glamour of working with a great star. Gleason plainly had a gift for making even trivial moments of intimacy seem special. Almost all his TV series colleagues, even those who admit to not having liked him, recall with exceptional clarity some small, personal encounter that gave them the feeling of a special bond with The Great One. Whether any of these moments had the same importance for Gleason is not so clear, although even his critics describe his intense and unyielding loyalty. Gleason associates delighted in retailing his personal oddities: his habit of describing a Scotch on the rocks as "a crumb bun on ice," giving an earthy and domestic feeling to the focus of his addiction; his penchant for designing gifts for the staff, everything from cocktail napkins to jewelry; his passion for trying all the arts—he even painted the original oil for one of his record album covers; his boundless, adolescent appetite for practical jokes, such as the time he bribed a waiter at Shor's and spent most of a morning sitting in wait, all to validate his offhand boast to Toots the night before that Jackie was so hardworking that he would show up for lunch before Toots even started his day. Gleason was happy in most of his boss-and-subordinate relationships, perhaps because he could control them. But at least one relationship where he had been treated as only an equal started to break down during his months of relative invisibility.

Bullets Durgom, the manager who had guided Gleason from the late fifties—and who believed, with some justice, that he deserved credit for shaping Gleason's career—was demanding more and more while doing, in Jackie's opinion, less and less. Bullets was sympathetic to Gleason's yearning for a rest, for scaling back. But he worried about a loss of momentum and, even more, a loss of income. A star may seem to be the height of individuality, pure personality projection. In fact a star is a business, with many mouths to feed. Jackie bridled when Bullets reminded him of that. Although the open break would not come until later, colleagues trace the first hairline fractures in the relationship to the period of Jackie's sabbatical. Ultimately the split would end in litigation over money, with Bullets claiming, among other entitlements, his share of Jackie's annual hundred-thousand-dollar exclusivity payment from CBS for the life of the contract. He sought similar cuts of projects conceived but not yet executed during his tenure as manager. Gleason would retaliate by basing at least two characters in his subsequent dramatic projects on Durgom —one alive and obnoxious, the other dead and unmourned.

By late summer of 1958, Jackie decided he was ready to face the public again. Hollywood was not beckoning, at least not with the right role; Broadway looked like an awful lot of work for not enough money, even if anyone had put forward an attractive project, which in fact nobody had. So he came back to television and, because of his exclusivity deal, of course to CBS. He seemed edgy about the period of inactivity and went out of his way to give the impression that he had been burning with creative fire. He told interviewers that he had been, among other things, writing a book. Sometimes it was two books, one a novel, the other a book about television—"the only enterprise in America that *starts* on a red light." Jackie liked the idea of himself as author. Indeed, for the next couple of decades, whenever he had been out of the public eye for a while he would leak the news that he was at work on a book. He could often be seen making notes or scratching out long paragraphs on a yellow legal pad. But he was neither disciplined nor patient, and no book by him ever materialized, not even a promised as-told-to autobiography. Although such volumes are not exhausting work, he lost interest in even the minimal effort it would have required.

Jackie was right to be defensive. A great many people thought he was through, and some of them were gleeful about it. Jack O'Brian, his early promoter (until the unseemly wristwatch episode), had written months before, "It has been inconceivable to us that a comedian carrying the towering impact of Jackie Gleason should flop so completely as he has." O'Brian blamed Gleason's personality: "his large ego, his unmerry, moody, melancholy guise as a TV tycoon who owned a large and bustling business whose assembly line's end product had to be either excellently manufactured laughter or show business bankruptcy."

Far from accepting the image Jackie sought to convey of himself as a natural genius, a man who could do anything, O'Brian snorted, "He found it impossible to deal creatively with Arnie Rosen and Coleman Jacoby, the comedy writers who started him at DuMont, who created a good deal of his successful comedy inventions. Gleason pampered his own personal whims, dominating the music, dancing, writing, direction, production, costuming, selection of pretty girls, the band's tempo and other departments normally parceled out to true experts."

Perhaps most reflective of the temper of the times, O'Brian lambasted what would later be recognized as Gleason's supreme creation, *The Honeymooners.* "We thought from the start that Ralph and Alice Kramden were his flimsiest cardboard characters," O'Brian wrote. His summing up also embodied Gleason's worst fears: "He went the way of all TV flashes."

While O'Brian was surely the most vehement of the naysayers, his attitudes were prevalent. Rather than an established star returning from a well-earned rest, Jackie was a man with much to prove. He was returning, moreover, to a television environment markedly different from the one he had left. The three networks were entering their Western craze. Eight of the top sixteen shows in the Nielson ratings for 1957–58 were Westerns, and their popularity accelerated as the season wore on; the following season, Westerns amounted to twelve of the top twenty, prompting Audrey Meadows to quip, somewhat plaintively, "Whatever happened to Easterns?" Some social critics saw the fondness for Westerns as a reaction against the post-Sputnik rise of Soviet influence and consequent loss of American confidence. Others linked it to a yearning for traditional male authority at a time when women were beginning to assert themselves. Some worried about a public taste for action and violence. In truth, the whole shift in taste may have been cyclical and whimsical. By the early eighties, comedy was again being written off as a commercial failure and the hour-long drama was all the rage; at the end of the decade, the situation had completely reversed. But whatever the reasons, the fact was that comedy had a harder time than ever before in Gleason's television career. *Life* magazine ominously summarized the shift as reflecting the "anti-comedian" feeling among audiences.

In response to the widespread belief that the separate season of *The Honeymooners* had been an aesthetic mistake, and perhaps in reaction to his own need to demonstrate he could succeed without Carney and Meadows, Gleason tried a whole new format. His show was a half hour, not an hour. It was mostly comedy, with much less music and dancing girls. It appeared on Fridays, not Saturdays, and thus, instead of Perry Como, its principal opposition was ABC's Walt Disney hour, which started half an hour earlier. Jackie's lead-in show was *Trackdown*, a Western starring Robert Culp that did not survive the season; it wasn't much help in providing a carryover of general popularity or in attracting Jackie's specific type of audience.

But the biggest change was in Jackie's choice of sidekick. His co-star—albeit in a more secondary situation than Carney's—was Buddy

Hackett, a chubby babbler whose basic humor arose from seeming to be mentally defective. One of the cardinal rules of partner comedy had always been the pairing of opposites. One should be loud, the other quiet. One should be dark, the other fair. One should be gentle, the other volatile. Above all, one should be fat and the other skinny. Gleason readily acknowledged that he was gambling by breaking with tradition pairing two loud, volatile, dark, fat men—although at moments over the summer he vowed that he would be "the skinny one of the twosome" by going on another of his crash diets. Hackett was a stand-up comic, not an actor like Carney or for that matter Gleason, and he was coming off an aborted sitcom, *Stanley* on NBC, in which he had played the manager of a hotel newsstand. The show had been notable only for featuring Carol Burnett in a secondary part and for having its debut episode written by Neil Simon.

The opening episode of Gleason's new show offered a Reggie sketch punctuated by one of the character's best-ever one-liners. Asked in a courtroom where he had been on the night of August 12, 1956, the playboy tippler lifted his head and drawled, "I was coming home from a New Year's Eve party." But for the most part the show was a critical failure. John Crosby of the *New York Herald Tribune* after saying the new series didn't work, quoted a contentious Jackie asking why comedians needed to be lovable on television. "It bothers me that all the comedians must be nice guys," Gleason said. "Why can't a guy be a schnook? Look at W. C. Fields. He was great. You believed him because you thought he really acted that way at home. He really kicked babies and drank booze by the gallon, so when he did it on screen, you laughed." But if Gleason thought he was breathing life, or at least verisimilitude, into his by now shopworn sketch characters by investing them with his off-screen quirks and failings, critics disagreed. *Time* magazine judged the new venture a loser and said, "Perhaps Gleason's biggest mistake [was] replacing Art Carney and Audrey Meadows, who were actors and could play up to Gleason's roaring diatribes and outrageous double takes, with Buddy Hackett, a lowbrow buffoon funny on his own but not much help to Jackie Gleason."

In truth, it rapidly turned out that Gleason had really replaced Carney and Meadows with nobody. Although Hackett had a contract guaranteeing he would appear in twenty-four of the twenty-eight scheduled shows, he was excluded from three of the first seven and downplayed in most of the rest, ostensibly because the writers couldn't think of anything for him to do. Hackett was polite and philosophical, in public at least. "The arrangement isn't going as well as we thought it would," he said, "but that's not Jackie's fault, nor mine. That's just the way the cookie crumbles. The Gleason show is Gleason's show. Every time I see him he says, 'Hackie, my boy.' He gives me a few 'my boys' and there we are."

The next time, Hackett said, he'd probably choose to work in a series where he was making the rules. But there wasn't to be a next time. Although he remained a familiar talk show figure, he never got another series lead.

People began to predict the same fate for Gleason when he announced in December that he would shut down his series early in the new year. He blamed the schedule—"A half hour is too short for comedy-variety"—and the writers, his old familiar crew—"There just isn't enough good material for a weekly series." He didn't blame the network or admit that they had urged his decision. "I've known for myself," he explained, "since the third week."

Yet he retained at least a hint of the old bravado. As his third series in four seasons sank into oblivion, this time faster and more ignominiously than ever, Gleason told syndicated television reporter Anthony La Camera that he planned to go off and compose. "I want to write a couple of symphonies and a ballet score I have in mind," he said. These were big ambitions for a man who could not read music, played no melodic instrument and could not find middle C on a piano.

Two things kept the waning years of the fifties from being an utter disaster for Gleason's television career. One was a dramatic performance, his first of consequence in three years. The other was a series of radio and TV talk show appearances that were meant to rehabilitate his interviewer, Arthur Godfrey, but that turned out mostly to resuscitate public interest in Godfrey's guest.

The Time of Your Life, William Saroyan's fizzy stage cocktail of maudlin sentiment and big-hearted optimism, exactly suited Gleason's taste, Although Saroyan's reputation had dropped steadily from the heady early years when he was regarded as a Nobel Prize candidate (and has never really revived), this play was what Gleason thought of as art: some laughs, some tears, for-giveness for everyone and a moral for the au-dience to carry into the night. The title is a shortened version of Saroyan's central apho-rism: "In the time of your life, live." Jackie played a sort of Reggie Van Gleason with a con-science—"a young loafer with money and a good heart"—who befriends the careworn ha-bitues of a San Francisco waterfront saloon. Also appearing were Betsy Palmer, Dick York, Bobby Van, Jack Klugman and Dina Merrill in the pivotal role of Mary L., a self-pitying drunk. Jackie's friend A. J. Russell wrote the ad-aptation. Gleason himself was credited as com-poser and conductor, and he collected the biggest salary in the history of the series on which the show aired, the prestigious *Playhouse 90.* The wage, reported to be somewhere in the low five figures, was comparable to what Gleason got for an episode of his variety series. But it was twice as much as any Broadway performer had ever been paid for an eight-performance week, and *Playhouse 90* was TV's nearest approach to Broadway.

The critical response was mostly glowing. Jack Gould of the *New York Times* rated it "touching and compassionate, quite possibly Gleason's most winning performance on TV. If any viewers [presumably among them Gould himself] thought Gleason would employ the broad strokes of his vaudeville characterizations, they found themselves in happy error." The performance, captured on tape and maintained in the archives of the Museum of Television and Radio in New York City, still holds up more than three decades later as one of Gleason's finest. When one realizes how quickly it was done, under the additional pressures of launching a comeback series *The Time of Your Life* aired six days after Gleason's season debut with Hackett—the drama stands as even stronger testimony to Gleason's intuitive theatrical gifts. For him, however, the biggest thrill came not in the show's capacity to endure, but in its immediate impact. The performance was so good that Clark Gable, who was Gleason's screen idol but whom Jackie had never met, hunted him down by telephone at a golf course to convey unstinting admiration for a fellow actor's craft. Yet even in the face of such praise, Gleason found it hard to take himself seriously as an actor. To one critic who remarked on how effective he had been in a drunk scene, Jackie replied, "Why not? After all, I'm supposed to be one of the top men in that field."

Jackie's appearances with Godfrey were the brainstorm of Oscar Katz, a longtime employee in the CBS research department who had been made the first vice president for daytime programming at any network and who would soon become the overall chief of programming for CBS. Katz's opening instructions from Stanton and Paley were to attempt to revive the fading fortunes of Godfrey, who in the early fifties had had no fewer than three CBS television shows plus a daily network radio show and who back then had personally accounted for an eighth of the entire company's profits. "I had a sitdown with Godfrey," Katz recalls, "at which I summarized his problems. After years of being a sort of Peck's bad boy, not unlike Gleason, Godfrey had turned himself into a real bad boy by buzzing the control tower at Teterboro airport in New Jersey while piloting his private plane. The public also had never forgiven him for the abrupt on-air firing of the singer Julius LaRosa, whose career he had more or less ruined. Godfrey had become such a strong ego that the other performers on his show were frightened into being monosyllabic. And he had turned into a complete bore with only three topics of conversation: his own airplane; General Curtis LeMay and the United States Air Force; and Godfrey's farm and pet horse Goldie. I told him what he needed to do was invite in performers who felt themselves equals and would stand up to him and have free-form conversations that would let the public in effect discover the charms of Godfrey all over. At the time I was suggesting this, I had not even met Gleason, although I had worked at the network for about twenty years. But I told Godfrey he should start with Gleason because I knew Jackie was a good talker with a quick mind and a wide range of interests. Plus there was the contrast in lifestyles. Gleason would come in seeming to have stayed up all night and be a barroom philosopher as he did the show before going to sleep. Godfrey seemed to have arisen at six A.M. and to be full of wholesome, homespun pap."

The conversations, which came just a few weeks into the season, caused a sensation. Newspapers covered them day after day in detail and critics started speculating about a permanent talk show spot for Gleason, perhaps in tandem with Godfrey, perhaps on his own. For Jackie's co-workers and acquaintances, there were no revelations in what he said. The ideas and anecdotes were familiar. The spontaneous wit was mostly mild. But for the public accustomed to seeing Gleason only in character sketches or in lamely executed monologues, the steady flow of his intelligent conversation was impressive. Few performers have enough interest in the world beyond their own careers to sustain hours of unedited talk. Few have the nerve to try. The Gleason-Godfrey conversations wandered from atomic weaponry and the cold war to youth gangs and the quest for social justice—although, as ever,

Jackie said little that engendered outright controversy.

As a public relations venture by Gleason, the conversations with Godfrey were a striking success. A noticeably more respectful tone toward him emerged in the press, and it was sustained even in the bleak period when his series folded just a couple of months later. Godfrey, too, prospered, although as it turned out, Katz's brainchild made little difference in prolonging the redheaded, ukulele-playing pitchman's career. Godfrey canceled all his shows the following spring after he was found to have lung cancer, saying that he did not want to expose audiences to the discomfort of watching him waste away. Ironically, surgery on Godfrey's lung was successful and he lived on for more than two decades. But the self-imposed cancellation proved to be pretty much permanent. Although he continued to work occasionally, he never enjoyed any real prominence again.

Reading excerpts of the Gleason-Godfrey talk leaves one wondering why journalists were so excited. On paper the exchanges sound banal or at best faintly funny, and most of the quips and repartee seem decidedly inferior to what Gleason had been saying via the gossip columns for so many years. On the matter of the press, for instance, Gleason revisited familiar ground: "I've made a few million dollars in my lifetime. When I think that the guy sitting behind a typewriter makes a couple of hundred bucks for telling me

316

that what I've been doing is all wrong, then I feel pretty good." On his lack of humility, he asserted, "Talent is a gift of God. Why be humble about something that comes from God?" Godfrey buttered him up, saying, "There's an essential difference between you and me. You do have talent. You have something to be egotistical about. I can't do anything but bang that ukulele." Gleason smiled and nodded and weakly joked, "I'm beginning to like you."

His most striking comments came later, after the variety series folded, when he was interviewed by assorted critics and columnists about the idea of reuniting with Godfrey more permanently. Rather than insist that he was foremost a comedian and actor—or writer, director, composer, conductor, painter, designer and impresario—Gleason embraced the idea. "Any time that quality has a deadline," he said in one typical conversation, "it's got to deteriorate. You can strive for quality week in and week out, but you won't often get it. It can't be manufactured within a specific time. It's a luxury, that's what it is. Quality needs care and unlimited time. That's why I'm crazy about doing this ad lib show with Arthur. Here we don't need plot lines, or sets, or choreography. It's completely unprepared, and what comes out is really pure, honest humor. It's the real thing. When I want to perform on TV, there'll be time for occasional specials, time to perfect them qualitatively. With an ad lib show, I'd be both rich and happy."

Although those remarks sound rambling and offhand, they contain revealing dualities. Gleason had the highest esteem for quality in his craft, but he found the task of achieving it increasingly onerous. As the years went on, he would become ever less happy about the idea of long labor. Art Carney, his most consistent collaborator, would eventually describe him as "by no possible definition of the word a workaholic." CBS executives would label Gleason flat-out lazy. As an actor, moreover, Gleason excelled at invoking a variety of characters, sometimes several within the same hour. Despite his complete lack of formal training, his performances in dramatic roles were becoming increasingly surefooted and effective, full of emotional clarity and vulnerability and rarely cluttered with inapposite mannerisms from his vaudevillian days. Yet increasingly Gleason was enchanted with the idea of presenting himself to the public in the role of himself, offering his considered opinions and spur-of-the-moment bon mots. He saw a talk show or, failing that, a game show as the ideal way to unburden himself of the need for co-stars, designers, directors and, above all, writers. He saw spontaneous chatter as the escape from the tedium of rehearsals and the pressures of having to remember movement and lines.

Naively—there are none so blind as those who will not see—he envisioned himself gliding into a studio five minutes before air time, inserting a fresh carnation into his lapel, dusting his jowls and pouring his personality into the camera with the same seductive effectiveness as in the days when he had been known as the best table comic in the business. A talk show, he thought, would be no work and would run forever. And if he could charge the network as steep a fee as for a costlier variety show, arguing that the point wasn't his outlay but the rating he delivered, then he could stuff far more of the proceeds into his own wallet. Over the next two to three years, virtually every series project that Gleason brought to CBS was either a talk show or a game show. He deflected suggestions that he return to variety. He abhorred situation comedies. He urged the occasional drama; once he envisioned an hour series in which he would play "a public relations man with great connections, the kind who can get President Eisenhower on the phone." But CBS was interested in Gleason solely as a comic, so that proposal went nowhere.

Most of the time, the person to whom Gleason brought those ideas was Oscar Katz, the executive who by pairing him with Godfrey had put the whole talk show idea into Jackie's head. The relationship between the two men was feisty and combative. Nominally, Katz was the boss, but in fact Gleason had the upper hand. Programming chiefs would come and go, and their role was mostly to *spend* money. Stars *earned* the money by attracting the public. The interaction started at a level close to combat.

"At the end of my first day as vice president

for programming," Katz recalls, "I got a call from Jackie's chief agent, Herb Rosenthal. Now at this point I had absolutely no idea what my level of authority was, I hadn't had any chance to think about the job and I was really scared about meeting with a major talent like that. I had no idea what Jackie wanted, but it was a safe bet he wanted something. He wasn't calling just to wish me good luck. Anyway, I reluctantly agreed to join him the next afternoon at the 21 Club for cocktails. When I got there, sitting at the far end at a table with a checkered cloth were Gleason, Rosenthal and Jack Philbin. They had obviously been there for a half hour or so already, although I was right on time, and that immediately put me on the defensive. I could also see that Jackie had been drinking. His first words to me did not include any form of 'hello.' He just said, 'I'm going to sue you. You've got me under exclusive contract. You obviously have no intention to use me. That's a violation under the Fourteenth Amendment of the Constitution, which has to do with slavery or involuntary servitude.' Philbin and Rosenthal were speechless. My genuine impression is that they had no idea what Jackie was going to say. He went on, 'No one at CBS has ever liked me, and the money you pay me I spend at the corner store on cigars.' At one point he said, 'Bullshit,' and he liked the sound of that so much he repeated it a few times.

"He went on for about twenty minutes, stating his position over and over again in different words. I tried to persuade him. 'Everybody at CBS likes you,' I said. 'You're the top sketch comic around, one of the major comedians of our time, and we do want to develop programs with you. It's very important to us to get you back onto our air.' Jackie wouldn't have any of it. He started up again with 'Bullshit' and 'I'm going to sue you.'

"Let's fast forward. By now it's eleven P.M., we've been there for at least six hours, Jackie is blotto, people are coming in from the theater for late supper and looking over to see who these boors are making all that noise. Herb Rosenthal is a tall guy but he has slumped so low in his chair that he's practically under the table so no one will see him. Philbin is silent. Jackie is saying, 'All right, if you mean it, give me money for a script.' Finally something flashed through my mind and I said, 'I don't have the authority to do what you want. But I can tell you, Gates Avenue is never going to bullshit Halsey Street.'

"Jackie looked at me as though seeing me for the first time and said, 'You're from Gates Avenue? I love you, pal.' He said it a couple times more. Then pretty soon he was asleep and the crisis was over.

"It wasn't simply that I was another Brooklyn boy. In fact, the kids around Gates Avenue, the area where I lived, were all Jewish, just as the kids who lived around Halsey Street, where Jackie was from, were mostly Irish, and the two groups hated each other. If they came into contact, it was apt to be gang warfare. The psychology was this. In that neighborhood, or any neighborhood like it, when a new kid moved in, someone in the gang would pick a fight with him. If the kid ran away, he would never be accepted. If he fought, even if he lost, he would fit in. That's what Jackie was doing to me. He was testing to see whether I would stand up to him.

"Time and again, after that, a new executive in programming would come up to me and throw his chest out and say, 'Guess what? I've been invited to come spend the weekend with Jackie Gleason.' I always knew the guy was going to get the shit kicked out of him.

"Out of that meeting, we developed several projects for Jackie, all of which he rejected. He would read the proposal and drop it onto the floor of whatever restaurant we were in. In turn, he would come back at us with ideas for a talk show or game show. He would say he wanted something where he could, to use one of his favorite phrases, 'just wing it.' We fought him off on that for years.

Frustrated by the logjam at CBS and unable to sell the movie studios, as yet anyway, on an idea he had for a sort of homage to the great silent-era comics, Jackie returned to the situation he said he loved best, the live theater. His chosen vehicle was *Take Me Along*, a musical adaptation of Eugene O'Neill's only comedy, *Ah, Wilderness!* Set on the Fourth of July at the dawn of the twentieth century in a prosperous town in Connecticut, O'Neill's play is an uncharacteristically sweet and optimistic story of young love and emerging manhood. The central characters are an adolescent boy, blossoming with equal excitement into first infatuation and the gorgeous realm of ideas, and the boy's father, an eminently pragmatic newspaper executive who nonetheless retains vivid recollections of his own youthful immersions into poetry, philosophy and puppy love. The problem with the project as a vehicle for Gleason was that Jackie would play neither of these roles. His part was to be Uncle Sid, a tipsy and irresponsible newspaper reporter, full of brains and charm, who had squandered his chances for both advancement and marriage by drinking too deeply, and literally, the wine of experience. The role could be beefed up a bit with songs, and in the O'Neill original it offered both splendid comedy and poignant glimpses of self-destruction. But it was unmistakably a supporting presence for a man who considered himself a star, the Greatest Entertainer in the World.

The show was being produced by David Merrick, and Gleason liked that. He didn't know Merrick, and as it turned out they grew to detest each other. But Merrick, then in his heyday, employed more actors and backstage people in his various shows than any producer ever had before, and he dominated the Broadway scene as no other producer ever would until in the early nineties Cameron Mackintosh offered simultaneously

Cats, Les Misérables, The Phantom of the Opera, Miss Saigon and *Five Guys Named Moe*. Even then, it was a measure of Merrick's abiding reputation that Mackintosh was widely described as "the new Merrick." Just as Jackie had wanted to be with CBS because it was the biggest network, so he wanted to be with Merrick because he was the biggest man on Broadway.

Gleason held true to form in other ways. When Merrick offered the part, he emphasized that Gleason could not expect to be paid as well as he was in television. Of course Jackie's name would help sell tickets, and he should be compensated for that. But with a maximum of about twelve thousand seats to fill every week, versus the millions who watched a television show, the economics of the business were necessarily different. Jackie's response was vintage Gleason. He demanded to know what was the highest wage that had ever been paid on Broadway before. The answer, it seemed, was five thousand dollars a week to Alfred Drake, a masterful singing actor, in *Kismet*. Fine, said Jackie. Then I will do the show for five thousand and fifty dollars a week, so that my salary is the biggest ever—plus, of course, a few perquisites. He demanded that Merrick provide a white stretch limousine to be on call to Gleason twenty-four hours a day, even when Jackie was asleep or sick or having a day off. He required expense allowances, personal servants, a dressing room telephone with unlimited toll calls. And to the eventual detriment of the digestion of all the stage managers and fellow cast members, he insisted on being excused from the standard requirement that he arrive a half hour before show time. Instead, Jackie would slip in through the stage door, costumed and wearing what little makeup he tolerated, just fifteen minutes before curtain.

Gleason's demands were widely reported as "outrageous," in part because Jackie used that word himself in describing them to reporters. He delighted in the image of himself as a pampered supremo bringing the money men whimpering to their knees. Merrick, whose own ego was well-nigh uncontrollable and whose icy rudeness was legendary, unhesitatingly accepted Gleason's terms. He was confident that he could handle Gleason, as he had handled other self-important performers. And although Jackie would be expensive, if his presence sold tickets as effectively as Merrick expected, Gleason would be well worth the price. His name made the show virtually review-proof.

To launch the tryout with proper publicity, Gleason suggested reviving a device he had used to great effect before, a press party aboard the train carrying the actors toward Boston, complete with nonstop jazz music and an eternally open bar. Reporters would have lots of color and glamour to convey and might be cheaply seduced by the sheer ebullience and effrontery of the exercise. In addition, they would have the opportunity to interview the show's creators and its rather glittery stars, who in addition to Gleason were Hollywood veterans Walter Pidgeon and Ruth Warrick (replaced during tryouts by another movie name, Una Merkel), British stage luminary Eileen Herlie and, as the boy, Bobby Morse, already a Tony-nominated Broadway star (for the straight play *Say, Darling* the previous season). Morse would later achieve a rare double, winning the Tony as best actor in a musical for *How to Succeed in Business Without Really Trying* in 1962 and again for best actor in a play for *Tru*, a one-man show about author Truman Capote, in 1990. Also in the cast, as an unheralded chorus girl, was a young comedienne named Valerie Harper.

The train ploy worked beyond Merrick's imaginings. According to Harvey Sabinson, the press agent for *Take Me Along* and now the executive director of Broadway's main trade organization, the League of American Theater Owners and Producers, both *Time* and *Life* magazines came on board. So did all the New York City newspapers and the major wire services. Best of all, NBC's *Today* show filmed a feature piece that suggested that the jazzy party atmosphere would be reflective of the finished play as well as its opening promotion. Oddly, after insisting on the idea, Gleason proclaimed the event too noisy and soon retreated into his private room.

Jackie had been in a slightly weird mood from the outset of the day. As they strode through the train station in Manhattan, publicist Pete Mc-

Govern spotted a quarter lying on the ground and reached for it, only to hear Gleason say, "We go divvies. I saw it first but I can't bend over to pick it up." Once installed in Boston, where the major portion of the out-of-town run would take place, Gleason became even more stand-offish. He tried to skip most of the all-cast photo call, although union rules required him to be available for four hours and common sense would suggest that he and the producer might want to see his picture in the paper stimulating ticket sales. Gleason waved his arms after the opening shot and said, "Okay, that's it. I'm through." Publicist Sabinson rushed after him and pleaded, "Jackie, never mind the Actors' Equity rules, you're not giving me any ammunition here." Gleason grudgingly heard Sabinson out while Pidgeon, Warrick, Morse, Herlie and others submerged their own professional egos and dutifully waited. At last Gleason reluctantly consented to stay for about half the scheduled four-hour shoot. Having negotiated star billing, Gleason had little reason to complain about that, but he grumbled to a Boston entertainment reporter, "Any time you can see the name of the show I'm in, my billing isn't big enough."

For the most part, Gleason cooperated in rehearsals out of town. He showed up on time, learned his lines (without demonstrating his vaunted "photographic" memory, as fellow cast and crew members recall it) and mastered his songs and dance steps. He didn't even complain much when one of his numbers was thrown out and replaced by something entirely new, because the replacement item, a song about drunken hallucinations called "My Little Green Snake," worked better and brought down the house. But in other ways, Jackie played the star. He insisted on breaking character at points to wink at the audience or to introduce bits of familiar body English, such as the "Away We Go Shuffle" or the Poor Soul's trademark slump of the shoulders. He didn't do this in the big dramatic moments, if only because he didn't want to spoil his own scenes. Instead he used these movements to milk his laughs or to get laughs in scenes that more properly focused on others.

At one stage he suggested that he be introduced into a tender moment between Pidgeon and Morse when father and son discuss the reproductive facts of life. Jackie thought Sid should watch from halfway up the stairs, leering and offering silent erotic encouragement. The impulse was so plainly wrong that Gleason accepted a forceful putdown from director Peter Glenville. On other matters, however, he got his wish, and for Morse some memories still rankle, "The play *Ah, Wilderness!* is about the boy," he says, "and the musical was supposed to be, too. But Jackie wanted to be the star and while we were in Boston my part kept getting smaller." During the actual Broadway run, Gleason felt Morse was beginning to impinge, getting too fidgety and antic while Gleason was supposed to be the center of attention. So in the pivotal scene between them, Gleason kept blowing smoke from a lit cigar directly into Morse's face. The younger actor choked, his eyes teared up and he had vocal trouble the rest of the night. As they met offstage minutes later, Gleason stared at Morse and snarled, "Don't ever fuck with The Great One." (Even more bitter for Morse, however, is a memory from after *Take Me Along* was over. One night Gleason came to Morse's dressing room to greet him before a performance of *How to Succeed.* On hearing that Jackie was heading off to dinner, Morse entreated, "Why don't you stay and see the show?" With a dismissive wave of the hand, Gleason said, "Naaah. I know what you do.")

For a while, the return to the live stage bolstered Gleason's morale and satisfied his ego. In Boston, he had an audience with Richard Cardinal Cushing, the powerful prelate and Kennedy family ally. He addressed the Massachusetts House and Senate. He had a practice session with the Boston Bruins hockey team. He threw a party for theological and medical dignitaries at which he demonstrated his skills as a hypnotist. But most remarked upon and most revealing was the night after a performance when he got drunk in a bar, jumped up on a table and recited a couple of Shakespeare soliloquies from memory. Soon after, he was floating rumors that his next role would be the Bard's most famous. "Where in Shakespeare," he demanded, "does it say that Hamlet is a skinny guy with legs like Barrymore?

I want Hamlet to be a fat guy." Some of this was vainglory. Gleason didn't really mean it, at least not entirely, when he added moments later, "Compared to my profile, Barrymore's is amateur night." Nor did he really want to face either the critics or his natural audience, the TV variety show audience, while spouting Shakespeare, even though he twice announced he'd do a two-hour, cut-down version of *Hamlet* for CBS. In his later years, agent Sam Cohn repeatedly tried to induce Gleason to play Falstaff, a role that is really Ralph Kramden with swordplay, and Jackie always sidestepped the idea, no matter what the money or the circumstances. Never once, so far as one can tell, did he appear in a role written before the twentieth century. But he did sincerely mean the characteristic gush of enthusiasm for any project in its early stages and the particular delight at facing live thousands rather than unseen millions.

His joy in his performance in *Take Me Along* was widely shared. Publicist Sabinson recalls watching the show over and over, filled with awe at an overpowering presence appearing in a role just right for him. Neither Carol Channing in *Hello, Dolly* nor Rex Harrison in *My Fair Lady* gave Sabinson the same total satisfaction, he says. "The only other times I ever felt that way were with Lucille Ball in *Wildcat* and Lena Horne in *Jamaica*. I admit, when push came to shove, it was still Jackie Gleason onstage. He wasn't playing the Poor Soul or Ralph Kramden, but there was still this added layer that he was playing it through the filter of Jackie Gleason—it was 'Jackie Gleason as Uncle Sid.' He would even break character to wink and nod to the audience. Yet he was still very much in keeping with the character. And he had enormous technical gifts, even if undeveloped. He wasn't a trained dancer, but he danced beautifully. He wasn't a trained singer but he sang beautifully." Charles Blackwell, a stage manager on the show who saw virtually every performance, says, "He performed the role in a big way but his emotional immediacy was equally enormous. He did not sentimentalize to get the audience's sympathy. There was a drunk scene, his most important emotionally, that he played beautifully—except on the nights when he had had a little bit too much to drink offstage. Then, ironically, he wasn't as sharp or as touching. I admired the fact that he didn't cheat. The scene had to leave you feeling sorry for him, but also a little disappointed and even angry with him for the way he had destroyed his own life and that of the woman he loved. He didn't wink at the audience to make them like him, to say, 'I'm really not such a bad fellow.' He did it right, and with bravery."

Fellow actors were equally admiring. Sir Tyrone Guthrie, the director who helped found leading classical theaters in Minneapolis and in Stratford, Ontario, hailed Gleason in a *New York Times Magazine* article as "a great entertainer" and described his gifts as equivalent to those of the foremost classical actors. "He can move to

331

laughter or to tears and dance so expressively, so beautifully, that clowning becomes poetry." Laurence Olivier, the true Great One of the stage, not only came to see and admire the show but sent a thank-you note that began, "Dear Great One. . . ." (Astonishingly, Gleason threw out this memento, which any other American actor would have framed and pointed out to visitors. The keepsake was rescued and preserved by Gleason's *Take Me Along* dresser, Herb Zane, who showed this writer the original.)

As always with Gleason, the newspaper critics were less extravagant. By theater historian Steven Suskin's assessment, *Take Me Along* drew two raves, three favorable notices, one mixed and one unfavorable, but no absolute pans. Even those who liked Gleason tended to hedge their acclaim. While John Chapman in the *New York Daily News* hailed Gleason's "engaging sweetness" and his soft-shoe duet with Pidgeon in the title number, he considered all the principals "wonderful," so Jackie could hardly feel he had made a singular triumph. Frank Aston in the *World-Telegram and Sun* liked the broadly comic first act but not the meaty second; Brooks Atkinson of the *Times* felt just the reverse. Aston said no better of Jackie than that he "lends popular pull." Atkinson deplored Jackie's "vaudeville exuberance," which he said "made a cheap-jack out of the half-tragic figure of Uncle Sid." He also judged that Gleason's style and strength of personality "destroyed the values of the O'Neill source book."

Richard Watts said much the same thing, if more gently, in the *New York Post*. Walter Kerr of the *Herald Tribune* hailed Eileen Herlie as both the most poignant and the funniest presence on stage and kissed Gleason off with the single word "genial."

The reviews were disappointing to Jackie. But he soon found he had a much bigger problem to contend with. Having been away from Broadway for a decade and having never before worked a long run in a show where he was pretty much obliged to stick to a written text, Gleason had not really thought through what it would mean to commit himself to a full year's contract. At first, doing Uncle Sid was challenging. Then it was gratifying. But not long into the run, he began to find it aggravatingly tedious. The show eventually ran 448 performances, and Gleason was around for all but about the last twenty-five or thirty. He missed a few others along the way— Pete McGovern says two or three, stage manager Blackwell says ten or twelve—mostly owing to illness. On occasion he had a sore throat and cold, which an angry Merrick accused Jackie of deliberately inducing by leaving the window open in winter. Once Gleason claimed he had a stomach upset, at which Merrick snapped, "Gleason with a bellyache is like a giraffe with laryngitis." At least a couple of his absences were for acute intoxication or even worse hangovers. But beyond the times when Gleason actually missed a show were the countless performances when he showed up too drunk to be in good form yet went on anyway—or started the show at the brink of being plastered and then fell over the edge after taking slug upon slug from the wine bottles he kept in his dressing room.

The rumor of his condition each show would spread through the chorus boys, who had to contend with him first, in his opening number. "Oh, he's hot tonight," they'd say. The bad news would reach Morse, who had some scenes with him, and then Eileen Herlie, who had most of her important moments, including two big ballads, in his proximity. If Jackie were gassed enough, the cast members knew, there was no telling what dance steps he might improvise or what impromptu lyrics might issue from his lips. At his worst, he once was so legless he failed to mount the old-fashioned streetcar on which the cast entered and instead trailed in behind on foot. Morse, who has declared his own alcoholism, says flatly that Gleason was an alcoholic. "He would fall and falter and I don't know how he got away with it. You'd show up at the theater and wonder what wreck you were going to see tonight. On Jackie's last night, he somehow got into a fight with Walter Pidgeon, one of the sweetest men in the world. The chorus people had to pull them away from each other." Blackwell acknowledges that Jackie "had a lot of bad performances when he was more or less out of control." Dresser Herb Zane saw Gleason in his cups frequently and says Jackie was always at his worst when he and Honey Merrill had had a fight. Most of the time she remained at the theater with him throughout each performance. When she stayed away for a few days in pique, Zane says, Jackie would telephone other women. Some were call girls. But one was Marilyn Taylor, whom Jackie had tracked down and repeatedly implored to re-enter his life. As far as Zane could tell, Marilyn had given up on Gleason and she just hung up when he called.

Despite the frequency and depth of his indulgence—climaxing in a day when he and Broadway columnist Ward Morehouse consumed ten bottles of wine between them at lunch at Sardi's before Jackie staggered across the street to the theater to attempt a matinee—Gleason was in deep denial about his behavior. He told columnist Earl Wilson that he never drank before or during a performance and rarely had even a sip afterward, because the eight-show-a-week schedule was too demanding if one didn't stay in shape. After uttering this balderdash with apparent sincerity, Gleason then bemoaned his boredom: "A hit show is like a concentration camp with music." Indeed, he later said he was going to have prison bars and an identification number painted on his dressing room door. He vowed to have the shower taken out to install a working bar (there is no record that this actually happened, and the last thing the management wanted to do was to stimulate Jackie's alcohol consumption backstage).

Gleason was so self-deluding about his own drunkenness and deportment that he reacted with horror at the abusive meanderings and eventual electronic disappearance of Irish playwright Brendan Behan during a transatlantic video hookup hosted by Edward R. Murrow in November 1959. Appearing on an installment of the series *Small World,* Gleason assured Behan the connection was clear: "You're coming in one hundred proof." On hearing that he was one of four people Behan wanted to meet in the United States—along with Eugene O'Neill's son, Harvard University professor Harry Levin, who is a James Joyce scholar, and novelist Norman Mailer—Gleason exclaimed, "Good God!" But when Behan showed up a few months later and visited Gleason backstage, they hit it off famously and Gleason attached himself to Behan for much of the rest of the Irishman's visit. Gleason had no romantic love for Ireland itself—Herb Zane remembers hearing Jackie refer to thatch-roofed cottages as "those slums"—but he cared deeply for its language and literature, which he had heard about at his mother's knee. When Behan's *The Hostage* had its opening night party at Downey's, an erstwhile Irish steak house on Eighth Avenue in midtown, Gleason showed up roaring drunk and belligerent. Actor Malachy McCourt, who was there, considered Gleason "irresponsible and reprehensible" for urging Behan to drink, indeed almost haranguing Behan on the point, even though Jackie knew full well that the Irishman was on the wagon and risked mortal illness if he resumed boozing. (He eventually did, and died of it.) Gleason was also so possessive about Behan that, as publicist Pete McGovern recalls, Jackie repeatedly pushed away bodily a well-dressed, mild-mannered Hibernian who kept trying to approach the guest of honor. The man Gleason was treating so harshly, it turned out, was the Irish consul in New York, there to present Behan with a proclamation and a gift. Eventually Gleason was thrown out of the party. McCourt describes watching him, for long minutes afterward, pounding on the window, shouting and making faces and demanding that he be let back in. "It was like a pantomime, seen through that thick glass," McCourt says. Gleason later redeemed himself, minimally, by challenging Behan to a buttermilk-drinking contest for a charity benefit. Behan said forgivingly, "What I like about Gleason is that there is a certain amount of sadness, of truth in his jokes." An example, he noted, was Gleason's line "loneliness is particularly wretched to the actor because there is no audience to witness his misery."

Part of the reason most people love show business is that it provides a family. The negative side is that it provides this bonding over and over, then destroys it over and over, as each cast or crew assembles and disassembles, so that over the years one loses many more friends than one keeps. Gleason, as reserved at *Take Me Along* as he had been at CBS, mostly chose not to be a part of the intimacy. He was polite but distant to his colleagues, with the exception of a small but bold boy about nine years old, a replacement member of the cast, whom Gleason called "the Shaughnessy." Some onlookers thought the child reminded Gleason of himself, or perhaps of the son he never had. The only other times Gleason tended to join in were the moments of ribaldry. Jackie obviously enjoyed a party at which one of the chorus boys appeared in complete, and very convincing, drag. In a somewhat less mild instance of sexual daring, one of the chorus girls was dating the actor Forrest Tucker, who was rumored to have been amply blessed by nature in the organs of reproduction. No cloistered convent maiden, she brought in and passed around color photographs that purported to show Tucker in a state of full arousal. Jackie held them long and studied them hard. A few years later, when Jackie was Milton Berle's guest at the Hillcrest Country Club in Los Angeles, Tucker walked into the locker area. Berle, who is similarly well endowed (and has made a lifelong practice of discussing the fact), recalls that Gleason spotted Tucker and shouted out to everyone nearby, "All right, we got the two kings of endowment here. We got the East Coast king and the West Coast king. Who's bigger? My money is on Milton. I'll put up two hundred dollars even money." According to Berle, the bet was taken up and within a moment, eighteen hundred dollars had been wagered. Berle professes to have no recollection about what, if anything, Tucker said during these slave auction–style discussions. But Berle claims his own reaction was to beg off. "I wasn't shocked, I mean, I've been through this before, and we're all men. But it seemed kind of silly. So I said, 'Jackie, enough.'

"And he looked at me and said, 'Milton, just take out enough to win.' The place broke up. It was maybe the funniest spontaneous line I ever heard."

This taste for the coarse was no problem in private life, but Jackie got into trouble at least once for indulging it onstage. In a dream-sequence dance, the women appeared in scanty costumes featuring large dicelike attachments along the bust. One fast-moving chorine shed her dice and, in the process, wound up barebreasted. Most of the audience noticed immediately. But Merrick would have preferred the cast to stay quiet about it. He fined Gleason five hundred dollars, according to McGovern, for shouting from the sidelines an apt crapshooter's term, "You're faded."

That was far from Gleason's only contretemps with Merrick. The impresario shrewdly grasped the essential personality of actors. "No matter how big they are," he said, "they all need the constant attention of their producers." If ever that was true of an actor, it was true of Gleason. Merrick, with a perverse disregard for the wellbeing of his show, refused to humor Gleason's need. Gleason considered Merrick a tightwad.

339

The Great One considered himself insulted by the modest, tasteful size of *Take Me Along*'s opening night party and by his own limitation to a single table for twelve (not unreasonable in a show with five stars). Merrick considered Gleason a piggish spendthrift and got back at him in the most enraging way possible, by docking him for real or imagined infractions. At one point, a press agent attempted to broker a compromise by claiming that Jackie's portrait at Sardi's had been "stolen" and then having it "reappear," much larger and fancier than before, in a ceremony conducted at Merrick's expense, a sort of substitute opening night bash. But the two men continued to squabble. Gleason had golf balls made up with Merrick's mustachioed face on them to "inspire" his drives. Merrick sniped back but reserved his deftest gesture of retaliation until a few years later, when Gleason was no longer in his employ and thus posed no risk to Merrick's empire. When Gleason offered his Peekskill residence for sale, by this time including an ultramodern round house that Jackie, a UFO fan, called the Mother Ship and an outbuilding he dubbed the Saucer, Merrick sent for the brochure and then offered about ten percent of the asking price, telling all the columnists that the house was a grotesquerie and he was bidding based only on the value of the land. Despite their malice, both men got what they wanted out of the relationship. Merrick got a long run for a modestly received show. Gleason got a comfortable income, enhanced prestige, a dramatic platform that quickly stimulated major stardom in the movies and, of course, the Tony Award, the final imprimatur of acceptance on Broadway. Having been declared best actor in a musical, beating, among other nominees, Anthony Perkins in *Greenwillow* and his co-stars Morse and Pidgeon, Jackie left Broadway on October 20, 1960, never to perform there again in the twenty-seven years left of his life.

A couple of years before, Jackie Gleason had been considered washed up. He was now entering the most fecund period of his career. While *Take Me Along* had been on, he had completed his appearance on CBS's *The Fabulous Fifties,* replicating his number "Sid, Old Kid" from the show. He had narrated *The Secret World of Eddie Hodges,* a June 1960 glimpse of childhood featuring a puckish child star. He had filmed a golf match with Arnold Palmer during which Gleason claimed to have sunk a sixty-foot putt; Palmer didn't remember it that way. Gleason did confess to one fiasco, a quintuple bogey ten on a par five hole. "That was the perfect hole," he quipped. "I used every club in the bag." He had been billed as composer and conductor of musical selections on a show also starring Kate Smith, another amply built client of Jack Philbin. Jack O'Brian had written of the offerings, " 'His Melancholy Mood' is a good, fat, lush, popular piece, undoubtedly his best. The others reflect a dilettante talent for composition, pastiches all. The rhythm instrumentals, arranger's trifles, entitled 'Dan Dan Dandy,' 'Bear Mountain Blast,' 'Toll Gate Treat,' uniformly were exhibitionistic and thin. Gleason's own lyrics proved to be banal, derivative, a random imitation of the type of song in which someone cites all his ultimate memories for romantic emphasis. As a conductor, Jackie didn't stay too far off the beat."

Jackie had brought back Ralph, Reggie and Joe the Bartender for a variety special called *The Big Sell,* the nominal theme of which was a spoof of American salesmanship, from Coney Island barkers to Madison Avenue image makers. He had begun developing a game show, *You're in the Picture,* which would air in January 1961 and quickly metamorphose into a talk show, thus fulfilling in one (albeit short-lived) vehicle both of his enduring wishes for an easier approach to television. He had cajoled CBS into accepting his concept for an original drama, a kind of unconscious parody of O. Henry's short story "The Ransom of Red Chief," in which Gleason at the height of his mid-fifties popularity would be kidnapped, and network executives would coarsely debate whether it was worth paying the money to save his life; he, meanwhile, would make himself so odious that his captors would ponder just dumping him, before finally being paid off in an ingenious trap of Jackie's devising. (The actual making of the show would be deferred until months after Gleason left Broadway.)

Gleason claimed to Kay Gardella to be at work on *Go on Red,* his longpromised but never completed (or started?) nonfiction book about television, and *Brother Miracle,* a melodrama about a novice monk with psychic powers, blending the religion he was born into with the spiritualism he had found for himself. He also said he would be producing a sports stunt show, a forerunner of the trash sports phenomenon that has persisted unabated from the seventies into the nineties, and another show about people who had overcome physical handicaps. None of these materialized. But then, even the most fertile producers suffer the occasional barren harvest.

Most important, Gleason was about to reenter the movies, this time on the big-star terms he had been seeking for decades. Within little more than two years after he left *Take Me Along,* he would complete work on five major Hollywood films. One was a project he conceived and developed himself. A second was a star vehicle in which he played the title character. The other three would give him character roles of varying size but unrelenting emotional intensity; in each case, he might not be the star but he was the emotional crux of the story. His fellow actors in these endeavors would include Anthony Quinn, Steve McQueen, George C. Scott and Paul Newman, and his directors would include Gene Kelly and Robert Rossen. The material would range from sentimental comedy to stark drama and Gleason's persona would range from loser to amiable also-ran to formidable villain. By themselves these five films would constitute an amply accomplished career. Although Gleason would go on making films for another two decades and more, some of them vastly more popular and lucrative, a few of them artistically worthy, for the rest of his life his reputation would rest primarily on the single season of *The Honeymooners* and this two-year burst on the big screen. Indeed, while the rest of the country might think of Gleason as the man who created Ralph Kramden and *The Honeymooners*, for the final third of his life Gleason always defined himself, whenever he felt his standing or judgment was remotely called into question, as the man who created *Gigot*. Nothing he ever did on television would mean so much to him, or express his worldview so satisfyingly, as this story of a fat, unkempt, unsober Saint Francis of the sidewalks. In that year of elation on Broadway, from the moment when the script of *The Hustler* was brought to him backstage at *Take Me Along* to the moment when he won the Tony Award, from the jubilation of breaking ground on his Peekskill Shangri-La to the tender evenings of Honey looking after him in Manhattan, no moment thrilled Gleason more than the moment when he got studio approval to make the movie he had been gleefully envisioning almost shot by shot. "We're going to Paris," he bellowed to his secretary Sydell Spear. "We're going to Paris. We're going to Paris."

He spoke no French. He had no love of travel.

His palate was not delicate for food or brandies or wines. But he was, Spear remembers, "the most like a little boy that I ever, ever saw him." Televison had been the making of him, Broadway the confirmation of his popular appeal. The movie *Gigot* would be Jackie Gleason's message to the world.

CHAPTER NINE

The unmistakable rooftops of Paris, quaint but slightly dowdy in the morning sun. Glimpsed from middle distance, a milkman's horse-drawn cart in the rutted lane behind an outlying square. Next, seen a little closer, an orange cat following the dribble from the milk cans through the scarred turf, then cutting off to scamper into a cul-de-sac, down ramshackle stairs and into the dungeonlike cellar quarters of a very fat, extremely disheveled, thoroughly unshaven man, who awakens to a tender feline licking of his face. Snuffling and stretching, the man arises and tends first to his temporal duty of feeding the animal, then to his spiritual one of kneeling in prayer, before washing, before dressing, before tearing a crust from the battered bread that provides his meal.

That is the opening sequence of *Gigot* as first conceived by Gleason and described to various columnists in the late 1950s. It is also, virtually frame by frame, the opening sequence as achieved in Paris during the nine months of preparation and shooting in 1961 and 1962. Whatever else Gleason may have claimed undue credit for over the years, *Gigot* was, in ambience and flavor and in practically every detail, his and his alone. The influence of Chaplin and his little tramp was evident, to be sure, and so was the impact of the postwar French and Italian cinemas, with their emphasis on the working classes and the streets as the centers of real life. Closer to home, the debt to Coleman Jacoby's Bachelor and Poor Soul was hard to miss, and the film's episodic structure called to mind the loosely related, sketchbook style of a variety show. But any art must come from somewhere. Through a succession of announced or proposed directors, writers and producers, through two years of rumor and worry, the essence of *Gigot* always came from its star.

So many of those jottings on the yellow legal pads had come to nothing. No books. No articles without a ghostwriter's help. A few ideas for sketches in variety, the germs of a couple of television specials made by CBS chiefly as a concession to its biggest and brashest male comedy star. Never, before *Gigot,* a movie—and never afterward, either. If the World's Greatest Entertainer were to sustain his claim of protean talent, this tale would have to serve as his strongest evidence. Like most of the stories and characters Gleason favored, it was at once deeply pessimistic and cynical, in its view of how often cruelty goes unpunished and kindness unrewarded in a hard world, and deeply optimistic and redemptive, in its view of the way that decency and brotherly love can flourish in a few souls despite a hailstorm of rejection.

The title of the piece is French for "leg of mutton," and that is the nickname by which everyone in a rowdy and predatory neighborhood addresses the local version of the village idiot—a mute of surpassingly sweet nature and extremely limited intellect. For Gleason, as for many religious people, there wasn't much moral distinction between the innocence and simplicity of sainthood on the one hand and the innocence and simplicity of child-mindedness on the other. Gigot is set up as a born victim, harassed by urchins, taunted by their parents, cheated of even the few coins he does earn by a double-talking landlady-cum-employer. Ragamuffins pin an ass's tail on him. Men bully him into drinking brandy to the point of blackout. Women scorn him or shy away in fear. Only the cats and dogs adore him, not least because he takes whatever pocket change he has to the butcher or baker to buy treats for them. His only personal pleasure is to attend funerals, whether he knew the deceased or not, and to have a good cry over the harshness of fate.

All of this is sketched in the kind of bright color and emotional distance associated with religious parable. Given the depth of Gleason's spiritual preoccupation, he must have meant the story to serve the same purpose as an apt sermon or reading from Scripture—to get audiences to recognize a direct connection between principles they espoused in the abstract and human beings around them whom they might initially be apt to shun. To emphasize further the purity of Gigot's mind and heart, Gleason has him happen upon a prostitute on a rainy evening and take her home—with no bawdier purpose than giving her and her young daughter a modicum of shelter for the night. The child's presence introduces Gigot to some of the joys of fatherhood; he winks at her, plays parlor games, tears paper in lacework patterns to entertain her. Then he takes her to a public park, pays his last sou to put her on a merry-go-round and, as it speeds up, fearfully chases ever faster around the outer circle to keep her within his protective glance. (This scene involves several pratfalls over gates and other obstacles, which Gleason insisted on performing, unpadded. He was black and blue for days and could easily have sustained an injury that halted filming and imperiled the project. Characteristically, he had envisioned the scene being shot in a fashion that ensured that no double or stunt man could be used and would not hear of any alteration.) While this merriment is going on, the mother resumes her trade. Gigot fights with the first man who picks her up and is about to threaten another when she tells him off and steams away, grabbing the child with her and leaving him to howl silently, like Charles Laughton as the Hunchback of Notre Dame, lacking only the bell tower.

Even a saint may succumb to bad companions.

When Gigot's harlot-houseguest threatens to leave unless he produces some money—taking with her the little girl who has brought laughter to his life—he impulsively seizes on an opportunity to steal from the baker. Still, the moral dice are loaded on his behalf. Not only has the baker been clearly established as a mean-minded cheat, but even in his moment of theft Gigot cannot break himself of the habit of honesty. Along with the sack of money he grabs a few broken cookies and automatically leaves the usual steep payment for them on the counter. Like all fools, he is soon parted from his money—buying clothes for the mother and child, champagne for the neighborhood wastrels in the bar and only a decent meal for himself. He dances with the child, then looks out through the window to see that even in the middle of this feast the mother has embraced another man, so he sobs anew at this reminder that his happy little "family" is a fraud.

While the mother is off catting with an old boyfriend who regularly beats and abuses her, Gigot is taking the child into his secret hideaway, a back room of the cellar where he sometimes plays with a mouse that lives in the wall and emerges when enticed by cheese. Abruptly the ceiling beams give way and the child is knocked unconscious. Gigot carries her to a nearby church, seeking divine intervention to save her. Leaving her with a priest, he returns to his ruined lair to dig out his old gramophone, a toy that used to please the girl and that he hopes may revive her now. As he leaves with the bulky object, he is spotted by an angry, pursuing mob of neighbors; he hitches up one arm from the hip and turns full profile to the other side, in classic "Away We Go" fashion, and then galumphs away.

The ensuing chase is as elaborate and slapstick as any in silent comedy. Gigot upends a sack of potatoes and a cart of fish, over which his posse flounders. He escapes into a riverside mill, ascends a conveyor belt, disappears into a thresher and is presumed dead when his hat is seen floating in the water—while he hovers hidden beneath stairs nearby.

The child slowly recovers. Gigot is eulogized at a funeral, which he cannot resist sneaking into. (Presumably Gleason read at least a synopsis of *Tom Sawyer* sometime.) At the pivotal moment of this florid if insincere tribute, dogs sniff Gigot out, bark to herald his attendance, call him to the notice of everyone else—and he bolts and runs anew, as the credits roll with his erstwhile mourners still in hot pursuit.

Gleason never explained what this narrative meant to him, from what recess of his subconscious it emerged, how it took shape in his conscious mind and why it became such a personal quest. Doubtless he saw a great deal of himself in the well-meaning and misunderstood Gigot. Both were figures isolated from their fellow men despite the substantial difference in their respective saintliness quotients. The fact that Gigot has what amounts to a private back-cellar stage and derives his greatest joy from performing for the little girl, an audience of one, surely connects to Gleason's own deep sense of identity with his craft. Jackie must have resonated, too, to the element of turning to the church in a dark hour. During a turbulent time in his life he went to Mass in Beverly Hills with Jack Haley. As they crossed the threshold, Gleason said to his friend, "Do you feel the place rockin'?" At another troubled juncture he asked Flo Haley to pray for him, to which she replied, "Oh, so you *do* believe in something? Well, pray for yourself." But in all probability, Gleason liked *Gigot* best for the ways in which it was *not* like him. Faced with far worse poverty for a far longer period of life, enduring far harsher treatment and living with a disabling handicap, the title character in *Gigot* seems to feel none of the obsessive anger that beset Gleason, only a benign forgiveness. For Gleason, *Gigot* may have been a redemptive fantasy, an opportunity at least on camera to inhabit a more truly Christian soul and thus to know what unhesitating, unskeptical faith would be like.

On a more pragmatic level, friends joked that Gleason wanted to play a mute because it would free him of having to memorize lines and thus allow him to roister more freely on and off the set. Jackie plainly believed the film would be both commercially lucrative and a career gilder. Although it is considered unspeakably bad form in

Hollywood to predict that one's work may win an Academy Award, Gleason said repeatedly to friends and even in interviews that he anticipated that this film would win him "a big award" or even, flat-out, "one of those Oscars." Indeed, he thought it might bring him credit for several, because he would be cited on screen for contributions to the original story and the score and would be generally acknowledged to have wielded complete creative control, no matter who was nominal director or producer.

Studios were not so confident about the project. It took Gleason at least two years and repeated tries to get a commitment from Seven Arts as producing company and Twentieth Century-Fox as distributor. Time and again Jackie committed himself to would-be colleagues who proved unacceptable to studios or incompatible with his vision of the film. At one stage he solemnly assured columnists that in all the world only two people were remotely right for the project, Orson Welles as director and Paddy Chayefsky as scenarist. But Welles, famed for excesses of temperament and expenditure that made Gleason's conduct seem monastic, could not pass muster with the number-crunchers. And Chayefsky wanted to transplant the story from Paris to Brooklyn and from the horse-and-buggy era to his own day, which Gleason thought would wrongly jolt the fantasy into bleaker truth. He was interested in metaphysics, not sociology. At another point Jose Ferrer became the director of record; for a time it was William Wyler; even the name of Fred Zinnemann, an action specialist and an unlikely choice, was floated in print. A similar variety of writers was rumored. Ultimately the screenplay job went to John Patrick, playwright of *The Teahouse of the August Moon,* in which he had demonstrated his skills at tragicomedy and delicate cross-cultural musing. Gleason, however, continued to insist to subordinates that Patrick did little more than "check The Great One's spelling"; it was always difficult for Gleason to admit that a writer made any significant contribution, and on this highly personal project it proved next to impossible for him to accept a need for help. The ultimate director was, oddly, Gene Kelly, presumably because of his Oscar-winning work in *An American in Paris,* which Kelly choreographed and performed in. But Kelly's genial, nice-guy humor had almost no point of connection to Gleason's plot, with its rituals of cruelty and submission, and the schmaltzy, romantic center city of *American* in no way echoed the *Gigot* Paris of rotting suburbs, petty merchants, peasant mores and stark survival. By the time Kelly came on board, however, Gleason was for once prepared to tolerate compromise. He wanted, and in career terms needed, to get this movie made. Besides, Kelly met two of Gleason's absolute requirements: he was a "top man" in his own field of dance and he was a "pal" by proxy, having made *On the Town* in 1949 with Jackie's old chum Frank Sinatra.

The mood on the set was unusually festive for a Gleason production. Jackie mingled with the cast and crew far more than he ever had during his days on television, and he partied night after night in Paris. Numerous celebrities dropped by, including Milton Berle who, for reasons even he has forgotten, brought a fifty-pound sack of beans that he shouldered in and dropped in front of The Great One. Although Gleason made no effort to learn any French, he delighted in communicating by grimace and gesture, claiming exuberantly to his secretary Sydell Spear and to other colleagues that he could get across any notion he wished. As far as Spear could see, it was true. This may have been typical Gleason bravado, but it was also a valuable acting exercise. He was, after all, playing a character who was mute and "spoke" only through facial expression and movement. Scornful as he always was of the Method and other acting techniques, Gleason in this instance followed the most basic Method precept—finding a correlation between moments in his own life and the life of Gigot. The bond between Gleason and Kelly survived inevitable clashes of ego and even a Kelly-imposed exercise regimen for the leading man (Jackie ran up and down flights of stairs, huffing and puffing, and tacked up a dressing room sign saying, "Gene Kelly is always right"). Jackie, astonishingly, also forgave Kelly's scheduled departure for another project before finishing the crucial editing of the film. As a result, the final cut, the selection of scenes and pacing, rested entirely with the studio. Jackie grumbled publicly that the result was not as good as it could have been, although without giving any specific reasons why. But he never criticized Kelly.

The quality of Gigot remains a matter of dispute among Gleason's allies and admirers. Some regard it as genuinely of Chaplinesque scale and delicacy. Others view it as embarrassingly bathetic. Coleman Jacoby, who created the Bachelor character from which Gigot derived, particularly detested the film and told Gleason so. "It's not comedy, Jackie, it's mental retardation," he said in a conversation that chilled the relationship more than Jacoby's threatened lawsuit over rights and royalties ever had. Estelle Parsons, who joined Gleason some years later in the film of Woody Allen's *Don't Drink the Water*, found herself forced by her plump and preening co-star to sit through a screening of *Gigot*. "I don't remember it very well," she says, "because I was drinking rather heavily at the time. But I remember having to say how wonderful it all was, and I remember thinking that really it was pretty one-note." Hollywood, in general, certainly didn't share Gleason's awe at his achievement. In the highly competitive year of *Lawrence of Arabia*, *To Kill a Mockingbird*, *The Music Man*, *Bird Man of Alcatraz*, *The Miracle Worker*, *The Days of Wine and Roses*, *The Longest Day*, *Divorce—Italian Style*, *Sweet Bird of Youth*, *Long Day's Journey into Night*, *The Manchurian Candidate*, *Lolita* and the

Marlon Brando remake of *Mutiny on the Bounty*—not to mention *Whatever Happened to Baby Jane?*—*Gigot* was passed over completely in the major Oscar nominations. That wasn't surprising. The film had mixed reviews, it was less than a smash at the box office, it came out in one of the finest postwar years of American film-making—and, of course, it had been made in Paris, employing an almost entirely French cast and crew, so in jobs-conscious Los Angeles it stirred a special resentment. *Gigot* did draw one secondary nomination, for its adapted score, but even that served as a subtle slap at Jackie. Despite his claim of having composed the theme music, the nomination did not mention Gleason, only Michael Magne.

From today's perspective, *Gigot* is neither the unsullied masterpiece that Gleason thought he had created nor the maudlin muck that its contemporaries often dismissed it as. In the attempt to pay homage to the great silent clowns, Gleason adopted, consciously or not, many of the structural flaws of early film comedies. The story is fragmentary rather than cumulative; the tone wobbles; the action frequently lapses into mere bits and routines, without the attention-grabbing authority of conflict driving toward resolution. The star performance, while mostly natural and touching, has moments of self-consciousness, even calculation, that might be permissible in other kinds of movies but that are ruinous in a tearjerker. The ending is a deliberate nonending, with Gigot's fate and future left willfully unresolved. That may be realistic; few people with his handicaps, living in his time and place, would wind up happy. But for audiences, seeing this sad, sweet man left alone and in flight from pursuers is the exact opposite of a payoff and probably contributed to the film's mediocre word of mouth and box office results. With all that said, *Gigot* remains an extraordinary first film from an auteur of great promise, one who would likely have gone on to make far more surefooted comedies of equal originality and daring. The film's failings are those of detail—of timing and taste and technique. Its strengths are the central ones of ambition and passion. No wonder Gleason cherished the film to the end of his days and cited it as, in his mind, the knockout blow in any battle over his judgment in artistic matters. Perhaps the greatest artistic tragedy of his life is that in the quarter century remaining to him he never again made a film in which he originated the material, controlled the circumstances of production and significantly contributed to shaping the final outcome. Admittedly, he might not have grown from movie to movie. On television he was to display a confining reliance on the familiar. But Gigot was the debut of Gleason the artist, not merely the performer or entertainer. It was also very nearly the swan song of that Gleason. Although he had two dozen working years ahead of him, only in the next two or three of them would serious people be looking for evidence of true greatness in The Great One.

Before Gleason could get to Paris to make *Gigot*, shooting on another film intervened. For years Jackie had promised himself that his triumphal return to the wide screen would be in a vehicle of his own devising. But he had reckoned without the ingenuity of a producer, director and screenwriter named Robert Rossen, whose distinguished work included the Oscar-winning adaptation of Robert Penn Warren's Pulitzer Prize novel *All The King's Men*. Rossen had a role to offer in a new picture, one he expected to serve as the capstone of his career, for which his first and only choice was Jackie Gleason. The part was not especially big. It was not particularly sympathetic. It would not pay well, because the whole film was being made on a very modest budget. The only pluses were that it was vivid, that the scenes were concentrated at the beginning and end of the film, when the audience forms its most lasting impressions, and—by far the crucial selling point to Jackie—that the character made his living playing pool. Of all the things Gleason was vain about, his skill with the cue stick was what he vaunted most. He would eventually own dozens of custom-made cues and in every house he built he would center a room, usually the largest, around his table. To play a poolroom shark would allow him to revisit the first success of his youth and would exhibit the undiminished prowess of his middle age. Besides, however edgy Gleason might be about film acting, he had absolute confidence that he understood the psychology of a pool hall warrior.

Rossen sent the script through intermediaries and negotiations stretched on awhile, with Gleason eventually extracting a stiff penalty clause for long shooting days as well as the more usual one for extra weeks. These provisos, according to Gleason spokesman Pete McGovern, ultimately more than tripled Gleason's salary. But on this as on other matters, McGovern may have been misinformed by Jackie himself. Gleason, with his characteristic taste for the dramatic if imaginary scene, had Rossen delivering the script in person to Jackie's dressing room at the Shubert Theatre during the Broadway run of *Take Me Along*. When the producer started to depart after the exchange of the script and a few pleasantries, Gleason claimed to McGovern, the fat actor imperiously told him to wait; Jackie would look over the scenes during the show, in his few minutes offstage and the fifteen minutes of intermission, and would render an answer on the spot. Did this happen? Rossen said not, and he had no reason to suppress—indeed, every reason to promote—such a colorful tale if it were true. Despite Jackie's description of this moment, it probably didn't happen so neatly. He probably did receive the script backstage. But given the physical demands on Gleason during the actual performance of *Take Me Along* and the psychological seriousness of committing to his first film in more than a decade, it was both emotionally and logistically unfeasible for even so impulsive a man to have reached a decision so fast.

However arrived at, Jackie's choice was the right one. In the judgment of most critics, *The Hustler* was the finest film he ever participated in and featured his finest performance on the big screen. His character, Minnesota Fats, was yet another in Gleason's gallery of life's losers, but this version had several subtleties. Fats was meant to be a genius at his game, technically adept, nerveless and physically inexhaustible despite his overburdened frame. His vulnerability, a love of gambling leading to a fistful of unpayable debts, was to be revealed only slowly, so that Gleason could not hope to enlist the audience's sympathy until the film was nearly over. The emotional residue that the character should leave was chill ferocity, not poignancy; he should arouse fear more than compassion. Most actors, especially established stars, resist playing this kind of role. They know that what truly distinguishes them is not talent but likability, that what brings in the big checks and the above-the-title billing is the audience's affection. Gleason, however, had a taste for distasteful characters. He didn't often opt for outright villains—who can solicit audience affection in another way, as characters one loves to hate—but instead repeatedly took on no-larger-than-life characters who were petty, crude, selfish and mean. Whether he was playing a loathsome comic in the television dramas *The Laugh-maker* and *The Million Dollar Incident* or, later, repulsive financiers in *Mr. Billion* and *The Toy* or an odious sheriff in the *Smokey and the Bandit* trilogy, Gleason delighted in detestability. It was as though he was exploring the outer limits of his public appeal, seeing just how ugly his character's behavior could be without alienating his fans.

The pool shark of the film's title was played by Paul Newman, who in the opening scenes is working himself up to a big-money match with Fats, the greatest player in the game. But the term *hustler* also expressed the mentality of all the players in a craft that, like show business, requires both talent and psychological maneuver. The confrontation was shot in an actual New York poolroom, and Gleason's character was based on an actual player known as New York Fats—at least until the release of the movie, when the man changed his nom de cue to Minnesota Fats. At the outset of this first big scene, almost everything goes Newman's way. Racking and breaking long into the night, he climbs tens of thousands of dollars ahead. Then, in the epiphany for which Gleason won his only Oscar nomination, as best supporting actor for 1961, Fats pauses to pull himself together. He splashes water on his face, rinses his hands, pats himself down, and steps out, as fresh as a new day, with the simple words of challenge "Let's shoot some pool." He proceeds to pick Newman clean, then leave in triumph, a model of the maxim that age and cunning will always win over youth and strength.

He does not reappear until the film's climactic confrontation, when Newman, avenging the death of a woman he loved, returns to the same poolroom to challenge Gleason anew. This time Newman wins. The real victory is not over Gleason, whom by now the audience sees as merely a skilled pawn, but instead over George C. Scott, the gaming tycoon who at various points has financed, and dominated, both men. Fats has become a figure of pity. Having seen in detail the Newman character's humiliating submission, the audience can guess at Gleason's. The movie is a metaphor that Rossen, Gleason, Newman and even Scott must have appreciated. It argues that everywhere in the world, no matter how much the artists may seem to be succeeding, real power always resides with the money men, whimsical and philistine.

Apart from his acting, *The Hustler* demanded of Gleason his considerable skills with the pool cue. Willie Mosconi, the world champion of the sport, served the film as a technical adviser and is credited in reference volumes with having supplied the trick shooting. But Gleason insisted ever after that he did all his own cue work for the film and also asserted that he, rather than Mosconi, taught Newman how to fake expertise with the stick. In fact, Gleason claimed to have won an elaborate bet from Newman involving a supposedly unmakable shot—and according to Jackie, Newman paid off with fifty dollars in pennies, unrolled and poured onto the floor.

The Hustler was released in September 1961 and promptly brought Jackie unstinting critical acclaim. Bosley Crowther of the *New York Times*, who had never even deigned to notice Gleason's prior film performances, called him "excellent—more so than you first realize—as a cool, self-collected pool expert who has gone into bondage to the gambling man. His deceptively casual behavior in that titanic initial game conceals a pathetic robot that you only later perceive." The movie was still circulating widely three months later when it brought Jackie the ultimate media accolade of the era, a cover story in *Time* magazine. Writer John McPhee, later a New Yorker essayist and best-selling author, began with a description of the first pool match with Newman, which he deemed unforgettable. McPhee said the performance demonstrated that "inside the master jester, there is a masterful actor." Gleason, he said, was "emerging as a first-rank star of motion pictures." The story mentioned *Gigot,* then some nine months away from release, and a third drama, *Requiem for a Heavyweight,* which Gleason was at that very moment filming in New York, for release mere weeks after *Gigot* in the fall of 1962.

From Gleason's point of view, the role in *Requiem* had much in common with the part in *The Hustler.* Once again he was cast as a desperate man in debt to gamblers. Once again he was seen perverting talent in pursuit of a quick buck to save his life. The difference was that in *Requiem,* the skills he subverts are not his own but those of the fading prizefighter he manages—and on occasion bets against—played by Anthony Quinn. Unable to relinquish the boxer as a meal ticket even after doctors decide that one more fight might render the man blind, the sleazy manager manipulates his supposed friend into entering the humiliating arena of professional wrestling, where the competition is phony and the emphasis is on the tackiest kind of show business. Bosley Crowther of the *New York Times,* who had reverted to disdaining Gleason when it came to the "ponderous, maundering and soggy" *Gigot,* viewed his depiction of manager Maish Rennick as "brilliantly underplayed."

Making *Requiem* was not a particularly pleasant experience, and it seems to have put into Jackie's mind, for the first time since he crowed about California in the forties, the serious notion of moving away from New York. He found Manhattan in winter nowhere near as enticing as Paris in autumn. Gymnasiums, where many of the indoor scenes of *Requiem* were shot, had none of the happy personal associations for him that the pool halls of *The Hustler* did. Everywhere he went seemed to be wet, dark and cold.

He and co-star Quinn got along after a fashion, sharing a taste for various kinds of ethnic food and a resentment at the power brokers in Hollywood. But they clashed on acting technique. Quinn, a committed Method man, liked to spend half an hour or so before a big scene getting into character. Jackie dismissed this approach as "marinating." As ever, his philosophy was to do the scene with total concentration once the camera started rolling but to attempt almost no preparation beforehand. He generally got the moment right nonetheless, and almost always on the first take.

This approach made Jackie almost undirectable, as many a noted filmmaker would discover. He was sometimes superb, sometimes embarrassing, rarely anything in between. After he performed his version of a scene, he would listen politely to suggested alternatives from a producer or director. He would say, "Right, pal. Got it, pal." And then he would perform the scene exactly the way he had before. Or, if he changed anything, it would be in some manner altogether different from what the director had requested. The only real way to manage Gleason as an actor was to cast him correctly—not, as is usually the case with actors who must be carefully cast, because he was so limited, but simply because he was so willful.

Gleason would make two more films before returning full-time to television. In *Papa's Delicate Condition* he portrays a drunken, doting father in turn-of-the-century Texas who had been affectionately recalled in his real-life daughter's memoir of childhood. Gleason's director, George Marshall, and producer-screenwriter Jack Rose said they viewed Jackie's sad-eyed performance as Oscar-worthy, but no one else did. The character was, or became at Jackie's urging, a variant of Aubrey Piper in his favorite play, *The Show-Off* a foul-up who can do nothing right but who is so transparently loving and emotionally needy that all is forgiven. In the narrative's high (or low) point, Papa buys an entire circus, with money he doesn't have, just to obtain for his beloved daughter a pony that she momentarily fancies. At another point, he sings to a dressmaker's dummy. He paints his house purple to annoy an obnoxious neighbor. He embarrasses his wife and her stuffy politician father. Through it all he abuses alcohol in a way that Gleason meant audiences to see as cute or endearing but that now looks (and should have looked then) both pathetic and destructive. Naturally Jackie thought a drunken father was, or at least could be, the best kind. He had been one. But he should have known better, because he had also had one.

The other film, released in November 1963, about eight months after *Papa,* was called *Soldier in the Rain.* A thoughtful melodrama, it features a half-wit rather in the fashion of *Gigot* and, arguably, Papa, but this time that was not Gleason's role. Instead, as in *Requiem,* he was the half-wit's keeper. The setting was an army training base and Gleason was the gruff, savvy and, underneath it all, kind master sergeant, looking after a hapless hick portrayed by Steve McQueen. Gleason got to flirt with Tuesday Weld, duke it out with a couple of MPs to protect his friend, muse aloud about retiring to a tropical island and gently die on screen—all in all, an actor's dream gallery of attitudes. Bosley Crowther, pretty much as ever, hated Jackie's performance, but most critics admired it. The movie wasn't nearly good enough to contend for Oscars, and Jackie didn't have a serious chance at a personal nomination in a year when those chosen for best actor included almost nothing but major stars, mostly in career-best performances—Alben Finney in *Tom Jones,* Paul Newman in *Hud,* Richard Harris in *This Sporting Life,* Rex Harrison in *Cleopatra* and the winner, Sidney Poitier in *Lilies of the Field.* Once again, the only faint sop to Gleason came in the music categories, where "Call Me Irresponsible" from *Papa's Delicate Condition* won best song.

As a real-life papa, Gleason found his responsibilities winding down even as his long-term negligence became ever more public. His older daughter, Geraldine, was finishing college, and Linda was on her way. But after years of being kept carefully away from the destructive effects of the limelight—Gleason's wisest and kindest move as a father—Geraldine went public with a bang in October 1960. She gave an as-told-to interview to *Good Housekeeping,* which was also widely syndicated to newspapers, that was plainly meant to be affectionate and forgiving but that wound up being hurtful. Friends say that Jackie was thunderstruck by its assertions and that Geraldine in turn was appalled at how supportive conversation was recast as criticism. The family, once burned and twice shy, refused to be interviewed for the *Time* cover a few weeks later, even knowing that Jackie was cooperating fully with that story. They also have avoided the press almost entirely ever since, including declining, through family attorney Richard Green and business manager Jack Philbin, to be interviewed for this book.

The basic point that emerged from the headlines about Geraldine's piece was Gleason's longtime paternal absenteeism. *The New York Journal-American* billed its opening installment of the syndication "My Father Is a Stranger." Within the context of the interview, it was clear that Geraldine really meant to convey above all the sense of distance felt by almost every child of a famous person, between the public figure glimpsed on a television screen and the parent who tucks a toddler into bed. But of course there were darker truths as well. One telling sentence read, "I don't remember his being around the house much." The same idea was repeated in later installments. Another passage described Gleason as a compulsive eavesdropper who had listened in to neighbors' conversations on the telephone party line and eventually rigged up a primitive wiretap so he could overhear other people's talk for hours without detection. The article offered no serious analysis of why he wanted to do this—whether he was amassing material about human nature, working out a deep loneliness, trying to find out what other personalities were like in true privacy or simply, as he phrased it to his daughter, "enjoying other people's ulcers."

Geraldine was a further source of unintended pain to her parents when she married in September 1961. In reporting on the event—held at her mother's parish church, St. Paul the Apostle, and the Waldorf-Astoria and attended by twelve hundred people at a cost of almost twenty-five thousand dollars—the *New York Daily News* told millions of the city's residents, in a story picked up nationwide, that the senior Gleasons had "reconciled." The truth was that Jackie and Gen had buried the hatchet long enough for him to fly back from the making of *Gigot,* give his daughter away, and dance one waltz around the Waldorf's Empire Room with the bride's proud mother. In the *Daily News* version of events, Jackie and Gen had negotiated a full reconciliation with the help of their old friend Bishop Fulton J. Sheen—a neat trick, given that Gleason was living in Paris, filming full-time and residing with his mistress Honey Merrill—and the reunited pair supposedly had gone off after the wedding for "an intimate dinner to observe the occasion of double joy." Accosted by a *News* hound, Genevieve declined comment, saying tearfully, "Please, my private life is my own affair." Jackie ducked reporters. But the *Daily News* confidently went with its story. Had it been true, both husband and wife would have hated having the whole world watch their trial reunion. Because it was false, it only spoiled what should have been a reassuringly amicable day for the whole clan.

Genevieve apparently raised no objections to the lavish scale of the wedding, although Pete McGovern says that she and Jackie still fought frequently over his presents to his daughters. She felt that he was buying their favor and that any indulgences to them should come through her, as custodial parent. Once, McGovern remembers, Gleason got so angry that he abruptly stood up and knocked his heavy armchair to the floor while still on the phone, shouting. The cause of the dispute was a couple of hundred dollars' worth of Easter hats, which Gen thought unsuitably grand. "In Brooklyn," Jackie roared, "we had three forks and three cans of beans and that was it. If I want my daughters to have better and I can pay for it, I will."

Geraldine married John Chutuk, a budding show business executive who is now a personal manager for actors, including Burgess Meredith. Although Meredith has no recollections of making a movie with Gleason (Otto Preminger's dire *Skidoo* in 1968), he recalls meeting Jackie at the Chutuk household for a few quiet evenings, which he describes as offering "great warmth but not much conversation." His most vivid memories, however, are of hearing the Chutuks remark in Gleason's absence about how little they saw of him and how much they wished he would visit. Despite the sad Gleason marital history for at least two previous generations, Geraldine's union has endured more than thirty years. Linda was married a couple of years later, without Jackie's benevolent approval, to actor-dramatist Jason Miller. For a while Jackie so disapproved of the union that he barely spoke to them. But father and daughter grew closer, especially after Linda and Jason were divorced in the mid-seventies, a split that Miller attributed to his wife's discomfort with his success, as a film actor in *The Exorcist* and as the Pulitzer Prize–winning playwright of *That Championship Season*. Having grown up in the shadow of one famous man, Miller said, Linda was unwilling to live in the shadow of another. One measure of Jackie's distance from his younger daughter is that when Linda Redfield—the widow of actor William Redfield, with whom Gleason made a movie— would occasionally call to say hello, he invariably and gushingly mistook her for his daughter Linda. Mrs. Redfield does not know if their voices sound much alike. But it is surely unusual for a man not to recognize the vocal tones of his own daughter.

Almost everyone has a vision of the dream house he or she might build, if only money and other practicalities did not get in the way. By the time of *Take Me Along* and the lucrative relaunching of Gleason's movie career, money was certainly no obstacle to any of his wishes. And he had never, even in debt and despair, let practicality get in his way. So he bought a piece of land in Peekskill, north of the bustle of Manhattan, and started to invent yet another identity for himself: Jackie Gleason, country squire. The land he acquired—just how much is unclear, with Gleason himself having described it as any number of acres from ten to twenty—seemed more than sufficiently beautiful. It came with a comfortable old farmhouse, suitably nestled on the site and appropriate to the area. But for Jackie it was, predictably, just too ordinary. He didn't tear it down—that was too profligate even for him—but he decided to install a new and distinctive structure at a much more prominent site on the property. Its odd quality virtually shouted the eccentric traits of its author.

The house was described as round, and was, more or less, although both inside and out it consisted more of intersecting curves. There was scarcely a right angle to be found. This made it extremely difficult to build. Jackie compounded the construction difficulties by specifying such materials as marble (for which workmen had to be brought over from Italy) and ship's timbers (which had to be soaked for months to be bent along the requisite arcs). The place prompted many wisecracks, the most frequent being that it was a bar with a bedroom attached. In fact, by Gleason's count there were twelve bars in the house and, sure enough, only one sleeping space. The house was meant to accommodate parties but not overnight guests. Elaborate wiring and speaker systems connected the whole space to a state-of-the-art audio system, including enough turntables that Gleason could line up his choice of records and then go on a two-day drunk before he would have to touch another album. Predictably, Jackie paid almost no attention to pragmatic concerns like waterproofing and drainage but lavished attention on the installation of technological whizbangery, including a lighting system that could make the hillside blaze like Times Square. Even as a party house, the place had one shortcoming: its host, who was growing ever more reclusive. He exhibited the place a lot when it was first finished, especially to the press; he even invited *Life,* with whom he was feuding, because, as he explained to Pete McGovern, "We want to reach the most people, and they have the readers." CBS program executive Oscar Katz was invited during this opening round of hospitality to Sunday afternoon cocktails for fewer than a dozen people. What he remembers most vividly was the arrival of two local officials who walked around wide-eyed, then asked each other sotto voce what assessment they had given the place on the property tax rolls. "Jackie thought he was currying favor," Katz says, "and instead he was just costing himself money." Although Katz continued to work with Gleason for years and was later offered a job running his production company, he was never asked back to Peekskill. Other Gleason colleagues were never invited at all. Even Jackie himself stopped going after a while. He was too busy. The house was too far from the city. It wasn't located right on a golf course, and golf had become his outdoor obsession. Above all, he had built it to show off, and the excitement of that had worn off. He was left with a house that had cost him anywhere from six hundred fifty thousand dollars to twice as much, and that simply wasn't very comfortable.

Throughout the period of *Take Me Along* and the movies, for nearly four years, Gleason steadfastly avoided returning to the grind of weekly television. CBS, which had not been very interested in him when he halted his half hour with Buddy Hackett at the beginning of 1959, grew avid as he piled success upon success in other media. Technically Jackie remained an employee of CBS. He was still being paid one hundred thousand dollars a year not to appear on any other network. But he and the network remained deadlocked about what kind of show could actually restore him to CBS air time. The brass, from Paley and Stanton on down, wanted Gleason in a variety show. They regarded that as an essential format to have on the schedule, and it was what he had done so well before. Gleason, on the other hand, saw his future as being in films and wanted his television ventures to be less time-consuming and creatively demanding. Over and over, he brought to meetings his proposals for game shows and talk shows. Over and over, Katz and the CBS team turned him down. For one thing, they were convinced that Gleason seriously underestimated what it took to succeed in either format. They felt he would not do his homework, would not accept any scripted material, and would not only wear thin but erode the public's fondness for his persona in comedy and variety, nullifying his usefulness for the longer term. Their resistance was based, deep down, on their own exhaustion at dealing with Gleason's quirks and tantrums, his arrogance and unpredictability. They no longer liked Jackie very much, and they believed that if his true personality became known the general public would not like him either. They also didn't think he had very much to say, or at least not much they would like to hear said. He was opinionated but not particularly informed. And he was potentially much too volatile and controversial for the bland entertainment standards of the time.

Eventually, however, Jackie got the better of the executives, the suits. Appearing Friday nights at nine-thirty on the fall 1960 network schedule was a new and not very popular series, *Mr. Garlund,* about a tycoon of uncertain origins. According to Oscar Katz, Jackie and the executive producer of a proposed game show, Steve Carlin, went directly to the sponsors of the series and suggested it be dropped in favor of a Gleason vehicle to be called *You're in the Picture*. The sponsors and their ad agencies were eager to make the change and CBS could offer no sound reason for continuing with *Mr. Garlund,* which was both low-rated and lousy. So, faced with a fait accompli, Katz and company agreed to put *You're in the Picture* in its place. The show's concept, such as it was, derived from an old-fashioned attraction at Coney Island and other amusement parks in which customers would poke their heads and hands through holes of a photographic backdrop depicting cowboys or bathing beauties or whatever and be snapped—creating a sort of instant travel memento without the trip. For the TV version, celebrity guests would poke their heads into pictures they could not see and would have to guess, based on hints and wisecracks from Gleason, just what sort of picture they were in. As a game show this concept had two monumental shortcomings. First, there was no real competition. That may have seemed a godsend in the still-pungent aftermath of the quiz show scandals just a couple of years before, but it eliminated almost all dramatic tension. The celebrities could never know before Gleason did, and he would remain in almost total control of just how fast they could guess correctly. Even worse, there was no way for the viewing audience to play along, except perhaps by keeping its eyes shut the entire time and just listening, like the celebrities, to Jackie's wisecracks. If the viewer has to keep his eyes shut, he might as well listen to the radio.

In after years, Gleason's version of events was that network executives had urged the show on him and told him it was the funniest thing they had ever seen, but they had all been wrong and so he had deluded himself. Katz and Mike Dann, who were running programming at CBS, and Frank Stanton, who was president of the parent company, say that the executives knew perfectly well prior to air time that the show was terrible, but they had nothing to gain from announcing their feelings to the star, the producer or the two hundred or so CBS affiliate stations, who were instead solemnly assured of a hit in the making.

Once *You're in the Picture* actually debuted on January 20, 1961, however, nobody had the slightest doubt that it was a stinker. Critics hooted. The public howled. Katz summoned Carlin and suggested massive changes in format, which the producer conceded were probably necessary but which he felt personally unable to accept. By midweek there was no producer, hence no show, and only a single episode left to be aired—if CBS could stand the further embarrassment. Then Jackie showed up unannounced and proposed a classic Gleason go-for-broke gesture.

He arrived at Oscar Katz's office already in his cups and accompanied by his own managers, people from the production company and representatives of the sponsors and their advertising agencies. Bellowing that what he had in mind was something he doubted Katz would have the authority to approve, he demanded, "Where's the football player?" This was Gleason's not so-friendly nickname for James Aubrey, then the president of the network and a former All-American at Princeton. Katz mollifyingly explained that Aubrey could not be summoned on such short notice, particularly not at that hour; he was at the weekly meeting of the company's editorial board, along with Paley and Stanton and the top executives of the news division, to discuss issues of national politics and foreign policy and how CBS should cover them. But, Katz added, of course he himself would be honored to hear and if possible put into effect whatever Jackie proposed.

Gleason's idea was, in short, an apology to the American people. He would explain how easy it was to be misled in show business, how in his own career Broadway shows that had seemed to be in big trouble out of town turned into hits, while others that seemed headed for standing room only somehow flopped within a week or two. He would recall some of his own prior failings and mention other legendary entertainment goofs. As Gleason laid out this chat, with charm and humor, it seemed to Katz a burst of inspiration. He accepted Jackie's argument that approval was vital immediately so as to make the deadline for the last edition of the evening newspapers, telling people that the turkey had been plucked from the next evening's schedule and would be replaced by this delicacy of wit.

Jackie's self-condemnation was an immense hit. Critics hailed its easy manner, its candor, its barrage of one-liners. The public warmed to the idea of a big star eating crow. "Honesty is the best policy," Jackie told his listeners. "We had a show last week that laid the biggest bomb. I've seen bombs in my day, but this one made the H-bomb look like a two-inch salute." He had the crew haul on a piece of scenery from the previous week's show and cracked, "Notice the stagehands have their backs to the audience. Even they don't want to be associated with this thing." After the first telecast, he said, he returned to his hotel, opened the window to see if it was snowing and found that the firemen had the nets out below in case he decided to jump. He ended by promising to return next week. "I don't know what we'll do," he said, "but I'll be back."

Others may have been amused, but Oscar Katz watched with mounting dismay. He realized that he had been had. Jackie had promised to say that the game show was fixable and would return in a few weeks. Instead he had buried the corpse forever. There was no way now for CBS to bring the show back, in any form and by any name. That meant that at least one already filmed episode, which Katz had expected to slip in unnoticed in six or eight weeks after the return, would now have to be junked without ever airing. Worse, Gleason had promised in public to be back next week. There was no workable way for him to do so that fast, except in the talk show format that CBS had been so assiduously avoiding. Short of calling one of its biggest starts a liar in public, the network was going to have to let him keep his pledge to return.

The next day, it turned out that things were

even worse than Katz thought. Gleason had appeared on the apology program holding a coffee cup which he had refilled periodically with a fluid that he strongly hinted was not coffee. One of the show's two sponsors was irate at being publicly linked to the apparent consumption of alcohol, and short of a further public apology from Gleason on this matter—which was assuredly not forthcoming—the company would not sponsor any subsequent installments of the chat to be known as *The Jackie Gleason Show*. When CBS threatened court action to enforce a signed sponsorship contract, the corporation in question—Katz says he is unsure of its identity at this remove—replied that it would countersue if its name were so much as mentioned in association with this heinous, antifamily, booze-promoting show.

During the next eight weeks, Gleason's guests would include Art Carney, Jayne Mansfield, Bobby Darin, Mickey Rooney and a chimpanzee. But always the focus was Jackie. Mike Dann recalls it as "the least successful thing Jackie ever did, because it depended on displaying the real Jackie Gleason, and there was no real Jackie Gleason, except perhaps for the belligerent depressive who emerged when he was drunk." Katz, characteristically, is a little kinder, and so were some of the critics. But no one except Jackie thought the show was a smash, and the network jettisoned it as soon as it could. The episode seems to have muted Gleason's drive to become a pure personality rather than a performer, although he remained an avid lifelong watcher of talk shows and a willing and frequent guest. In his later years, talk on TV or radio was almost the only programming he enjoyed. He professed distaste for most dramas as too violent and most comedies as too vulgar, but he never shied away from any topic if discussed in real-life terms. His puritanism was limited to art.

According to Katz, the total losses from the apology episode—including the unaired game show installment, the lost advertising and other costs—amounted to half a million dollars at a time when that was a substantial portion of prime-time profits. Aubrey reassuringly told Katz, "It was worth it. You got him out of your system." He had no use for displays of star vanity and felt Katz had catered too much to a probable has-been, not worth the trouble. His tune would change once Jackie's movies began to debut.

Jackie's impulsive, provocative ways caused Katz another big headache in April, a month after the talk show wound down. *The Million Dollar Incident,* Jackie's original drama about an imaginary kidnapping of him at the height of his network fame in the mid-fifties, was two days away from airing when former manager Bullets Durgom obtained a court injunction prohibiting the show from being broadcast. Durgom, still squabbling with Gleason over money and over the erosion of what had been an intense friendship, claimed that the appearance of a character based on him and bearing his name held him up to public ridicule. He had never signed, nor had Gleason sought, a release to permit that his identity be used in the drama. CBS, facing what it described to newspapers as a potential five-hundred-thousand-dollar loss if it canceled the show, compromised by bleeping out Durgom's name wherever it appeared, and the injunction was lifted. The solution did not satisfy Durgom, who insisted that the character was still recognizable and still constituted an invasion of his privacy, but the court rejected his arguments. As far as Katz and Mike Dann could tell, Durgom was not trying to extract a payoff, although he may have been. The felt he was motivated by vengeance of plain rage. Gleason, off in Paris making *Gigot*, retaliated by ensuring that a cemetery scene would include a headstone with Durgom's name on it. Lawyers assured him there was nothing Durgom could do to protest that.

The Million Dollar Incident was Gleason's funniest piece of self-impersonation, and very nearly his darkest. In it he portrays himself as hugely resentful of the demands on a star, from meeting "Miss Pizza" to accepting a snake from a Boy Scout troop; through virtually the entire narrative he is either drinking or hung over. He is at once bragging and self-mocking about his high, wide and handsome style of spending. For a promotional trip to Detroit, he announces, he needs an entourage of eighteen, including four secretaries and four stenographers—all blonde—a

Dixieland jazz band and a personal golf pro. The dialogue is snappy, epitomized by the crack "I don't eat the olives. I just used them to keep track of what I drink." (Off camera, this was a favorite Gleasonism, as was a similarly spirited line he voiced to his *Take Me Along* dresser Herb Zane: "New Year's Eve is for amateurs.")

Jackie makes himself as odious to his kidnappers as to his employers, and the bandits very nearly release him without being paid, sure that no one would ever want the irksome presence back. The network executives do stump up, but only after assuring themselves the payment is covered by insurance and is also tax-deductible. Compassion never enters their calculus. Gleason himself devised the kidnappers' clever twist of having the ransom sent back via a dozen homing pigeons and the law enforcers' even cannier response of releasing only eleven, then following the twelfth by helicopter. The ideas may not have been practicable, but they were certainly novel and arresting—and further evidence of Gleason's persistent creativity.

CBS welcomed *The Million Dollar Incident* with only slightly more warmth than it felt for *You're in the Picture.* "We did things with Jackie because he was a big star and we couldn't say no to everything," Mike Dann recalls. "But we knew that anything we agreed to would be expensive and a pain in the ass and above all a major consumer of executive time. Jackie was our Orson Welles. He needed an awful lot of stroking and he was very unpredictable. What we really wanted, of course, was to get him back in a variety series." To this desire, however, Gleason kept saying no, privately and publicly. Typical was the interview he gave the *New York Herald Tribune* television magazine during *Take Me Along.* "The whole thing with TV," Jackie said, "is the material. Without good material, you're dead. So, automatically, weekly TV is out for me at any rate."

At long last, however, his outlook changed. Maybe the trigger was the frustration of the film business, where so many of his projects had brought less honor and lucre than he thought he deserved and where none since *Gigot* had been under his control. After *Soldier in the Rain,* Gleason would not have another film released for five years. Maybe it was the yearning for steady money after his gush of expenditure on the Peekskill house. Film work was profitable but undependable. Maybe it was simply a longing for that old gang of his. Jackie had always reveled in maintaining a giant personal payroll, in operating an industry rather than merely a personal career. Only a weekly television show could give him the wherewithal, or reason, to resume that grander existence, to travel through life like royalty, forever surrounded by minions. Whatever his motives, Gleason came to Oscar Katz one day and said what CBS regarded as the sweetest words in the English language: "I have an idea for a variety show."

Gleason's notion, as yet unnamed, was to

evolve into *The American Scene Magazine.* In the current video age it is almost unimaginably quaint that a television entertainment show thought it would lend itself importance and credibility by purporting to be a print reflection of American life. But Gleason was enchanted with the notion of treating recurring sketch situations as akin to the sections or departments of a magazine—particularly because he could designate the pulchritudinous "Glea Girls" as the "editors," or introducers, of each skit and thus relieve himself of much of the monologue and emcee speaking that he did so badly and with such discomfort.

As soon as he had quickly outlined his idea, Gleason told Katz, "I need twenty-five thousand dollars to develop a script." Katz recalls, "I had no idea at that moment whether my superiors would approve the expenditure, but psychologically it would have been wrong to say, 'I'll get back to you, Jackie.' So I went ahead. Now, I may have been overly sensitive to the nuances of my relationship with Gleason. Half the time you couldn't be sure if he even knew who you were, because he always called everybody 'pal'— like Desi Arnaz, who called everyone 'amigo,' except that you absolutely *knew* Desi didn't know your name. Well, Jackie banged his hand on the table and said, 'Pal, I'll promise you one thing. I'll lay the best damn script you ever saw on your desk.' "

This was a promise Gleason would fail to keep

in at least two ways. First, he decamped to Florida, for the weather and the golf, and spent most of the CBS advance flying writers down for meetings. By the time the twenty-five thousand was gone, he had only half a script, although it was ultimately enough to permit a judgment that the show was feasible. Second, Gleason had no intention of laying the document on Katz's desk in person. He wanted Katz to come to Florida to get it. This aroused the programmer's ire, both because he had just spent two weeks either preparing around the clock in New York or testifying in Washington before the Federal Communications Commission and therefore didn't want to leave home and also because the journey would make him a supplicant rather than a boss. But a colleague in business affairs (the network office charged with negotiating contracts) persuaded Katz that it would not be a career boost to have Gleason call Paley and complain, "Your program department has so little regard for me that it's closing out its fall schedule without even coming to see me and discuss my ideas."

So Katz and Mike Dann flew down, along with Gleason's agent Herb Siegel. Delayed for hours by a snowstorm, they eventually commandeered an available, but slow and small, private plane and did not arrive until about ten-thirty at night. They headed to a golf club, where Gleason was playing poker with cronies and enjoying the effects of several drinks. Katz and Dann had agreed that the only plausible spot for Gleason's show was at his old fifties stand, at the start of Saturday night. But almost as soon as conversation began, Gleason summarily rejected that time slot as bad for a variety show. Katz heard him out, noncommittally, and said to Dann, "We go back to the hotel. We read the script. We have a breakfast meeting. If he won't yield on the time, we just leave. No bargaining. We have to be ballsy and firm." Gleason apparently sensed Katz's stubbornness and opened the meeting the next morning by saying, "If you will concede that I am a great comedian, I will concede that you are a great scheduler and I will go where you put me.

Despite the bravado, this speech verged on the humble. Plainly Gleason, for whatever reason, was aching to get back to weekly television, the venue that had made him a star. And on September 29, 1962, he did. Jackie had lasted all or part of eight seasons in the fifties. He would last eight full seasons through the balance of the sixties. He had traveled the world from the Great White Way to Gay Paree. Now, once more, Jackie Gleason was home.

CHAPTER TEN

The television industry to which Jackie Gleason returned in that autumn of 1962 was considerably bigger, tougher, more lucrative and more businesslike than the mom-and-pop sort of operations he had known in the early fifties or even the maturing semimonopolies he had left less than four years before. ABC, NBC and especially his employer, CBS, were entering a heyday that was to last two decades, during which the ownership of a network, or of a local station affiliated with one, was widely described as a license to print money. With exceptions so infrequent that they became national news stories, network-affiliated stations never had to ask themselves whether they would turn a profit for the year; the only question was how ample it would be. Every demographic, economic and social trend was working in the networks' favor. The national population was swelling with the baby boom. Beyond that, the television audience was enlarging even more rapidly, as production efficiencies made sets relatively cheaper and as evolving public perception turned owning one from a luxury into a necessity. The long arc of postwar prosperity had, for the first time, given the mass of

Americans a substantial income to spend on matters beyond the basics and had thus helped launch the consumer culture—a kind of identity-through-materialism that television proved singularly effective in selling, both through its advertising and through its entertainment programs, with their emphasis on suburban ease and comfort. Even the civil rights movement turned out to be an economic boon to the networks, by bringing empowerment and opportunity to millions of the previously excluded, who proved just as eager as their white brethren to acquire the trappings of the good life. CBS was particularly well positioned to take advantage of this growth, for it dominated the industry. During Jackie's first season back, in 1962–63, CBS would have eight of the top ten series in the Nielsen ratings, and sixteen of the top twenty. Moreover, under president James Aubrey the network introduced accounting techniques that enabled executives to assess exactly how much revenue each show generated, as well as all its direct and indirect costs, and thus gauge exactly how profitable every item on the schedule would be. This information was closely guarded, however, not only from advertisers and their agencies, but also from studios and individual performers. All the networks paid on the basis of what the market would bear, and that market was determined by salary competition among individual entertainers, not by an objective assessment of fairness in the overall sharing of the pie. For performers, the share was much smaller than it would become starting about a decade later.

As always, Jackie prided himself on being the highest-paid performer at CBS, and if judged by direct salary alone, that was technically true. In overall compensation, Lucille Ball made out better. But much of her pay was in development deals with her studio. (The Desilu adventure show *Mission: Impossible* turned out to be a hit, for example, but was placed on the CBS schedule in 1966 solely to persuade its owner, Ball, to renew for another year of her *Lucy Show*.) Red Skelton, whose show actually outrated Gleason's every year, albeit with the help of more favorable scheduling, also had complex capital-gains-oriented deals. Jackie never liked accounting complexities and often turned down percentage deals on films for that reason. He loved straight cash. Of course, he would still try to sweeten the arrangement. Each year, after extracting and publicizing his top-dog wage, Gleason would add to his sense of triumph at the network's expense by lobbying for extras—a limousine here, a hotel suite there, items that would sound swank to the man in the street and that would provide a ritual assurance of how much Jackie was needed and wanted. But these postcontract lagniappes, put together, never amounted to more than a few thousand dollars per episode. They were meaninglessly small—compared, that is, with the massive way in which Jackie, like almost every other performer of the era, was being underpaid.

That very word *underpaid* was volunteered in separate conversations on two coasts between this writer and Sal Iannucci, who oversaw CBS network business affairs during most of the sixties; Mike Dann, who was chief of CBS programming for much of that time; and Frank Stanton, the most senior executive at the parent company except for the late CBS owner and founder William Paley. In the first season of Gleason's return, for example, he was paid one hundred ten thousand dollars per episode, or something akin to four million dollars per year—as Jackie, characteristically, could not wait to leak to his friends in the press. But out of that sum he had to produce an entire hour variety show, and he was contractually obliged to use CBS production and editing facilities, at rates that not only offset the network's overhead but added on a substantial profit, thus recouping a chunk of Jackie's fee. Toward the end of his eight-year run, the budget per new episode had more than tripled and Jackie had been allowed to move his show to Florida, where he got municipal subsidies in the form of free, or at least very cheap, technical facilities, and he pocketed the resulting savings. By then his personal take probably exceeded one and perhaps two million dollars per year, and he had convinced himself and a lot of naive entertainment reporters that he was robbing the network blind. According to the CBS executives, however, the truth was that by then the Gleason show was accounting for about ten million dollars in annual profit to the network. While Jackie, as he never tired of pointing out, carried by himself the creative burden—the development of scripts, the pressures of performing and the struggle to retain popularity among a public easily bored or sated—CBS, by virtue of holding a near monopoly on the means of distribution, was raking in fully eighty to ninety percent of the net.

The advent of computers and the professionalization of the agenting business eventually changed this one-sided arrangement. In the end it became possible for almost any performer to grasp his economic value to the network. The most significant catalyst in that process was no artist or agent but Pete Rozelle, chief executive of the National Football League. Using public information and contacts at ad agencies, he simply totaled the revenue that the networks reaped from telecasts of NFL games, subtracted fees to affiliates and other overhead, and determined that what was left amounted to an unacceptably large multiple of what was being paid to his organization. That was, in contract maker Iannucci's view, one of the half dozen pivotal moments in the history of American television as a business—and one that Gleason, as a sports fan and as a hater of network executives, must have enjoyed. But its ramifications came by and large in the seventies and eighties, too late to enrich Jackie.

In programming as in business management, the television environment of the early sixties was changing in ways uncongenial to Gleason. The Western craze was beginning to decline, although in the season before Jackie's return the three highest-rated series were *Wagon Train, Bonanza* and *Gunsmoke,* and a separate show of *Gunsmoke* reruns ranked eighteenth. But the dominant forms of the succeeding decade would be hour-long urban dramas and half-hour situation comedies, virtually all made on film and on the West Coast. Variety and sketch comedy, at which Gleason excelled, were formats in decline. Live performance, from which he drew most of his psychic energy, made network executives horribly nervous, not least because it put performers in control of content. The networks vastly preferred the smooth, controlled, mistake-free quality of conventionally filmed series, made with long lead times and meticulously rendered bland by in-house censors.

Yet CBS was thrilled to get Gleason back on any terms, and so, it seemed, were the citizenry. Certainly his admirers in the news media were ecstatic, for his photogenic antics and off-camera revelry made him guaranteed good copy. The week the variety series debuted, *Life* magazine put Jackie on the cover—dressed in a particularly sporty blue and gold houndstooth jacket and an old-gold paisley vest, with his trademark carnation blazing scarlet in his lapel—and termed him "the hottest performer in all show business today." The spread inside featured Jackie amid balloons, Jackie strutting with a showgirl aboard a train, Jackie crowing about sinking a short putt, Jackie with his new TV "wife" and sketch partner Sue Anne Langdon, and Jackie with Art Carney in the role of Ed Norton.

The latter photograph was to prove particularly misleading: whatever else *The American Scene Magazine* turned into, what it most emphatically was *not* was *The Honeymooners*. For the four seasons that *Scene* ran before evolving into a wholly different name and format, Gleason broke away almost completely from his most celebrated character, his signature material. He never really explained why, even to those most closely involved. It wasn't that the material had lost popularity: by this time the 1955–56 season of thirty-nine filmed episodes had already begun to achieve classic status in reruns, occasionally drawing a bigger audience than brand-new shows on competing channels. Nor was Gleason unable to cast *Honeymooners* episodes. Carney, although unwilling to come back on a weekly basis, remained amenable to doing occasional shows. When asked about *American Scene* he remembers it as one of the blank spots in his relationship with Gleason. "I don't know anything about it," he says. "I wasn't involved in the show. I wasn't even in contact with him then. I can't say I cared much for the show. It had no *Honeymooners* and very few comedy sketches of any kind. It was mostly monologues and musical numbers, as I recall it. But we had no cross words about that or anything else at the time."

In fact, Carney did come back at least twice beyond the opening week—on January 4, 1964, as the host of a tribute to Jackie's "thirty-five years in show business," a chronology dating from Jackie's first amateur appearance on the stage of the Halsey Theater in Brooklyn, and some two years later, on January 8, 1966, in a special that tested the concept of full-length musical versions of *The Honeymooners,* for what soon turned into the format of Gleason's final four years in weekly television. Yet in general, Carney is right. Gleason made no significant use of him during the early and middle sixties, nor of Audrey Meadows and Joyce Randolph, nor of the vehicle that had displayed them all so well. Initially, Jackie had intended to do more of *The Honeymooners,* but with a new, young and curvaceous Alice played by Langdon, who joined him on the cover of *Life,* sporting a pixie haircut and a peekaboo lace negligee with plunging neckline and ample cleavage. Long gone was the battle-ax bride portrayed by Pert Kelton or even the progressively more groomed but consistently housewifely version enacted by Meadows. Langdon was twenty-six, fully two decades younger than her "husband" and co-star, and her slinkiness was meant to emphasize the presumed sexual appeal of Jackie. He wanted his on-screen persona to invite envy, not just pity. Thus, although he remained mired in poverty and despair back in Brooklyn, Ralph Kramden acquired a new "trophy" wife. The pairing lasted only half

Langdon quit because she wasn't getting enough to do. Gleason professed annoyance at her impatience and impetuosity and hinted that there had been something unsatisfactory, although unspecified, in her performance.

In truth, the problem was almost certainly the absence of Carney. Gleason as Kramden needed the dual foils of Norton and Alice to play off, and for over-the-top comedy Norton was the more important. The character of Alice had long since been established, in the writing and in the years of Meadows's performance, as practical, plainspoken and deeply rooted in reality. She could never join her husband in, let alone help devise, the harebrained schemes that allowed Gleason and Carney to glow. Gleason could, of course, have had Carney back, at least occasionally. But he didn't want a co-star. He wanted subordinates. It had irritated him throughout the fifties when people spoke of him and Carney as a team, à la Laurel and Hardy or Abbott and Costello, for that implied a relationship of equality. As Carney recalls, "Gleason was the boss, and things worked so long as I never challenged that." By the time of his return to CBS in 1962, as the toast of Broadway and Hollywood, Jackie clearly felt more entitled than ever to solo star status. To bring Carney back in a variety of sketch roles would be to risk losing the high ground he had fought so hard to gain.

He certainly wasn't averse to repeating himself per se. He brought back many of the other elements of his show from the fifties, including the June Taylor Dancers as the opening act, the writing team headed by Marvin Marx and Walter Stone, announcer Jack Lescoulie and a host of sketch characters, such as the drink-sodden Rum Dum, the fast-talking salesman Stanley R. Sogg and the two mainstays since his first weeks on *Cavalcade,* the Poor Soul and Reggie Van Gleason III. In the second season he added a sassy butler played by Sid Fields (conceptually a ripoff of Jack Benny's valet-with-verve Rochester) and a pair of lovelorn tenement stoop sitters, Arthur and Agnes, played by Gleason and Alice Ghostley.

The most important addition was a character resembling Norton at his most brain-damaged and named, Jackie always claimed, for a childhood companion, Crazy Googenham. In this role, Frank Fontaine, a nightclub singer and comic of no prior renown, became a national celebrity. The format never varied an iota: Crazy entered, told some preposterous malaprop tale accompanied by much rolling of his eyes, twisting of his mouth and clutching at his battered hat, then ended with a syrupy rendition of some bygone ballad, the more melodramatic the better. Jackie joined Fontaine each time in his favorite monologist's guise as Joe the Bartender—swabbing at the counter with a rag, patting at his white apron and, in a happy reversion to vaudeville days, getting some of his biggest laughs of the night through silent facial reactions to Crazy's outlandish tales. Gleason might have been back at El Rancho in Vegas, watching Chas Chase eat his shirt. Colleagues joked that he loved these sketches because they didn't require him to rehearse or learn lines. They weren't entirely joking. Sometimes it was unclear to network executives, and even to Fontaine himself, whether Jackie knew what Crazy was going to say before he said it. They feared that Gleason might come out for a live show not having glanced at that part of the script at all, relying instead on his favorite admonition to "just wing it, pal." Mike Dann and Irwin Segelstein, CBS programming executives of the era, both have vivid memories of coming upon Fontaine an hour or so before show time as he paced back and forth, feverishly muttering his lines. Asked when his dress rehearsal would be, Fontaine looked at them, genuinely astonished that they did not grasp the depth of his weekly plight, and said, "I'm having it right now."

Artistically, *The American Scene Magazine* was the low point of Gleason's television career, and maybe the low point of his career altogether. Having spent his entire adult life striving for, and having at long last achieved, the pinnacle of celebrity and esteem, he dissipated his reputation in mediocrity. He proved himself on Broadway, then left forever. He proved himself in films, then stopped making them for five years and didn't make another really good one for nearly two decades after that. He proved himself in situation comedy, then abandoned it. Faced with an abundance of options while still in his physical prime, he chose to come back to CBS in what remained, for all but a few moments of its four seasons, a fundamentally pallid show. It won no big awards, garnered few rave reviews, spawned no imitators and, most significant, later on brought in almost no money from reruns, making Gleason the grand impresario of a troupe of highly dubious value. The most perplexing thing is why he chose to do a show so ill fitted to his talents. Some of the material was meant to be topical, and relevance had never been Jackie's strong suit. Very little of the writing called on him to do serious or subtle acting, for which he had such demonstrated gifts; quite a bit, especially in the opening moments of Joe the Bartender sequences, called on his sub-minimal aptitude for stand-up. Gleason ballyhooed the show as having "the feel of a Broadway musical," but if so, it was a musical from his youth, when that form meant a revue rather than a cohesive story with a sustained plot and theme. The musical sections were frequently given over to so-called discoveries, the majority of whom did not go on to great fame, or deserve to. Above all, the program allowed Jackie to repeat the same shticks, the same gestures, sometimes literally the same sketches he had been doing for a dozen years and more. If the definition of life is growth, then Gleason was committing a form of artistic suicide. The only thing that saved him was that he was still so energized a performer. Audiences will forgive almost endless repetition—indeed, once a phrase or gesture becomes a player's trademark, audiences will demand to see it again and again—but they want the performer to trot out his tried-and-true material with unflagging panache and the apparent delight of someone showing it off for the very first moment. Gleason could do this, infallibly, if he avoided working without a crowd. He could always rise to the challenge of an audience if he faced the scare of "winging it" sans preparation. This need, even more than laziness and a general distaste for detail, was what kept him from rehearsing. He wanted to serve spontaneity. Maybe other actors could rehearse diligently, yet still find the material fresh. Gleason couldn't, or at least feared he couldn't. He didn't ever want to endure anything remotely like the drudgery of the final months of *Take Me Along*. He knew that the essence of his appeal was the brand of nervous energy, of visceral joy in performing, that makes onlookers feel exuberant too—and that is something that rehearsal and rote repetition cannot teach, only take away.

On occasion, when *American Scene* was organized around a theme, the show's quality rose a bit. There was a kind of sweetness to the New Year's installment in which Jackie gave center stage to a group of comics who had never quite made it to the top. Instead of competing, he just appreciated and applauded. There were tributes, in music and sketch, to the Gay Nineties and

World War I. More often, and less charmingly, the tributes were to Gleason himself: an evening of musical compositions credited to him; celebrations of his fifteen years in music, thirty-five in show business, fifty of just being alive. The "host" of the half-century birthday bash was, in a fitting bit of show biz hypocrisy, his old adversary Milton Berle. The huge ego that CBS executives had sought to conceal by keeping Gleason away from game and talk shows revealed itself to the fullest on these occasions. Jackie might make token attempts at humility, but he exhibited almost none of the poignant vulnerability that had made a nation love Ralph Kramden or the Poor Soul or his other acting creations. He was loud, boisterous, even aggressive. And as the decade wore on, his style of dress and speech, his values and demeanor, almost everything about his persona began to seem more and more dated, less and less hip. Having risen to favor by beguiling the young and affluent families who owned television sets in the early fifties, Jackie was in the process of becoming the favorite, instead, of those who were older, poorer and much less interesting to advertisers.

The recollection of CBS executives, admittedly colored by ego then and by the passage of three decades since, is that Gleason had been almost desperate in his eagerness to return to weekly television. He yearned in equal measure for the fame, the money and the vast live audience, and thus he settled for a very reasonable price. It didn't take long, however, for his relationship with CBS to sour, and during the course of the decade the contretemps between the comic and the cost controllers would become far more passionate than any during the fifties. Jackie started, a few weeks into the 1962–63 season, by demanding a meeting with Aubrey, Mike Dann and Sal Iannucci to protest alleged overcharges and inefficiencies in CBS studio operations. Virtually point by point, he got his way on everything. Iannucci recalls, "We resolved things and made adjustments in his favor because the show was working and he seemed to be committed to it."

By the middle of the year, it was time to consider renewal. (Network scheduling decisions for the new season were made much earlier then, because the standard order was for thirty or more episodes of a show, versus the twenty-two that are considered a full season today, and it took longer to get them all made.) Gleason's agents reported that Jackie was prepared to sign for a second season. The only hitch was that this offer would expire almost immediately. Hating the idea that his fate and fortune lay in the hands of network executives, whom he regarded as uncreative and for whom he felt almost universal contempt, Jackie tried every year to take control of at least the timetable. It was unthinkable to just wait and let CBS executives get back to him when they were good and ready. The network would have to meet his deadline, he declaimed, or the deal was off. Iannucci, Aubrey and even Stanton were familiar with this quirk by now; after all, that was the way Gleason had always behaved, ever since he buffaloed Jack Van Valkenberg one lunchtime into awarding The Great One's very first CBS contract, back in 1951. But Aubrey disliked Gleason as heartily as Gleason disliked him. After all, when Oscar Katz's decision to allow Gleason to lambaste *You're in the Picture* on network air time cost CBS almost half a million dollars, Aubrey's only response had been, "It was worth it. Now you have him out of your system." The CBS president had spoken of affection for the fat comic, or even belief in Jackie's talent, as though it were a virus.

When Iannucci heard from Gleason's agents that Jackie was ready, he recalls, he telephoned Aubrey with something approaching elation. "Jackie had been saying, 'Maybe I'll work, maybe I won't,' his usual routine, and we wanted it behind us. He demanded more money, of course, but it was a good deal for us as well as for him. We could accept the terms without any trouble. The only hitch was that Jackie wanted it settled with some dispatch, that very week, and it was already Thursday or maybe early Friday.

"I call Aubrey on the West Coast with the good news and he says, 'Don't answer yet. I want to hang Jackie out to dry for a while.' Now, this is getting uncomfortable. Jackie would have to know that I was dealing with Aubrey, because that's the way things worked. But I have my orders. I call Gleason's agents and say maybe it will get settled over the weekend, otherwise next week.

"The next thing I know, Gleason himself is calling me and he says, 'That's not good enough, pal. Unless I hear from Aubrey by the end of business today, there's no deal, and I'm not working next year.' Now I know that Jackie has always resented having to deal with Paley, going into the big office suite with the staff of servants, the living room and the dining room and the conference room all full of museum-quality art, so he always makes sure to put us lower-level guys through the drill. I don't mind much. I just want it done. I call Aubrey back and explain the situation. Aubrey, in his inimitable way, says, You heard what I said before. You can't reach me. I'm out of touch. We haven't spoken.'

"Now I have to call Jackie. He's obviously been drinking a lot. He demands that I come over to his hotel and wait with him for Aubrey to return my call there. I say no, I have a family engagement. I'm not going to sit there with Jackie while he's drunk and going crazy, because he certainly isn't going to get any *happier* when Aubrey doesn't call. The upshot is that Aubrey sits tight and Gleason does cancel.

"A week later, I get a call from Aubrey. He starts, 'What can I say, I always do the work for you. I've got the Gleason deal closed.' And he sure did—but for about five percent more than if we had closed on that Friday. That display of macho cost about two hundred fifty thousand dollars of the network's money."

Gleason, a man whose street-smart intelligence was almost as sizable as his ego, surely recognized Aubrey's behavior as a calculated insult. It reinforced Jackie's rage and cynicism toward his bosses and made him much more temperamental and difficult toward Aubrey's subordinates and successors. Extracting the additional money, pleasant enough in itself, served as a means of getting even, of making Aubrey pay—albeit not out of his personal pocket.

But the bigger lesson Jackie learned was that twice within three months CBS had readily agreed to his demands for lower costs or higher fees. Perhaps the time had come for a much bolder stroke.

As he entered the fall of 1963, Gleason had built up a list of interlocking discontents. First, he was disenchanted with New York. The long months of cold, wet weather depressed him, and they made much of the year unsuitable for his favorite recreation, golf. The saloon society he had reveled in during the forties and fifties had faded. His own contemporaries had grown into the responsibilities of middle age. Many of his older heroes were dead or in retirement. Modern wives were less indulgent of endless boys' nights out, of copious drinking and wolf-pack conviviality.

For that matter, Jackie himself had become less of a carouser. He was still drinking heavily, sometimes very heavily, but he was trying (in the manner of many a self-deluding drunk) to substitute wine for the hard stuff. His relationship with Honey Merrill had become more domestic, more nearly monogamous, and the raunchy stories that colleagues recall from his youth have almost no parallels in these middle years. Larry King, the radio and TV talk show host who got to know Gleason about this time and who is himself a multiply married connoisseur of pulchritude, recalls numerous occasions of sitting with Gleason as conspicuously attractive women walked by. "He didn't try to pick them up. He didn't flirt. He didn't follow them with his eyes. He didn't even look, didn't even notice. I know his earlier reputation, but by the time he was pushing fifty, this was simply not a sexual man. I don't say he never did anything, just that it didn't drive him anymore, not in private. Of course it remained a part of his public persona—a part of his act."

Professionally, New York was no longer so enticing either. Except for what awestruck ex-vaudevillians still called the "legitimate" stage, most of the entertainment industry was rapidly shifting to Los Angeles. Gleason had given periodic interviews deploring this trend and calling on Manhattan's municipal government to take corrective measures. His counsel had gone unheeded, to his deep offense. In personal terms, too, Gleason had very few close friends left in New York other than employees and business associates, who could move with him. The kick had long since worn off his occasional visits with the old gang from Brooklyn, and whatever sentiment he had for the borough of his youth was mingled with a lot of bitter memories. Leaving New York would not mean leaving much of his emotional life behind.

The major thing connecting Jackie to the New York area was his home in Peekskill, the folly he had constructed to prove himself a man of exacting standards and distinctive taste. But when the initial publicity died away, Gleason found the house uncomfortable and unsuitable. He didn't really want to go up to the woods. Watching the house take shape during the run of *Take Me Along* had fascinated him no end. This was his San Simeon, his architectural assertion of arrival. But watching leaves flutter in the wind or chipmunks scurry across the meadows did not satisfy him at all, despite his loud public protestations that he was a born nature lover. For a man who worked in Manhattan, on an irregular schedule with many night hours—and who ended many of those nights in something akin to a stupor— the house's location was simply too distant to be practical. Also, like so many of his residences since he had left Genevieve, it just wasn't homey. The space age geometry was fine for parties, but how many of those did this loner want to throw, and why throw parties way up there? Would his city friends even attend, especially without overnight accommodation? By the end of 1963, Gleason was claiming to a *Newark Evening News* writer that he had visited the Peekskill property only three times in the previous three years. "I've got about a million dollars in it," he said. "And if I just had the time to enjoy it, I'd keep it. That place is like heaven. But that's the trouble—while I'm still alive, I can't get there."

Jackie may have been exaggerating in saying he'd been only three times—although the period included some protracted absences for film work—and he probably didn't even know exactly how much money he had poured into the construction, although a million was the kind of nice, round, rhetorically effective number that Jackie liked. Whatever the true amount, it was surely of that magnitude, and it probably represented a blotting up of nearly all of Jackie's liquid assets. Jackie's income in this period had leapfrogged up and down, but rarely approached, let alone surpassed, half a million dollars a year. Out of that sum, he paid close to a third to agents, managers and Genevieve, and on the remainder he faced the era's comparatively steep income tax rates. He appears to have been more consistently solvent in this period than five or ten years before, when in cash terms he was often all but broke. Still, Peekskill required that a lot of cash be expended in a short time. And it didn't prove easy to get the money back out. Gleason's taste was not exactly universal. Once he decided to sell, he discovered that the house's celebrity associations were far outweighed, for most buyers, by the unaccommodating eccentricity of the floor plan. No serious bidders emerged. So, after months, Gleason offered to renew for a third season of *American Scene* only if CBS would move the show to a warm climate and take the Peekskill house off his hands.

This not-so-modest proposal caused consternation among the senior ranks at the network. They worried, rightly, that they would be establishing a precedent and opening themselves to ever more frivolous demands from future stars. They also wondered what to do with the property itself, which Oscar Katz described as "suitable only for the establishment of a new cult religion." But Iannucci argued to his colleagues that if the overall cost of the deal made sense, it shouldn't matter whether some of it involved real estate as opposed to salary or license fees for shows. In Iannucci's vision, CBS would in effect pay Gleason with his own money—just as it would, at about the same time, divert money from Red Skelton's show into acquiring a studio from him to suit that star's financial and tax needs. The ironic upshot, Iannucci recalls, is that CBS made what amounted to a profit on the deal. In his recollection—which current officials at the network said they were unable to confirm—CBS in effect donated the Gleason property to a charity. The network took a tax deduction for the full amount at which the estate was valued in the contract with Jackie, approximately one million dollars, even though the true resale value was somewhere around half that. Says Iannucci: "In Gleason's mind, in his bonnet, this was quite a coup. But my attitude was, 'Why get caught up in the emotions of the deal?' We were still not paying anything close to what we could have afforded to pay him." Gleason announced through his sometime friend, columnist Earl Wilson, that his new deal with CBS would be for six million dollars. Jackie was quoted as saying, "I'm told that it is the biggest one-year contract in the history of television. With this money, I can afford to hire four thousand writers. And away we go—to Florida."

At the time he leaked his new contract terms to Wilson, Jackie wasn't sure whether he was heading to Miami or Fort Lauderdale or Palm Beach. He liked them all, regarded them as virtually interchangeable for his purposes, and was prepared to go to the highest bidder. CBS executives, dreading the addition of a new and distant venue to their regular shuttle between the East and West coasts, persuaded Jackie to leave open the possibility of moving to Los Angeles if no suitable facility could be found in Florida—meaning, in Jackie's mind, if no sufficiently lucrative deal could be struck. As ever, Jackie counted on the network to meet his show's technical demands, whatever the problems with local facilities, as a matter of corporate self-interest. Gleason had absolutely no desire to move to Los Angeles under any circumstances. He still harbored a grudge for the way Hollywood had failed to embrace and advance his talents twice during the forties, and his recent film success, most of it achieved on location rather than in studio back lots, had not much softened his resentment. Moreover, in California he would be just another star among many. Anywhere in Florida he could be Mr. Show Business, the biggest act in town. That would be immensely flattering to his ego. Just as important, it could be immensely profitable. Hotels and nightclubs would beseech him for endorsements. So would golf courses and cruise lines. Where a restaurant in New York or Los Angeles might ask permission to photograph him during dinner and put his picture on the wall, a proprietor in Miami might pay for the privilege or at least arrange a useful barter. And that was just the small stuff. Jackie rapidly discovered that real estate speculators were prepared to offer a mansion-size residence absolutely free, just for the privilege of advertising to prospective buyers in the surrounding development that Jackie Gleason would be their neighbor.

Local governments proved just as receptive as the private sector, and with good reason. To begin with, the Gleason show would pump millions of dollars directly into the economy of whatever town landed it. If the performance setup were to be as Jackie envisioned, in front of a live audience in a large theater, the chance of getting tickets to see his show would become a tourist attraction generating many millions more for local hotels, restaurants, merchants and the like. The very fact that the show's locale would be featured in film footage and countless verbal references would, moreover, serve as a massive promotional campaign, stimulating not just tourism but also more general economic development. Given the undeniable benefits to whatever town he settled in, Jackie's expectations of giveaways or subsidies looked eminently reasonable.

Miami, as Florida's biggest city and most highly developed tourist center (in those pre–Disney World days), was the logical place for Jackie to go, and he did in fairly short order. Sources differ about exactly what Miami provided and how the deal evolved over time, but two things are generally accepted. First, credit for making it happen belonged equally to a canny local public relations man named Hank Myers and to Gleason's longtime manager and producer Jack Philbin. Second, the savings from the deal, on items for which CBS continued to pay full price but which Miami provided cheap or free, effectively doubled Jackie's take-home pay overnight. Of all the things Philbin had done for Jackie in an association already well over a decade long, this was probably the most lucrative and therefore in all likelihood the most endearing to his temperamental employer.

Philbin already was, and during the Florida years he became ever more strongly, Gleason's principal point of contact with the CBS corporate world. Network executives fondly remember him as a gentleman, a diplomat and a professional—although, curiously, such close Gleason associates as public relations man Pete McGovern and personal secretary Sydell Spear go out of their way to emphasize that they worked for Jackie, not Philbin, and that they reported only to the boss, never to his aide de camp. They say nothing harsh about Philbin. But they don't volunteer anything affectionate either. Whatever level of trust Philbin may have enjoyed among these subordinates, he certainly had the ear of his principal. He was Jackie's producer in some projects, his partner in others. Unlike his predecessor, Bullets Durgom, he apparently never clashed with Gleason over money, at least not strongly enough to generate public controversy. He stayed with Gleason to the end and still plays a role in managing the affairs of the Gleason estate. CBS programming executive Mike Dann, who says he relied on Philbin as an irreplaceable go-between and peacemaker, recalls, "He would never tell Gleason what to do and he would never confront him, as far as I could see. But he had a way of being able to push him into things. He could gradually bring Jackie around to a reasonable position. He was extraordinarily good at reading his moods. He would let us know when it was the right or wrong moment to have a meeting or to bring something up. He would tip us off when Jackie had been drinking extra heavily and might be especially difficult. In my experience, Philbin was always a man of his word. Besides, he was basically on our side, because as the producer of the program he shared our interest in seeing it continue."

As producer, Philbin oversaw a tense and complex operation. But his primary duty was to cater to the needs and whims of the star. Jackie liked to have the theater's air conditioning operate at full Arctic blast, for example, even in midwinter, because he was convinced that a comfortably warm audience might be apt to doze off. It was left to Philbin to handle the complaints from, and eventually obtain jackets for, the June Taylor Dancers, who were shivering in their low-neckline scanties between routines. Gleason, who liked to help erstwhile stars in decline, was fond of bringing Orson Welles onto the show every season or so to perform a magic act. It was up to producer Philbin to try to see to it that Welles got paid in cash so that the Internal Revenue Service, with whom the actor was having troubles, could not garnishee his check. Jackie, who liked rehearsing less than ever, would nonetheless sometimes schedule a full run-through on the day of the show, then abruptly throw his hand to his head and announce that he just couldn't go on and insist that "all these people" leave at once. Then it would be up to producer Philbin to disassemble the cast and crew with a maximum of speed, a minimum of fuss and no acknowledgment whatsoever of the oddity of Jackie's behavior. When they were out in public, at a restaurant or club, it was Philbin who talked to the waiters,

Philbin who deflected the autograph seekers, Philbin who handled the parking attendants and the coat checking and the bills. Sometimes he was a producer. Sometimes he was a partner. But even more often he was an upscale valet.

Moving to Florida had a major effect on Jackie's lifestyle and conduct that he seems not to have anticipated. It made his show much more of a family and brought him much closer emotionally to its individual members than he had ever been in New York, as a sort of pater familias. He realized the significance of uprooting whole families and he recognized that many of the underlings, ignorant of the full financial significance of the shift, thought it might prove a whim that he could reverse at any moment, to their vast collective inconvenience. They needed reassurance and more visible leadership. They were too much on their own. In New York, the workers on the Gleason show had been part of a large show business community. Almost every one of them knew other people in the field; some of them, from technicians right on up to co-star Art Carney, worked with great frequency on other shows. In Miami, the Gleason people were virtually the only show business professionals in town and had no one to talk to. Although Jackie had sold the locals on the idea that by himself he could turn Miami into the new Hollywood, there was as yet almost no film or television production going on. Thus the employees of *American Scene* had to provide moral and emotional support for each other, and they looked far more than before to their employer to set the communal tone.

Gleason frequently rose to the occasion with a courtly or compassionate gesture. When a hurricane imperiled the area, felling trees and cutting off power lines, he personally telephoned every member of the company—starting, according to publicist Pete McGovern, not with the top brass but with the fathers and mothers of the biggest broods of children. He sent a dozen roses every week to every June Taylor dancer—by some accounts, to every woman on the permanent staff—and he tried to arrange trips, gifts and other perquisites for them. Although stern in handling slackers and incompetents, he fiercely defended solid workers against the slings and arrows of visiting stars. When Milton Berle dressed down makeup woman Ruth Regina for an error the staff considered to be Berle's fault, Jackie demanded that Berle render a public apology and send the woman flowers at his own expense.

Yet however much chummier than in his Manhattan days, Gleason remained mostly remote. While such stars as Lucille Ball made a point of arriving on set as early as anyone, mingling with the company, eating the same catered lunch as the lowliest stagehand (and not being served until everyone else had been taken care of), Gleason preferred princely isolation and splendor. He chatted with a few people because he liked them or because they were well connected. Dancer

Mercedes Ellington, for example, readily acknowledges that a key point in her early friendship with Gleason was his admiration of her grandfather, composer Duke Ellington. Feeling ignored was a far more common experience. Trudy Carson, who danced with the June Taylor troupe for two years before returning to New York City to resume a more varied show business career (and ultimately marry comic Soupy Sales), recalls that Gleason did not speak to her before approving her hiring at the final audition, nor ever in rehearsal, nor ever after a show. In two years she had two brief conversations with him, both at cast parties. Throughout her two seasons, she remained amazed that Gleason would run the risk of emerging live, week after week, into the finale of a dance pattern he had never seen performed. "I just couldn't understand how he could do it, or why. He wouldn't even rehearse the walk-out. His stand-in, Barney Martin, always did that. I heard that he would sit somewhere else during dress rehearsal and watch on a monitor, so that's how he handled it."

Carson, a former Rockette at the Radio City Music Hall, rated the Taylor regimen as much harder than the Rockettes'. Both troupes relied on precision, but the Taylor team had fewer dancers, increasing the audience attention on any one of them. The camera, moreover, exposed minor errors far more mercilessly than the naked eye operating at long distances from the stage. Rockette routines stayed in a show for an entire holiday season, months at a time, while the Taylor dancers had to master new numbers every week. And Gleason loved having the dancers use tricky props—golf clubs, canes, banjos, English racing bicycles. These technical demands, plus the ego-swallowing fact of never being a soloist, just one-sixteenth of a complex human machine, might have made the job unappealing to young talents. But the Taylor troupe had become the highest-profile dancers in the country. The pay was also the best. When Mercedes Ellington started, she got one hundred fifty-five dollars a week, double the eighty a week she had been getting in her last job, in the chorus line of *Pal Joey* on Broadway with Bob Fosse.

One outsider who got a revealing if brief glimpse of Gleason's fondness for isolation was Alfred Chadbourn, known as Chip, a painter and commercial illustrator who also taught at the Famous Artists Schools. Philip Morris was sponsoring Gleason in 1965, in virtually the last gasp of permissible cigarette advertising on television. A company vice president who owned some of Chadbourn's work arranged for him to be commissioned to paint portraits of The Great One and nine other stars whom the company was underwriting. The idea was sent down via Jack Philbin for Gleason's approval, and Chadbourn later heard that the conversation went like this:

"Does this guy play golf?"

"No, Jackie, he doesn't."

"Does he shoot pool?"

"Apparently not."

"Well, does he drink?"

"Yes, he says he does."

"In that case, have them send him on down.

Despite his lack of interest in golf, Chadbourn accompanied Gleason in the cart once or twice to observe his subject and sop up local color. Jackie, meanwhile, was sopping up straight vodka between strokes. "He and his companions talked a lot about inside show business matters," Chadbourn recalls, "and they were playing some complicated gambling game for very high stakes. They all used his catchphrase, 'How sweet it is,' about a hundred times, until I got sick of hearing it." On other occasions, Chadbourn watched Gleason nestle at home with Honey Merrill or simply sit silent and alone (save for the painter in the corner). "He was very subdued, seemingly sick of being surrounded by yes men who laughed at everything he said and relieved to be with someone who didn't want something from him. He would stare at objects for a long time and he rarely had much to say. I think he would have been a rough guy to get along with if you crossed him—I was at a studio session one day when someone showed up late and was fired on the spot, right in front of me and everyone else—but he was definitely less crazy than some of the other people I painted for that commission. At one point, while I was sketching him, he did a little sketch of me. He said he had fiddled with cartooning when he was young. It wasn't brilliant, but I remember how graceful and delicate his movements were in making the drawing. What separated us most was that he couldn't understand how eager I was to get back to New England, where there would be something to paint. He said, 'You mean you like that cold, wet weather?' To him Florida was not flat and dull and uninteresting to look at, but a different and wonderful world. As an artist, he would not have seen *things*. But he clearly saw people very perceptively."

At about the time that Chadbourn was sketching him, Jackie experienced what he considered one of life's major pleasures, the settling of a score. CBS President James Aubrey, who had sneered at Gleason as an addiction for program executive Oscar Katz and had wanted to "hang Gleason out to dry" in the middle of contract negotiations, came down to Miami to make obeisance at Jackie's forty-ninth birthday party. The festivities were said to be wild, and those to which Aubrey went on, later in the evening, were said to be wilder still. When the man whom Gleason derided as "the football player" flew back to New York a day later, it was to be summoned forthwith by the company's top executives, William Paley and Frank Stanton, and dismissed. Aubrey wasn't sacked simply for his misbehavior in Florida, although it was emblematic: he had developed what the company considered an unseemly reputation as a playboy. But Aubrey had been in trouble for much more pervasive managerial reasons. Practically everyone in the business, however, thought that he had been ousted chiefly for his immediate conduct, and they credited Jackie with both Dionysian tastes and Machiavellian cunning.

The departure of Aubrey did not, however, much change Jackie's tortured relations with CBS. Contract maker Iannucci recalls, "We still went through the same ritual every year of waiting to see whether Jackie would commit. Only he and Lucy were allowed to negotiate on this annual basis, although we had continual contractual problems with Red Skelton and every so often we had a very tough renegotiation with Ed Sullivan. I remember flying down with Mike Dann or Irwin Segelstein to meet with Gleason and Philbin and Jackie's agent Sam Cohn. It was obvious that Jackie took great delight in making us wait for him for hours so that we could begin to beg him to work another year. I don't think he held any of the past against me, although shortly after the deal where Aubrey made trouble, I saw Jackie at the 21 Club in New York and he yelled from a couple of tables away, 'Iannucci, I don't like you!' I thought he was pulling my leg, but with Jackie you didn't always know. In any case, he made us all go through this yearly mating dance. He would raise one problem after another. Then Philbin would resolve things for him and convince him that whatever was obsessing him at that moment would not be as difficult as in years gone by. Jackie liked to intimidate, that was his style, and he liked to make you pay homage. One year he was being honored by some organization in the Miami Jewish community and he insisted that Mike Dann and I fly down to attend this testimonial. It was at a big hotel or restaurant, and Dann and I didn't want to eat the kosher meal and drink the Manischewitz wine, so we ordered in the main dining room and periodically sneaked out of the testimonial to eat a regular dinner course by course. He would have been furious if he knew."

Gleason's intimidation worked particularly effectively on Irwin Segelstein, who for a while served as the program department's principal contact with the show in Miami, flying down for the opening and closing installments every year and a couple of others in between. "I went there with the follow-spot on me," Segelstein says, sounding faintly cowed even now, "because I knew that if he didn't like me, I wouldn't keep my job." In his efforts to ingratiate himself with Gleason, the normally abstemious Segelstein on one occasion consented to down three martinis by nine-thirty A.M., then call his network president for a business conversation. (The inebriation showed, his boss told him later.) On another occasion Segelstein accompanied Jackie to a party where the "entertainment" was a pianist without fingers who hit the keys with his stumps of knuckle. "Jackie found this highly amusing," Segelstein recalls. When Jackie demanded for his show the same long-focus lens that CBS was using for covering the launch of space satellites, Segelstein agreed without a murmur. Although he attended the show a dozen or more weekends and on several occasions visited Jackie at home, Segelstein never got the least gesture of acceptance that might have allowed him to relax—but that might have cost Jackie some of his competitive edge in negotiations. "Never once," Segelstein recalls, "did he actually speak any part of my name. I don't know for sure that he ever, for even a moment, actually knew my name. He always called me 'pal.' I did whatever he asked and I still went away feeling that to him I was just another network fink. He was formal and courteous, never abusive. But the whole fortification of handlers around him was such that I never felt I got past the official visit."

Sometimes Jackie was rude even when he meant to please. Oscar Katz, who had left CBS to run the Desilu studio, was asked by Gleason to consider creating a similar operation for him. Katz viewed the idea with some skepticism, both because of his vivid memories of Jackie's erratic nature and because of doubts about good faith on CBS's part. "In that situation, I knew the networks would not be rooting for Gleason's shows to succeed, because then he would get rich and wouldn't have to perform his own series anymore, while what the network wanted most was to keep him on the air." Nevertheless, the prospect was too intriguing to refuse, so Katz accepted the free

424

trip to Florida and arrived at the appointed hour at Jackie's home.

"I rang the bell and finally Honey Merrill answered but didn't actually open the door. It was at least nine and maybe ten A.M., and we were supposed to have breakfast, but she said, 'He's over at the clubhouse waiting for you.' So I went over and when I got there he was either already loaded from that morning or still loaded from the night before. I no sooner got there than Jackie said, 'Pal, I'm of no use to you. I'm going to go take a nap and I'll catch up to you later.' That was absolutely the last I saw of him. For the next three days I was taken out on the town by June Taylor dancers at Jackie's expense and then, not having had one word of conversation with him or any sign that I was going to, I flew home. And that was the end of the whole idea of this production company."

By the middle of his second season in Miami, two things were becoming dramatically clear to Gleason. First, the experiment had been inspired. Although Philbin and Pete McGovetn and Sydell Spear and the rest of the entourage had moved down half-expecting that Jackie would change his mind a month later and move everyone back, he loved being his adopted town's Mr. Show Business and he wanted to stay forever. Indeed, although he would move several times, for reasons ranging from seeking bigger quarters to rebuilding after a disastrous house fire, Florida remained his permanent home for the rest of his life. The second thing that Jackie realized was that if he wanted to reside in Miami as a weekly television series star on CBS, the concept and format of his show were going to need a lot of remedial work.

Jackie always claimed to feel more appreciated in Miami than he had ever been anywhere else. Almost all performers have out-of-balance egos, accepting praise and even adulation as their due but recoiling at the faintest sign of disaffection or criticism. This syndrome was particularly pronounced in Jackie, and it seemed he loved Miami chiefly because it treated him with the awe he thought befitting a star of his magnitude. He said that on the day he arrived he realized he had come to the right place, even before the motorcade from the train station brought him to a welcoming luncheon full of dignitaries. As the cars passed a pool hall, he recalled, the players lined up outside on the street, their cue sticks held aloft in a gesture of salute.

Over the next few years he repeatedly cited instances of similar salutation. But with a shrewd sense of public relations he insisted that what these moments really showed him was how friendly the Miamians were. "It's not that anyone thinks I'm sensational," he claimed. "It's that the people here are so naturally nice." This argument didn't make a great deal of sense—were the pool players out on the street every day, saluting just anybody?—but it allowed Jackie to revel in being revered as The Great One without gloating openly about it. In interviews and other public appearances (of which he did at least as many in Miami as he ever had in New York, to the astonishment and delight of the Florida media) Gleason also made a point of hailing the facilities he was being afforded. "That auditorium just turned out to be a natural," he said in a radio conversation with his new friend Larry King. "It has an amazing lighting system and a fine air conditioning system to handle the heat from all those lights. We have the best color on the network, bar none, and CBS has sent men down here to see how it is done." Discreetly, Gleason avoided discussing, in this and other interviews, the auditorium's finest feature from his point of view: its nominal price and the consequent increase in his income.

However congenial he found Miami emotionally or technologically and however uncritical the weekly audience of locals and tourists tended to be, Jackie realized by the final months of 1965 that his national audience was beginning to erode. That meant he was in trouble. The first two seasons of *American Scene,* those emanating from New York, had ranked respectively seventeenth and fifteenth in the Nielsen ratings. The two Miami seasons dropped below the top twenty. CBS accepted that Saturday was an unfavorable time slot—so many people went out for the evening that it was customarily the least-watched night of prime time—but that factor had not changed, so it did nothing to explain the downward trend. The competition had become a little tougher. In the first two seasons, Jackie was opposite shows that folded at the end of the season. By the second season in Miami, NBC had him stacked against *Flipper,* a show about a dolphin popular with children (and featuring, that year, a Scandinavian blonde popular with many of their fathers) and the debut of the fantasy sitcom *I Dream of Jeannie,* which would run five years; both are still omnipresent in reruns. But the officials at CBS began to wonder if the public was once again tiring of Gleason. Jackie, knowing that his program was expensive and that the inconvenience of its coming from Miami was considerable, rightly feared that the network might think about phasing him out. He detested the thought of being canceled, the public humiliation of failure. In addition, he was feeling again the too familiar anxiety of trying to generate fresh ideas for thirty or more variety shows every season. And at moments he admitted he was starting to get bored.

The solution that rejuvenated him is one of those successes for which everyone wants to claim credit. CBS programmer Mike Dann remembers very clearly that it was the network's idea to ask Jackie to bring back Art Carney and revive *The Honeymooners.* People from the Gleason camp, including agent Sam Cohn and publicist Pete McGovern, are equally sure that the idea originated with Jackie. Carney knows only that he was in the hospital or fresh out of it—recovering from the exhaustion of a Broadway triumph as the original finicky Felix Unger in Neil Simon's stage play *The Odd Couple*—when Gleason cheered him enormously by inviting him down to Florida to work again. For all the past difficulties of working with Jackie, the late scripts and the lack of rehearsal and the general hurly-burly, Carney remembered the relationship as having been unusually creative and productive. Carney recalls, "It made me feel just wonderful, the exuberance and joy that he expressed that I could come out of the hospital and work with him again. It seemed particularly right for me then because one of the reasons I enjoyed doing Norton was that he was an extrovert and gregarious, which I'm not, and I was a little down in that period."

On Broadway, Carney had once again found himself a sort of second banana to a louder, more assertive star. Walter Matthau won the Tony Award as chaotic, bullish sportswriter Oscar Madison in *The Odd Couple*. The play, the playwright and director Mike Nichols were also honored, while Carney wasn't even nominated. The relationship between the two leading men was not too terrific either on or off the stage. Carney said later that he had hoped to do the inevitable film version of the play, but without Matthau. Gleason, he said, would be his ideal costar as Oscar. (Gleason also loved the play but told Larry King he wanted to play Felix, Carney's part.)

As it turned out, Hollywood kept Matthau instead of Carney and gave Art's role to Jack Lemmon. Playwright Simon was and remains an avid fan of Carney, but insists, "Carney never spoke to me about Gleason in any way, including what it was like to work with him. I mentioned my own unhappy experiences and he gave the feeling that he understood, but he was extremely discreet. In any case, there is nothing I ever wrote that I would have considered putting Gleason into, with or without Art, because I like comics who are vulnerable, who come from a down position. Gleason always seemed to me an arrogant man. He could make me laugh sometimes, but I could always see through to the arrogance. He was like a J. P. Morgan without the money. In Carney there is a Stan Laurel—he really makes me laugh—but in Gleason I saw no Oliver Hardy." Simon credits Gleason, perversely, with launching his whole career as a playwright. During the nights and weekends over three years as he labored on his debut hit, *Come Blow Your Horn*, what kept Simon going was "the thought that I did not want to get to be a middle-aged man waiting for the phone to ring so I could go to work writing gags for some abusive, unappreciative shit like Jackie Gleason. It was my personal vision of hell."

For the theme of the one-hour reunion show with Carney, Gleason revisited what had always been his favorite *Honeymooners* of the fifties, an episode in which Ralph and Alice temporarily become parents. The subject appears to have had deep psychological resonances for him. To the extent that the Kramdens may, in his mind, have symbolized his parents, he could have wanted subconsciously to reassure himself that his arrival had strengthened rather than sundered their marriage. To the extent that Ralph was his alter ego to the world, he could have thought that showing paternal tenderness might help make up for his decades of real-life parental neglect. But even if these things were true, Jackie would surely have waved away such Freudian probings in favor of pragmatic show business observations: the voluntary childlessness of a long-married couple raises problems of empathy in the minds of family audiences, while the yearning to secure a baby has a surefire sentimental appeal. So the plot was built around the Kramdens' application to an adoption agency and the interview they would have to pass. For this revival the original sets were available—one of Jackie's underlings, set designer Phil Cuoco, had been canny enough to store them and then ship them to Florida at the time of the move—but the format expanded from a half hour to an hour, the presentation from bleak black-and-white to cheery color, and the style from vaudeville sketch to musical comedy, complete with song and dance. The episode was a huge hit with critics and viewers and CBS promptly started importuning Jackie to do a clutch of such *Honeymooners* specials.

By the spring of 1966, Jackie's agents and the

network had devised a motley assortment of projects to get him through the 1966–67 season. There would be, it was decided, ten musical *Honeymooners*. There would be ten other musical book shows, collectively giving Jackie a variety of roles but calling on him to play only one per night. There would be ten quasi documentaries featuring footage of animals being cute and quirky, over which Jackie would ad-lib his sardonic comments. And there would be four to six variety specials of the kind he had been doing, but focused on themes—holidays, his birthday, musical tributes and the like, sometimes with a guest host. In hindsight, and presumably at the time, the disadvantages of this package were obvious. It would not provide the viewer something consistent and predictable. It would greatly increase the pressures on Jackie to rehearse and learn lines or heighten the perils of his not doing so. The animal shows would amount to nothing less than reviving the talk show that CBS had fought so hard against and had considered such a fiasco when, in the wake of *You're in the Picture*, Jackie had forced it on them. All in all, it is baffling why CBS agreed. Mike Dann explains: "We expected the more undesirable elements of the plan to disappear, and we certainly did not expect to get a full season as described. With Jackie the contract was always just theoretical. We wanted as many *Honeymooners* as we could have and we figured we would fill in the rest with other variety specials from Jackie, reruns of his shows or movies and specials of our own. Getting Jackie to agree to work at all was tough. He retired every day. Every show was going to be the last one ever. Our policy was to agree to what he wanted and then, with the bad ideas, to wait until he didn't want them anymore."

CBS was right. At first Gleason made a good-faith effort to develop this tripartite series. But the animal shows soon fell by the wayside. Of the ten book musicals other than *The Honeymooners,* he approved a script for only one, despite hiring Sid Caesar's producer from the *Your Show of Shows* era, Max Liebman, to coordinate the project and a talented roster of writers including Saul Turtletaub, later the creator of *Carter Country* and other series, and Jackie's first TV variety writer, Coleman Jacoby. The script that Jackie approved, credited to Turtletaub, Keith Fowler and Terry Ryan, was called *The Passing Politician* and featured Jackie as the fading mayor of a small city and Carney as his campaign consultant. Although broadly comic and uninspired—its best moment was a fish-out-of-water sequence in which the mayor went to a disco and tried to relate to rock music to drum up the votes of young people—the script won Gleason over because it fulfilled a long-thwarted ambition. Although the writers didn't realize it when they proposed the idea, Jackie still burned over having been denied his chance at the film of *The Last Hurrah.* This script amounted to another version of the same story, if coarse and jokey instead of elegant and poignant. Turtletaub remembers that all the writers were working in New York and that periodically he and Liebman would fly down to Miami to show Gleason new scenes and get approval or instructions for rewrites. "It was not an easy, fun job," he recalls, "although he and Jack Philbin treated Max Liebman, who was pretty old by then, with great deference and respect. I had heard that Jackie was a screamer and could really carry on, but I saw none of that. Jackie definitely knew what was best for him, as most comics do, but it never got ugly, with him yelling, 'This isn't me, change it.' I don't remember any of the ideas he rejected, which probably means there was no great injustice in his decisions." *The Passing Politician* aired at the start of the season; the balance was taken up with *Honeymooners* musical hours interspersed with standard variety.

For the permanent cast that fall, Audrey Meadows did not take the role of Alice, to the best of everyone's recollection because she was not available. Joyce Randolph would not have been willing to move to Florida, either, but says she was not even asked to reprise Trixie, ostensibly because if Gleason was recasting one wife he felt he ought to recast both. "I always felt there was more to it than that, but I never knew," she says. Jane Kean, Gleason's pal from vaudeville days, got the role. For Alice, Gleason opted for another young and pretty blonde, like Sue Ann Langdon. His choice was Sheila MacRae, who had been married to the Broadway singer Gordon MacRae and later wed Ronald Wayne, a sometime producer of Jackie's TV shows from Florida.

MacRae says she thinks a large part of the reason she was chosen was that she shared Gleason's interests in matters spiritual and supernatural. "He would question me constantly about these things," she recalls. "He showed me his gold-bound box with the ectoplasm in it. We talked about the parapsychological research at Duke University. It started right from my audition. He called up the professional psychic Peter Hurkos, whom he knew, and asked what Hurkos could tell him over the phone about the person whose hand Jackie was holding. Hurkos said I had hurt my back as a child by being knocked over by a big dog, which is true. He said I would stay with Jackie, which I wasn't sure I wanted to but eventually did, and then he said I would be a very different Alice and Jackie should never try to make me like the other one.

"I really got to know Jackie and he got to know me and it felt like we did read each other's minds. Once we had to ad-lib a scene of two people talking about when they first fell in love and we were so mystically in tune, Jackie said to me, 'Tonight, kid, you joined the ranks of the pros.' Another time Art Carney missed a cue to enter when I was singing and Jackie came on, took off his uniform jacket and started improvising unpleasant remarks about Alice's mother. Then he took me over to the window and whispered about Art and we just made up the rest of the scene, all live before an audience. After he died, I often felt his spiritual presence with me." (MacRae caused sharp intakes of breath around the room and a sort of mini-scandal when, at a swank black tie tribute to Gleason after his death sponsored by the Museum of Broadcasting in New York City, she declared that she felt his spiritual essence in the room at that very moment. Gleason's widow, Marilyn, was reliably reported not to be amused.)

Commercially, the shift back to the *Honeymooners* format was a huge success. *The Jackie Gleason Show* vaulted up to fifth in the Nielsen ratings that season, Jackie's highest finish since ranking second to *I Love Lucy* in 1954–55. But almost all of the attention—and yet another Emmy Award, to be followed by still another a season later—went to Carney. The press stopped referring to Carney as a second banana and Carney, his confidence burgeoning, stopped referring to himself that way, too. He told *TV Guide,* "I'm not a stooge anymore. I used to be." Although Gleason professed to be delighted at Carney's success, which after all ensured the longevity of a series that only Gleason and not Carney owned, it rankled a little that Jackie needed a partner to find the popularity he craved. Some of the publicity was, in Jackie's view, downright insulting. The New York *World Journal Tribune* bannered its Sunday television magazine with the cover line HOW CARNEY PUT GLEASON BACK ON TOP.

As ever, Carney played peacemaker. Franklin Cover, who went on to a decade of sitcom popularity as the white husband of an interracial couple featured on *The Jeffersons,* recalls appearing twice on the musical *Honeymooners* episodes. He wasn't asked again, he says, after he declined a summons to work Thanksgiving Day in Miami when he had a family reunion planned in Ohio. The pay was enticing: seven hundred fifty dollars per show, plus four hundred fifty dollars spending money plus accommodation at the Algiers Hotel and first class airfare. "This was for having maybe one speaking line as an Irish cop, something like, 'All right, Kramden, why don't you shut your big fat mouth or I'll run *you* in,'" he recalls. "Under his breath, on air, Jackie would be saying, 'Wait for it, pal, wait for the laugh,' as though I wouldn't know enough to do that. He would use every swear word you've ever heard. He'd be hung over and snarling. I remember saying to Jane Kean, who was an old friend, 'How can you stand it?' She replied, 'For this money I can listen to those words. I've heard them all before.' After one rehearsal broke up almost immediately because Jackie had a tantrum or an anxiety attack or whatever you want to call it, Art Carney drove me back to the hotel. I went on and on about Gleason's behavior and how unprofessional it was and all Art would put in was, 'That's right' and 'It *is* unusual.' He was very careful not to say a negative thing against Gleason, although you could sense that he agreed."

Jane Kean, who observed the same willingness to absorb abuse and not answer back, said of Carney, "He's not a fighter. If he has to fight, Art won't do it. He will never, never fight." Periodically, Carney dealt with the pentup frustration by going on a bender. Agent Sam Cohn says, "We figured we would lose Art for at least a show a season. But what he did the rest of the time made it worth it." Typically, the dynamics of the relationship continued to be such that, instead of recognizing he had driven Carney to drink, Gleason saw himself as the benevolent boss indulging a subordinate's weakness. Even in Florida, where Carney was forced to live part of the year so he could do the Gleason show, the two actors almost never socialized. Between seasons, they did not see each other. Theirs was almost entirely a business relationship. Privately, each thought the other deeply troubled.

The pairing still yielded fine comedy, however. While the musical *Honeymooners* episodes rarely achieved the exquisite blend of cartoon imagination and gritty reality of the hallowed thirty-nine episodes from the single sitcom season of the fifties, the new hours were generally entertaining and at least one was truly inspired, a farce worthy of Feydeau. Its premise was to have Kramden and Norton "meet" Gleason and Carney. As chairman of his Raccoons lodge dance, Ralph boasts of being able to get a celebrity to attend and thereby boost ticket sales. Ed tries to be helpful by pointing out that Brother Kramden has long claimed to know Gleason. Ralph, unwilling to admit a lie, temporizes. Meanwhile word spreads through the neighborhood that Gleason is definitely coming, and tickets sell by the fistful. Finally Ralph and Ed, in desperation, camp out at a hotel where Gleason and Carney are ensconced producing a show and plead in vain for an opportunity to see the two stars. By chance, each happens to spot the other's lookalike coming out of the elevator, but the two nobodies are too dumbstruck at seeing a genuine star in the flesh— "Do you know who you are? You're Jackie Gleason!"—to ask for help. As usual, Alice saves the day, writing a full and frank letter to Gleason that persuades him to come. (The bait: her recipe for anchovy pizza.) Most of the crosscutting between the famous duo and the nonentity duo is done via lightning changes of costume and manner, performed live, and it all amounts to a Broadway-quality display of theatrical timing and technique. Only Gleason's unseen but loudly heard final "appearance" at the Raccoons Hall, as Ralph stands in the next room listening, involves an obvious use of recording equipment and other television techniques.

Most of the other musical episodes revisited themes established in the fifties: Ralph losing a large sum of money and going into a panic; Ralph misunderstanding some action of Alice's and feeling hysterical jealousy; Ralph at last getting a chance to fulfill his ambition, a momentary appearance on television, at which he freezes in stage fright; Ralph becoming convinced that Ed is somehow a danger to him. While these plots might fairly be faulted as unimaginative and as depriving the characters of growth, the counterargument is that Gleason was fiercely protective of his creation. Larry King recalls being invited to attend a session at which Gleason's writers outlined in detail, with funny gags and acted-out bits of business, a proposed installment. Ralph, in financial trouble, was supposed to stage a rent party, where he would provide food and music and collect an entry fee at the door. Jackie laughed uproariously, heard the story through, and then said at the end, "Kill it. Kramden would never hold a rent party, no matter how tough things got—not with his pride." The judgment was right, and it was shrewder than that of writers who had been creating Kramden sketches since the character was born.

At the end of the first season of the *Honeymooners* revival, Gleason reentered the movie business. Over the next four years he would make films annually in the summer break following the end of the TV season. In every case he worked with major stars. Most of the time he was working with celebrated producers, directors and writers. Without exception the results were awful. Had Jackie devised a plan to render him dependent on television and to kill off his career completely once the network no longer wanted him, he could not have schemed better than to make, in succession, *Skidoo, How to Commit Marriage, Don't Drink the Water* and *How Do I Love Thee?*

On *Skidoo* his only accomplishment was off-screen, upstaging the legendary ego of director Otto Preminger. Former CBS executive Oscar Katz was invited to visit Jackie on the set one day and, knowing the director's bullying reputation, listened with delight as Jackie kept him waiting. With mounting peevishness the cinema auteur finally shouted—himself, rather than through a toady—"Is Mr. Gleason ready?" Jackie shot back in falsetto, "Coming, *Otto,*" the lilting tone only underscoring the intended insult. The film centered on Jackie as a retired mobster being blackmailed back in for one last hit on a Joe Valachi-type squealer played by Mickey Rooney. The rest of the cast included Groucho Marx, Cesar Romero, George Raft, Burgess Meredith, Frank Gorshin and Carol Channing, all abysmally used.

On *How to Commit Marriage* the director was Norman Panama and the co-stars were Bob Hope and Jane Wyman. The plot, a pathetic attempt at trendiness then, is hopeless hokum today. It is a farrago of irrationalities about hippies, rock bands, trial marriages, secret divorces, gurus and drugs. Gleason was cast, somewhat aptly, as a father outraged by all the sexual freedom and antiestablishment shenanigans of the younger generation. This was exactly the line he was taking in interviews and, with hilarious hypocrisy, at a "Rally for Decency" in Miami in

March 1969, a few months before the film's release. That rally, organized ostensibly by teenagers to protest an appearance by the rock band The Doors (at which lead singer Jim Morrison had been said to expose his genitals), promoted "God, parents, patriotism, chastity and brotherhood" and condemned "indecency" in entertainment. "I believe this kind of movement will snowball across the United States and perhaps around the world," Jackie told a crowd of thirty thousand people in Miami. He was apparently unfazed by any contrast between what he preached and what he practiced in his own life, which had included precious little regard for the conventions of religion, parenthood and sexuality. "These are my kind of people," he told the throng assembled in the Orange Bowl. In fairness to Gleason, it should be noted that the rally organizers emphasized that they were not speaking out against anyone, but rather for specific values, and that although Jackie congenially shared the stage with Anita Bryant that day, he seems not to have taken any role in her anti-homosexual crusade in Miami a few years later. He was not, at least publicly, a hater.

Of all the movies in this period, the biggest disappointment for Gleason was surely *Don't Drink the Water,* an adaptation of a Woody Allen play that he had loved. Although Allen's sensibility and Gleason's would seem as far apart as their physiques, personas and ethnic backgrounds, Gleason admired the reedy, neurotic

Jewish comic and repeatedly went to see him perform. Larry King recalls going with Gleason to an appearance by Allen in Miami at which the budding performer told what eventually became one of his most famous stories, a long-winded yarn about a man who shoots a moose, discovers it's not dead, takes it back with him to the city and enters it in a Halloween costume contest. The moose wins only *second* prize, losing to a husband and wife dressed in a moose suit. The upshot is that the man takes the moose back to the woods, shoots it again and discovers he has killed his friends instead. They were Jews, and the trophy of their costume, the punch line explains, now hangs in a very "exclusive" (meaning anti-Semitic) private club. "Now Jackie had never heard this story before," King recalls, "but as it unfolded he would turn to me and whisper, 'Moose not dead' and 'Halloween contest, moose loses' and finally 'Wrong moose.' He just had this amazing show business intelligence. I asked him how he did it, and he said, 'It was just logical, there was nowhere else that it could go.' When he used to say that he could watch the first minute or two of a sitcom and know how the whole half hour would go, I believed him. He had that much street smarts and, especially, experience."

The problem with *Don't Drink the Water* on screen is that it wasn't directed by Woody Allen. Instead the director was Howard Morris, an erstwhile writer for Sid Caesar who did not seem to grasp the basic wellspring of the humor. The story concerns an unsophisticated caterer from New Jersey and his wife who, by a combination of accident and international incident, wind up trapped in the American embassy of a small Eastern European nation. Onstage the concept was that the embassy was tiny, so crowded with these extra guests that laundry had to be hung in the living room to dry. Morris moved the action to quarters as expansive as the Capitol rotunda. Charles Joffe, who produces all of Allen's movies including this one, says flatly, "Howard Morris destroyed the play with this huge, lavish set. I knew it was a disaster the first week but I was a novice producer and I was scared to speak up. I think Jackie sensed it that early, too. He certainly knew by midway through the picture, but he was very cooperative. He didn't beat up on the director, he gave no trouble to the other actors, he didn't just walk through his lines only half-acting. The only time he let on that he knew how bad it was came near the end, when he said, 'We all went in hoping for the best. All you can say is that we tried.'

"Everything that I had been told about how difficult he could be absolutely did not come true.

"He wanted his own trailer, his makeup and hair people from the TV series, but those are not unusual demands in this business. When you buy a star, you buy a package. He could have gotten very nasty because he basically did the picture for nothing, for free. He took a salary of union-scale pay, which was very low, at most five thousand dollars or so for the whole ten weeks of shooting, because he needed a picture at the time, he loved the play and our schedule fit his. He took a big piece of the back end—that is, he was supposed to get a large percentage of the adjusted gross profits—only there weren't any and you could tell there weren't going to be while we were still filming."

Gleason requested very little rewriting on the script, he did not complain about camera angles and, while he did not fraternize in the least with the crew, he threw only one moderate tantrum, on a day when he had to wait three hours for the lighting to be set up on his final shot of the afternoon. Joffe wasn't thrilled with Gleason's interpretation of the central role, a man used to his own world who cannot cope with change and thus gets in everyone's way. Gleason, he felt, was too eager to maintain the ebullient strength of his television persona and to reach for broad comic bits instead of subtle reactions. He was more concerned, Joffe thought, with getting momentary laughs than with building up believability. But he appreciated Gleason's candor: "At one point, Jackie decided he was working too hard and called me in and said, 'I have to have a shorter day, pal. I'm no good after three o'clock. I just don't have it then.' Well, I had figured this was coming. I knew he thought I would go away and try to eliminate some scenes, cut down the number of takes, that kind of thing. Instead I said to him, 'Fine, Jackie, I can do that. But will you make the call to CBS to tell them that you're under contract here and you're going to be two weeks late starting your series?' He roared with laughter. 'So you got the date, you smart sonofabitch! You got the date!' That was all he said. He had been testing me, and I passed. The subject was dropped and he was very nice. The next time I saw him, which was at a birthday party for Sam Cohn, Jackie came up from behind and grabbed me and said, 'Hi, pal, when are we going to find another piece of shit to do together?' "

Estelle Parsons, who played Gleason's wife in *Don't Drink the Water,* had met him in the fifties when she was a charter staffer of the *Today* show and married to journalist Richard Gehman, a magazine freelance writer who became part of Jackie's crowd at Toots Shor's. She says, "Personally Jackie was a lot like me, I thought—cantankerous and vengeful—but I didn't get to know him too well because that crowd treated me as just a wife. Jackie wasn't flirtatious, he wasn't smutty, he wasn't much interested. They would all just stand around and drink. I don't think those guys even talked much among themselves. I had always found him very shy and private. And after my husband and I split up, I didn't see him anymore. In the fifties I drank with him and smoked pot with him at our house but I didn't even know where he lived. I certainly was never invited there. So I was surprised that he sort of treated me as an old friend when we did the movie. By then, of course, I had the Oscar for *Bonnie and Clyde*. Once we started rehearsing the movie he talked about *Gigot* all the time and finally screened it. I certainly didn't think it was a good representation of him. He didn't sparkle. But of course he wanted me to say it was wonderful, so I did. He wasn't hard to work with. Whatever he got upset about always seemed to me to be a justifiable complaint. Howard Morris didn't have the same sense of humor as Jackie or Woody or the play. And Jackie would keep explaining things to him. Jackie was very smart about how to make his kind of humor work. He was also very generous with creative impulses for others. Eventually he gave me a photograph, which I don't recall asking for, inscribed, 'You deserve an Oscar just for walking on the set.'

"I must admit, I would not call him an actor. I thought of him as a comic or a personality. I felt he was always doing Jackie Gleason. He was a creative genius, but he wasn't malleable. Personally, you couldn't be devoted to him. He always picked up the check—he would, wouldn't he?—and he wanted the bill to be right. But he did not encourage friendship in the way that normal people do. So I never saw him again after the film."

At the end of his 1969–70 season Gleason made the last of this run of four films, *How Do I Love Thee?*, a tedious sentimental comedy of interest only because it prefigured so many of the themes that Gleason would revisit, far more ably, in his final film, *Nothing in Common*. Both movies cast Gleason as a combative father estranged from a successful son. In both he falls ill and only then achieves a rapprochement with his offspring, who turns out to be much more like him than either generation has realized. But where *Nothing in Common* would aim at drama, *How Do I Love Thee?* sought to be a trendy generation gap comedy. The fulcrum of its inane plot was Gleason's taking a poem given to him by an old flame, Shelley Winters, submitting it to a poetry contest and winning the then-staggering sum of ten thousand dollars—all the while with nobody, even the poetry contest judges, recognizing the poem as the hugely famous sonnet by Elizabeth Barrett Browning, known to every schoolgirl, that begins with the words of the movie's title.

Many of the people who worked with Gleason in films during this period, and most of the reviewers, faulted him for not choosing better material. It is remarkable that a man who could so shrewdly attune *The Honeymooners* or *Gigot* to his gifts, who could so quickly spot the potential of *The Hustler* or *Take Me Along*, should have squandered himself in such shlock just a few years later. But the truth is that Gleason simply did not have that much choice. Producers with first-rate scripts were apt not to come to him because his television persona was so well established with audiences that it would get in the way, or at least blur the edges, of whatever character he was playing. Besides, Hollywood still believed, with some solid evidence to back up the opinion, that the public resisted paying movie ticket prices to see performers it could view for free at home. Jackie's physique disqualified him from many roles, and so did the seemingly inescapable forcefulness of his personality. In all likelihood he accepted the most promising of what was brought to him, primarily hackneyed material that his popularity was a key to getting financed. And most of it, like *Don't Drink the Water,* probably looked better on the page than it ended up being on the screen. It is a sad show business truism that there are dozens of ways a show can go wrong and only one way to succeed—for absolutely everything to go right.

As the sixties turned into the seventies, Jackie's public persona came to seem more and more dated and irrelevant. In dress and manner, in style and sense of humor, in his taste in music and his choice of material, Gleason remained rooted in the forties, when he was young and just beginning to make it. Other performers of his time had tried, if ineffectually, to remake themselves. Jack Benny was determined to keep up with the new. So was Bob Hope. Gleason seemed to lack their suppleness of spirit. He was drinking more heavily than ever, getting tongue-tied and legless in the company of his producers and co-stars of his movies and sometimes imbibing during performances of his television show—at grave peril to his once infallible timing.

Perhaps the worst year of his life was the last year of the sixties, when everything seemed to fall away from him. *Don't Drink the Water* was a disaster. The CBS series, after a couple of seasons of heady ratings, again fell out of the Nielsen top twenty. By the end of 1969, the show was relying heavily on reruns. On the personal side, things were, if possible, even worse than they were professionally. Honey Merrill, Jackie's companion for a dozen years, had given him a deadline for marriage. So in 1968 he sued Genevieve for divorce, on the reasonable grounds that the marriage had ended long before. She refused, invoking both the Catholic church's ban on dissolution of a marriage and her undeniable financial rights as his prospective widow, which would end with a divorce. Gen was only a year younger, so it almost amounted to a curse for her to presume she would outlive him. Jackie won the first legal round against her, in February of 1969, when a New York State Supreme Court judge ruled that Gleason was entitled to seek the disunion even though he was the "guilty party," applying retroactively a law that had taken effect in 1966. But in New York State the Supreme Court is a trial court. In October of 1969, Jackie lost a three to two vote of the superior appellate division, which said that in the absence of specific retroactivity instructions from the legislature the court would exceed its authority to grant that right unilaterally. Throughout, Jackie took a battering in the newspaper headlines. Typical was the *New York Daily News*: GLEASON SEEKING DIVORCE; HE SAID HE NEVER WOULD.

While the court case dragged on, Jackie's relationship with Honey, often stormy, deteriorated sharply. In April of 1969, just after Jackie had won his initial court battle and marriage to Honey at long last looked possible, she left him. Consciously or not, she marked her departure with a gesture that for Jackie had chilling echoes of his father's running away all those years before. Pete McGovern, Gleason's publicist, can still recall the look of unutterable sadness in his boss's eyes as he said, "This time I think she means it, boys. She took all the pictures with her."

By the time the next round of court action came, setting back his plans for freedom, Jackie had already lined up a new spouse-in-waiting. Once again she was blonde and decorative. She had been introduced to him, friends say, by the wife of his producer Jack Philbin. Her name was Beverly McKittrick, and she was a secretary from Baltimore. For Gleason, on the rebound from Honey and bitter about Genevieve, the infatuation felt like love at first sight. His friends were not so enthusiastic. The next few years would prove them right.

But of all the events of 1969, none quite matched what was to come in the first few months of 1970. By then Gleason was emotionally exhausted, as depressed as anyone had seen him

451

in years, and ready to give in to whatever befell him. He sensed that the ax was about to fall and braced for it. Robert Wood, the tough new president of the CBS network, objected to the runaway cost of Jackie's show. The advertising sales department had targeted Jackie, Ed Sullivan, Red Skelton and other holdover stars as being popular in the wrong way—they attracted older, more rural and less affluent viewers instead of the well-heeled young urbanites that advertisers wanted to reach. Jackie's ratings, while still strong enough to merit renewal by the standards of the time (and high enough for megahit status today), were slipping. Gone were the executive pilgrimages to Florida, the elaborate rituals of deference, the mating dance of renewal. The network's strategy shifted to making Jackie quit: demanding more and more work, offering less and less money. Then, with negotiations pending, without warning, in a meeting that no representative of his was invited to attend, CBS canceled its weekly slot for Jackie Gleason. No one can quite remember how Gleason was told, but agent Sam Cohn thinks Jackie endured the added insult of finding out by reading it in a newspaper. Ostensibly this was to be just a rest, a chance for audiences to rediscover their hunger for Gleason and for Jackie to refresh himself and retool his offerings.

The truth was that Jackie was through in weekly television. He would show up a couple of times a year in specials, reprising *The Honeymooners,* doing other sorts of sketches, on a couple of occasions playing substantial dramatic parts. He still had ahead of him a national tour of a major Broadway comedy and at least seven feature films. There would be tributes and talk show appearances, lucrative commercials and cheering crowds at parades. But in essence Jackie Gleason had been forced into semiretirement by the medium that had made him so visible a workaholic. And although he would keep working steadily and profitably to the end of his life, he would never again control the means of production. Except for scattered *Honeymooners* specials, he would not be the owner, just a hired hand. He would never again employ a vast entourage. He would slowly disappear from the headline attention he so loved and hated. He would keep the honorific, but in name only.

In reality he would never again be The Great One.

CHAPTER ELEVEN

On a winter day in 1968, a group of CBS programming executives including Mike Dann and Irwin Segelstein sat in a small conference room and watched a videotape of a situation comedy newly popular in Britain. Called *Till Death Do Us Part,* it centered on a short-tempered, intolerant, blue-collar head of household, Alf Garnett. The humor was acrid and mean-spirited but undeniably truthful. When the show was done, Dann and Segelstein looked at each other and said two words, or rather one name: "Jackie Gleason." Adapting this series for American television, they felt, might be the ideal way to modernize and reinvent Gleason's persona. And Gleason in turn would invest the rather harsh central figure with some of the accumulated affection that audiences felt for Jackie and for his principal characters, especially Alf Garnett's closest correlative, Ralph Kramden.

But CBS did not get the rights. A movie and TV producer named Norman Lear, along with his partner Bud Yorkin, did instead. They sold the concept of the show, then titled *Those Were the Days,* not to CBS but to ABC. A pilot was cast, made and rejected as just too tough for

American television. Then another was made and, after longer discussion, met the same fate. Lear and Yorkin at last took the show to CBS, which bought it, renamed it and apparently offered it to Jackie one last time. (On this point, memories sharply differ.) But Jackie was furious with CBS for canceling him. He still wanted to do a variety show. He considered the new series a degenerate version of *The Honeymooners*. Above all, he rejected the character of Archie Bunker and the show, now called *All in the Family*, as "not funny." So if the role was offered, as it seems to have been, it was promptly spurned.

That decision was the turning point in the last two decades of Jackie Gleason's working life. If he had done *All in the Family*, and if it had succeeded as thoroughly with him as it did with its actual cast and production team, he would have transformed his passé image, made himself a star with a whole new generation, cemented his claim to be the most enduring male performer in the American history of the small screen and vastly enlarged his bank account.

He always insisted that he did not regret the decision, at times so vehemently that it was hard to believe he was telling the truth. He called the show "cheap humor, like telling a dirty joke. It's easy to get laughs with ethnic humor. But there is nothing genuinely funny about it, or about menstrual periods. These are not suitable topics." He was pleased and touched that Carroll O'Connor, the actor playing Bunker, paid tribute to Gleason's pioneering sitcom acting, and he eventually wrote words of praise for O'Connor's performance, although he remained queasy and noncommittal about the show as a whole. Deep down, Gleason's disavowal of interest may have reflected a realization that the show was, in fact, far better without him than it would have been with him. He and Lear, both giant egos, would have clashed monumentally. Jackie, aggressively Republican and a particular fan (and sometime golfing partner) of President Richard Nixon, would have raged at Lear's deliberate attempt to show Bunker, a Nixon supporter, as bigoted and ignorant and so inattentive to current events that he did not know his favorite president's correct middle initial. Most people who worked with Jackie considered his attitudes toward women antediluvian. He resisted the least hints of women's liberation on *The Honeymooners* for as long as the network would let him and would almost certainly have raged against the underlying feminist agenda that evolved season by season in *All in the Family*. About the only area of rhetoric in which he would have felt comfortable was Archie's assertive belief in the unquestionability of parental authority—and Lear even poked holes, albeit more gently, in that.

The only thing one can say for certain about Gleason's lack of interest in *All in the Family* as the seventies began is that it left him unemployed, almost devoid of income, bored, depressed and increasingly drunk. "Those were pretty tough and lonely times," Sam Cohn recalls. "It was hard being Jackie's agent. It got to the point where he would call and it would be two or three or four days before I would call him back. There was just nothing, no interest, no one asking for him to do anything. Finally I had a conversation in which I laid it on the line for him. He said, 'Just so long as our friendship is still okay, pal. That's what really matters. As long as we talk, that's all I ask.' "

When CBS canceled his series in 1970, Jackie said he would devote himself full-time to making movies. But except for *How Do I Love Thee?*, to which he had already been signed, Gleason didn't make a film for almost seven years. A few roles were floated as possibilities, including the coach in the ultimately misbegotten screen version of *That Championship Season,* the Pulitzer Prize-winning play by Jason Miller, the estranged husband of his daughter Linda. But nothing came of any of them. Except for doing celebrity commentary on the Jackie Gleason Inverrary Classic, a golf tournament that emanated from the course alongside his fourteen-room mansion near Fort Lauderdale, he did not appear consequentially on CBS or any other network for almost three years. Then it was to do yet another *Honeymooners* revival, for which Art Carney kindly consented to appear. After that it was almost a year more until he came back, once again as Kramden. By then Carney was busy filming *Harry and Tonto,* which in 1975 would win him the Oscar for best actor, so Gleason turned to Julie Andrews, of all people, to play the role of Norton. (She also sang the part of Eliza Doolittle in what seems to have been a trip down memory lane for both parties.) Jackie occasionally showed up on talk or interview programs, especially in Miami, and once, in 1974, he joined Bob Hope in drag to tape a Hope special in New York City's Central Park. By then Gleason was no longer getting his hundred thousand dollars a year from CBS and had a one-year deal with Hope's longtime network, NBC. Although the two-day shooting was open to the public and was free entertainment, it drew a crowd estimated by the *New York Times* as only about fifteen hundred people, an alarming index for Gleason of how much his popularity had fallen.

He had been slow to accept the necessary dissolution of his empire. While most of the cast and crew of *The Jackie Gleason Show* went off the payroll as soon as the series was canceled, he held on to his oldest, closest aides a good deal longer. Publicist Pete McGovern, with Gleason since 1952, recalls that he was retained for eight months during which he had nothing to do, then was let go by Philbin during a time when Gleason was traveling. "I'm sorry," Philbin said to him, "but Jackie still doesn't know what he's going to do so there just isn't any need for you." When Jackie found out about it, McGovern says, "He didn't bring me back, but he sent me a year's pay as severance."

Gleason repeatedly claimed to journalists that CBS was constantly imploring him to return and that the other two networks were desperately eager to sign him to series deals. But in truth, when CBS tried *Honeymooners* reruns in early 1971, the ratings were dismal, and pilot scripts for a proposed half-hour series based on Jackie's Joe the Bartender character were rejected as unfit even to be taped and tested. The hundred thousand dollars a year that CBS paid him annually through 1973 had plummeted in value since the mid-fifties, and even back when it started Jackie had derided it as "cigar store spending money" by his standards. Gleason wasn't broke. He had enjoyed too many perquisites and free items during the good years and had been protected by too many shrewd managers to have strewn away quite everything. But he did not have enough to live indefinitely in the style to which he had become accustomed. And sooner or later he would need the psychic income of highly public work, not just a retainer and the odd guest appearance.

He did not retreat totally from public view. Actress Jane Alexander, a Tony and Emmy winner and four-time Oscar nominee, recalls Gleason's coming backstage to meet her and the rest of the cast of Harold Pinter's dark, obscure *Old Times*. Although it was 1972, for her the memory is as fresh as yesterday. "He wore a dark blue jacket and had a carnation in his lapel and the holders and handlers were all around him. I was pretty thrilled. I had already won a Tony Award for *The Great White Hope* but, I mean, Jackie Gleason—this was a star. I thought to myself, what an odd choice for him, this old vaudevillian, this sketch comic, not what you immediately thought of as an educated or intellectual man, but he liked the play. He said, 'Do you know what this play is about?' and I said, 'No, I don't think even Pinter does.' He said, 'I don't know either, but it's a good evening.' "

Most of the time, however, Jackie was at home in Florida with his new wife, Beverly—whom he had wed in July 1970, ten days after the divorce with Gen became official—and sometimes with his grandchildren. Now and then he showed the intuitive wit of a storybook grandfather in the matter of endearing himself. His secretary Sydell Spear recalls a day when Linda's son Jason (now film star Jason Patric) saw a favorite toy animal run over by an automobile in a parking lot. The boy ran in crying. Gleason snatched the ruined animal up and announced that he could inflate it back to perfection with his own lungs, then carted it out of the room and dispatched Sydell with money to buy another. Minutes later, he returned, huffing and puffing as he held the new animal and then proclaiming, with the last "restorative" gasp, that it was all fixed. "Oh, Grandpa, you can do *anything*," the delighted child cried, words that any grandparent would be happy to hear but that Gleason particularly wanted to believe. An increasing percentage of the time, however, Jackie was spending the whole day drunk and disorderly, if not outright disabled. Virtually all of his friends considered Beverly a bad influence. She had nothing in common with Jackie, they said, except golf and drinking. She knew nothing of show business and did not encourage him to perform. She was possessive and consequently mistrustful of his old friends. Flo Haley found her more humorless even than Genevieve and sexually jealous of Jackie's tiniest affectionate gesture toward Flo, a woman whom he had known and trusted more than thirty years and whose husband had been a kind of surrogate father to Jackie. Mercedes Ellington says, "Beverly encouraged the dark side of Jackie, the drinking, the carousing, the staying up all night, the being out of shape and not taking care of himself." By his own admission, in this period Jackie often got only two to three hours of sleep a night. His weight began to seesaw again, a condition even more dangerous than permanent obesity according to researchers, and his temper, never entirely controlled, often flared.

The marriage seemed not to agree with Beverly, either. She aged rapidly in appearance and looked haggard by the time she and Jackie divorced in November 1974. If Marilyn Taylor had been determined not to be perceived as the cause of the breakup of Jackie's first marriage in the fifties, by now, as Marilyn Taylor Horwich, she was apparently perfectly willing to be seen as the reason for the end of Jackie's second wedlock. Marilyn had reentered Jackie's life at a lunch he had with Marilyn's sister, his longtime choreographer June Taylor. June brought Marilyn, by now a widowed mother of a pubescent son with her as a surprise for Jackie. According to some old friends, Gleason asked, "Who's the cute blonde?" He either failed to recognize his paramour of two decades before or wanted to pretend he didn't recognize her, for reasons never explained. The relationship with Beverly was already doomed—"As a real marriage, it lasted about a weekend," says one crony—and Jackie had never quite forgotten Marilyn. They started keeping company and he announced his engagement the instant his divorce was final, just as he announced his engagement to Beverly long before the divorce from Gen was final. For a man who lived like a carefree bachelor through most of his adult life, Gleason achieved the remarkable feat of being married for all but a few weeks of his entire manhood.

Before the nuptials with Marilyn could be completed, however, came a bizarre reunion with Beverly, never publicly explained. About a month after the divorce, Beverly said, "Jackie moved back into the house without warning, bag and baggage. And he was drinking then. He wasn't drinking when he left. I tried straightening him out. I cooked him corned beef and cabbage. I got him off the booze. We lived as man and wife." Then, said Beverly, she and Jackie started fighting again, in her judgment because he started pill-popping. "Anytime he's not drinking, he's taking prescription pills for his weight," she said. "And then he's against me, because I'm strictly against pills." Jackie remained in the fourteen-room, eight-bath house, living in a guest bedroom, as he may have been wont to do during prior spats with Beverly and was definitely known to do in later years, when he was being too sullen for Marilyn to put up with him.

During this truce, he and Beverly encountered each other, fittingly, at the game room bar, where each laid claim to one end, divided by a neutral zone. Jackie was still in residence in March of 1975, and so was Beverly, according to a report in *People* magazine. At this stage the fighting seemed to be strictly over money, with no hint in the air of a peaceful reconciliation. Beverly claimed that Jackie had given her only two hundred dollars in cash for household expenses during a three-month span. His lawyers countered that she had run up more than ten thousand dollars in bills on credit cards until Jackie cut off her accounts. Beverly claimed that Jackie had a net worth of more than three and a half million dollars and said she would settle for half of it. That would have been pretty steep, considering the brevity of the marriage and the fact that almost none of Jackie's wealth was earned during it. Gen, married to him eight times as long, had finally settled for a hundred thousand dollars a year. But Jackie was prepared for divorce to be costly. He said simply, "It's the law."

Things got particularly nasty when the annual

Jackie Gleason Golf Classic rolled around that year, with President Gerald Ford in attendance. Jackie had Beverly's membership at the Inverrary Country Club revoked a week beforehand so that she could not attend as a member and interfere with Marilyn's position as his official hostess and consort. Presumably at his behest, the club's president even asked Beverly to move out of the house for the duration of Ford's visit, to avoid embarrassment. She refused.

What seems to have been behind all this is not romance, although it is just possible that Gleason may have toyed with a rapprochement, but rather a calculated move by Jackie to hold on to the Inverrary house, his favorite residence and the place he lived longest in his entire life, until it burned down in 1983 as a result of faulty air conditioning.

It is definitely the case that Beverly sought to receive the mansion as part of her settlement and that Jackie gave her cash instead. One can only speculate that his lawyers advised him he might have a better chance of persuading the divorce court not to award Beverly the house if both of them, rather than she alone, were living there. If Jackie went back as coldly as that and misled Beverly as to his intentions in the way she claimed, it seems almost inconceivable that he would not have had Marilyn's full understanding and connivance. Why else would she have taken him back so readily after he had returned to co-habiting with the woman he was supposedly leaving? Soon after this bizarre episode broke into print in the spring of 1975, Jackie and Marilyn married and at long last made legal what had started as an illicit flirtation almost a quarter century before.

The same year that Jackie shed Beverly and finally wed Marilyn, he consummated another "romance" that the public had been encouraging for at least as long. After decades of talking about playing Diamond Jim Brady to her Lillian Russell, Gleason at last teamed with Lucille Ball in a trio of playlets about middle-aged lovers. It was a measure of how far Jackie had fallen in clout that the production was assembled by Lucille Ball Productions Incorporated, with Ball listed as executive producer and her husband Gary Morton as producer and Jackie ranking only as a hired hand. Indeed, CBS labeled the evening "A Lucille Ball Special," with Gleason given subsidiary billing. The title credited the skits to Renee Taylor and Joseph Bologna, but another writer, James Eppy, was listed as the author of the script, suggesting that Taylor and Bologna had spied impending catastrophe and escaped or had shrewdly gotten themselves fired at some point during this dreary exercise. The hour package was reviewed by *New York Times* television critic John O'Connor, without the least hyperbole, as "disaster at its unmitigated worst."

In one sketch, Ball and Gleason played a married couple trying to reinvigorate their marriage on a trip to Rome. In another, they played lovers who were married but not to each other, meeting on the sly in a cocktail lounge. In the last, they played domineering parents of grown children, endeavoring to keep their offspring home for a "traditional" New Year's Eve. The plotting was hopeless, the dialogue worse. But the problem went deeper. There was no chemistry between television's greatest male star and its greatest female star. Their personalities did not kindle each other. Their styles did not mesh. Each brought out the abrasive excesses in the other. And each made the other seem terribly old-fashioned. What had been touted as a landmark pairing proved a career deflater for both. Ball's weekly appearances had ended a season and a half before, Gleason's five and a half years before. She would have only one comeback, a short-lived flop. Jackie, despite much bravado-laden talk about how all three networks were after him, would never seriously be considered a potential weekly star again.

A few months later, Jackie suffered another body blow to his ego. The golf tournament named for him, originally at Doral and then at the Inverrary course where he lived, was suspended and replaced, ostensibly "for one season only," by the 1976 Tournament Players Championship at the same Inverrary links. Jackie bitterly denounced the tour golfers as "greedy con artists who come to town, gobble up all your money and then treat sponsors shabbily. They think they can walk in with no obligations. I guarantee you we celebrities could put on our tournament and outdraw the pros for four days." What the celebrities could not have done, of course, was get a longterm television contract for their golf or build a pro tour that networks could profitably cover. The only skullduggery afoot seemed to be that the tour no longer felt it gained much by putting Gleason's name on a tournament and so, despite what he said were promises to feature him in advertising of the Tournament Players Championship, Gleason simply got shoved aside. He was a fading celebrity, a falling star.

Only two things went right in 1976. Near the beginning of the year, he reunited with Audrey Meadows and Art Carney for a twenty-fifth anniversary salute to the Kramdens. Once again Joyce Randolph was not asked back, although she was eminently available to play Trixie again, and the role went to Jane Kean. When a group of fans accosted Gleason to question the casting, he explained lamely that it was the twenty-fifth anniversary of the Kramdens as a couple, not of *The Honeymooners* as a sketch. The truth was simply that Jane Kean was an old friend and Joyce Randolph was not someone he had been close to, or for that matter had even seen since 1957. She didn't act any too intimate toward him, either. When she had seen *Take Me Along,* she hadn't gone backstage or even let him know she was coming. She didn't correspond with him or offer herself as available to work.

The special was officially directed by Gleason, and he told a lot of television critics in telephone interviews across the nation that it was the forerunner of a nonmusical hour series, for which all three networks were bidding. If they met his financial demands—"which have always been atrocious," he said—he would sign on. "They have to come up with the Taj Mahal, let me direct and let me do it from Florida." Alas, the network executives felt as critic Arthur Unger of the *Christian Science Monitor* did after watching an advance cassette prior to the interview: "It's a very long hour." So there was no weekly series. But ABC aired three more *Honeymooners* specials over the next couple of years, giving Jackie a renewed source of income. Remembering the golden days, he had the effrontery to try to sweeten his deal by asking the Miami Beach Tourist Development Authority for a forty-thousand-dollar subsidy in exchange for plugging the town in the specials. Local officials quite reasonably objected to giving taxpayer money to ABC, a large and thriving company, or to Jackie, "who has more money than any of us." As an ABC loyalist, Jackie soon afterward spurned an invitation to be part of CBS's fiftieth anniversary festivities. He might have come, he said, if his former network offered more money and made him a co-host of the event.

Later in the year came Jackie's other big boost,

his return to the movies. *Mr. Billion* was a silly comedy about a man who inherits a fortune provided he gets to San Francisco in a specified time to take charge of it. Jackie plays a wily lawyer who wants to obstruct the young man so that he can maintain control of the wealth himself. Much of the filming was done in Rome, which delighted Jackie. Almost as soon as he arrived, Gleason swept into his orbit the distinguished actor William Redfield, whom Jackie greeted as an old friend on the basis of their having worked together in Jackie's early sixties TV drama *The Million Dollar Incident.* Redfield actually recalled that episode as rather unpleasant. His role had been small, and when he had attempted to invest it with a little personality, Jackie had wheeled on him, stabbed a finger and said, "You say that line straight!" Redfield had come home speaking of Gleason as a bully. But by the time of *Mr. Billion,* Jackie was grateful for the esteem Redfield showed him and appreciative that a serious actor might like a fallen comic. The Gleasons and Redfields spent a great deal of time together.

As he was making the film, Redfield was terminally ill with leukemia, although he did not realize the severity of his disease. He died about a month after shooting had finished, and almost all of his scenes, as well as much of his social time, had been with Gleason. Jackie and Marilyn called and wrote and sent flowers. They invited Linda Redfield, his widow, to the Inverrary house when she came to Florida. Years later, Linda

Redfield ran into the film's producer, Steven Bach, in Rio de Janeiro. His reaction on hearing of Jackie was to say, "Don't mention that man's name to me. I hated him." But both Linda Redfield and the actor's son Adam, himself a player of some accomplishment, recall Gleason as having been warm and kind to a colleague who he did not know was dying. The film, alas, did neither man any honor. The *New York Times* aptly reviewed it as "aimlessly harmless" and expressed bafflement that it should have been chosen as Radio City Music Hall's Easter movie for 1977.

By the time *Mr. Billion* came out, Gleason had already gone on to take a role as a Southern sheriff in an accidental hit, *Smokey and the Bandit*, that pushed him right back into stardom. As the apoplectic, arrogant and bonedumb Buford T. Justice, Gleason provided both the villainy and the biggest laughs in this good-ole-boy comedy about truck racing across the Southeast. Much of the reason the film reached a wide enough audience to gross a reported two hundred fifty million dollars at the box office and spawn two profitable sequels, released in 1980 and 1983, was the cunning construction of Gleason's bad guy. Country audiences could enjoy Gleason's constant frustration because he represented law and order, the force that keeps you from drinking and racing and doing whatever else you want. For Northern, city audiences Gleason was fun to hate because he was playing a corrupt bigot, the stereotypic image of redneck bureaucracy.

Gleason claimed to have improvised much of his role, which is not implausible given the general state of the script, and he inspired Burt Reynolds to describe him as the greatest genius Reynolds had worked with (one must note that Olivier, Gielgud, Kurosawa and Ingmar Bergman do not adorn Reynolds's resume). Reynolds came back for the first reprise, in which Jackie not only repeated his role but essayed a gay brother to Buford, his first known homosexual part, played with a minimum of stereotypic offense, and for good measure threw in a cameo as a Canadian Mountie. In Part III, which Reynolds bypassed save for a walk-on, Jackie in effect became the protagonist.

In taking on *Smokey* at all, Jackie showed his shrewdness. Agent Sam Cohn urged him not to do it, saying, "It's not worthy of you." But Gleason made a major financial mistake in turning down a percentage of the gross and insisting on a higher salary instead. "I don't want to go through anybody's books, pal," Gleason said to Cohn. "Just get me the most cash you can up front." That decision cost Jackie millions of dollars in tax-favored capital gains.

Viewing the rushes for *Mr. Billion* and *Smokey and the Bandit* led Gleason to another key career-rejuvenating decision. He decided, after sixty-one years of hard living, that he needed a face lift. His eyelids were puffy and saggy, his jowls as droopy as a basset hound's. He explained, "I felt I owed it to the audience. They see some decrepit-looking fellow running around and they get worried." At the time of the face lift, Jackie described himself in interviews as planning a stage version of *The Honeymooners,* which never happened, two CBS dramas, which he never made, and a CBS miniseries based on his life for which he would compose the music, also never assembled. On the old show biz theory that if you tell a story enough times it becomes true, Jackie determinedly portrayed himself as all the way back from retirement.

Jackie's next move in his campaign of self-rehabilitation was, Sam Cohn recalls, "one of the biggest shocks of my life." Jackie, who hated to leave Florida, hated to get on airplanes, hated to rehearse, hated to memorize lines and hated to have to perform the same material day after day, announced his willingness, nay, eagerness, to return to the live theater—not on Broadway but in a national tour of a vehicle that had already starred three other actors. The play, *Sly Fox,* was a retelling of Ben Jonson's *Volpone,* set in 1880s San Francisco, and was written by Larry Gelbart, whose credits ranged from the musical *A Funny Thing Happened on the Way to the Forum* to the TV series *M*A*S*H.* Gleason had talked in the fifties of playing Volpone for real, under the direction of Orson Welles. Now he would have a chance to revisit, in modified form, that unfinished business.

Like Ben Jonson's 1606 original, *Sly Fox* is a

cartoonish satire of gluttony and greed, lechery and license. Jonson's signal contribution to English literature was the "humour character," a concept of comedy based on the idea that every character should embody the most extreme and obsessive form of a single humour, or mood. A character who is greedy should be nothing but greed; a character who is lustful should be nothing but lust. For this monomaniacal emphasis on a single trait or flaw, Jonson might reasonably be interpreted as the spiritual father of the modern sitcom. Thus, although it is doubtful that Jackie ever read the original play or anything else written by Jonson or any other writer of the era except Shakespeare, he brought to the genre the wholly appropriate lessons of a lifetime in vaudeville and sketch comedy.

The central figure in both the original and Gelbart's retelling is a man so struck with the love of money that he halfway believes he *can* take it with him. Surrounded by sycophants whom he scorns and mistrusts—because he suspects, rightly, that they are just after his pile—he fakes a mortal illness. That allows him both to test the worthiness of potential heirs and to see what rich presents he can extract from those with hopes for the future. George C. Scott created the role in Gelbart's version, giving an exuberant, eyes-rolling performance that Jackie saw on Broadway and loved. Despite mixed response from critics, the show appealed to audiences enough that Scott went on to complete his contractual run and be replaced first by Robert Preston, then by Vincent Gardenia. As the show settled in to a long stint on Broadway, two things were agreed upon among the creators, author Gelbart and director Arthur Penn, and the producers, the Shubert Organization, Lord Lew Grade and Martin Starger. First, there clearly ought to be a national tour. Second, selling the tour to theater owners and skeptical audiences would require a marquee name, a star of the first magnitude. The suggestion that the star be Jackie apparently came from the ever-loyal agent Sam Cohn, who also represented Penn. The idea was seized on by the Shubert Organization officers, Bernie Jacobs and Gerry Schoenfeld, who considered Gleason to be box office insurance in the heartland. Penn and Gelbart describe themselves as having been less enthusiastic right from the outset. They knew of Jackie's reputation for being demanding and difficult. They wondered whether he could accept a situation in which he was, no matter how highly paid and deferentially treated, in the end still just an employee. And they questioned whether he had the discipline to act the lines as written and stay within the confines of the character. Cohn, who had to honor Penn's interests as well as Gleason's, tried to reassure them. In any case, balanced against these worries was one enormous consideration: everyone thought Jackie's residual popularity would bring in a lot of money.

From the beginning, Jackie made sure he was

the mountain and they were all Mohammeds. The deal was sorted out in a succession of meetings in late 1977 and early 1978, all held at Jackie's mansion within the gated community of Inverrary. Despite themselves, almost all the visitors were impressed—not least because the route that Jackie's office suggested they take went past a giant advertising billboard emblazoned with Jackie's face yards high. Says author Gelbart, "He was letting us know he was the king of Fort Lauderdale." Once inside the house, which qualified as a mansion but not as a museum, either in size or in style or in worth of contents, what the visitors perceived was mostly bland good taste, lots of brown and orange but mainly beige, giving an overall feeling suitably sunny and bright for the landscape outside. Manny Kladitis, who was to serve as associate general manager of the tour, felt particularly envious of the game room. It was the house's largest space, something more than thirty feet by twenty feet, filled with equipment for dozens of games, either set up or stored at hand. In the center was a sunken bar surrounded by high stools, so that the booze hound could literally look down on the bartender. The basic plan was not unlike the layout of the main room at the round house in Peekskill. Both expressed Jackie's idea of comfort wedded to elegance. To him, the era's ubiquitous conversation pit, inverted to become the inebriation pit, was the quintessence of style and class.

As he showed them around the house and then

settled in for discussions in the library—over cocktails but not food, for Jackie almost never served meals to guests at home—Gleason was, in Gelbart's recollection, "graciousness itself."

In truth, Jackie was desperately eager to go back before the public, to be loved and applauded again, to feel the electrifying danger of performing live and the better-than-cocaine rush of laughter. But it would have violated every principle of street corner bargaining and punk one-upmanship to let on that he was doing anything more than granting a favor to some amiable gentlemen. The event was, director Penn recalls, "alcoholic—appropriately alcoholic, without any sign of a potential problem in that regard." Penn pressed Gleason hard at a couple of points on the one vital creative issue. "My basic question was, 'Are you going to subvert the Jackie Gleason persona, Ralph Kramden and *The Honeymooners* and Reggie and all the rest, and play this play as written, speaking the words the author spoke and creating the man the author had in mind?' I certainly expected, and may have acknowledged, that we thought a few embellishments were inevitable, that the audience might demand some Gleasonisms. But I was very clear that he had to relate to the other actors and stay within the basic frame of reference of the play. I wanted a performance comparable to the best of his film performances. Both Larry and I came away not quite convinced that Gleason was going to be able to do it, but we did believe he was going to try. Meanwhile, there was a lot of enthusiasm among the owners of quite big theaters around the country, so the deal looked smarter and smarter."

Kladitis, the only attendee of those early meetings who wound up truly liking Gleason, was also, ironically, the only one to perceive danger signs right from the beginning. When conversation turned to the question of the standard eight performances a week (some stars try to bargain down to seven or six), Jackie impulsively shot back, "We'll do nine!" Although he hated to fly, Jackie never stopped to question how he would get from San Diego to San Francisco, or from San Francisco to Chicago, with only one or two days off between engagements to arrive at the next town, settle into new lodgings and check out a new theater, usually with a differently configured stage. Although Jackie disliked leaving Florida, or for that matter even leaving his home, except to play the golf course alongside it, he was talking about spending peripatetic months on the road. And this man who was used to the constant attentive presence of a wife or mistress was going to spend much of the time on his own. Says Kladitis, "I remember thinking, 'He wouldn't be asking for nine performances a week if he had any memory of how much work eight performances are.' I never believed that Jackie understood this undertaking in any way. Hearing this man talk, you could tell that he was not dealing with the artistic or practical realities of the situation. It was evident that it was running through his mind that his career was slipping and might be over. What he saw in this was the answer to his worries. That was as far as it went."

At Jackie's insistence, rehearsals took place in Fort Myers, Florida, near enough to his Fort Lauderdale base to allow him a last little interval of living at home before he faced the rigors of the road. This was just the first of a series of demands that added hugely to the show's budget and to the headaches of its managers. But at that moment it was accepted philosophically. "Given Jackie's style of living," Kladitis recalls, "we figured it would cost almost as much to bring him up to New York as to bring everyone else down to Florida." Rehearsals turned out to be anything but a vacation in the sunshine for the other actors. It was impossible to work outdoors when the cast included someone as famous—and as shameless at playing to a crowd—as Jackie. No suitable indoor theater space could be found in time, so the actors worked in an empty storefront, mostly without props and furniture, a hellish shortcoming in a show as dependent on physical business as *Sly Fox*. To keep from attracting public notice, the company covered the windows with thick brown paper, so the actors rarely glimpsed the sun. Although rehearsals were scheduled for three weeks in February of 1978, Jackie attended only nine days of them. He was often half an hour late and he cut out frequently for midday sessions with the various designers and technicians.

Although a road show is normally an exact reproduction of the Broadway original, modified only to reduce costs or to accommodate frequent setups and tear-downs of the scenery, Jackie insisted on shaping the show to suit him. He instructed the costume designer on what he would wear, right down to the shoes (which one Chicago critic shrewdly spotted as "more suitable for a Florida country club than San Francisco in the late 1880s"). Says Gelbart, "He really, truly seemed to care more about the width of the shoulder on his jacket than about what he was to say and whom he was to say it to." Jackie also started altering the direction, changing bits of business he didn't find funny or groupings that did not give him enough solo attention at center stage. Most significantly, he started rewriting the play, in violation of all his promises. He changed elements of the plot. He changed the first act curtain line to "Aw, shit." On some occasions he substituted "And away we go," a phrase that he might choose to employ in half a dozen random spots per performance. Other Gleason catchphrases popped up here, there and everywhere. When Gelbart confronted him, Jackie looked outraged and cited what, in his television days, would have been unheard-of generosity. Said Jackie, "I allowed your name to go over the title."

To Gelbart, this was war. In the theater, a playwright of any standing almost always has his name over the title. He controls the rights. It is his property. The star, not the writer, is the hired hand. In this particular instance, the property had been a success long before Jackie got involved, while he hadn't yet faced a single audience. But he was already presuming to know how to make it better. Instinctively, Gelbart did the one thing likeliest to enrage Jackie. He walked away. "I said, 'Why don't you go fuck yourself?' and turned on my heel and headed out. From behind I heard this bellowing animal, 'Come back here! Nobody walks out on Gleason!' " The situation, and the dialogue, may well have had an eerie echo for Jackie. In his first season at *Cavalcade* back at DuMont, just as his star was starting to rise, he had gotten into a fight with his producer, Milton Douglas, who weighed literally half what Jackie did, and the frightened Douglas started to sidle away. Jackie lunged for the smaller man, grabbed him by the lapels, hoisted him into the air and roared, "Nobody walks out on me when I'm telling him off." In 1950, Jackie could get away with that. In 1978, he couldn't. He didn't dare touch Gelbart; he just screamed on in fury. The playwright kept walking and thought about trying to cancel the entire deal.

Jackie's treatment of his fellow cast members proved even more of a problem. The other featured players included Irwin Corey, a holdover from vaudeville who specialized in double-talk, and Cleavon Little, a serious actor like Art Carney rather than a comic. It soon turned out that Little had some of the same sensitive, brooding temperament as Carney. Gleason spotted the weakness and, characteristically, bored into it, taunting Little unmercifully for no reason except that he rose so satisfyingly to the bait. Little, who is black, played Gleason's servant at a time when it was becoming politically very uncomfortable for black actors to take such roles. After irritating Little the first few days by calling him "Cleveland," Gleason one day addressed him with the condescending epithet "boy," and Little froze. No one around the two men viewed this as a serious expression of bigotry on Gleason's part. Indeed, Gleason had been known for his openness to black talent. His hiring of Mercedes Ellington was probably the most publicized example, but he also was one of the first TV producers to include a black musician in a predominantly white on-camera band. He hired a black Glea Girl, a professional beauty with no other substantive role, several seasons before he took on Ellington. He gave repeated exposure to comedian Timmie Rodgers, whose trademark phrase "Oh yeah!" constituted the bulk of his act but who was, unaccountably, a very funny performer. After he died, Gleason was hailed by the popular black magazine *Jet* as having been a particular friend of the black community. But for some reason it appealed to him to ride Cleavon Little. Perhaps the explanation is as simple as the fact that Little was more secure onstage and was thus giving a much better performance. In any case, once he discovered that "boy" worked to such attention-grabbing effect, Jackie never dropped it. That left most of the cast detesting him, but he seemed to enjoy that.

As rehearsals wound down, the finishing touches were put on what almost everyone but Kladitis regarded as a punitive, "sticking-it-to-you" kind of contract. Jackie's straight salary, which worked out to something over ten thousand dollars a week, was not out of line. While on the high side even for a major star, it was not a precedent setter like his Broadway wage in *Take Me Along*. Moreover, it was composed in part of a share of the gross ticket sales, so that for Jackie to really clean up he would have to be generating income for all the other profit participants, too. The problem, as always with Gleason, was the perquisites. Jackie would pay for his own housing during the tour. But the show's management was responsible for finding him, at his option, either a house directly on a golf course or a luxury suite in a downtown hotel, and he was to be the sole judge of whether the lodgings met his standards. He was to be accompanied by a chauffeur and a valet, both of whom were normally on his personal payroll. The chauffeur would drive Jackie's personal limousine, a maroon yacht that he repeatedly described as the longest in the United States by a matter of two inches. He told several of the people involved in the show that he had had the limousine sent back to the manufacturer, sawed apart and made longer, just to safeguard its claim to be the longest in the country. The valet or, in stage parlance, dresser was paid twelve hundred dollars a week, more than most members of the cast. "That was very important to Jackie," Gelbart recalls with still-hot resentment. "He insisted on it." The most objectionable stipulation of all, and the costliest, was that Jackie not fly by commercial jet, even first class, but instead be taken from city to city by private plane. He further specified that the craft had to be of a particular size, which added to the cost. To Gelbart and Penn and general manager Gene Wolsk, this seemed like just another thumb in the eye from Jackie. Only Kladitis thought he saw some legitimate purpose behind it. "You have to understand," he says, "that Jackie didn't just dislike flying, he was terrified of it. It literally made him sick. If he had flown on a regular plane he would have had to lurch to the bathroom or use the air sickness bag in front of all those other people, which would have been a terrible affront to his sense of dignity. And a small private plane wouldn't have a toilet, or at least not one he could fit into. What he really wanted, I think, was a plane where he could be sick in private, and when you think of it that way, it doesn't sound so unreasonable."

While the business deal was getting more and more unpleasant, director Penn was getting more and more frustrated about the creative side. "The whole damn experience," he says, "was a lot less than I had hoped. Once the rehearsals started it was clear that there was simply no way that Jackie could stay inside the role. He kept trying, and I kept saying, 'No "Away we go," ' and he would do his best. But the whole basis of his appeal as a performer was that there was this wonderful uncensored part of him. He was a creature of his impulses, a true primitive. That was his charm and it was what made him interesting. It did not, however, make him a directable actor. He was able to do the lines and get them more or less right, at least when he wasn't consciously changing them, but they would slowly blur into his own diction. There was another ego at work besides the playwright's, and it was saying, 'Hey, look, my stuff is funnier.' He had his own style and before you could even finish a sentence he would say, 'Got it, pal,' and then he would do his own version of what he thought you said, not having really heard you. I didn't come away with a corrosive feeling. I did not think he was mean-spirited. In fact, I had a feeling of tenderness for him. We spent a few evenings together. I'm not that charitable, ordinarily, but I had a couple of evenings with him where I would get a portrait of this lonely, detached, disconnected man."

Jackie's favorite toy in this period was a telescope. To Gelbart, with whom he was not sympatico, he would describe the heavens and conventional astronomy, leaving the impression on the playwright of "great enthusiasm and greater ignorance." To Penn, however, he opened up more and described staying up most of the night peering into the ether for aliens from outer space. Jackie had believed in them most of his adult life, and he was firmly convinced of a government conspiracy to conceal their visits. "He left me," Penn says, "with this vivid picture of this fat old man in his bathrobe watching for extraterrestrials. He was not in fear of them. If anything, I had the sense that he probably longed for them. They made him feel all right. I almost felt he believed he would relate better to them than he did to the people around him."

A measure of how emotionally needy and unsettled Gleason felt during this period is that he ventured onto customarily taboo conversational terrain with Penn, a relative stranger. "We had a few discussions about his early life," Penn recalls. "He was still very angry toward his father. That was why he was still rebelling against authority. I was able to work with him, but you could not squeeze that man into a spot he didn't want to go to. I'll bet a lot of television executives have bleeding stomachs to this day because of him." Jackie also talked a bit about his romances. Penn, like everyone else connected with *Sly Fox,* liked Marilyn enormously, thought she was a good influence on Jackie and lamented that she would not be by his side for every minute of the tour. If she were, they were convinced, their own lives would be a lot easier. Instead she was just to make occasional visits. She struck them as more a mother to Jackie than a partner in passion. Says Penn, "I have an abiding feeling that there was an inclination in him toward a more saintly relationship with women. I have no basis for saying it, but I got the feeling from him that he had basically retired from sex."

Penn still speaks of Gleason with great depth of feeling, although he terms him "a man unavailable to ordinary friendship and common conversation, holding you at bay equally with his easy charm when sober and his absolute intractability when in his cups." But the relationship was based on the work they shared, and the bonds started to crumble the instant rehearsals gave way to performance. When the show opened in San Diego in March, the critics were kind but business was only mediocre. It turned out, moreover, that there was a double edge to Gleason's crowd-pulling appeal. Many of the people who came to *Sly Fox* seemed never to have been to a straight play before. They had no theater manners and no sophistication. They were disappointed to see Jackie in some role other than his TV characters. And some of them were horrified by the play's bawdy, even raunchy humor, which Jackie had taken to accentuating. One night early in the run, a man sitting very close to the front of the theater stood up, denounced Jackie as an obscene blasphemer and stormed out, followed by his wife and son. The episode made Jackie even more acutely aware that, far from rescuing his career, this play could further damage it. He might erode his support among his continuing bedrock admirers, many of whom were modestly educated middle Americans accustomed to being shielded by network television's puritanical censorship. From that point, says Penn, "It all started to slip away. Jackie couldn't bring himself to do the character and stay within the play, and I just couldn't hold it together. To be honest, I was gone. I accepted that he was taking this play out as a personal vehicle, that the bookings were based on his name and that there was just no way to protect Gelbart."

By San Francisco, the tour was plainly doomed. Ticket sales continued to be weak, and the critical response was much less generous than in San Diego. Advance sales in other cities were also disappointing. Jackie knew that everyone put up with his tirades and shenanigans on the theory that he was popular. Once he failed to generate money, his ability to put on the prima donna act would swiftly be curtailed. From the point of view of the tour's organizers, the situation amounted to the moral equivalent of fraud. They had agreed to a complex and expensive contract, had endured countless headaches and had tolerated infuriating artistic compromises in order to make money. Now they had only the problems and none of the rewards.

Jackie took to just standing there at his first entrance, waiting for the applause to come, willing it, virtually demanding it by his frozen posture. That mood-breaking gesture set the tone for a full evening's disregard of the text and plot, in favor of Jackie's improvisations. It also established a kind of ugly dominance in his relationship with the audience, more frank perhaps than his false modesty of the fifties but much less attractive. He still had his funny moments, especially when disguised as a judge; he gave the jurist a spot-on Carol Channing voice, presumably learned during the time he and she filmed *How to Commit Marriage*. But the whole performance had the tang of "flop sweat," the comic's term for the too evident need to be appreciated that is the swiftest and surest killer of an audience's pleasure and laughter. Backstage, Jackie started drinking a little more, usually before rather than during the performance—albeit nowhere near as much as he had during *Take Me Along*. He responded to the exhaustion of so much work, after so long a semiretirement, by smoking even more than his customary five to seven packs a day and eating to excess by even his own indulgent standards. Sam Cohn flew out to San Francisco to steady him. After a performance, they went out on the town. "Jackie got sodden drunk and said, 'Let's find a jazz place.' We did, and he saw an oldish couple who were whizbang ballroom dancers. He got up and in a courtly way cut in, then danced impeccably, better than the husband, who was terrific. His manners never failed him with strangers. I once saw him, falling-down drunk, carry on a gentlemanly conversation with two nuns. But he was far, far gone in the bottle this particular night."

Defiance had always been Jackie's instinctive response to any constraints. The more he felt burdened by a situation, the more he insisted on displaying what he believed were boundless capacities. Back in 1951, he had been appearing onstage in Hartford in comic sketches to promote *Cavalcade* when he went into a cartwheel and got stuck standing on his head. After a moment he came crashing down. Coleman Jacoby, who was along as writer-director, and Peggy Lee, who was also featured on the bill, all but carried Jackie back to his hotel room and tucked the fevered comic into bed. His collapse, they felt, resulted from a combination of a slight flu, exhaustion and an excess of food and drink—including two consecutive dinners, one Italian and the other Chinese, just before he went out onstage to perform. "As we were putting him away for the night," Jacoby recalls, "we asked if there was anything else we could do for him. He nodded and beckoned me closer, then said, 'Pal, you could get me a big pepperoni pizza.' What really made it funny was that I could see he was absolutely serious."

The passage of nearly three decades had not much tamed Jackie's physical bravado. His excesses got more and more extreme. But his nerve, his inner strength, had started to crack. He began threatening not to go onstage each night for the performance. He had become as erratic as in his naughtiest days at CBS. He could not explain what his complaints were, he could only communicate that he was deeply unhappy. He was especially incensed that the producers were not calling him daily or, better yet, flying out to pay homage. He felt abandoned by them and was desperately afraid of failure. Unable to reach anyone higher, he took to calling Manny Kladitis, whom he addressed as "Bellyache," apparently because their relationship consisted almost entirely of Jackie bellyaching about something. At first Kladitis would be alarmed by these calls, then touched by a great star's desperation. "I realized," he recalls, "that Jackie did not really want to skip the performance. Why would somebody go to the theater, get into costume, put on makeup and then call from there to say he was not willing to do the show? It was too much trouble if he just wanted to quit. But Jackie was easily worked. I'd say, 'All right, Jackie. You don't have to go on. What are we going to tell all your fans? There are thousands of them lined up, waiting, and they came just to see you.' He'd mutter and grumble and then say, 'All right, Bellyache, I'll go on tonight. You tell those fuckin' producers that I'm not going on tomorrow night.' "

By the time the tour reached Chicago, Jackie was a bundle of nerves. He could not stay in a house along a golf course—none was close enough to the theater—so he agreed to take a hotel suite in the center of town. The local press agent, Margie Korshak, arranged a couple of options, but they did not strike Jackie as grand enough. Once again Kladitis was called in. His attitude was that stars were supposed to be difficult, that was what made them stars, so he didn't mind trying to placate Jackie. The city's Ambassador Hotel was in the middle of a massive renovation, and normally one would not expect a friend, let alone a star, to stay in a construction site. But the hotel was eager for publicity and was prepared to offer a highly concessionary price on a suite consisting of two smaller suites knocked together. Moreover, the hotel pledged to divert its refurbishing crews to that one spot and get it ready in little more than a day, working around the clock. The capper was that the suite had once been occupied, eons before, by Frank Sinatra. So Kladitis called Jackie to tout the suite's features, its rooftop terrace, its greenhouse, its penthouse location, its brand-new fittings just for him. "Then I mentioned Sinatra and I said, 'Jackie, this is what you deserve because of what you have achieved, your stature in life.' I was sweating because I had already basically made the deal with the hotel. Jackie said he'd look at it, but he'd also have to wait and see what Marilyn thought. She was finally joining him for this leg of the tour, much to our relief. We got into the limo, leaving the place where Jackie had been, accompanied by literally dozens of suitcases. We got out, went up, Jackie looked around and finally he said, 'Bellyache, you did it. Now we're going to eat.' He had a rack of

491

liquor and a stack of food sent up, enough for five very heavy eaters, and we ate nonstop for fifteen minutes. There were oysters, clams, shrimp, pastries. Even Jackie couldn't begin to finish this food. Then he thanked me and I went back to New York. Two days later, Marilyn called to tell me that they had moved *again*. Jackie just could not be satisfied."

Gleason was equally scornful of the accommodations at the Chicago theater, where he spent virtually all day on Saturdays and Sundays, because he had only a couple of hours between matinee and evening performances. Gelbart recalls Jackie's complaints as almost irrationally grandiose, on the order of "I'm supposed to use a toilet that some stagehand has been using, and I won't do it." General manager Gene Wolsk drily noted that the dressing room had been sufficient for eighty years' worth of actors before Jackie, some of them quite famous. But Kladitis once again thought compromise the better approach. He arranged to bring in a Hollywood-style trailer for Jackie and to build a little covered bridge connecting it to the stage door. He says, "My goal was to get him to continue to perform. I think some of my colleagues may have viewed things differently because sales weren't going so well and they might have preferred to have Jackie refuse to go on. Then they could have collected the insurance contingency payment instead."

They didn't have long to wait. Jackie was further spooked by weak sales in Chicago and the continued disheartening word from future cities on the tour. Worse, he and the show got a killer review from Linda Winer of the *Chicago Tribune.* Winer, now the drama critic of New York's *Newsday,* says, "I still have this feeling of dread about that performance. I didn't like the show and I hated what Gleason did. I thought it was gross and egomaniacal." What she actually wrote in the newspaper was a little gentler, but phrased in a fashion particularly devastating to Gleason's self-image as a family comic. "The show has too much talent to be so coarse," Winer opined, "too many inspired moments to stoop so low, and two hours too many boffo penis jokes for me. It also has Jackie Gleason, who, oddly enough, is not usually enough to matter. . . . Gleason has little spontaneous fun with the role. As the judge, however, he overcomes his drabness and becomes his own sight gag. The face doubles over on itself. The legs climb around the bozo stomach." Gleason, incensed by the aspersions on his talent and decency, booked himself onto columnist Irv Kupcinet's local TV show for the specific purpose of denouncing Winer's review and all her other works. He sounded like a man aggrieved. In fact, he was a man whose heart had been broken.

Jackie had felt increasing pain in his chest night after night and at one performance was barely able to finish. The role of Foxwell Sly required much running and jumping and had already had to be modified to accommodate Jackie's physical limitations. But there was no way to cut it down further, and in any case Jackie was too proud of his professionalism, his indestructibility and his macho to admit that something was wrong. Until, that is, suddenly *everything* was wrong. Ten days after Winer's review appeared, on May 30, 1978, Manny Kladitis got a call in New York from Marilyn Gleason, who fortunately had remained with Jackie in Chicago. Her husband had had a heart attack, she said, and the doctors doubted he could return to the show anytime soon.

Over the next couple of days, as further medical information emerged, it became plain that Jackie had not had an actual coronary, only a severe angina attack. But the result was the same. He underwent a triple bypass operation almost immediately and was explicitly forbidden by doctors to return to the stage for months. Neither George C. Scott nor Robert Preston was available to step in. Not even Vincent Gardenia could be rounded up—and, as Kladitis points out, "You don't sell people tickets on the basis of Jackie Gleason and then give them Vincent Gardenia." So the tour was over. The insurance money was duly paid, although the unrecoverable expenses and losses of the tour had wiped out essentially the entire Broadway profit of the show. Ended, too, was Jackie's career onstage, and maybe all the rest of his career. For a while the production team feared that Gleason might lose his life.

Gelbart set about, detective-like, reconstructing Jackie's final couple of days in the show. The

494

author termed the actor's collapse "foodicide." Gleason had eaten five bowls of pasta, richly sauced, on the day of his near-mortal agony, and had drunk red wine in proportion. "I really think he wanted to take himself out," Gelbart says. "I think of him as a pathetic figure, because I think he thought of himself as one." Wolsk doubted the suicide theory, in part because it might evoke compassion. He came away thinking of Jackie as "the worst person I ever worked with in my entire life, and it's not even close. He wanted to be feared and kowtowed to. Power was what interested him more than love. He really didn't give a shit about anyone else, and when a star takes that kind of attitude out in front of an audience, it's inevitably self-defeating. He was killing his own career." Penn, who had been appalled by how little sleep Gleason got and how frazzled he seemed emotionally, did not regard the angina attack as a surprise. Even the noblest constitution can absorb only so much abuse. He thought of Jackie as "a man who enjoyed punishing himself, physically and in every other way."

Once again only Manny Kladitis felt much sympathy for Gleason the man. He sent flowers to the hospital and later to Jackie's home in Florida. He also noted how few other people did. "I realized that Jackie Gleason was basically friendless. He had his family and he had the people who worked for him, but almost nobody outside of that. During the whole tour, he wasn't getting fruit or flowers or even 'hello' from anyone else in show business. With all stars, the worry starts about why people are around, about who wants what from them. He had let that worry isolate him almost completely." About Gleason's lack of friendship, Kladitis has only intuition. But Dick Green, Gleason's attorney since the early fifties, says much the same thing based on ample facts: "Jackie had golfing buddies, whom he didn't see for anything but golf. He had Jack Philbin and me, but I didn't see much of him socially after the fifties, when we were both free agents. There was June Taylor and Sydell Spear and maybe Sam Cohn. Way back, there was Toots. And those were about all the intimates aside from women in his love life."

Of all Kladitis's memories, the most vivid is of a moment with Gleason in the maroon limousine on the streets of Chicago, about a week before the angina attack. Kladitis was in back, riding in comfort. Jackie was, as usual, up front with the driver. Abruptly he told the driver to pull over to the curb, lowered the window and yelled to two teenage girls, "Hey! Hey! Do you know who I am?" Then, roaring with laughter, not giving the girls a chance to reply, he brought the window back up and pulled away. Kladitis still asks himself why Gleason did it. Was he trying to impress himself with his celebrity? Or, on the other hand, remind himself of the fleeting quality of fame? Was he playing to Kladitis? Was he flirting, oddly if harmlessly, with the young women?

Gleason didn't explain. Kladitis never got a chance to ask, nor does he think he would have had the nerve to, anyway.

But the episode lingers because it seemed to speak to Kladitis's deepest judgment about this star in decline. "I don't think Jackie Gleason felt he understood *why* he was Jackie Gleason. He was constantly testing everything, himself, his reputation, his audiences. By then, at least, I don't think he actually believed he *was* Jackie Gleason."

CHAPTER TWELVE

Inside every artist are two people, the one who thinks and expresses great ideas and the one who snores and peruses the grocery bills. One figure is unique and remote. The other is commonplace and approachable. For performing artists, whose success usually depends on mass appeal, there must always be a delicate balancing act in the display of these two personalities. The performer must seem ordinary enough to serve as a surrogate for the average man or woman. And he must seem extraordinary enough to justify garnering all that money, all that attention, all that fantasy-laden admiration as he cavorts in a pool of light amid the darkness. During the last not-quite-decade of Jackie's life, from the bypass operation onward, he found himself increasingly the object of summings-up from critics and other chroniclers of popular culture. After his self-promoted image of merry immortality was dispelled by this thudding blow, after it became more or less official that he would never have the stamina to face a prolonged live stage engagement or a weekly television series again, reviewers shifted from talking about Gleason's latest particular effort to assessing the entire body of his work. The experience resembled hearing his funeral eulogies, or reading his obituaries, while he was still alive—on the one hand hugely flattering to the ego, on the other hand immensely thwarting to what remained of his ambition. From these analyses, an image emerged of two Jackies, one entirely the everyday man within each artist, the other almost entirely the abstract genius. The ordinary Jackie was a vulgar roisterer, a go-for-the-gusto celebrant of the good life who made coarse movies such as the *Smokey and the Bandit* series, *The Sting II* and *The Toy.* This Jackie filmed a celebrity commercial for MasterCard as the human epitome of carefree spending. This Jackie was a real-life Falstaff, although he continued to resist Sam Cohn's blandishments to play the role—an aging rowdy whose snowy hair and raddled features turn his cavorting into foolishness, an ogler of female flesh he can no longer waylay, a pathetic sot. Trapped in the lifestyle and bad habits of the forties while living in a society obsessively self-absorbed with the health consciousness of the eighties, this Gleason was merely a clown, the only interesting element about him the hint of willful self-destruction in his sprees.

The extraordinary Jackie was the artist who had created Ralph Kramden and Gigot, Fats in *The Hustler* and Maish in *Requiem for a Heavyweight,* and who went on creating high art to the very end. He joined Laurence Olivier for *Mr. Halpern and Mr. Johnson,* a beautifully made television movie, and teamed with Tom Hanks, one of

Hollywood's hottest young leading men, for *Nothing in Common,* a splendid family drama given wide release in movie theaters. He dug up "lost" episodes of *The Honeymooners* from the variety shows of the early fifties and released them to an adulatory world in a coup that vastly replenished both his fortunes and his esteem. This Jackie had both a fan club bidding for *Honeymooners* memorabilia and a scholarly mystique that made him the subject of tributes on *60 Minutes* and at the Museum of Broadcasting. From moment to moment, Gleason vacillated about which was the true Jackie. Of course, with him as with any artist, both were. The public just found it hard to reconcile the shy, sensitive thinker with the bellowing playboy. But then, Jackie had always found it hard to reconcile the two himself.

For a while it looked as though *Sly Fox* would be the humiliating finale of Jackie's career. The reports of his behavior did not exactly enhance his reputation for professionalism. The weak results at the box office suggested that the triumph of *Smokey and the Bandit* the year before had belonged to Burt Reynolds and Sally Field, not Gleason. And his health was now a potential issue in every casting decision. A man in his sixties who has just endured a triple bypass and continues to drink, overeat and smoke several packs of cigarettes a day is a poor risk. Even if a director were willing to take that risk to secure Jackie's talents, the production company would require that Gleason qualify for insurance in case a medical catastrophe halted his work. If Jackie died with, say, just a week of absolutely necessary scenes left to shoot, the loss could be equivalent to virtually the entire production budget of a film. Everyone wanted to wait and see. Sam Cohn did his best to reassure Jackie, but except for a *Honeymooners* special already delivered to ABC, there seemed to be nothing doing.

Quite a few people, in Hollywood and elsewhere, were questioning whether Jackie still had the gift to entertain. He looked ravaged, his face seamed, his hair swept from one side of his head over the middle in a hapless attempt to hide a bald spot, his once fine nose grown bulbous with age and drink. The face lift had disquietingly altered the contours of his visage, making him look somehow inauthentic, a cartoon-cheerful, plastic version of his old self. A great many of the people who had admired him and profited by him— Coleman Jacoby and Joe Cates, Mike Dann and David Merrick—no longer found him funny. His tragedy, they said, was the tragedy that sooner or later befalls all comics: they dry up, they cease to get laughs, their brittle energy hardens into a shellac that deflects audiences. Of course, all these men, and many others who doubted Jackie's enduring appeal, admitted that their vision was colored by their flat dislike of him. Nonetheless, their opinion was shared increasingly widely in the entertainment industry. Once again Jackie floated his familiar claims that all three networks were begging him, with large sums of cash as the lure, to return to weekly television with *The Honeymooners*. But only the most credulous or cooperative columnists believed and printed that.

Fortunately for Jackie, he had a few things on his side that combined to resuscitate his career. First, *Smokey and the Bandit* had been such an enormous hit that its producers desperately wanted to profit from a sequel. Second, whether or not audiences might have accepted another actor in Jackie's role as the endlessly pursuing sheriff, star Burt Reynolds would not, and the producers blanched at the thought of losing both male stars for the sequel. Reynolds, a plainspoken pragmatist who had worked in a lot of inferior movies, explained his support this way: "I have always prided myself on being able to make chicken salad out of chicken shit, but Jackie can make it into cordon bleu." So Gleason was cast again and once more enhanced the film with improvisatory hijinks. The film's style was so farcical that no matter how over-the-top his acting was, he could not be called excessive. And his salary, for a mere fourteen days on the set, was one million two hundred thousand dollars. That amounted, admittedly without adjusting for inflation, to more than his earnings from his entire first six seasons on television. It matched his earnings for an entire season of television in the late sixties, when he was in his heyday and was the highest-paid star in the medium. And this was for three weeks' work in a second banana role. Small wonder that Jackie felt driven to keep working, now that the good times were rolling for performers.

He presented himself to the public as virtually back from the dead. "I'm going full tilt with everything," he said. "I don't see any sense getting a heart operation if you're not going to live after you have it." In keeping with this almost mythic sense of indomitability and rebirth, he granted a cover story interview to *People* magazine at the time of the film's release in which he began burnishing anew some of the tall tales about his past. The article was headlined AFTER 53 YEARS IN THE LIMELIGHT, JACKIE GLEASON REVELS IN SWEET IT STILL IS. The "53 years" meant since the age of eleven. Jackie, who earned his first professional money as an emcee at nineteen—and who for a CBS special had generously dated the start of his career to age thirteen, when he had been the host of amateur nights at the Halsey in Brooklyn—now pushed his debut back two years earlier. It came, he told *People,* while he was working as a trick diver. He trotted out the old interview standby of his having taken a risky high leap when asked to fill in for another performer. But this time the details were all brand-new, fresh as paint and just as highly colored. "When I was eleven years old," Jackie said, "I was in a traveling water show. I remember one time we were in Bangor, Maine, in an armory. And we had a high dive into a canvas tank. One day the guy who usually did it was drunk, so he told me to do it. I knew I had to, so I went up sixty-five feet and jumped off. Then I said, 'That's it, I'm not doing that any more.' And the guy said, 'Well, you're fired.' I'm in Bangor, Maine, for Christ's sake, and I'm eleven. How do you get home? I borrowed enough money to get the bus." It says a great deal for Jackie's skills as a storyteller that *People* bought this story wholesale and even built a headline around it. Under other circumstances a reasonable person might have questioned the likelihood of a two-bit traveling show's being able to erect a diving structure taller than a six-story house. Similarly, a reasonable person might have doubted the plausibility of such a show's having adopted an eleven-year-old into its company—in, after all, the late twenties, not the dark ages—and of then having tossed him out for refusing to do a job not his own. A little research might have shown that Jackie had told the diving story many times before, but never quite so pathetically, and never with it set in Maine. (The usual locale was Atlantic City.) Above all, a skeptic might have asked where his possessive, clinging mother was during this time. There is no record, in the Bishop biography or anywhere else, of Jackie's ever having seriously run away from home, at eleven or any other age. And what mother would willingly send a child of that age off on his own to work with a carnival troupe? This story seems never to have appeared in Jackie's reminiscences again, neither in his interviews with biographer Bacon nor in those with Morley Safer for *60 Minutes* nor in any other major venue. This man, who claimed he felt honor-bound to give the same answer to a question every time it was asked, once again debunked that pious assertion. Jackie wanted, perhaps needed, to turn his interesting-enough life into Dickensian legend.

Smokey and the Bandit II employed Jackie and enriched him. But it did not, at least at first, ensure him a future. It was two full years before another movie of his reached the public and that one, too, starred a younger, hotter actor, with Jackie cast merely as villainous comic relief. In the interim, Jackie's name almost disappeared from the gossip columns and the entertainment trade news. Only he believed the rumors he periodically floated about some big special or miniseries in the offing. To be sure, he did get some offers, but mostly from impresarios who did not have financing for their inglorious undertakings and who were counting on Jackie's celebrity to get their projects made. Jackie was not altogether incapable of enjoying semiretirement. He remained, as both Sam Cohn and Art Carney characterized him, "one of the laziest men on earth," fond of sluggish idleness, averse to exertion and psychic effort. "Things don't have to be challenging for me to enjoy them," Gleason said. "I'm perfectly prepared to turn something down that will be educational and not fun." But this posture of serene indifference was much more satisfying when Jackie was sure the choice was entirely his own. Instead, he found himself in the position of nearly all actors other than the biggest stars. He had to take what roles were offered and choose them because they were available to him, not because they were high art or a showcase for his talents.

Never was this more true than with Jackie's next movie, *The Toy*. Nobody close to Jackie, not even his boosterish secretary Sydell Spear, claims he took the slightest pride in this borderline-racist farce. The director, Richard Donner, and the writer, Carol Sobieski, had fine credits. The balance of the cast included veterans Ned Beatty, Wilfrid Hyde-White, Virginia Capers—and even that seasoned actress Marilyn Gleason. (At Jackie's behest his wife was also given roles in *Mr. Billion* and some of his other projects.) Everyone involved ought to have been savvy enough to have recoiled at the film's inescapably offensive premise. Jackie was to play a tycoon whose bratty, neglected nine-year-old son asks for a human being as a "toy." The chosen object, an out-of-work reporter turned waiter who is in dire financial straits, was to be enacted by comic Richard Pryor, a black man. The evocation of slavery was dangerous, if not impossible, material to wed to a broad farce. With the best political intentions in the world, social comment does not complement bowls of soup being spilled into laps, dogs urinating on people's feet or a car chase that ends with a literal splash, into a swimming pool. Certainly the gritty opening scenes of racial exclusion and poverty could never have comfortably co-existed with Jackie's spluttering cartoon of a plutocrat.

In most of Jackie's past fiascos, he could at least claim credit for effort. Burt Reynolds was right in praising him for rising above weak material. The first great exception to that craftsmanship is *The Toy*, in which Gleason seems to telephone in his performance. It is stilted and noisy, lacking in energy and almost entirely devoid of imagination. Perhaps he regretted having accepted the script. Perhaps he was slipping into the periodic deep depression that old friends would remark upon as they saw him over the next few years. At least some of the time during filming, he was simply drunk. Biographer Bacon begins his book *How Sweet It Is* by bragging about having been thrown off the set of *The Toy* as an "evil companion" for Gleason—a concept he reasonably characterizes as incomprehensible, given what Jackie was like all on his own—after a day when the two shared a long, liquid lunch. By Bacon's account, Jackie's midday meal was "his usual, six double scotches with no ice, no soda, no water and no food." Gleason then returned to the set for his scheduled reaction shots, only to find himself ordered to drive a golf cart across acres of greensward in pursuit of Pryor. According to Bacon, this was the day when Gleason crashed the cart into a swimming pool for the cameras, and the scene's watery climax was entirely accidental. If that is so, it more than explains why the production team panicked. Jackie could have been injured badly enough in the incident to miss the rest of the filming. And if he really was permitted to drive while known to be roaring drunk, the insurance company might quite understandably have refused to pay off. In any case, having his old friend and future biographer thrown off the set must have soured Jackie's mood. Maybe it is just sullen fury that coarsens and stiffens his performance.

A few months after *The Toy* came another dismal film, *The Sting II,* a pitiably inferior remake of the comic con game that a decade before had earned seven Oscar Awards including best picture. The new script was by David S. Ward, an Oscar winner for the original, but this time the machinations seemed less sprightly and more convoluted. The setting was the forties, versus the thirties of the original film, and Gleason and Mac Davis were cast as the presumably faded versions of matinee idols Paul Newman and Robert Redford. (Confusingly, the characters' names were changed, but only slightly, while the basic plot structure was all but identical—leaving audiences uncertain whether these really were supposed to be the same men, but in no doubt at all about whether to trust the tricky twists on which the "surprise" plot depends.) Jackie loved wearing the too-spiffi clothes of a gambler from his own personal heyday, and he enjoyed playing the slick man-of-the-world with a hint of a benevolent twinkle in his eye. His hopes for a film of popular and critical appeal to match the original were dashed as soon as he saw the leaden final version, but the critics' responses to him personally were the best he had received since his first rush to film stardom in the early sixties. The *New York Times* said, "Mr. Gleason, looking very unlike himself, performs smoothly." The *Los Angeles Times* asked rhetorically, "Who's better with a gimlet eye than Jackie Gleason, a Damon Runyon character brought to life in the ample flesh?" *Newsday*, the giant Long Island daily, said, "Gleason seems to be very much his bombastic self, playing the nattily dressed grifter with the sly demeanor of a man who would sell you the incorrect time of day. In one nicely turned scene, where he's hustling Karl Malden at the pool table, The Great One performs a masterpiece of shifty-eyed one-upsmanship, strutting around the table like an overblown shark, ready to cue his opponent to pieces." The scene thus described was, of course, a sort of personal homage, Gleason's nod to his own electrifying work in *The Hustler*, a film where he had appeared *with* Paul Newman instead of in place of him.

The *Smokey* movies, *The Toy* and even *The Sting II* thrust forward the everyday Jackie, the vulgar Jackie, the common man. His next job, a fifty-five-minute, low-budget movie for cable television's Home Box Office, brought to the forefront Jackie the artist. It paired him with the foremost actor of the century, and against that competition Jackie more than held his own. *Mr. Halpern and Mr. Johnson* was the story of a brief and confessional encounter between two time-worn men, one the widower of a newly dead wife, the other her devoted if platonic secret lover throughout her forty-two years of marriage. The piece's theme was that marriage is often only the simulacrum of intimacy, that beneath the pretense of sharing, both partners often go on living separate lives. Mr. Halpern, the bereft husband, was written as a roughhewn manufacturer of cardboard boxes. Mr. Johnson, the wife's paramour, was supposed to be a refined accountant with style and clothes sense. Each man had to envy what the other possessed—the husband longing for the trust and confidences he never received, the lover longing for the everyday pleasures of connubiality and companionship. The setting was ostensibly metropolitan New York, the actual filming was done in Bristol, England, and in spirit the story took place in no particular city or time. The words were meant to be poetic, their import rather like a parable.

From the outset the British and American co-producers agreed on the two actors they wanted. One was earthy, edgy Jackie Gleason. The other was elegant, ethereal Laurence Olivier. They were natural casting for, respectively, the widower and the mysterious lover. But Olivier was not sure which role he wanted to play. Almost until shooting started, he dithered back and forth about whether he would rather be the husband, listening and occasionally expostulating, or the lover, smoothly unfolding his stories of the inner woman that her own husband never knew. Jackie was amenable to playing either part. If Olivier felt he could handle either role, then Gleason would be no less daring. In the end Olivier opted for the husband and Jackie became the lover. For both, this was a physical challenge. Olivier had to seem petty and unglamorous, while Jackie had to seem more polished and assured than the great romantic idol. Olivier had to say obsequiously, "You're a man of distinction, class. Anyone can see that." And both men had to make this comparison between them seem unmistakably true.

Olivier, seventy-six years old and in steeply declining health, could work only a few hours a day and welcomed the fact that nearly all the scenes took place with both men seated, first in a bar, then in a restaurant. (Ironically, although he was nine years older than Jackie and in much worse shape, he would outlive him.) Save for the opening and closing scenes at the cemetery, the show amounted to a filmed version of a one-act play. As a man supposedly of English origin who had moved to the United States four decades before, Olivier adopted the mishmash of stateless sounds that he always mistook for American speech. He has perhaps the funniest moment, demanding in a vaudeville snarl, *"You* contributed to *my* happiness? This I gotta hear!" He also has the most heartfelt, when he strangles over the words "If Flo were here, I'd murder her." Jackie was lumbered with the pompous diction he was given to in life and, so often, in art—the extravagant display of vocabulary that reveals a recently self-educated man. In the opening scene, at the dead woman's uncovered grave, he asks permission to toss on a flower and Olivier turns on him, full of suspicion, to say, "You're not Jewish." Jackie replies, in his chesty, mellow baritone, "Is it that obvious? Have I committed a sartorial indiscretion?" Perhaps no other actor alive could have spoken those pedantic words without placing vocal quotation marks around them, without distancing himself sardonically from this grandiloquence. Jackie played the phrase straight, unself-consciously, and thus did nothing to break the emotional tension of a pivotal moment. It was his very aura of confidence—in his big body, his sweeping gestures, his decorated but swaggering masculinity—that made him such a believable counterpoint to Flo's painfully contained husband as evoked by Olivier.

Mr. Halpern and Mr. Johnson ushered in a final few years when almost everything Jackie did was treated with admiration. Olivier hailed Jackie as one of the finest actors he had ever worked with and told interviewers, "I don't think there's much opposite about the backgrounds of Jackie Gleason and myself. His is every bit as respectable as mine." To be sure, their approaches to acting were different. At about this same time, Olivier was pouring the last of his great creative energies into filming an exquisite *King Lear*. Jackie said in conversation with various friends—although not, as far as one can tell, to Olivier—"Could I play *King Lear?* Yes. Do I want to? No. I don't need the challenge." Tom Shales of the *Washington Post,* by then perhaps the nation's premier newspaper critic of television, wrote of *Mr. Halpern and Mr. Johnson,* "Gleason is not only indisputably a man of distinction, he also gives the better of the two performances. . . . A case could be made that Gleason is, in television terms, the better actor of the two." Two decades before, Gleason had read and tossed aside Olivier's salutation of him as The Great One. Now he had something better. He had an incandescent hour of videotaped proof that Olivier, the nonpareil of the century, accepted the boyo from Brooklyn—indeed, worked to keep up with him—as a peer.

While filming *Halpern and Johnson* in England in March of 1983, Jackie began feeling pains in his left leg. At the end of shooting, when he flew home to Fort Lauderdale, he checked in almost immediately to the city's Imperial Point Hospital. There he underwent surgery to unclog his arteries and spent several days in intensive care. Because he was in danger of an embolism, Marilyn stayed by his side around the clock, actually taking a room in the hospital. In their absence from home, an electrical fault in the air conditioning burnt the Inverrary house to the ground. Thus, when Jackie left the hospital, it was not to return to his beloved game room, his inebriation pit, his trophies and memorabilia. Instead he and Marilyn installed themselves in a Pompano Beach hotel to wait out the year-long reconstruction. Jackie tried to be cheerful about it. Had they been home, he said, "We could both be part of a sand trap on the Inverrary golf course today." But behind the public bravado was a keen awareness that his vigor and maybe his years were dwindling, that months of comfort lost now could never be regained. Gleason had always prized luxury—to the point, says agent Sam Cohn, of "having a phobia about getting to places and finding there was nowhere to sleep and nothing to eat. Some childhood trauma made him want to nest at home." For the moment, that place of reassurance was gone, up in smoke. While Jackie was not too concerned about the vanishing of keepsakes—"Things like that never mattered much to him," says his longtime attorney Dick Green—the disappearance of the house and its contents was also a sort of symbolic equivalent to the disquieting nature of life in show business. Accomplishments are quickly forgotten; ones greatest achievement, reputation, is especially fleeting. An actor's critical standing is only as good as his most recent reviews; his employability is only as secure as the box office results of his last venture. Says Gleason's friend and dancer Mercedes Ellington, who continued to see him a couple of times a year until the end of his life, nearly two decades after their last business connection, "Jackie was always very aware that in entertainment, your last job may turn out to be your *last* job." He had money in the bank and he had options. But when the house burned down in the spring of 1983, before *Halpern and Johnson* had been seen, his life accumulation and lifework had both been reduced almost to ashes.

What a difference a year makes. In that summer of 1983, Jackie Gleason was homeless and unhealthy, prosperous but not proud in his career, a sad and secluded man whose best years lay decades behind him. By the autumn of 1984 he was a national treasure, a living monument. Jackie the vulgarian was crowded out of view, seemingly forever, by Jackie the artist. He knew that whatever indignities lay ahead, as his body inevitably betrayed him, he would not have to face eternity as a half-forgotten, half-dismissed old buffoon.

Four events burnished his standing. First was *Mr. Halpern and Mr. Johnson*. Second was a convention attended by more than two thousand three hundred *Honeymooners* obsessives, banded together to form the Royal Association for the Longevity and Preservation of the Honeymooners, or RALPH. Third was an exhibition of a few "lost" *Honeymooners* sketches, to crowds stretching round the block month after month, at New York's Museum of Broadcasting. Fourth, and by far the most significant to Jackie, was Morley Safer's interview for *60 Minutes*.

Jackie had no movies out in 1984. He had nothing to promote, nothing to sell. He had always approached publicity pragmatically, as part of the marketing process, accommodating reporters when he had a financial reason to do so, stiff-arming them (save for a handful of old friends) when he did not. So he was not even in attendance for the public events of that year and granted few if any interviews to promote *Mr. Halpern and Mr. Johnson* or the *60 Minutes* appearance. But at home he basked in receiving, at long last, what he thought was his due. And he dreamed up a way to convert this new esteem into a windfall.

The RALPH convention was held in Greenvale, Long Island, at the C. W. Post Center of Long Island University. It was in part a nostalgia session—Joyce Randolph, director Frank Satenstein and some cameo players attended, although Gleason and Carney and Audrey Meadows did not. In part it was a shlock variety show, with impersonators aping Kramden and Norton and songwriters plugging such campy items as "It's Honeymooner Time" and "I Want a Wife like Alice Kramden." Part of the atmosphere was a sleazy bazaar of souvenirs and memorabilia, posters and statuettes, mugs and hats, even stomach-sinking food items, such as pig knuckles with sauerkraut, that are mentioned in one or another of the thirty-nine shows. Many of those in the audience professed to have seen each episode dozens, if not hundreds, of times. They described watching *The Honeymooners* as a part of daily life, like getting up and going to work. The peak event of the festival day was the screening of two episodes not part of the canonical thirty-nine, culled from rediscovered kinescopes of the fifties variety show. One plot has Ralph Kramden dabbling in astrology. The other, which had no ending because the show ran out of time in mid-skit, embroils Kramden with gangsters.

Hearing of the public zeal for these *Honeymooners* odds and ends and reading Frank Satenstein's claim that "hundreds" of such sketches were locked up unexploited in CBS vaults fired the imagination of the Museum of Broadcasting's curator, Ron Simon. The museum had been launched with money donated by CBS founder William Paley, and the operating budget came in large part from various networks' grants, so Simon felt confident that if any such kinescopes did indeed survive at CBS, he would be able to locate and extract them. It turned out that there were indeed some "lost" *Honeymooners* episodes squirreled away at CBS, but only four of them. The question of who owned the rights to the shows was tricky, so the museum sidestepped it and simply exhibited the four shows—complete with monologues, dances and the rest of the original context for the sketches—without clearing the venture with Jackie. Between the convention and the museum exhibit, newspaper and TV entertainment reports were chockablock with stories about the immortal nature of *The Honeymooners* and in particular about Gleason's eternal artistry. Every such story emphasized the tragedy that so much of his early work had disappeared. This media buzz in turn brought out would-be entrepreneurs. Cable and videocassette companies kept calling the museum, wanting to put together a package of the "lost" and found material; Simon and museum president Robert Batscha prudently and persistently explained that they had no rights to sell it and referred all comers to Dick Green, Jackie's lawyer. Meanwhile, a daughter of Snag Werris, one of Jackie's early writers, called to say that she, too, had old *Honemooners* episodes, mostly from *Cavalcade of Stars* but also including Jackie's first-ever appearance on CBS, re-creating the inaugural *Honeymooners* sketch, with Pert Kelton as Alice and a pre-Norton Art Carney as a policeman. Originally done on *Cavalcade,* the skit had been restaged for *The Ed Sullivan Show* to promote Jackie after he signed his CBS contract. Werris's daughter had been trying to sell the kinescopes, which were historic, if blurry and filled with light flashes, but had not found a buyer to meet her price. Eventually she donated them to the museum. The problem with them as a commercial entity, apart from their horrendous visual quality, is that they do not have the beloved quartet in the cast. Meadows did not become Alice until CBS days. Says curator Simon: "We have found there is simply no significant interest in the musical *Honeymooners* or any other material not including those four particular performers."

Jackie's agent Sam Cohn confirms that judgment. Throughout the search and bidding, Jackie stayed mum, by implication confirming the assertions that all his career-establishing CBS variety shows had vanished forever. The enduring appeal of *The Honeymooners* was also the impetus for the *60 Minutes* interview, of which Jackie later wrote to Safer, "The result just made me feel wonderful!" Alan Weisman, one of the CBS News show's myriad unseen producers, had pitched the idea of Gleason as a man who had not been on television regularly in nearly fifteen years and yet who was, through reruns, on television every night. Safer hesitated, he recalls. "I was aware of Gleason's reputation for being difficult and egocentric. I had never met him and had no idea how cooperative or forthcoming he would be. But I agreed with Alan that Gleason was, in the context of our industry, a classic performer, one whose work had permanent value. Then I called Sam Cohn, whom I did know somewhat. He called Jackie. Then I called Jackie. And finally Jackie called me back. From that point, the arrangements were easy. Gleason was accommodating about schedule. He did not have major acting commitments, although he was very excited about the possibility of getting involved in what eventually became the film sequel to *The Hustler*, called *The Color of Money*. He said he was talking to Paul Newman about that although, in the end, it didn't happen for him. He explained we couldn't shoot at his home because he was still reconstructing from the fire. So we had to use a hotel that had a poolroom and bar, which we let double for his house—not the perfect journalistic thing to do, but the only practical one under the circumstances. He seemed very honored that we were doing the piece because *60 Minutes* was where serious stuff gets talked about, and therefore he was being treated as a totem, an American landmark.

"Once we got there he was completely professional. He did not ask for a lot of hand-holding. He did not want questions in advance. He was a bit nervous at the beginning but he seemed to be committed to trying to give honest answers. He wasn't drinking heavily when we were there. He was impulsive. It was the height of televangelism and he was just obsessive about that. He just went crazy about these guys using this wonderful medium for a con game. Marilyn was around with him but she seemed a bit shy. He talked about her but she certainly wasn't pushing to have a place in the piece. [Indeed, the interview suggests she was doggedly determined not to say anything the least bit controversial, to the point of denying that her husband had a big ego, something he had always conceded and promptly conceded anew.] He gave no indication of taboo or sensitive areas and I think he thought of his answers as completely honest, whatever their precise relationship to fact. I liked him enormously. What he was—and this is rare in an interview—was wonderful company. He had a terrific ease with the crew, not a put-on familiarity with the blue-collar groups, just a naturally winning way. He was spontaneously funny. I felt he still had one foot in the Club Miami back in Newark. He saw himself as a trouper who still had to suck it up and get out there and who could die at any performance."

The way Safer remembers the interview is much the way it appeared to audiences. Instantly it became regarded as one of Jackie's more memorable moments and as one of 60 Minutes' highlights. The footage offers a poignant glimpse of a man who never escaped the deprivations of childhood or the fears besetting his early career. Yet it conveys the serene and almost contemplative quality that Jackie had on his happier days. The whole thing is, of course, a performance, carefully suppressing the anger, the depression, the compulsive and addictive and self- destructive fixations, the bottle, the battles, the grudges, the grief. It bears the same relationship to the inner Gleason that Ralph Kramden does: it is a dark-seeming portrait that has in fact been considerably brightened from a still darker truth. Gleason wrote to Safer describing the depiction, accurately, as "kind and generous," adding, "Marilyn and I watched the program, and as the minutes went by our smiles grew bigger. Thanks, again, and I hope we meet sometime in a pub where we can rattle a few corks." He signed his name "Jackie," his perfect penmanship re-creating the all-lowercase letters of his stationery imprinted with his name but no address. He closed with the term "your friend," and below his signature he could not resist adding, perhaps with just a hint of a smile, "The Great Gleason."

If 1984 had been the year when Jackie was saluted for the lasting value of *The Honeymooners*, then 1985, he decided, would be the year to cash in on it. To the amazement of his former costars, his former network and the archivists at the Museum of Broadcasting, Jackie let slip, soon after the *60 Minutes* interview, that the "lost" years of CBS shows were not lost at all. As their producer and owner, he had meticulously preserved the kinescopes for more than three decades, latterly spending five thousand dollars a year just to provide air-conditioned storage. While the Museum of Broadcasting had been interested in recycling complete shows, he soon discovered that the main bidders for the "lost" material were interested only in The Honeymooners. Some sketches were as short as eight minutes, others nearly an hour. But the bulk were thirty-three to thirty-eight minutes long. In total they amounted to more than seventy hours. Viacom, a CBS spin-off which owned the syndication rights to the beloved thirty-nine hours, was interested in acquiring the rest. So was the cable television channel Showtime. Finally the two united on a deal that would bring Jackie nearly six million dollars over a seven-year span, with the potential for more on renewal. Best of all, Jackie did not seem to have to share the cash.

Although he never explained his long silence and subsequent secrecy, presumably his caution arose from a desire to have his lawyers check over the ownership and royalties questions. CBS apparently had no residual rights; it had simply purchased initial use. Jackie's ex-manager Bullets Durgom seemed not to have a claim, either; the two men had settled their mutual obligations two decades before. Of the writers for and performers on the show, no one but Audrey Meadows appeared to have any rights—she had negotiated a perpetual royalties clause from the beginning—but Jackie eventually yielded to AFTRA actors' union demands for payments to some of the others rather than risk litigation. Once he had the business situation arranged, so that no embarrassing negotiations need take place amid the glare of publicity, Jackie and his two purchasers announced the "discovery." The "lost" shows would be grouped into a few hour specials and some seventy-five half-hours, lightly edited from the originals. Jackie agreed to provide opening and closing comments on camera for each episode and to help publicize the effort.

At a press conference in New York City to launch the "new" shows, Jackie had plenty of jokes ready to sidestep any serious questions about the backstage aspects of the deal. "Until Ralph found them under the backseat of the bus," he cracked, "we didn't know they were there." He added, "I think this is the right time. I'm sick of watching those other ones." Carney pleaded illness and skipped the press conference. But Meadows came, and so did Randolph, for her first up-close glimpse of Gleason in twenty-eight years. Their encounter, she says, was cool but friendly. She didn't mention all the times he had passed her over for *Honeymooners* revival shows, nor did Jackie. She didn't say how exploited she felt in retrospect. She came, she said, "because this role is what people know me for, and I still get a kick out of that."

Although the occasion was celebratory and lucrative for Jackie, he grew arrogant and short-tempered pretty quickly. After the main session, he agreed to a short photo call and brief print and TV interviews at the 21 Club, scene of much of his past bad behavior, including his near-catastrophic first meeting with CBS programming executive Oscar Katz. The individual demands on him were not unreasonable, but there was so much cumulative press interest in the "lost" shows that his total commitment amounted to a full, indeed hectic, day's work. Photographers Bob Sacha of *Time* and Robert Deutsch of *USA Today,* for example, were asked to share a fifteen-minute session. When Jackie came in, he announced he was cutting that to one minute and in reality stayed for about three. He composed the single shot he would offer, let the two men squeeze off eight or nine frames and left. His language was not vile or abusive. But his attitude, both say, was scornful. At the end of the day he granted a longer session to Fred Bernstein of *People* magazine. "It was bad planning by his publicity people," Bernstein recalls, "because by then he was obviously inebriated. He was much too drunk to stick to the party line he took during the press conference, which was that these shows had been miraculously found and admitted he had gotten tired of paying for the storage and thought the time had come for the best possible sale." Gleason strayed from the publicity program in other ways. The conversation with Bernstein was long and rambling, about death and illness, money and friendship, and eventually it touched on some of Jackie's crackpot theories about human biology. Bernstein, then in his twenties, is dark and bearded, with a slightly receding hairline. He suddenly found Gleason demanding that he roll back his sleeves and unbutton his shirt to the navel, so that Jackie could test his notion that men with a lot of body hair start to bald sooner than average. "I couldn't quite believe it was happening," Bernstein says. "I look back and I know I should have told him to stop. But I wanted the interview and he had a very forceful personality. It never even occurred to me to write about that aspect of the meeting."

While in town for the publicity trip, Jackie took Marilyn, by then looking more plump and matronly than the glamour girl he had courted, to a Broadway performance of the August Wilson play *Ma Rainey's Black Bottom*. Set among black musicians, it was replete with blues numbers Jackie savored. Although the night was chilly,

525

Jackie dressed as though in Florida, in an open-neck shirt and a sports jacket, sans overcoat. After all the surgery and worry, he was determined to assert once again his superior capacity to survive.

Later that year Jackie joined James Cagney for an eighty-sixth birthday party at the Hotel Carlyle in Manhattan, and on hearing that the Cagneys did not have cable television at their upstate farmhouse, he promised to come visit with a complete set of the "lost" *Honeymooners* episodes. Gleason wisecracked all night, as ever on the boundary between mirth and bad taste. He said to his wheelchair-bound host, "I don't think I can leave here until Cagney does a dance on the table."

Toward the end of 1985, as he approached his seventieth birthday and the twilight of his working life, Jackie found himself back in Hollywood, the scene of so many disappointments. He was there to make one final movie, the one that friends say he considered his best and most significant work since *Gigot.* He took second billing to Tom Hanks, a romantic lead, and accepted that the film would be built around the younger man. Hanks said the major appeal of the film to him was the chance to work with Gleason. "Here's a guy I grew up with in my living room, and I get to be in the living room with him. Both Mr. Gleason and I danced around on the phone a lot before deciding to do it. I gotta say that I approached him like my own father, really, with love and a little fear." The title of the father-son epic conveyed its whole theme: *Nothing in Com-*

mon. Although directed by Garry Marshall, the maker of such sentimental TV as *Laverne and Shirley*, it was highly astringent in tone. The role Jackie played, a failed salesman—a sort of bargain basement Willy Loman—was economically miles away from Jackie. But in other ways the role was autobiographical. His character was a spiritual holdover from the forties, in taste and dress and manner, who loses his job and busts up his marriage and still cannot stop drinking and partying and going to jazz clubs all night. He is diabetic, as Gleason was, and eventually loses a foot to neglected gangrene. He is a man incapable of compromise, fierce in asserting his independence, truculent in the face of kindness, embarrassed by affection. Jackie has two scenes of overpowering poignance, and he plays them for gut truth. In one, as he boasts of his contacts in the business, a boss who is in the process of firing him gestures to take in a whole convention floor and challenges Jackie to name a single person there. Forced to face the truth, Jackie ages twenty years in an eye blink, his face crumpling and his eyes going dead. In the second key scene, while attempting a reconciliation with his wife, he blazes in self-righteous anger. Nothing, not even the fast-encroaching physical need for help with his illness, can make him bend. He epitomizes the macho of another age, railing in anger and confusion at how the rules have changed.

Much of the film was made on location in Chicago, and Richard Christensen, then the entertainment editor of the *Chicago Tribune*, visited him in his trailer. "He seemed subdued for the whole forty-five minutes," Christensen recalls. "He never stopped smoking and he often blurred on details, which Marilyn would fill in for him. He was not drinking, and he was certainly not the 'Away We Go' Gleason that I so admired. As a young man in New York I had seen the final couple of minutes and curtain call of *Take Me Along* about a dozen times, when they used to fling the doors open just before the end to let the crowds get out and it was thus possible, if you timed it right, to sneak on in for the finale. This Gleason seemed very reflective and soft, not at all the boisterous fellow I remembered, and maybe a little sad. He said he liked the character because he was complex and almost wholly unsympathetic, and he thought that would be good for him. He praised the script and said all the right things about Tom Hanks as a real comer. He just didn't give any sign of joy."

The finished film took no Oscar awards and did not really clean up at the box office. But it was a succès d'estime, a perfect swan song for Gleason's career. The *Los Angeles Times* wrote, "Never has Gleason been better. . . . He doesn't cheat, never playing for laughs in his dead-on portrayal of an insensitive, cold-eyed, hard-living man with whom time has caught up." Most other critics were equally quick to praise Jackie's uncompromising interpretation. Sam Cohn says Gleason loved the film because it had "overtones of our own relationship, his and mine," and because Jackie felt he had escaped the performer's incessant trap of trying to make himself lovable.

In the wake of *Nothing in Common* Jackie completed a MasterCard commercial for which he was paid eight hundred fifty thousand dollars for a reported three hours of work. He was offered CBS movies in which he would play Boss Tweed (deferred pending script rewrites) and P. T. Barnum (declined because it involved filming in London and Paris, while he wanted to stay home in Florida). He stayed home, as well, for his induction into the Hall of Fame of the Television Academy of Arts and Sciences, accepting the Los Angeles-based honor from his Florida house by videotape as a form of retaliation for the years when the Academy denied him a competitive Emmy or even a nomination. He was snubbing the Academy, too, for the fact that he had not been in the first group of inductees but was deferred to the third annual selection, along with retired CBS executive Frank Stanton and such other inferiors—in Jackie's view—as producer-director Fred Coe and puppeteer Burr Tilstrom. Besides, although he seems not to have known yet that his resilience was at long last fading, that he was about to enter the final year of his life, there was something telling him that he had made public statements aplenty, that the time for privacy was at hand.

Amid the succession of triumphs in the last few

years of his life, Gleason had only one major aesthetic failure. Yet it too represented unfinished business of the most urgent kind. For more than three decades, since *The Laughmaker,* he and Art Carney had spoken of combining in a dramatic vehicle outside the confines of Gleason's variety show. Many a project had gotten to the idle talking stage. A few had been put forward as scripts. But those almost always amounted to a reprise of Kramden and Norton under other names, which did not appeal to either man in the least. What both wanted was something lively and vital, something that would take advantage of their extraordinary creative chemistry, something that would enable them to feel that their partnership transcended the confines of a Brooklyn kitchen.

Carney wanted one more thing, although he was too much the gentleman ever to insist on it in public. He wanted, for once, to work with Gleason as an equal, not a subordinate. That meant he wanted the same billing and the same pay. Several projects had run aground over this quiet insistence on Carney's part and over Gleason's louder determination to maintain the upper hand as the bigger star. But a canny veteran producer named Robert Halmi spotted a way around this impasse and so, in 1985, before *Nothing in Common,* the fat one and the flaky one reunited one last time in an amiably airy nothing called *Izzy and Moe.* The script was based on the true story of failed vaudevillians Izzy Einstein and Moe Smith, who became Prohibition agents in the twenties and relied on impersonation and disguise to bolster their investigations. Halmi had read of their adventures, which had also been the subject of a long-forgotten Broadway play. He considered the potential for shtick and disguises a natural for Gleason and Carney. "In the beginning," Halmi says, "neither one of them wanted to do it. They didn't want to work with each other. Finally Carney, whom I already knew well, said, 'You get Gleason and then you come talk to me. I won't let you down. Just get him first.' To get Jackie I had to go to Florida four or five or six times to talk conceptually. Later on, Jackie insisted on involving himself in every line of the script. It was rewritten for three solid months under his supervision. But the problem was still that Gleason wanted to be paid more than anyone else."

One day, during these "conceptual" discussions by which Jackie was promoting himself from hired hand back to de facto producer, a chance remark showed Halmi how to resolve the situation between his stars. Gleason suggested that the film be heavily scored, with music behind the action almost nonstop—bright and perky stuff in Dixieland style. "I could compose it in a minute," he boasted, "and conduct it, too. I've been doing both for forty years." Here was the answer. Jackie and Art would get the same wage for acting, which would meet Carney's demand. But Jackie would get paid an additional fee as composer, which would satisfy Gleason's ego by giving him a bigger take overall. Both actors agreed.

Jackie's first round of "compositions" arrived by Federal Express package soon after, which was a little odd. Normally composing is not completed until after the film is shot, because each piece of music must be fitted precisely, down to a fraction of a second, to the length and emotional arc of the film it is to interpret. In its way the process is as delicate and precise as lip-synching dialogue. When Halmi opened Jackie's package, he recalls, "It contained a pile of yellowing old sheet music, standard arrangements of nightclub and saloon songs. I began to wonder what was going on, but the first order of business was to get the film shot."

There were no rehearsals—Jackie flatly refused to have any—so Gleason and Carney met on the set mere moments before they were to start filming together. Carney's diplomatic version is that the two men embraced, after not having seen each other for nearly a decade, and it was instantly "just like old times." Halmi viewed it a little differently. "I was scared shitless. I knew perfectly well that these two men had been very reluctant to work with each other. The way it worked out was that for the next five weeks they saw very little of each other except on the set. They went into each other's Winnebagos only for publicity purposes, when reporters were there. In all that time Jackie never once invited Art to lunch or dinner. Twice he had Carney into his trailer while he was being interviewed and both times Art came back after about fifteen minutes and told me he couldn't get a word in edgewise so he left."

In most regards, Carney reluctantly confirms Halmi's harsh portrait. But he remembers at least one "conversation" not in the company of reporters, lasting forty-five minutes or so, involving few words and much silence. "It was the first time," Carney says, "that I had seen Gleason look really old. He seemed genuinely miserable. He took no pleasure in what he had achieved or what he had amassed. My heart just went out to him. I knew he was a diabetic but he wouldn't stop drinking, which was crazy. He was in a lot of pain and I thought he might have diabetic neuropathy, which I have had and it's awful. The way he felt physically had a lot to do with how he felt about not being number one man anymore, which he obviously hated. His spirit was just not there. The joy had gone out of him."

Whatever compassion Gleason may have aroused in Carney, he evoked little or none from the rest of the cast and crew. Nandrea Lin Courts, who was twenty-two, had the first big job of her career, playing Jackie's daughter. In the absence of rehearsal, she decided to knock on Gleason's Winnebago door and introduce herself. "I told him I'd be playing his daughter and he took one look at me, up and down, and said, 'Who the fuck cares?' Then he slammed the door in my face. He drank constantly on the set and always had lackeys whom he would order around to get him a Kleenex or a cigarette already lit. He seemed angry through every minute of his work. He wouldn't work late. He wouldn't do another take on a scene if he was satisfied with himself in the first one, no matter what else had gone wrong, and so we lost a lot of scenes that way. It was not exactly a secret that he disliked and disrespected our director, Jackie Cooper. In one scene that was shot without sound, when we were supposed to be laughing, what he said to get the laugh going was mocking and insulting things about Cooper. That made us his unwilling partners in laughing at the director. He was violent with a crew member's heirloom china that we were using in a scene; he understood the situation fully and just enjoyed making that person nervous. Carney had a very diplomatic way with him. The worse Jackie got, the more Carney would back off. Gleason was being the pig of the earth and Art, who could have objected greatly, just didn't and instead told wonderfully funny stories about their days on *The Honeymooners*. He was so gentle."

Halmi and Carney say that Jackie was imbibing on the set. He got drunk by the end of almost every day. "For the last three or four hours each afternoon," says Halmi, "he was simply useless." Jackie was uncooperative to the point of refusing to go visit owner William Paley at CBS, which was once again Jackie's network. He gave a few press interviews but dealt with them brusquely. Arthur Unger, retired from the *Christian Science*

Monitor, remembers, "He granted me an hour but he was clearly just going through the motions. Afterwards, my editor asked why I had dwelled so much on the dark and depressed aspects of him, but they were what I saw. He had the body language of a defeated man." Yet if downcast, Jackie could still be mulishly intransigent. Jackie flatly refused to speak lines he didn't care for or to perform physical business he found uncomfortable or unfunny. And no matter how much he said he wanted to get away from Kramden, in every scene he slipped into familiar Gleasonisms. "Still, he managed to dominate the film," Halmi says, "by knowing all the tricks. He positioned himself so that he would be the only one fully in focus in scene. He interpolated movements that distracted attention from other actors' speeches." Adds Halmi, "I did this show because the casting guaranteed it would get made and get aired and make a profit. In pure business terms, it was a no-brainer. But I knew going in that we would all pay the price physically and emotionally and psychologically, and so we did." At the wrap party at the end of shooting, Jackie pushed aside the drummer in the band that was performing and insisted on bashing out a few rounds himself. It was the last time he and Carney ever saw each other. They did not even speak again until Carney, ever the gentleman, telephoned on hearing that Jackie was dying. The last words he remembers Gleason speaking were the ones he had always wanted Jackie to say and mean: "I love you, pal." It was, Carney admits, a smallish side of Gleason, this tender and affectionate stripe. But it was the side he chooses to remember.

For Halmi, the pain of dealing with Gleason was only partway over. The next phase was to get the movie scored. In addition to the batch of faded arrangements of Dixieland standards, Jackie eventually sent along three original songs that he said he wrote himself. This was not such a big claim for a man who also asserted he had written dozens of other songs, much of his television and movie theme music, a ballet and a symphony. To assist Gleason in hiring musicians and coordinating their work, Halmi brought in a twenty-seven-year-old named Irwin Fisch, who had grown up in a household possessing one of Jackie's many record albums. The relationship started off shakily. Although Fisch found Jackie the soul of warmth, Gleason disliked some of the young man's arrangements that had been prerecorded as a working score and arbitrarily threw them out. Says pianist Frank Owens, who participated in all the recording sessions, "There was nothing wrong with the arrangements. It was Jackie's whim, really. But as the music director of record, he had the right to do it." In place of Fisch's work, Jackie insisted on recording almost thirty Dixieland standards plus his own three songs. In the arrangements he chose, which were quite elaborate by television budgetary standards—one required twenty-eight string players plus other instruments—the combined numbers would go on considerably longer than the contractual running time of the film.

Gleason had some notion of where the particular songs would go. But he did not grasp the idea that music ought to arise organically from the emotions of a scene rather than overpower the action, nor did he comprehend that music cannot be allowed to shout down the dialogue. "He certainly had a correct sense of musical gestalt, of what was the right kind of piece for a particular scene or situation," says Fisch. "But whatever his credits said, it was perfectly obvious that he had never had anything to do with putting music to film before. This kind of stuff was just too basic for him to have forgotten. How could he think of recording four minutes twenty seconds of song for a three minute ten second scene? Of the three songs he said he had written, he didn't really seem to understand any of them. He didn't grasp the harmonics, and forget about the chord structure. Don't even think about the orchestrations, which he admitted were done by someone else. In my opinion, there was no way he could have completed the basic melodies of those songs.

"When it came time for him to conduct, it looked like a routine from the variety show, a vaudeville strut with wavy arm movements. He didn't even indicate the tempos, which is the basic thing a conductor has to do. The first time

537

he started up, we got a few bars in and everybody was all over the place. Jackie, who had a reasonable enough ear, made them stop, and one of the violinists said, 'I guess we sort of lost the beat,' meaning that Gleason never gave one out. I put Frank Owens, the pianist, just out of Gleason's sight and he conducted while Jackie went on waving his arms and thinking he was conducting."

Marilyn accompanied Jackie throughout the sessions, at which he stayed sober although he joked constantly with her about booze. He smoked nonstop. Various crew members politely placed ashtrays at his feet—four of them, eventually—yet he continued to stub out each butt on the beautifully polished hardwood floor of the studio. Ultimately the entire fruits of the recording session had to be junked, except for a few fragments, and the film was scored yet another time, uncredited, for still more money. Producer Halmi says flatly, "It was fraud. He cheated me. I could have sued him or refused to pay. But I got what I wanted, which was to get the picture made and then to get him back down to Florida and out of my life."

Fisch's charges seem sweeping and could easily arise out of a young man's resentment at having his work rejected. But interviews with half a dozen of the musicians at that recording session, some of whom also worked on the albums credited to Jackie in the fifties and sixties, and with Pete McGovern, Sam Cohn, Larry King, Mer-

538

cedes Ellington and others, confirm the key points.

Jackie had absolutely no idea how to conduct. "He never claimed he did," says McGovern—a statement flatly contradicted, alas, by countless publicity claims put out in Jackie's name. He purported to conduct on film, on records, on live television. It was all a sham.

As a composer, he may have had some ideas but could at most hum four bars, then listen and make alterations while someone else plinked out on the piano what sounded like Jackie's idea. To turn a phrase into a song, he relied on uncredited composers, arrangers and orchestrators whose contribution was always far greater than he acknowledged. Some material that Jackie claimed to have written had nothing to do with him at all. Sam Cohn says, "He might have hummed the first four bars of some of those songs. That was about as far as it went. But he could listen pretty good." Mercedes Ellington confirms, "I don't believe he could have done anything technical with music, although he had ideas about everything. He had instincts devoid of formal education." Max Ellen, an instrumentalist who worked several recording sessions with Gleason, says, "He had absolutely no idea what was going on around him. He was a stranger to music. He just liked it. As for the songs he 'wrote,' well, he might have whistled them. His arranger down in Florida did it all. Gleason didn't mind fooling the public when his name on a label made for good sales. But he wasn't crazy, so he didn't try to fool people in the business. At the recording sessions there was simply no reason for him to be there. He didn't conduct. He didn't supervise. He neither detracted nor contributed in any way."

As for the albums, Fisch is right when he says, "To do that many, forty in little more than a decade, and have them be any good, he would have to have been doing nothing else all those years." The idea that this recording work was in any meaningful way Jackie's was an obvious nonsense, but a nonsense that the supine media of the era never stopped to examine. The basic ideas of the records were Jackie's. He had a musical taste, a sense of what kind of innovative schmaltz would sell. He had no technical gifts, however, and he stole the credit of those who did. Pianist and sometime ghost conductor Owens says, "His name sold a lot of albums. I don't know whether you want to call it fair that he was credited as composer and conductor and producer when the most he may have done was to choose the tunes and sit in on the recording sessions." Larry King and others specifically credit trumpeter Bobby Hackett with creating and developing many of Gleason's early albums, the ones that established him in mood music. King adds that by Gleason's own admission to him, Hackett was often the conductor and musical director as well as lead horn player. Musicians assert that Gleason paid Hackett only the union minimum and placed the trumpeter under contract to prevent his re-creating the sound with anyone else.

It all amounts to an old, familiar tale among artists. Working in collaborative media, some of them yearn ever more desperately to become solo acts. Having one gift, they come to feel that they possess all gifts. Making some contribution, they become certain that theirs is always the vital contribution. And so, in Jackie's case, what may have started out as a business scam or a tongue-in-cheek effrontery slowly evolved into a fraud that seduced most of all the perpetrator. There was no mistaking the conviction in Gleason's voice when he talked to friends like Kay Gardella or business partners like Robert Halmi. He truly believed he could compose and conduct in a minute. And in the end, a minute's effort was virtually all he gave.

Of all the legends in the life of Jackie Gleason, the one he held to most stubbornly and circumstantially was this image of himself as a musical genius. It could have been intellectual snobbery, claiming accomplishment in the most abstract and technical of the arts when he was in truth an undereducated and intuitive man. It could have been the fallacy that equates intensity of emotional response, the sheer emotional expression he felt in hearing music, with intensity of creative gift. It could have been an elaborate practical joke on the world, or on himself. He was given to such jokes, and his humor was often impenetrable. Whatever else it was, to the end of his life, it remained The Great One's great lie.

At the beginning of 1987, Jackie agreed, through his longtime business manager Jack Philbin, to authorize a Museum of Broadcasting retrospective of his work. Jackie's role would include attending a ceremonial dinner, giving a speech or two, perhaps leading some seminars. The museum would show anew some "lost" *Honeymooners* episodes and also a range of his other television work, from the dawn of *Cavalcade* up through *Izzy and Moe*. The focus on Gleason would last for months and would include a handsomely printed scholarly catalogue plus all the other trappings to certify his artistic significance. Although he accepted, Jackie was oddly detached about the details. He did not request the right to read the catalogue copy. He showed little interest in what was to be exhibited. He was flattered that Dick Cavett came down to record a question and answer session for the exhibit, but in Cavett's description, "Gleason greeted philosophical questions with superficial answers."

What was happening was that Jackie was dying. He had been feeling uncomfortable for months and finally went to his doctors in April. After preliminary examination they told him they were almost certain he had colon cancer. They also suspected it had metastasized to the liver, a certain and swift sentence of death. But Gleason refused to undergo exploratory surgery, even a biopsy. He panicked and left. On the night of May 21 he was secretly admitted to Imperial Point Hospital, his customary place of treatment in Fort Lauderdale, with agonizing abdominal pain. Nurses who described themselves as Gleason fans later told reporters that their hero was unrecognizable, his face drawn and white, his robust looks aged to those of a man of ninety. In a three-hour operation, surgeons removed a large tumor that was blocking his colon and making him ill. But the cancer had clearly spread into the liver and into twenty-seven of the twenty-eight lymph nodes that the oncologists checked in Jackie's groin. The day after the surgery, the chief surgeon told Gleason he had six months to a year left to live. As the doctor must have suspected, the truth was even more grim. Jackie would be dead in a month. With mortality facing him, he threw all restraint aside. Hours after getting the bad news, he succeeded in getting his oxygen tent cut off so that he could resume chain smoking. On June 3 he underwent a second surgery for leaking intestines, which had made him painfully weak, and his abdomen was drained. Then, as soon as the nurses could strengthen him to make the journey, he went home to die.

He was conscious of having his wife and daughters there for Father's Day on June 22, then slipped into unawareness and died June 24 with Marilyn by his side.

In his final weeks he used his fading strength

to mail notes and autographed pictures to some cherished friends. He made up lists of people he wanted called with a personal farewell after his death. He spoke often of God and seemed, at least in public, to settle into the unquestioning religious faith that had eluded him all his life. He said he hoped he was right in the sentiment he had expressed to *60 Minutes* that "God isn't vengeful and if you've committed a sin he's not going to send you to hell for eternity." With stillness beckoning, he made peace with the world he was leaving behind.

Even in death he defied the rules. His heart did not kill him, despite all the abuse he gave it. His death could not be clearly attributed to his eating or drinking or smoking. He died of a pattern of cancer that attacks many people of much more abstemious disposition. And he surpassed the biblical three score and ten.

His passing was front page, evening newscast and magazine cover news across the United States. Two thousand people attended his wake or the funeral mass at St. Mary's Cathedral in Miami. Audrey Meadows flew in, the only major star to do so, and flowers came from Art Carney, Joyce Randolph, Bob Hope, Mickey Rooney and Perry Como. In the background at the ceremonies, recordings played of his old theme music, "Melancholy Serenade," and other compositions he claimed as his own. Per his instructions, no expense was spared on his funeral or on his mausoleum, a marble edifice overlooking the water.

The steps were incised with words he had specified: "And away we go."

In the months that followed, friends remembered his generosity. Larry King recalled the time when he was a novice radio interviewer in Miami and his friend Gleason got Frank Sinatra to show up for a live three-hour conversation, simply by calling in a favor Sinatra owed Gleason from a decade before. Jackie told me he called Frank and said, 'Remember the time you told me you owed me one? Well, this is the one.' " Pete McGovern remembered the night that he and his son were out on the town with Rudy Vallee, Honey Merrill and Jackie, the latter much in his cups. Hearing that the McGovern boy liked geography, Jackie promised him a present "that will take you anywhere in the world." The next morning, before Jackie could possibly have begun to conquer his hangover, before the town plows had even cleared away the previous night's snowfall, clanking up McGovern's Connecticut driveway came a delivery truck containing an electrified, lit-up, state-of-the-art globe. It symbolized a promise kept. Mercedes Ellington thought about the train ride through the South and Jackie's affirming embrace. Sam Cohn thought about the terror of his first meeting with Gleason, then at the peak of power, and about how Jackie did not seem to test or challenge him but just put him at his ease. Manny Kladitis thought of the time, years after *Sly Fox,* when he spotted Jackie at a show he was managing, a Broadway revival of

The King and I, and ran down to say hello. Gleason hailed him warmly, recalling all of his name and his nickname Bellyache, and made him feel a friend. Kay Gardella thought of her first meetings, when Gleason scooped her up into the company of the famous, and their last meeting, at a party in New York where they commiserated about their weight. Jackie admitted that he had never met his own definition of a star—the fellow who gets the girl. "If I hadn't been fat," he said wistfully, "you know, I could have been Clark Gable."

They all remembered the angry moments, the cruel moments, the cold and detached moments. But to them the real Jackie Gleason was the man who could choose to be so sweet.

On February 26, 1991, the seventy-fifth anniversary of Jackie Gleason's arrival on the planet, forty-five people gathered at a restaurant in Miami to salute his memory. Some, like Pete McGovern and June Taylor's associate choreographer, Peter Gladke, flew down from New York. Some, like Jack Philbin, newly turned eighty, lived nearby. The ranks would surely have been still greater, save for the fact that of those two hundred plus people who had moved to Florida with Jackie, many had gone on to other work in California and many more had died. Recordings attributed to Jackie played in the background. Speeches and conversation paid tribute to his vibrant memory. One important person was not in attendance. Marilyn Gleason had declined to come, saying she thought a Mass of remembrance would be a more appropriate tribute. But Sydell Spear, the devoted former secretary who arranged the party—she who had kept Jackie's office phone number as her personal one, she who in his retirement at times worked for him virtually free, she who saw him only as shy and kind—explained to Marilyn that she disagreed. Her words seemed true to The Great One, the public Jackie, and perhaps to the private one as well. "The Jackie Gleason I knew," she said, "would have much preferred a party."